"As *The Federalist Papers* pointed out, an enduring constitution must create not only a government strong enough to accomplish intensely difficult tasks but also controls over the government that preserve liberty and autonomy. Tracing, explaining, and evaluating these delicate balances over three centuries require an extraordinary historian. That person is Gary Gerstle and his book *Liberty and Coercion* will shape how we understand American governance for years to come."

—JENNIFER HOCHSCHILD

coauthor of *Creating a New Racial Order*

"*Liberty and Coercion* is a much-needed, cogent, and deftly executed exploration of the American state. Gerstle's lucid and widely informed argument provides insights never advanced before and will attract a wide readership. This book is a home run."

—DANIEL CARPENTER

Harvard University

LIBERTY AND COERCION

LIBERTY AND COERCION

THE PARADOX OF AMERICAN GOVERNMENT FROM THE FOUNDING TO THE PRESENT

GARY GERSTLE

PRINCETON UNIVERSITY PRESS

PRINCETON AND OXFORD

Copyright © 2015 by Princeton University Press
Published by Princeton University Press, 41 William Street,
Princeton, New Jersey 08540
In the United Kingdom: Princeton University Press, 6 Oxford
Street, Woodstock, Oxfordshire OX20 1TW
press.princeton.edu
Jacket art: Flattened US flags. © Bruce Peterson / Offset.com
All Rights Reserved
Library of Congress Cataloging-in-Publication Data
Gerstle, Gary, 1954–
Liberty and coercion : the paradox of American government
from the founding to the present / Gary Gerstle.
pages cm
Includes bibliographical references and index.
ISBN 978-0-691-16294-2 (hardcover : alk. paper) 1. Federal government—
United States—History. 2. Federal-state controversies—United States—History.
3. Abuse of administrative power—United States—History. 4. Political culture—
United States—History. 5. United States—Politics and government. I. Title.
JK311.G46 2015
320.473'049—dc23
2015002394
British Library Cataloging-in-Publication Data is available
This book has been composed in Sabon LT Std and Univers Lt Std
Printed on acid-free paper. ∞
Printed in the United States of America
1 3 5 7 9 10 8 6 4 2

In memory of Roy Rosenzweig
historian, mentor, friend

CONTENTS

ACKNOWLEDGMENTS

I owe a great debt to the several communities of scholars—most notably political and social historians, social scientists, and legal scholars—who have produced large and stimulating literatures on government in the United States from the revolution to the present. Without that scholarship as a foundation, a book of this scope would have been impossible to write. I am also indebted to many individuals who have taken time from their own work to educate me about the many subjects I needed to learn more about, to comment on my conference and workshop presentations, and to give me feedback on draft chapters. I hope this list names them all: Robin Archer, Jim Banner, Nicolas Barreyre, Sven Beckert, Herman Belz, Ira Berlin, Mark Brandon, Alan Brinkley, John Brooke, Margot Canaday, Nancy Cott, Gareth Davies, Mary Dudziak, Max Edling, Robin Einhorn, Lou Ferleger, Eric Foner, Jun Furuya, Jim Gilbert, David Grimsted, Pekka Hämäläinen, Joel Isaac, Richard John, Ira Katznelson, Alice Kessler-Harris, Alex Keyssar, Desmond King, Paul Kramer, Chuck Lane, Nelson Lichtenstein, Chris Loss, Jane Mayer, Noam Maggor, Suzanne Mettler, Ewan Morgan, Johann Neem, Bill Novak, Alice O'Connor, Adam Rothman, Steve Sawyer, Dan Sharfstein, Suzanna Sherry, Ganesh Sitaraman, Rogers Smith,

Jim Sparrow, David Stebenne, Tom Sugrue, Dan Usner, Barbara Weinstein, and Michael Zakim. The advice I received has had a profound influence on the shape and content of this book.

I have benefited greatly from opportunities to present my work as lectures or in workshops at these institutions: University of California at Santa Barbara, Vanderbilt University, University of South Alabama, University of Maryland College Park, Ohio State University, University of Michigan, University of Virginia, University of Pennsylvania, Columbia University, Harvard University, Boston University, Trinity College Dublin, Queen's University Belfast, University of Edinburgh, University of Sheffield, University of Nottingham, University of Cambridge, University of Oxford, London School of Economics, University College London, University of Sussex, Paris Sorbonne Université, Université Sorbonne Nouvelle, Écoles des hautes études en sciences sociales, University of Bielefeld, University of Tel Aviv, Seoul National University, University of Tokyo, and Universidade Federal Fluminense.

I first attempted to frame the ideas for this book in graduate seminars that I taught at the University of Maryland and Vanderbilt University. My thanks to the many smart students who challenged me to refine and rethink my views, and whose own deep engagement with questions of liberty and coercion persuaded me to turn what I had imagined would be a single article into this book. A number of students went on to write—or are currently writing—dissertations that intersect with the themes discussed in these pages. Their ranks include Jason Bates, Tim Boyd, Robert Chase, Rachel Donaldson, Clare Goldstene, Cheryl Hudson, Patrick Jackson, Alex Jacobs, Sveinn Jóhannesson, Steve Lipson, Linda Noel, Kelly O'Reilly, Matt Owen, Ansley Quiros, and Nick Villanueva. Their work has enriched my own.

My debt to two research assistants, Monte Holman and William Bishop, is large. Each worked for me for two years, and brought superb skills and great energy to the project. They responded to endless queries, pursued countless leads, and checked out so many books from the Vanderbilt library that we had to get special dispensation to raise my borrowing limits. They were superb collaborators, and the best of lunchtime partners. I salute them. My new assistant at Cambridge, Jonathan Goodwin, continues in their tradition, arriving just in time to perform indispensable cleanup work on the nearly—but never quite—finished manuscript. His expertise and good cheer helped me through the last months of the project.

Several wonderfully gifted and astute scholars—Dan Carpenter, Steve Hahn, Dirk Hartog, Sarah Igo, and Michael Kazin—gave me feedback on the entire manuscript and pushed me hard. So, too, did an anonymous reviewer for Princeton University Press. The book is so much better because of their engagement, encouragement, and critique.

I wrote this book during an itinerant portion of my career and life, and I would not have been able to finish it but for the hospitality shown me at my various ports of call. From 2006 to 2014, my home base was Nashville, where I was sustained by a community of historians at Vanderbilt University that was exceptional for its combination of intellectual intensity and collegiality. When Cambridge, Massachusetts, became a second port of call, Jennifer Hochschild and Dan Carpenter went out of their way to provide me with office space in and affiliation with Harvard University's Center for American Political Studies. Nancy Cott and Liz Cohen did the same at Harvard's Charles Warren Center for Studies in American History. These affiliations and work spaces—and the access to Widener Library that came with them—made a world of difference.

The year I spent at Oxford in 2012–13 as the Harmsworth Professor of American History proved crucial in terms of solving some of the toughest intellectual and narrative challenges posed by this book. Special thanks to the Oxford Americanists, especially Pekka Hämäläinen, Richard Carwardine, Desmond King, Nigel Bowles, Gareth Davies, Jay Sexton, Stephen Tuck, and Peter Thompson, for their intellectual engagement and conviviality; to the Rothermere American Institute, for its dynamism, resources, and good working environment; to Paul and Alison Madden, for making a home for me at Queen's College; and to Vyvyan and Alexandra Harmsworth for their deep commitment to the study of

US history in Britain, and for anticipating everything a visiting professor from the States might need, including tips for driving on the wrong side of the road.

The Harmsworth year quite unexpectedly led to my taking a permanent job in the United Kingdom, at an institution up the road and around the bend from Oxford. I have only just arrived at the University of Cambridge, but the welcome from members of the history faculty and the fellows of Sidney Sussex College has been extraordinary. A new project will soon rise from fresh academic networks that are already in formation, and from the phenomenal intellectual energy that pulses everywhere in this institution.

During my decade of migration, certain things have held fast. I have worked with Princeton University Press for twenty-five-plus years, and with Brigitta van Rheinberg for fifteen of those. Brigitta has been a great supporter of this book from the start and an outstanding critic. Our extensive and robust exchanges have repeatedly given the book and me lift. My deepest thanks to her, and to Quinn Fusting, Sara Lerner, Theresa Liu, Cindy Milstein, and other members of the Princeton team for patiently guiding this sometimes finicky author through every stage of the production process. Beyond Princeton, Destiny Birdsong stepped in with some timely editing work.

I cannot name all the friends who sustained me through the years of writing this book, but some need to be mentioned. I have listed them according to the lengths of time, often spanning decades, that I have known them: David Casey, Dan Sternberg, Debbie Cooper, Peter Mandler, Ruth Ehrlich, Stephanie Engel, Art Goldhammer, Jennifer Hochschild, Tony Broh, Elliott Shore, Maria Sturm, Steve Fraser, Jill Fraser, Michael Kazin, Rob Schneider, Sarah Mitchell, Deborah Kaplan, Ira Berlin, Martha Berlin, Dan Cornfield, Hedy Cornfield, Sarah Igo, Ole Molvig, Michael Bess, Kimberly Bess, Jim Epstein, Sherry Baird, and Tom Dillehay. We have shared magnificent experiences and seen each other through a lot. Your company and comradeship have so enriched my life.

Wherever I have gone, new friendships have blossomed. But some friends I have lost. This book is dedicated to one of them, Roy Rosenzweig. Roy was a remarkable scholar, a pioneer of the digital humanities, and a passionate democrat. He was also a great friend and mentor, and one very funny man. For thirty years, he read everything I wrote before it went into print. I miss him every day.

The greatest sustenance has always come from my family. My mother, Else Gerstle, is a pillar of strength and an inspiration to all those touched by her. My sister, Linda Gerstle, and her partner, Isaac Franco, make the sun shine while serving up meals worthy of a Michelin three-star restaurant. My in-laws, Robert and Barbara Lunbeck, have no peers as Scrabble players, and few peers in terms of the generosity they shower on their many children and grandchildren.

When I started writing books, my sons, Dan and Sam, were into fire trucks and *Star Wars*. Now they are accomplished men who outdo me in the vigor and range of their intellectual interests. Their contributions to this book and my life have been multiple and profound. It has been a great privilege to be their father. Liz Lunbeck, my wife, is still the best historian I know. Her courage, vision, and love make my world turn. Neither of us imagined that we would now be living the kind of life that we used to dream about but that we never really expected to come our way. It has been an incredible journey.

LIBERTY AND COERCION

INTRODUCTION

This book reconstructs the history of American government from its dem-ocratic, liberal, and federal beginnings in the eighteenth century to the Leviathan it has become in the twenty-first century. The story it tells is one of remarkable growth, innovation, and in the case of the states themselves, survival. It is a story full of contestation and contradiction, paradox and unintended consequence. It is also a story of how, since the 1930s, the federal government's efforts to solve economic, social, and political problems have been repeatedly subject to challenge and censure by Republicans charging that the central state had exceeded its constitutional authority, and with its regulations and prohibitions, threatened the very liberty that Americans fought a revolution to secure. Today the split between Democrats and Republicans about the proper scope of government constitutes a nearly unbridgeable divide. It is the source of many of the country's current discontents and has paralyzed politics at the federal level. It may portend the nation's decline. This book attempts to explain how the United States got to this point.

Unlike most efforts to explain America's troubled state, this one begins not in the twentieth century but at the moment of the country's founding, and it looks at two contradictory principles of governance that have shaped and confounded the deployment of public power ever since. The first principle, woven through the US Constitution, emphasizes the importance of limiting the federal government's reach by carefully enumerating and fragmenting its powers. The Constitution authorized the federal government to assume only those duties expressly given to it; unenumerated tasks were left to the states. It also split the power of the federal state among three branches of government—the executive, legislative, and judiciary—and granted individuals rights that no president, Congress, or supreme court would be allowed to abrogate. This determination to limit central government power is best understood as "liberal," in the classical sense of that term. Those who subscribed to this creed believed that the greatest threat to liberty lay in government tyranny and coercion. It was not enough to throw off the yoke of George III and his imperial British state. Citizens of the new republic had to be vigilant about identifying postindependence efforts to reestablish overbearing central state authority, and to expose and defeat all such efforts. This animus to concentrated federal government power runs like a red thread through the entire history of the nation, from the revolt against Great Britain itself to Andrew Jackson's attack on the "Monster Bank" in the 1830s to the Tea Party's assault on "Obamacare" in the 2010s.

The durable nature of this animus makes the second principle of American governance difficult to comprehend, for it gave individual states broad powers to shape public and private life and to engage in precisely the kinds of coercion forbidden to the central government itself. That states are dynamic players in American politics is indisputable. In the twenty-first century, states have vigorously pushed agendas on an array of issues, including immigration, gay marriage, the minimum wage, abortion, marijuana, global warming, and the right of public workers to organize. This activity, it turns out, is but a faint echo of the vast power that once inhered in these miniature Leviathans.

Consider these actions in which states engaged from the late eighteenth century to the mid-twentieth century. From the 1780s to 1860s, southern states stripped Africans and their descendants of legal and human rights; from the 1890s to 1950s, these same states denied African American citizens access to residential areas, jobs, parks, restaurants, water fountains, and toilets marked as white. In the early twentieth century, western states denied East Asian immigrants the right to own land. Various states denied people of all colors the opportunity to drink. Countless state laws regulated sexual behavior, forbade homosexual sex and many forms of contraception, and outlawed literature judged to be obscene, most famously James Joyce's *Ulysses*. As many as half the states forbade marriage across the color line. So-called blue laws ordered the closing of stores and the shutting down of commerce on the Sabbath. As late as 1928, Massachusetts was using a 1640 blasphemy statute to prosecute individuals who had allegedly taken the name of Jesus Christ in vain. So much for free speech in the place where the American Revolution began and that had always considered itself the cradle of American liberty.[1]

Why were these violations of free speech and other rights allowed to stand in a society in which the Bill of Rights had been part of the Constitution since 1791? As it turns out, state governments were largely exempt from having to observe the federal Bill of Rights from the early years of the republic until the middle decades of the twentieth century. This was the First Congress' intent. James Madison was almost alone in foreseeing that the federal Bill of Rights would be compromised if it offered citizens no protection against the tyranny of their state governments. States adopted their own bills of rights, but some of these documents were poorly crafted, and too easy to amend and violate. As a consequence, democratic voting majorities in the states working through their legislatures could intervene in and regulate the lives of citizens far more systematically than could the federal government itself, and many such legislatures proceeded to do so across multiple realms—economic, cultural, and moral.

States thus operated not in line with classical liberalism but according to the principle of "police power" that jurists set forth in the early nineteenth century. This power was grounded in an eighteenth-century British doctrine known as the "public police," which endowed the king with the authority and duty to look after the good and welfare of his subjects. Even as the American revolutionaries jettisoned kingship, they imported this royalist doctrine into state constitutions and state legislatures, thereby giving states a broad scope of action. Nineteenth-century judges made this linkage explicit, which explains the closeness in nomenclature between the American "police power" and the British "public police." Those who noticed this continuity were by and large untroubled by it. State legislatures, in their eyes, were nothing like the British Crown, for they expressed the democratic will of the people in ways that a monarchy governing by divine right never could. And the people, as a rule, would not use the democratic forum made available by state legislatures to tyrannize themselves. It was therefore acceptable for these state legislatures to wield power as broad as that exercised by the British Crown. Many Americans were blind to, or chose not to see, the coercion inherent in state governments that made too little provision for protecting the rights of minorities from the will of the majority.

That jurists in a polity consecrated to liberty would sanction an intrusive theory of rule and call it "the police power" is indicative of the paradoxes of governance in America. Liberty and coercion were bound together from the earliest days of the republic. Today, the police power doctrine is much weaker than it once was and largely unknown beyond legal circles. Many who argue for getting the federal government off their backs don't think much about what the consequences of restoring power to the states might be. Or they are surprisingly comfortable taking a libertarian stand with regard to federal government policies while supporting initiatives in their states that are plainly coercive in intent and effect. These latter initiatives have included mandating prayer in public schools, outlawing Sharia (the code by which observant Muslims live), designating homosexual sex as sodomy, denying gays the right to marry, and stripping women of their reproductive freedom. Those who have supported these campaigns while simultaneously taking strong stances against the exercise of federal government power in all its forms are living exemplars of how easily attitudes toward liberty and coercion still cohabit in the minds of single individuals. This cohabitation runs so deep and is so widespread that it deserves to be regarded as a core element of the American way. This book seeks not only to make sense of this phenomenon but also to trace its roots back to the founding of the republic. In the process, it tracks the history of the states' police power, from its emergence in the early nineteenth century through its remarkable resurrection after the Civil War to the all-out assault on it during the fiery 1960s.[2]

The story of the scope and durability of the power wielded by the states remains largely unknown. The story of how America's central state shed its roots as a government limited in its power and became today's Leviathan is more familiar but not well enough understood. Scholars tend to tell this story through the high-profile reform movements that sought to turn the federal government into a highly centralized, administratively capacious, and redistributionist instrument of reform. Those who led these efforts, including presidents Theodore Roosevelt, Woodrow Wilson, Franklin Delano Roosevelt, and Lyndon Baines Johnson, occupy outsize roles in American history, as do the programs of comprehensive reform with which their names became associated: the Square Deal, Progressivism, the New Deal, and the Great Society. What sometimes gets lost in underscoring the transformative influence of these individuals and their reform programs is this: that ambitious central state-building dreams often depended, for enduring success, on strategies to legally expand the capacity and power of the American central state beyond its constitutionally imposed limits. As a result, the ability to improvise often became as important to central state-building efforts as the ability to find and implement the right master plan. Indeed, this book argues that an emphasis on improvisation rather than transformation provides a better guide to understanding the manner in which the US central state grew as well as the techniques that Congress and the president employed to meet the nation's governing challenges.

Three strategies in particular powered the improvisational central state-building project in the United States: *exemption, surrogacy,* and *privatization*. Exemption entailed turning to the courts for permission to exempt certain central state activities from constitutional constraints. Activities of this sort, if they were carefully delimited in space and time, would strengthen the federal government's ability to pursue important objectives without formally compromising its liberal character. These activities involved either matters defined as beyond the polity's formal borders (war, international trade, colonial administration, and immigration) and thus judged beyond the Constitution's reach, or domestic emergencies, in the form of civil unrest, rebellions, and natural disasters that were thought to justify a temporary suspension of constitutional limits on central government power.

The second strategy, surrogacy, involved the federal government using a power explicitly granted by the Constitution to expand its authority into forbidden legislative terrain. Hence, for example, in the late nineteenth and early twentieth centuries, central state builders devised a way to police morality (an area of governance the Constitution reserved for the states) by creatively applying the federal government's power to supervise the mails and regulate interstate commerce. With the concurrence of the federal courts, Congress passed one law that forbade the post office from delivering "obscene" literature and another that criminalized the activities of those who were "polluting" interstate commerce by transporting female prostitutes across state lines. Neither law was as effective as blanket national bans on obscene literature or prostitution might have been. But each nevertheless permitted the central state to significantly expand its authority and power into areas where it possessed little of either. Over the course of the twentieth century, the central state would repeatedly use surrogacy to circumvent formal limits on the scope of its authority.

The third strategy, privatization, entailed persuading private groups to do work that the central state was not authorized or willing to undertake. The US government turned again and again to the private sector for assistance on a wide range of matters, such as building railroads, dams, and other forms of infrastructure; mobilizing the home front, economically and ideologically, for war; putting political dissenters under surveillance and sometimes in jail; staffing diplomatic missions and expanding American influence overseas; moralizing the poor and constructing welfare programs for those unable to help themselves; and contracting out a broad range of mundane government services. No one has ever quantified the number of Americans involved in the zone of governance defined by public-private interpenetration; even such a partial list as this of the kinds of activities that it encompassed suggests that the numbers and resources were vast.

Pressing this repertoire of improvisational techniques into service, America's central state builders found ways to make the federal government energetic. The repertoire offered those who wanted to expand the central state the authority to sustain projects that would otherwise have been hard to set in motion. The federal government grew substantially as a result, widening its area of authority and stoking its policymaking power. By the early twentieth century, those building this edifice were confident they had the tools necessary to establish the powerful central government that was the ticket of entry into the first rank of industrial nations. Improvisation appeared to be working.

But improvisation also had its limitations. A liberal central state that created an area of exemption that was too large or that lasted too long would ultimately cease to be liberal. Surrogacy could harm the reputation of a central state through overuse or overextension. At some point, critics might legitimately claim that the federal government had overreached by, say, using the post office to promote too many projects extraneous to delivering the mail, or the commerce clause to sanction reforms such as morals regulation that were not at their core about buying and selling commodities across state lines. The privatization strategy, meanwhile, risked putting too much public money and power in the hands of private individuals, groups, and corporations. Congressional leaders who turned to private corporations to provide vital services might claim that these institutions were publicly spirited, but too frequently these arrangements plainly became occasions for privileged private interests to feed at the public trough. This was as true of the building of the transcontinental railroad in the 1860s as it has been of the twenty-first-century delegation of nation building in Iraq for the likes of Halliburton and Blackwater.

Given the limits of improvisation, dreams of a more thoroughgoing transformation of government lived on in the minds of many Americans, both those who occupied the highest levels of the federal government and those, such as farmers and workers, mobilizing movements for change at the grass roots. Those dreams appeared close to realization in three convulsive decades, from the 1930s to 1960s, when a trio of crises—the Great Depression, a condition of near-permanent war arising from World War II and the Cold War, and the civil rights revolution—cumulatively overwhelmed existing structures of governance. These were the years in which the American central government grew into a Leviathan, amassing resources and power unprecedented in scope, scale, and permanency. In these decades, the federal government built a national welfare apparatus, regulated industrial relations and other economic matters, invested heavily in universities and science, and launched a Second Reconstruction to root out racial inequality. It also for the first time in American history stripped the states of their authority, undercut their police power, and made the Bill of Rights the law of the entire land. These changes were momentous. The thoroughgoing transformation of American government, so long envisioned, seemed finally to be at hand.

Yet this federal government was still burdened by its past. The enormous expansion in the central state's domestic reach after World War II took place without the benefit of a constitutional amendment transferring a portion of the power now denied the states to the federal government. This nonevent was hardly surprising; amending the Constitution has almost always been a notoriously difficult process. In the absence of such a potentially legitimating amendment, however, central state builders perforce relied on nineteenth-century strategies of improvisation to justify the expansion of federal power. But invoking these strategies was not sufficient to bestow on the federal government constitutional authority commensurate with its vastly expanded power. The central state's vulnerability grew alongside its reach. Indeed in the late twentieth century, conservative Republicans, led by Ronald Reagan, made the assault on "big government" the most forceful movement in American politics. From the 1980s to the present, the American Leviathan has been under constant siege.

The federal government did acquire one new tool for its state-building arsenal after 1945: "national security." In the 1940s and 1950s, liberals began to invoke this phrase not simply to battle Communism but also to strengthen their case for expanding the education, welfare, and infrastructural reach of the federal state. This form of surrogacy, like those built on the postal, tax, and commerce powers of the federal government, came with costs. The imperatives of national security justified an expensive and oligopolistic military-industrial complex. They gave rise to a largely clandestine national security apparatus in the 1950s and 1960s with the capacity, and often authority, to put large swaths of the American population under surveillance. At the very moment when the Supreme Court was securing for minorities access to their rights as Americans and for women powerful new protections for reproductive freedom, it was allowing for the rise of an imperial presidency with vast, often-unchecked power. In retrospect, it appears that the coercive power that was being drained away from the states was re-pooling in vital areas of the federal government, even as other parts of this government were championing Bill of Rights' liberties as they had never been defended before. The United States, thus, was still burdened by the paradox of liberty and coercion commingled that had bedeviled the exercise of governmental power since the republic's birth. This paradox continues to this present day, manifest in a dramatic expansion of liberty, the core achievement of the twenty-first-century movement for gay rights and gay marriage, and an equally dramatic expansion in reach of the national security state, the consequence of the never-ending War on Terror.

Writing the history of how liberty and coercion have shaped American government across 240 years of history is a complex task. Affairs of state were multitudinous; activities and agencies proliferated over time. I have attempted to be comprehensive in my approach while acknowledging that no one account can do it all.

I have organized my account chronologically. Part I, "Foundations, 1780s–1860s," looks at the contrasting theories of power underlying the central government and the states, and analyzes the successes and limitations of their deployment in the early decades of the republic. Part II, "Improvisations, 1860s–1920s," examines the improvisational initiatives of the central state during this time, covering a vast array of activities ranging from immigration regulation, morals control, and the acquisition of colonies, on the one hand, to the building of the transcontinental railroad, suppressing dissent in World War I, and managing a privatized system of electioneering, on the other. Part III, "Compromises, 1920s–1940s," analyzes the popular struggle to transform the central government in ways more fundamental than what improvisation allowed. Movements of farmers and workers spearheaded these struggles; they mostly met resistance until the Great Depression permitted a breakthrough in the form of Franklin Roosevelt's regime of positive liberty, known to us as the New Deal. Even then, however, opposition was strong enough to compromise the broader social democratic transformation sought by agrarian and labor insurgents.

Part IV, "American Leviathan, 1940s–2010s," shows how recently the nation acquired an enduringly large and powerful central state, and how this state was a product more of the Cold War than of the New Deal. It also reconstructs the success of this federal government in breaking the power of the states in the 1960s, and the fury that its ambitions elicited from conservatives who, since the 1970s and 1980s, have viewed them as a betrayal of the Constitution and the most important threat to their liberty. A conclusion assesses the condition of American governance today.

Throughout the book I have sought to enliven this history of political principles and structures with stories of individuals and groups whose activities influenced the shape as well as character of government power in America. Some of those individuals will be well known to readers but appear here in a new light. Their ranks include James Madison, Andrew Jackson, John Marshall, Herbert Hoover, J. Edgar Hoover, Franklin Roosevelt, Louis Brandeis, Dwight D. Eisenhower, Earl Warren, Hugo Black, Ronald Reagan, Lewis Powell, Sandra Day O'Connor, and Grover Norquist. Others are little known, yet through their social movements, the cases they brought before federal courts, and their struggles for influence in a range of government agencies (including the post office, Department of Agriculture, National Labor Relations Board, and Great Society's Community Action Program) had a measurable impact on the development of government in America.

This book is a work of synthetic interpretation, made possible by the superb work produced by historians, social scientists, and legal scholars over the last forty years. By and large, I have decided against discussing the many historical debates and controversies that have had a bearing on the interpretation that emerges in the pages to come. Readers wishing to learn more about my views on these matters can glean them from the commentary threaded through the endnotes. Nevertheless, it may be useful to indicate the three most important ways in which the interpretation offered in this book is distinctive. Two have already been mentioned. First, historians of the "American state" have generally ignored the states, and have had little to say about the theory of power animating the latter's actions. There are understandable reasons for overlooking the states. How, most immediately, does one take the measure of an institution that comes in fifty varieties? Nonetheless, the states are simply too crucial a part of America's governing edifice to ignore. They must be brought back into the conversation if we are to understand government power and its limits in the United States. This book offers one way of doing so.

Second, I steer the discussion about how the American central state changed over time away from a stress on crisis and transformation, and toward one focused on improvisation and incremental change. In so doing, I do not seek to minimize the significance of crisis in American history nor attempts at thoroughgoing transformation. There have been plenty of both.[3] I do argue, though, that efforts at transforming the central state have succeeded only in partial ways, and insist that the history of transformation must reckon not only with the forces propelling fundamental change but also with efforts to roll those forces back. Opponents of federal government power have regularly invoked the Constitution, both jurisprudentially and metaphorically, to make their case for a central state that ought to have limits on its reach restored.

Finally, I take a view of the Constitution and its influence on the shape of government in the United States that is different from interpretations of these matters circulating through the twenty-first-century Left and Right. The extraordinary buildup in the military and surveillance power of the US state across the decades of the Cold War and War on Terror has prompted some on the Left to trace the origins of that power to the earliest days of the republic. The Constitution, in this view, did not seek to limit the central state's power but to expand it across the North American continent, giving it the resources to expel or subdue whatever antagonists were in its way. From this perspective, which sees this early central state as all powerful, the word "liberal," in either its classic "hands-off" or modern meaning, is the wrong term to describe its character.

America's central state was, to be sure, an important instrument for those who wanted to sanction slavery and claim the entire continent for the United States. That this government promoted racialized conceptions of democracy and made war on Indians does not mean, however, that it constituted an American Leviathan from the moment of its foundation.[4] As I demonstrate in chapter 1, the army that Andrew Jackson took into battle to war on Indians, the British, and the Spanish between 1813 and 1819 was in fact small in light of the millions of square acres it was to defend and the number of enemies it was expected to vanquish. Jackson succeeded despite these limitations, with his army holding the United States together at a time when smart money was wagering that the new nation had overreached and was going to break apart. How did he do it? Was his military success a model for central state actions of any kind? Recognizing that America's central state faced formal limits on its powers helps us to pose—and then answer—these key questions.

Many on the Right, such as those who thrust the Tea Party into prominence in 2010, take a different view of the Constitution. For them, the ideal of limited government is sacrosanct, foundational, and constitutionally mandated. They revere the Constitution and tend to deify the men who wrote it. There is much to admire in the Constitution. Its concern with government as a source of tyranny was prescient in light of the totalitarianism that would disfigure politics in the twentieth century. The Bill of Rights pioneered a new way of thinking about personhood and its inviolability. But the Constitution was not perfect. It sanctioned slavery; it mandated electioneering practices, such as the electoral college, meant to limit popular sovereignty; and it did not anticipate—indeed could not have anticipated—many of the issues, from birth control and abortion, on the one hand, to the exorbitant (and corrupting) cost of elections, on the other, on which twentieth- and twenty-first-century courts have been called to adjudicate. And in deciding to exempt the states from an obligation to abide by the federal Bill of Rights, those who designed and ratified these first ten amendments generated an area of ambiguity regarding personal liberty that took more than 150 years to clarify and correct.

Because of these imperfections, we need to interrogate the framing of the Constitution in a way that is frequently missing from contemporary conservative discourse. As part of that interrogation, it is critical that we pry open the black box of the US government—that which contains the particulars about the powers originally given the states—and examine its contents. Such an exploration may well give some conservatives, or at least the libertarians in their ranks, pause about the virtues of originalism when it comes to constitutional interpretation. More important, it will give individuals of all political persuasions a fuller understanding of how governance in the United States has worked; what in this system has been strong, and what has been weak; and what needs to be fixed as America heads into its uncertain future.

PART I

Foundations, 1780s–1860s

1

A LIBERAL CENTRAL STATE EMERGES

Ralph Waldo Emerson may have been wrong in thinking that the first shot of the Revolutionary War was fired in Concord, Massachusetts, in April 1775. But he was not wrong in believing, as he wrote in 1836, that the battle of Lexington and Concord was metaphorically "a shot heard round the world."[1] This battle launched a major war of independence against one of the world's premier empires and inaugurated an age of democratic revolutions that would sweep through North America, South America, the Caribbean, and Europe over the next seventy-five years. In the United States—as in many sites of unfolding revolution—insurgents sought not only to topple the domestic and imperial lords who ruled their polities but to break with patterns of elite rule altogether. Those who embraced the Declaration of Independence's radical assertion that "all men are created equal" and "are endowed by their Creator with certain inalienable rights" believed that equality required that "the people" have a say in political decisions affecting their lives. A new era of popular sovereignty had begun. The American War of Independence ushered in the world's first democratic revolution.[2]

The word "democracy" was used sparingly in the eighteenth century to describe these events, for it connoted for many the rule

of the mob—thought to be composed of groups which, for reasons of poverty, sex, race, or uncontrollable passion, were unfit for
self-government.[3] Instead, the American revolutionaries thought
of themselves as creating a republic, by which they meant a polity
that derived its authority from the people and a commitment to the
public good, but in which full political rights were vested only in
those who were deemed economically independent and thus politically virtuous. The republics of the ancient Greek city-states and
Rome had shown that such a system of rule could work, and many
American revolutionaries imbued their thought with a healthy dose
of this classical republicanism. They also believed that the social
basis of the American citizenry would be much broader than what
had existed in earlier republics, for the abundance of land in the
United States and a relatively sparse population had put landownership (and hence economic independence and virtue) within reach
of most white heads of household. Imagining such a broad-based
citizenry made popular sovereignty seem a realizable goal, and generated ideas and movements that deepened the democratic character of the American Revolution.[4]

The American revolutionaries pursued a second goal that over-
lapped with the pursuit of popular sovereignty, but was also distinct from it: to make sure that no central political authority in the
United States would ever be able to concentrate power to the degree
that had made possible the misrule of George III. On one level that
meant declaring that America would have no king. On another
level, it meant constructing a central government whose power
would be limited and fragmented, and in which no executive,
judge, military leader, senator, or cabal would ever be able to assemble monarchical power. Ancient republicans had not concerned
themselves with designing governments in this way. Instead they
were preoccupied with creating economic and social conditions
in which virtue among citizens and rulers could flourish. Thus,
American revolutionaries turned to other forms of political thought
for guidance in designing a central state with limited powers. This
shift would point the American Revolution in a liberal direction.[5]

One important source of thought was that developed by English
Whigs—and by John Locke in particular—in the seventeenth cen-

tury. Locke's contemplation of his century's wars and revolutions against the absolutism of the British Crown led him to reject claims that English kings, and the monarchical states that embodied their will, were entitled to complete power over their subjects. Locke argued that societies had antedated these states, endowing the individuals who constituted them with rights to life, liberty, and property that no state (or monarch) could legitimately take away. These individuals, he posited, could agree to sacrifice some of their rights to a government capable of ensuring their safety and implementing a system of just laws. But this cession of rights was contractual and therefore reversible if the terms of the contract were violated.[6]

Locke regarded individualism and self-interest as natural human attributes. His governmental plan would both give scope to these attributes and, through representative government, manage the conflicts among the heterogeneous interests that would inevitably arise. Locke's discourse on contractualism, rights, and limited government circulated through Whiggish sectors of English society and the colonies in the eighteenth century, supporting both challenges to the excessive power of the king and his court and defenses of the rights of Englishmen in the name of liberty.[7]

By the 1770s and 1780s, another group of British theorists was developing ideas about economic liberty that paralleled Locke's thinking about political liberty. The Scottish political economist Adam Smith, a key figure in this group, wanted to enhance what he regarded as the propensity among humans "to truck, barter, and exchange one thing for another." Smith believed that "every man" should be "left perfectly free to pursue his own interest his own way, and to bring both his industry and capital into competition with those of any other man, or order of men." The primary obstacles to such economic freedom, or what Smith called "natural liberty," were overbearing monarchical states whose rigid mercantilist policies stymied commerce, technological innovation, and economic growth. Smith argued that the sovereign should be "completely discharged from . . . the duty of superintending the industry of private people, and of directing it towards the employments most suitable to the interests of the society." No "human wisdom or knowledge could ever be sufficient," Smith asserted, to support such an endeavor. Only by restraining the economic power of the monarch would the remarkable energies for commerce, industry, and growth that lay dormant in human intercourse be fully released. Smith was more concerned with freeing up the economy— fostering what he called a "simple system of natural liberty"—than with developing a theory of political rights. Nevertheless, his emphasis on limiting the power of the sovereign in economics dovetailed with Locke's focus on limiting the power of the monarch in politics.[8]

In the writings of Locke, Smith, and others, we can discern an effort to limit government and maximize economic and political freedom. This effort would come to define liberalism, and many of its eighteenth- and nineteenth-century proponents imbued this program with emancipatory hopes. It would, they believed, eliminate the bloated and suffocating monarchical and aristocratic states of eighteenth-century Europe while unleashing the energy and initiative of the people.[9]

These liberal ways of thinking about politics were not fully formed by the 1770s and 1780s. There was no liberal manifesto resembling what Karl Marx would produce for socialism in the nineteenth century, from which advocates could get their marching orders about how to build a liberal society and state. Yet everywhere in the emerging United States we can glimpse what political scientists Andreas Kalyvas and Ira Katznelson have called "liberal beginnings": in the antipathy to a powerful central state, in a deep commitment to natural and inalienable rights, in the articulation of a people's right to consent to the form of government under which they lived, and in a growing conviction regarding the centrality of representative assemblies to good government. In the process of constructing their own government, the American revolutionaries would demonstrate both an ability to advance beyond these beginnings and an inability to disentangle themselves from rival political philosophies, including republicanism, that were present in their revolutionary era and often in their own minds.[10]

Efforts to construct a central state out of this swirl of sentiments and ideologies unfolded in three political acts: the Articles of Confederation of 1781, the Constitution of 1789, and the Bill of

Rights of 1791. The Articles of Confederation was not as uniformly weak a system of rule as it is often thought to have been. As we will see, the Northwest Ordinances passed by confederation congresses in 1785 and 1787 were consequential bills that profoundly shaped land policy and related matters for more than a century. Still, confederation congresses came up short in too many areas, and the Constitutional Convention gathered in Philadelphia in 1787 to transform this compromised governing structure into something sturdier.[11] Out of it came the Constitution, ratified and installed in 1789. Its laws and blueprint still govern the United States, making it the oldest written constitution operative in the world today.

The Constitution gave the central government authority to regulate interstate and foreign commerce; lay taxes and tariffs; coin currency and borrow money; regulate immigration and naturalization; sponsor internal improvements, supervise the mails, and acquire, control, and distribute land; raise armies and navies for national defense and internal security; and establish uniform standards for weights and measures. These were substantial powers that cumulatively yielded a central government far stronger than what the Articles of Confederation had allowed.[12]

Still, this central authority had to operate within limits. The Constitution established a federal system in which a great deal of authority was left to the states. Meanwhile, the power of the central government was internally fragmented among three different branches of government to ensure that no single person, clique, or agency in the central state would ever be able to accumulate the sort of control that the despised George III and his ministers had allegedly gathered into the British royal government.

Even these constraints on the federal government's power failed to assuage the alarm of many Americans when they learned that the Constitutional Convention of 1787 had gone beyond its mandate—amending the Articles of Confederation—to produce an entirely new governing design. That the framers of the Constitution had done so in secret further raised suspicions that they were engaged in a conspiracy to reproduce the tyranny of George III.

The Constitution writers understood that these suspicions needed to be allayed, which informed their decision to ask each state to convene a ratifying convention, drawn from the ranks of each state's residents, to debate the merits of the new Constitution, and then vote on whether or not to adopt it. Affirmative votes in nine of the thirteen states would be required to make the Constitution the law of the land. This ratification process unleashed a remarkable debate on the place of a central government in American life.[13] The opponents of the Constitution, known as antifederalists (in that they opposed the strengthening of the *federal* government), failed to assemble enough votes to scuttle it, but they did wring a promise from the supporters of the Constitution that once ratification had been achieved, additional limitations would be imposed on America's new central state by elaborating rights for individuals that this new state would not be allowed to touch. These rights, assembled in the first ten amendments to the Constitution, came to be known as the Bill of Rights. They asserted the right of every person to speak freely; the right to have a free press; the right to assemble peacefully, with no restrictions on what could be said at such meetings; the right to worship in a religion of one's choice, or not to worship at all; and the right to petition the government for a redress of grievances without fear of reprisal. These amendments also set forth procedural safeguards to ensure that anyone charged with breaking a federal law would be treated fairly and humanely by the nation's criminal justice system.[14]

The Bill of Rights was liberal in the eighteenth-century sense, meaning that it was intended to identify a core area of human freedom, assert its inviolability, and protect it from the exercise of arbitrary government power. The ratification of the Bill of Rights in 1791 marked a major advance in the construction of liberal political theory and practice, not just in the United States, but in the world. Across the nineteenth and twentieth centuries, this collection of amendments would be a document studied and emulated by liberal-minded peoples everywhere.[15]

In eighteenth-century America, however, the import of the Bill of Rights was limited by the decision to exempt state governments from its strictures. A state could write a bill of rights into its own constitution, and many had. Indeed, the 1776 Virginia Declaration of Rights had influenced the shape of the federal Bill of Rights. But states could also decline to adopt a bill of rights, or design one with far weaker protections for individuals than that afforded by the national Bill of Rights. As such, while the First Amendment barred Congress from limiting freedom of religion, states that wanted to limit this freedom, such as Massachusetts and South Carolina, were able to do so. They were not bound by the terms of the First Amendment to the federal Constitution.[16]

That states themselves might become centers of government tyranny and might need to have constraints imposed on them troubled few who were active in American politics in the early 1790s. Even the most ardent antifederalists were largely oblivious to this possibility. They focused their antigovernment animus almost entirely on the federal government, seeing it as an institution external to the people and thus in danger of reproducing the tyranny of George III. State governments, in their eyes, operated on a different level. They were close to the people; in fact, in states like Pennsylvania, governments seemed to be indistinguishable from the people. Why would "the people" need to have protections for the rights of individuals in a polity in which "the people" were themselves the ones exercising power?

James Madison was one of the few to offer an answer to that question, and it was a good one. In the course of designing the Constitution, he had concluded that dissent and conflict among interest groups were normal, even desirable features of politics in the American republic. That reality meant that the Constitution had to include measures designed to protect the rights of minorities against the will of the majority. These minorities, Madison believed, would be as vulnerable to the whims of majorities in statehouses as they would be to those of majorities in Congress.[17] Madison therefore argued that any limitation on the power that Congress could exercise over individuals should be "secured against the state governments" as well. He himself proposed an amendment to incorporate states under the Bill of Rights—a measure that he came to regard as "the most valuable amendment on the whole list" that had come before Congress for consideration. His colleagues in the first Congress did not share this view. They did not see the problem that this amendment was meant to address. Madison's world was not yet their world. In a move that occasioned little comment or debate, they scuttled his "incorporation" amendment.[18]

The inability of many of Madison's colleagues to comprehend the fuss Madison was making about imposing a bill of rights on the states points to the piecemeal and incomplete way that the ideology of liberalism emerged in late eighteenth-century America. By the 1790s, it was coming to define the theory of power underlying the structure of the central state, but not the one that was animating the states.

This chapter focuses on the central government. It does not retell what is a well-known and well-chronicled story of the early republic: the contest between those, such as Alexander Hamilton, who wanted to increase the size and power of the central state, and those, such as Thomas Jefferson, who wanted to keep that state bounded in size and the orbit of its powers. The Jeffersonians and their heir, Andrew Jackson, won that battle, in part because their ideas for the central state corresponded more closely with the principles of limited government that were central to the Constitution, and in part because they were seen by a democratizing electorate to have far more fully embraced the dream of popular sovereignty than their opponents.[19]

What does bear examination is how well America's central state met its governing challenges given the formal limitations on its power and the long period of time during which it was ruled by a Jeffersonian party ideologically dedicated to keeping that state small. In 1803, Jefferson complicated this central state's governing challenges by purchasing the enormous territory of Louisiana from France. In theory, the acquisition of this land would allow Jefferson to pursue his dream of making every white male citizen a landowner. This was the surest route, Jefferson believed, toward creating circumstances of economic independence in which political virtue could take root, and in which a republic conceived in the tradition of Greece and Rome could flourish. But it was not clear whether the central state over which Jefferson presided would be able, in practice, to govern the territory he had acquired. Would it manage to settle the huge land expanse it now possessed, and to incorporate those territories and their white settlers into the nation?

Would it, in fact, be able to distribute land in a relatively egalitarian way in order to produce a nation of yeoman farmers? Would it be able to project sufficient power to implant the sovereignty of the nation in far-flung territories, and defend the borders of the United States against the Indian tribes and several European empires that threatened them?[20]

This chapter attempts to answer those questions. It contends that the central state succeeded in spreading settlers throughout its territories, in binding them to the new nation, and in vanquishing America's enemies. These were substantial achievements. Nevertheless, federal governance was a precarious enterprise. Several of the central state's greatest successes, such as Andrew Jackson's military victories over Indian tribes, could have easily turned into shattering defeats. Moreover, the central state exercised only limited and intermittent control over the white settlers spreading into the western and southern territories. It failed repeatedly to stop white settlers from invading Indian Territory even when it was the desire of the nation's leaders to do so. With respect to Indian matters in particular, a larger central government with a greater capacity for effective administration—both civil and military—would have had policy options that remained closed to a small government. These options might have made a difference not only to Indian-white relations but also to the degree to which the republic came to depend on racial solidarity among whites as an integument of nationhood. A full evaluation of America's central state must reckon with both its surprising strengths and consequential weaknesses.

TERRITORIAL EXPANSION AND SETTLEMENT

From the beginning, the founders of the new nation envisioned it not as a small collection of states clinging to the eastern shelf of North America but as a large, expanding, and continental nation.[21] This was partly a matter of ideology. Jefferson and his supporters wanted to create an "empire of liberty" in which every white male citizen could experience economic independence, thought to be the foundation of both political freedom and civic virtue.[22]

Claiming the continent for Americans was also a matter of geopolitics. Other nations, notably England, France, and Spain, had laid claims to parts of it, as did innumerable Indian peoples. In the mercantilist worldview that still dominated much of international politics through the eighteenth century's end, one nation's gain was regarded as another nation's loss (and vice versa). Thus, if the United States declined to expand across the continent, other nations would likely expand into and encroach on the United States, eroding its territory and ultimately undermining its sovereignty. From the end of the Revolutionary War through the end of the War of 1812, this threat was palpable, with Britain entrenched in the North and Northwest, the French controlling New Orleans (and hence all commerce whose conduit was the Mississippi River), and Spain dominant in virtually all southern lands other than New Orleans that bordered the Gulf of Mexico. For both ideological and geopolitical reasons expansion became a kind of imperative.[23]

Even before the Constitutional Convention of 1787, the central government had found a way to expand its territory and assert its control over lands in the Northwest. By the terms of the 1783 Articles of Peace with Great Britain, individual American states, including Massachusetts, Connecticut, New York, Virginia, North Carolina, South Carolina, and Georgia, gained title to huge reserves of western land that the British were compelled to relinquish. These lands might have remained with the states, as did many resources (and powers) under the Articles of Confederation. But the Northwest Ordinances of 1785 and 1787 shifted these territories to the central government, creating a national market in land while also stipulating terms of the land's distribution that would guide national policy for most of the nineteenth century. Getting the original thirteen states to cede their western lands to the federal government formed a crucial prelude to the framing of the Constitution, and, as it turned out, to making this government responsible for both the projection and protection of territorial sovereignty. The central government would never relinquish these powers.[24]

Once the Constitution confirmed federal control of the territories, the central government focused on populating them with settlers and putting them on the road to statehood. The first task was to survey the land so that it could be divided into parcels that could be easily distributed through gift or sale to land-seeking individuals or companies. Surveying entailed establishing uniform methods of boundary measurement throughout the United States and registering all measured land parcels in federal land offices whose authority was enforced by the central government. This surveying project was meant to make possible the emergence of a national regime of private landownership and exchange—a regime that the US government hoped would stimulate rapid settlement of its huge territories.

The Northwest Ordinances again set the precedent, calling for land to be divided into six-square-mile townships, established on north–south and east–west axes. Land in each town was then to be divided into thirty-six sections of one square mile each, or 640 acres, all of which would be sold, save for one section that the federal government granted to the territory/state in which the new township was established to support local public schools.[25] The success of this uniform system of surveying led to a rectangular system of landownership that took root in all the new territories of the United States—one that is still apparent to the eye today when flying across the country.

The uniformity did not happen all at once. The first thirteen states retained rights to land within their original jurisdictions, and some, such as Georgia, showed little interest in the grid system inaugurated by the Northwest Ordinances.[26] Settlers who flocked into the Louisiana Territory after 1803 were quick to make claims of land under the different systems of land measurement established there by the French and Spanish. And the survey system, even where it did establish itself easily, was no guarantee against abuses, both small and large, in transferring federal land to private control.[27] Nevertheless, across the nineteenth century, the federal government did implant its measurements through most of its domain, and in the process, created a single system for surveying, registering, and exchanging land. Its success in surveying the approximately 1.9 billion acres that would become part of the public domain and distributing almost two-thirds of that domain was one of the new republic's most important achievements.[28]

The government also managed to distribute its land to a broad cross section of America's population, though its success in doing so did not really become apparent until after 1815. At first, the government kept the minimum parcels of land that could be purchased large (640 acres) and set the cost at $1 an acre—not an astronomical sum, but at $640 for a minimum plot of land, well beyond the means of most family farmers. The government's expectation was that at these prices, private land companies would purchase most of this land and become effective distributors of it to individual families. By the early 1800s, this reliance on land companies had come to be seen as a Federalist policy more intent on creating a new landed elite than in spreading landed wealth among a polity of yeoman farmers. And so when they came to power, the Jeffersonians dramatically reduced the minimum parcel of land that could be sold, first to 160 acres in 1804, and then to a mere 80 acres in 1820. In addition, Congress began allowing purchasers to buy land on credit, demanding only a 5 percent down payment and allowing four years for full payment of the debt. It also asked the newly created General Land Office (established in 1812) to speed up the surveying of federal territory and processing of land claims—important elements of a mass land distribution policy.[29] The settlement of the West did not immediately take off, due to the presence of Indian nations on and European powers alongside much of the most desirable land. But once the United States checked the power of foreign nations on the North American continent through its victory in the War of 1812 and simultaneously broke the back of Indian resistance to American expansion in the Southeast, land sales mushroomed, from 1 million acres in 1815, to 2.5 million in 1818, to 4 million in 1819.[30] In the 1830s, land sales exploded again as the US government transferred more than 57 million acres into private hands.[31] Meanwhile, the US Treasury filled up with cash from these land sales until, by the 1830s, total sales amounted to 40 percent of all federal revenues.[32]

If the terms of the Northwest Ordinances gave the federal government control of the land in US territories, they also stipulated that new territories were to remain in federal hands only for a relatively brief period of time. A mere sixty thousand people were required to have settled in a territory in order to make it eligible for statehood. The Northwest Ordinances called for these new states to be endowed as collectivities with the same set of rights that the original thirteen states possessed (stipulations subsequently attached to other territorial acquisitions such as the Louisiana Territory and Mexican Cession). This meant that when the new states entered the Union, they would do so as the political equals of the existing states; their citizens would have the same rights as did the citizens of the original thirteen states. In some cases, states carved out of the Northwest Territories gave their people more rights than those enjoyed by individuals in the original states. For example, these Northwest states prohibited slavery and enforced freedom of religion.[33]

In 1805, only two years after the Louisiana Purchase, Congress applied the Northwest Ordinances' demographic threshold for statehood (sixty thousand settlers on the ground) to the New Orleans Territory. A mere seven years later, Louisiana was admitted as a state. This admission was marked as well by a profound departure from the Northwest Territories model: Louisiana was permitted to enter the Union as a slave state and limit the rights of citizenship to those who were whites. The racial dimension of American expansion and transformation of territories in states are subjects to which we will return.[34]

Both liberal and democratic principles fueled American territorial expansion. The liberal dimension is manifest in the attempt to enlist the support of white settlers throughout the United States by appealing to their self-interest: the government asked for their loyalty to the young republic in return for giving them an opportunity to own land, and dispose of the fruits of their land and related economic activity as they saw fit. The government would thereby be able to execute its commitment to expansion, and settlers would gain an opportunity to become economically independent and even prosperous. The promise of prosperity and freedom bound individual citizens to their federal government.[35]

The success of this system rested on more than self-interest, however. It relied as well on a democratic notion of popular sovereignty. The people of the new territories, in conjunction with the people in the existing states, would rule; they would determine the course taken by the governments—local, state, and federal—that played some role in their lives. This commitment to popular sovereignty is apparent in the determination to convert all new territory within the continental United States into democratic polities whose citizens would acquire precisely the same standing as those in the existing states possessed. Through the extension of the system of representation set forth in the Constitution to all citizens of the territories, the United States would deliver on its promise that the people would govern.

A radical naturalization law was part of this liberal-democratic mix. By the terms of the Westphalian system and mercantilist economic doctrine that dominated seventeenth- and eighteenth-century Europe, monarchical states claimed complete and permanent sovereignty over their subjects, reserving the right to control their movement within a kingdom's territory and their freedom to move beyond it. Because the strength of a monarchy was measured in numbers—the more people a sovereign could claim as subjects, the mightier the realm—European rulers were reluctant to permit their subjects to emigrate unless the latter were paupers, criminals, or some other class of undesirables. Subjects who did move to another state were still expected to give allegiance to their original state or monarch.[36]

The British colonists in North America had begun to challenge this European system for controlling population movement in the mid-eighteenth century, in part for pragmatic reasons: the North American appetite for settlers from Europe had become insatiable. But the colonists made this materialist demand for labor into a political principle. Even prior to the 1770s, they had started to develop rules for membership that were based on residence, consent, and voluntary loyalty rather than on birth, descent, and perpetual subjecthood. And when these colonists brought an independent

United States into being, they established two principles governing freedom of movement and ease of membership that were revolutionary in the context of the eighteenth century. The first principle was that people would be free to enter and leave the new nation as they desired; the second was that any free European immigrant of "good character"—regardless of nationality, language, or religion—could elect to become a citizen after a brief period of residence (two years) in the United States. Embodied in the naturalization law of 1790, this second principle made that statute the most radically inclusive measure of its kind in the eighteenth-century world—a judgment that holds even if we take into account, as we must, the racial restriction for which this law has recently become so well known (making nonwhite immigrants and Indians ineligible for citizenship). And even as subsequent congresses made naturalization tougher to achieve by mandating waiting periods stretching to five years and longer in some cases, the United States continued to distinguish itself by the ease with which European immigrants could gain US citizenship for themselves. Both the ease of joining the US polity and the ease of leaving it were part of the revolutionary settlement. So, too, was a willingness to accept into the polity religious groups that were excluded from public life in Europe. Thus the United States extended full citizenship to Catholics a half century before Great Britain and to Jews before the French revolutionaries had done so. The freedom of movement guaranteed by the new nation in combination with the generous terms of civic membership made the United States a magnet for Europeans and established America's reputation early on for being a nation of immigrants.[37]

Pragmatic considerations continued to drive the desire of US policymakers to open their country to Europeans in this way. In order to settle its western territories, the United States had to draw a substantial population from abroad. Congress imagined these immigrants as farmers with sufficient means (good character in the language of the naturalization law) to purchase their own land.[38] Prospective European settlers had to be guaranteed secure property rights in the United States in order to attract them in large numbers. In other words, they had to be convinced that whatever

title they gained to land in the United States would be theirs in perpetuity. In the eighteenth- and early nineteenth-century European
world, most individuals owned nothing in perpetuity—their persons and property were subject to the will of their monarchs. The
granting to immigrants of almost immediate citizenship in the
United States both freed the individuals from these Old World obligations and secured their rights as property owners against those in
America who would challenge their claims.[39]

Seen in this way, the offer of such generous terms of citizenship
was a form of liberal contractualism, an attempt by the federal government to draw the loyalty of foreigners by advancing their self-
interest—in this case, by enabling them to acquire and then protect
property. This contractual form of connectedness became mixed
up with a much more diffuse—but equally powerful—notion of
belonging. The naturalization law of 1790 signaled America's intention to be a country composed of individuals who had freely
chosen to join it. Unlike membership in most of the world's polities, membership in America was a matter of consent and free will.
Moreover, affiliating oneself to it meant joining a polity in which
the people were meant to rule. This notion of a republic by consent
was given dramatic form by the oath to the Constitution that every
immigrant aspiring to US citizenship was required to take.[40]

Significantly, making it easy for European immigrants to become US citizens required almost nothing from the central state in
terms of government administration and bureaucracy. Prospective
citizens simply had to appear at "any common law court of record"
in a state in which they had resided for at least one year and apply
for citizenship. Judges would inspect the applicants, and if satis-
fied with their qualifications, administer the constitutional oath
and grant them citizenship on the spot. By parlaying self-interest
into a powerful sense of belonging in the new republic with a minimum of intervention by government institutions, the first Congress
was demonstrating how a lean liberal central state could advance
its aims.[41]

As with the case of land distribution, mass immigration did not
take off until the United States entered a period of internal and external security after 1815. By the 1830s and 1840s, however, the

country had become a destination for millions of European immigrants—a pattern that would persist, with few interruptions, until the early twentieth century. In the hundred-plus years that transpired between the conclusion of the War of 1812 and the implementation of immigration restriction in 1924, the United States drew more than thirty million immigrants—the vast majority of them European—to its shores.[42]

THE BONDS AND BOUNDARIES OF CITIZENSHIP

In comparison to the administration of naturalization, the post office system developed by the early republic looked like a bloated bureaucracy. By 1831, it employed more than 8,700 postmasters, who made up more than three-quarters of the entire federal civilian workforce (11,491), and whose numbers exceeded those in the entire federal army by 25 percent (6,332).[43] In fact, it was hardly a bureaucracy at all. Although the postmaster general worked in a beautiful marble building in Washington, DC, where approximately thirty-five people toiled under his direction, the vast majority of postmasters worked alone or with only a few clerks in thousands of dispersed and unassuming locations: the basements of hotels, counters in the corners of stores, taverns, and even private homes. A leaner form of government administration could scarcely be imagined. To keep it slim, the federal government relied on private stagecoach companies to transport most of the mail. This arrangement proved conducive to the establishment of an extraordinary network of outreach that implanted a plain post office in virtually every town or hamlet in the territorial United States. By 1828, when this network was complete, it laid claim to being the most extensive such network in the world. At that time, the United States boasted approximately twice as many post offices as Great Britain and more than five times as many as France.[44]

The creation of this system resulted from the Post Office Act of 1792, which was as important in its implications for the US republic as the 1790 naturalization law. This act gave Congress the power to designate its choice of post roads, even if those roads were entirely within the territory of a single state. It granted generous subsidies for public papers and newspapers, ensuring that these documents could circulate across long distances for small fees or no cost at all. Under the terms of the act, the postmaster general was empowered to use the financial surplus from lucrative routes on the East Coast to subsidize lightly trafficked routes into the interior. The charge to send a newspaper more than a hundred miles was 50 percent higher than mailing it to a destination within a hundred-mile radius (1.5¢ versus 1¢ per newspaper), but no additional surcharges were attached to distances stretching for hundreds of miles or to mail heading for locales where only a handful of people lived. Finally, the act prohibited post office employees from reading private correspondence. In short, the act made it easy to extend the post office system across new territories, made it possible for mail to reach the most remote and most lightly settled parts of the country, and guaranteed the privacy of personal correspondence.[45]

Under these circumstances, the volume of mail exploded—a development that had less to do with the exchange of private letters than with the circulation of newspapers. Encouraging the circulation of newspapers had been a major purpose of the 1792 law, whose supporters believed that citizens' access to economic and political information was an indispensable precondition to the success of the American republic. A polity that put sovereignty in the hands of citizens expected these individuals to make informed, intelligent, and rational decisions. Here we see a manifestation of the republican emphasis on virtue, and of the importance attached to cultivating that trait in every one of the republic's citizens. Newspapers gave Americans the tools to do so.

The postal system had another effect, also a deliberate aim of the 1792 law: to use the circulation of newspapers to bind together people living in dispersed space, thereby giving them a sense of common identity, purpose, and peoplehood. It was almost as if an ancestor of Benedict Anderson were serving as an adviser to the 1792 Congress, offering its members advice on the value of print newspapers to the creation and sustenance of an imagined political community. That the post office would be the nation's largest "bureaucracy" testifies to the importance that the American central state attached to the sinews of nationhood and republican virtue that it expected a widely and densely distributed print culture to nurture.[46]

The aspiration to make citizens informed, virtuous, and self-governing flourished alongside a conviction that only a portion of those living in the United States could meet these lofty standards. And so some groups, such as women and the white poor, had access only to limited citizenship rights, while other groups, especially those who were not white and whose origins lay outside Europe, had no access to citizenship at all. Slavery had been a core feature of economic and political life in the British North American colonies, and remained so across substantial portions of the United States during and after the revolution. The power to define the boundaries of freedom and coercion in the new republic rested mostly with the individual states, and will be examined in that context in the next chapter. But some of that power rested with the federal government, as may be seen, for example, in the 1790 Naturalization Act, which was exceptionally generous toward Europeans and ruthless in its exclusion of everyone else. Two years later, Congress passed the Fugitive Slave Act, putting the power of the central government behind the efforts of slave owners to reclaim slaves who had escaped to nonslave states.[47]

Those revolutionaries who had immersed themselves in republican thought were little troubled by what looks to twenty-first-century eyes like a monstrous contradiction: a nation that had fought a revolution in the name of liberty denying an entire portion of its people the opportunity to be free and self-governing. The history of republics, as these eighteenth-century revolutionaries saw it, was one of failure, as citizens, lacking the requisite virtue, had invariably lost sight of the common good, sacrificed their pursuit of liberty, and allowed their polity to degenerate into dictatorship. The best insurance against the American republic succumbing to a similar fate was to limit citizenship to those capable of handling its weighty responsibilities. Any group judged to be deficient in the personal qualities deemed to be essential to good citizenship—independence, reason, and virtue—could be barred from political participation. From a republican perspective, political exclusion and even enslavement were compatible with the drive to establish a polity that imagined itself as consecrated to liberty.[48]

This contradiction between the promise of freedom and the reality of coercion was more problematic for those revolutionaries taking their cues from the emerging liberal discourse about equality and rights as the natural human condition than for those arguing from a republican perspective. Indeed, from the moment that the Declaration of Independence made its debut on July 4, 1776, all kinds of Americans used this call to arms to insist that the new nation live up to its principles and eliminate inequality wherever they found it—in slavery, capitalist exploitation, religious and gender discrimination, and the treatment of indigenous peoples.[49] But as we have seen, liberalism was new to eighteenth-century political thought, and its principles were understood only partially and applied unevenly. Its most powerful manifestation in the early republic is to be found not in the program that would define liberalism in the second half of the twentieth century—ensuring that all Americans, regardless of their religion, race, gender, and sexual orientation, would enjoy equal rights—but in the campaign to limit the power of the central state and thus free individuals from its grasp. Many eighteenth-century liberals believed that once freed from an overbearing government, individuals would enhance not simply their liberty but also their ability to engage each other in circumstances of equality. In other words, once the problem of government tyranny was solved, problems of inequality in civil society would take care of themselves. This is not what happened, of course. Policies conceived in a classically liberal mode would actually intensify some old forms of inequality and give rise to new ones.[50] Liberals would eventually take note of this unexpected development, and rework their ideology in consequence. Yet this reconsideration and reworking lay a century in the future.[51] For much of the nineteenth century, liberally minded individuals believed deeply that limiting government power would enhance liberty and equality.

WAR, CITIZEN-SOLDIERS, AND SOVEREIGNTY

If we measure central state institutions by their size, only one rivaled the post office: the military, which during peacetime employed about three-quarters of the number of those who found their calling handling the mail. During wartime, of course, the military could and did mushroom in size, becoming by far the largest and perhaps most important institution of the central state. Its work was crucial to protecting the United States against external antagonists and internal opponents, to holding an increasingly sprawling country together, and to making sure that the central government had the capacity to project its power—and hence assert its sovereignty—through every part of US territory.

The project of developing a military force capable of maintaining the territorial integrity and sovereignty of the United States prompted some of the most interesting decisions made by the early congresses. Few sentiments among these congresses were stronger than the aversion to a standing army, and few decisions were as important as the one to keep America's peacetime army small. In American eyes, professional militaries were tools of government absolutism and corruption. For most of the half century following the ratification of the Constitution, the professional army of the United States was minuscule, hovering during peacetime at levels somewhere between three and ten thousand men. England's post-1750 peacetime army, by contrast, was forty-five thousand strong, expandable to one hundred thousand (or more) during wartime with another hundred thousand deployed to the navy. And England's peacetime army was small by the standards of its chief European rivals, France, Germany, and Spain.[52]

In the United States, the place of professional soldiers was to be taken by citizen-soldiers whom the government would call on in times of need to defend the republic. These citizen-soldiers would emerge from two kinds of groups: state militia units and the US Volunteers. State militias called on upstanding and property-owning private citizens to become soldiers and serve their country in times of crisis. At first the states themselves administered these militias, compelling all able-bodied freeholders to participate in semiannual militia-training days. Increasingly, however, the states found it difficult to keep these militias stocked with their "better citizens." Local militia companies based on residence or ethnicity soon arose to take the place of state-sponsored groups. These militia companies often sought and received official recognition by the state governments in whose territory they resided.[53] In theory, the number of soldiers that could be turned out through these militias was vast: three-quarters of a million men were thought to belong to militias in 1816, and more than one million in 1827, when the total population of the United States numbered only nine million (in 1816) and twelve million (in 1827).[54]

These militias were thought sufficient for executing police actions and containing small-scale insurrections, but not for waging war. For the latter, the federal government turned to the US Volunteers—units that were to be raised from scratch to fight particular foes.[55] Typically, the federal government would send a request for a certain number of regiments to a state governor, who would then approach private citizens to raise the necessary troops. For much of the nineteenth century, this was the principal mechanism for raising troops.[56] Thus, America's nineteenth-century military system was built on the willingness of ordinary citizens to respond to their government's call to arms. Both the militias and US Volunteers depended on individual men of means and reputation coming forward to form military units and then lead them into battle.

But this does not mean that the US military lacked professional expertise. Congress had established a military academy, West Point, in 1802, and after an early reorganization, it acquired a reputation for turning out superior professional soldiers.[57] The government also developed a corps of army engineers that would play an important role in internal improvements, and established weapons factories that would produce guns and artillery. But the professionals could neither execute a war nor deploy their artillery without masses of citizen-soldiers who were willing to join the fight. The militia testified to one way in which classical republicanism influenced policy in the new American nation. The citizen-soldier had been the quintessential republican figure since the heyday of the Greek city-states. The citizen volunteering to defend his republic with his life was exemplary of the sensibility that military valor, sacrifice, and virtue were centrally part of the character of the American republic.[58] Many Americans spoke of militias and military service in these terms, even as they acknowledged that this republican tradition also served the purposes of those who wanted to create a liberal state—one that was lean, with a minimal number of regular employees, but that could scale up quickly to meet big challenges when the need arose.

The federal government was not averse to another liberal feature of these militias: drawing on the self-interest of these citizen-soldiers. A significant number of the settlers of America's western frontiers were veterans of one of the young nation's wars who had been promised a free bounty of land as a reward for their service. The government's generosity was simultaneously an opportunity to seed the frontier with former soldiers whose experience with arms and fighting made them a dependable line of national defense against aggrieved Indians. The federal government believed that these veterans could be relied on in part because they would be fighting not just for Washington, DC, but also for the security of their own lands and the safety of their own families.[59] The efficacy of the militia-volunteer system depended on fusing this self-interest with nobler sentiments: namely, a belief that the central government was their government, that it expressed their will and was concerned with their welfare, and that in acting to defend this government, they were acting to defend themselves and their families. How well did this system work?

Any evaluation must begin by moving away from a teleological view of the United States as a country destined for greatness and fated to become a mighty nation on the North American continent. From the perspective of the time, another view of America's early history is more plausible: that the new nation had overreached territorially, and was in danger of failing—or at least of breaking apart. One might have concluded in 1810 that the acquisition of the Northwest and Louisiana territories had saddled the United States with landmasses it could neither settle nor protect. It could have lost land to the British in the North and Northwest, to Spain in the South and Southeast, or to independent republics established either by white Americans hoping to multiply the number of "Anglo republics" on the North American continent or by groups of rebellious African slaves (often called Maroons) seeking a similar kind of freedom to that achieved by their counterparts in Haiti, Brazil, and other parts of Latin America, including Spanish Florida.[60]

Lower Louisiana seems to have been especially vulnerable to conquest, rebellion, or secession in the years after the Louisiana Purchase. Given the Port of New Orleans's importance to hemispheric and international trade, Britain and Spain were not ready to give up their claims to it. Many of Lower Louisiana's British, French, and Spanish residents, unhappy with their sudden incorporation into the United States, were not averse to working on a rival country's behalf to free the territory from American control. The preeminence of New Orleans as a site for hemispheric trade and the geography of the Mississippi Delta with its hundreds of hidden waterways made the area a natural haven for treasure-hungry pirates who swore allegiance to no nation or monarch. Lower Louisiana had also become a destination for refugees from the Haitian Revolution of 1791; abolitionists in their ranks soon set to work spreading revolutionary doctrines of emancipation among slaves working the plantations along the Mississippi River, contributing in 1811 to what one scholar has called the largest slave revolt in American history.[61] The preoccupation of the rival imperial empires with each other increased the leverage of Indian tribes in the area, allowing them to secure political arrangements that enhanced their autonomy.[62]

This swirl of multiple, contending, and opposing forces, and the shifting alliances among them, also drew opportunistic adventurers to the area. Some, like the pirate Jean Lafitte, built a commercial empire in the Mississippi Delta. Others, like Aaron Burr, believed that they could establish a republic of their own in the region, using New Orleans as a jumping-off point for expeditions—or filibusters, as they were called at the time—into Mexico, which was perceived as an especially vulnerable portion of a tottering Spanish empire. These adventurers imagined that they could conquer part of northern Mexico and, with territory taken from the southern United States, fashion their own country. They were betting that North America would follow a path that actually came to define South American geopolitics in the nineteenth century: a continent composed of multiple nations descended from a single imperial ancestor (and sharing a common language and other cultural affinities). Each of these nations, however, would be fiercely independent from the others in its politics. That Burr and those who followed in his footsteps lost their gamble should not obscure the fact that in the early nineteenth century, these wagers attracted a lot of smart money. The United States could easily have come apart.[63]

The US republic's success in beating the odds partly reflected the potency of its liberal-democratic principles. Promising people land (and the independence and prosperity that went with it) along with self-government was a powerful incentive—one that potential participants in the republic quickly understood and were eager to obtain. But the United States' ability to control the sprawling landmass it had acquired also reflected the effectiveness of its military. The army possessed an ability to scale up its force rapidly, to deploy it where it was needed, and to defeat Indians, slaves, rival imperial powers, and Anglo adventurers who challenged US sovereignty.[64] This military succeeded at several critical junctures, although none as important as the years from 1813 to 1819, when slaves, Indians, and the British threatened to fragment the United States in its vulnerable South. And no force was more crucial in defeating these threats than General Andrew Jackson and his largely Tennessean militia and volunteers. Their actions deserve a close look for what they reveal about the capacity of an army of mainly citizen-soldiers to defend a nation.

In 1812, Madison, the fourth US president, took the United States to war against Great Britain and several Indian nations over matters of sovereignty, trade, and territory. The British were seizing US ships, impressing American seamen into the Royal Navy, poaching on territory that the United States claimed as its own, and encouraging Indians to attack US settlers and thus destabilize the American frontier. In 1813, at the beginning of his second term, Madison called on Jackson, commander of the Tennessee militia, to raise a force to confront three threats to the United States in the South: first, an insurrection by Creek Indians in Alabama that was perceived to be part of a pan-Indian uprising stretching from the Great Lakes to the Gulf of Mexico; next, the determination of the British to land several armies on the southern coast, seize critical American ports (including New Orleans and Mobile), and reestablish British control over large stretches of North American territory and commerce; and finally, the flight of Africans from slavery on plantations in the American South to comparative safety and freedom in Spanish Florida. Jackson and the largely militia and volunteer forces he led played a leading role in defeating the Indians, British, and "banditti" of Spanish Florida, thereby ending the threat that each group had posed to the US republic.

Born in the Carolinas to Scots-Irish immigrant parents in the 1760s, Jackson migrated to the western territories of those states, rising quickly in the frontier society that became the state of Tennessee in 1797. Jackson amassed wealth as a planter, and served as his state's first US senator and one of its first militia commanders. The lower Mississippi drew his immediate attention, first for commercial reasons (this was the route through which Tennessee produce had to pass to reach East Coast or foreign markets) and then because of the region's geopolitical instability. Jackson understood how much other nations coveted control of the Mississippi River and New Orleans, and regarded the dense presence of Indian peoples in territory stretching from Tennessee south into Louisiana, Mississippi, Alabama, Georgia, and the Spanish colony of Florida as a perpetual danger. The future of his beloved American nation would not be secure until someone drove Britain, Spain, and the Indian nations out of the Gulf Coast. Jackson's opportunity to play a role in bringing this future to fruition arrived with Madison's request in 1813.[65]

Jackson's first assignment was to defeat a group of rebel Creeks in the Alabama portion of the Mississippi Territory. These Creeks, known as Red Sticks, were themselves warring against other Creeks. A key issue dividing them was how much to accommodate the Creek nation to the white settlers in their midst. The Red Sticks refused accommodation, and to drive this message home, attacked a US army outpost, Fort Mims, in southern Alabama in 1813, massacring hundreds of white settlers who had gathered there for safety. Reports circulated that the Red Sticks slaughtered women and children and cut the unborn from the wombs of pregnant women. The size and brutality of the Red Sticks' attacks were themselves frightening. But Americans feared that their significance was greater still, interpreting them as part of a broader pan-Indian insurrection inspired by the Shawnee leader Tecumseh against American settlers throughout the frontier states and territories, North and South. Because Tecumseh was known to be working closely with the British, any victory for his pan-Indian uprising would likely embolden the latter, whose naval forces were already probing American defenses along the Gulf of Mexico, looking for points of penetration. The stakes in the Red Sticks rebellion were therefore high, and Jackson was the man called on to put an end to it.

Jackson marched his Tennessee militia hard. Though he repeatedly outran his supply lines, generating near mutinies among his chronically hungry troops, Jackson nevertheless managed to assemble a force of more than four thousand for a March 1814 assault on a Red Sticks encampment at Horseshoe Bend, Alabama. Outnumbering the Red Sticks by a factor of four to one, Jackson's troops attacked from all sides, allowing the Indians no route of escape and showing them no mercy. By the time the fighting came to an end, an estimated nine hundred to a thousand Red Sticks had died, including many women and children. Jackson's troops suffered only fifty casualties. His soldiers mutilated the bodies of the Indians they killed by slicing off their noses and cutting strips of their skin to be used as bridle reins for American horses.[66]

Horseshoe Bend was the bloodiest single battle in the history of US-Indian warfare—a distinction it would never relinquish. It broke the back of Creek resistance in the South and damaged prospects for the broader pan-Indian rebellion. The defeat of the rebel Creeks significantly enhanced America's ability to extend its control and sovereignty over Indian land in Alabama and Georgia. The treaty that Jackson signed with the Creeks formally ending the Creek War compelled this Indian nation to relinquish twenty-three

million acres of their land to the United States. Among the signa-
tories to this treaty were Creeks who had supported Jackson in his
war against the Red Sticks. That support now won them no exemption from Jackson's broad land confiscation. Already in 1814,
Jackson had decided that the flourishing of his nation required the
expulsion of all Indians from territory that "rightfully" belonged
to the United States.[67]

Neither the government in Washington, DC, nor Jackson himself had much time in 1814 to savor the Horseshoe Bend victory.
The other news about the war that spring was bad. Together with its
European coalition powers, Britain had forced Napoléon into exile, and as a result, was now able to shift more of its military might
to North America. In summer 1814, the British sent a fleet into
the Chesapeake Bay, landed troops in Maryland, marched them to
Washington, and burned the American capital to the ground. The
torching of Washington humiliated the United States, exposing internal divisions about the wisdom and winnability of the war. In
New England, those gathering at the Hartford Convention talked
openly of secession. As they deliberated, a sixty-ship British ar-
mada was heading for New Orleans with eight thousand British
troops on board. Panic spread in the city, whose leaders wrote to
Jackson imploring him to bring his army to the city's defense.[68]

Jackson arrived in New Orleans on December 1, and found
there a scared and fractious population obsessed by the threat of
a British attack and by rumors of British sympathizers within the
city, especially among local African and Spanish populations.
Jackson placed the city under martial law and issued a warning
that anyone caught dealing with the enemy would be put to death.
He combined this ironfisted rule with a surprising openness to potential allies—his flexibility dictated by a need to bring troop totals
nearer to the numbers that he expected the British to throw into
battle. Thus, against the wishes of the local Anglo elite, Jackson
substantially expanded the ranks of the freemen of color militia,
and struck an alliance with Lafitte and his multicultural force of pirates who had built up a sizable and navigationally savvy military
force in Barataria Bay, seventy miles southwest of New Orleans.[69]

Jackson's American forces tangled with British soldiers on four different occasions between December 13, 1814, and the climactic battle of January 8, 1815, when British infantry charged into an American line of infantry and artillery batteries. The British had the advantage in numbers, with approximately eight thousand troops to Jackson's four to five thousand. But the Americans were well dug in and had the advantage of defense. Their artillery and sharpshooters poured barrages of fire into the British lines and cut down British troops in appalling numbers. The action was swift and devastating. When the smoke cleared and Jackson's scouts surveyed the fields of battle, they were stunned by the number of British soldiers who had fallen: three hundred killed, and more than seventeen hundred wounded—a full 20 percent of the invasion force. In comparison, the Americans had suffered only slightly: thirteen dead, and fewer than forty wounded.[70] The scale of the battle was epic, and its outcome decisive. Unknown to any of the combatants, the battle was actually fought after diplomats from both countries had negotiated a peace agreement in Ghent, the Netherlands, on Christmas Eve. This knowledge, when it came, did not diminish the battle's significance, however. Rarely had America won a battle of this size and complexity against a rival European power.[71] A report in *Niles' Weekly Register* declared that Jackson's victory had given the United States "the proudest period in the history of the republic," demonstrating "to mankind" America's "capacity to acquire a skill in arms to conquer 'the conquerors of all' as Wellington's invincibles were modestly stiled."[72] Celebrations broke out in numerous American cities, and exuberant parades were quickly organized. The United States had shown the world that it could protect its territory against the most powerful of rivals. Jackson became the preeminent American hero, his popularity eclipsing even that of George Washington, Benjamin Franklin, and Jefferson.[73]

Jackson was not finished. He now turned his attention to Spain, the remaining European imperial presence on the Gulf Coast. His concern was not with Spain per se, which was perceived to be weak and in a state of decline, but rather with runaway slaves and Indians—the so-called banditti—who were using Spanish Florida as a refuge from the reach of US law and military might. Spain no longer offered freedom to enslaved Africans who converted to Catholicism; however, many of these slaves and their Indian allies were able to achieve a state of de facto freedom in Spanish Florida, if only because Spain no longer exercised effective sovereignty over its one remaining North American colony. The freedom achieved by these refugees in Spanish territory encouraged more and more slaves and Indians to dream of an escape to Florida. Some who made the escape then used the safety of their Florida residence to organize raids on Anglo settlers in Alabama, Georgia, and South Carolina. The ability of Africans and Indians to live freely in Florida became a destabilizing force on racial hierarchies and slave systems within the United States—a development that America's Anglo majority would not tolerate.[74]

In early 1818, Jackson, now a major general and in command of the entire southern division of the US Army, arrived at Fort Scott, Georgia, with a force of three thousand regulars and volunteers and two thousand Indian allies. His aim was to invade Florida, drive the Spanish out, extend US sovereignty over the territory, and force Africans and Indians into submission to the republic's authority. In a three-week campaign, his forces burned hundreds of Indian villages, executed several prominent Indian chiefs as well as two British traders who had become Indian allies, undermined what was left of Spanish authority in Florida, and established in its place a provisional government under US control. Jackson exceeded his authority in executing the two British traders after convicting them in a military court of his own invention. This along with his unauthorized march on Pensacola, where he compelled the Spanish governor to cede control of the city to his forces, created an uproar both in Washington, DC, where senators brought motions of censure against him, and in international diplomatic circles. But Jackson's supporters in Washington defeated the censure campaign, and American diplomats turned his demolition of Spanish authority into Spain's formal cession of its Florida Territory to the United States. With his work of ousting rival imperial nations from the southern regions of the North American continent complete, Jackson fulfilled his obligation as a citizen-soldier: he retired from

military service in 1821, never to return. That same year, he became the first US governor of the Florida Territory. Eight years
later, the most popular man in the United States would become its
seventh president.[75]

Jackson's military campaigns in the American South from 1813
to 1819 reveal how active and successful America's central state
was in projecting and protecting its sovereignty. This central state,
concretized in the federalized armies that Jackson led, chased both
the British and Spanish from the Gulf of Mexico and broke the
back of Creek resistance in the Mississippi Territory. These were
big achievements. Moreover, this success came to a government
that was not impressive by the standards of nineteenth-century
European militaries. Jackson's military force rarely exceeded five
thousand troops and was composed largely of citizen-soldiers—
militiamen and volunteers from a variety of states, with Jackson's
own men from Tennessee usually providing its backbone. Jackson
had demonstrated how effective a lean and nimble government
with only a limited professional military could be in defending the
nation's interests. This United States had scaled up its professional
military to a total of ten thousand men for the duration of the War
of 1812. By the 1820s, with the British, Spanish, and most southern Indian tribes defeated, Congress scaled its professional military
back to a modest six thousand men, and refused Secretary of War
John C. Calhoun's request to maintain a larger force. In the eyes of
Congress, the militia and volunteer system had worked to give the
country the troops it needed in times of war, and it would continue
to rely on this system in future conflicts.[76]

A CENTRAL STATE BOTH
STRONG AND WEAK

The central government's military success was part of a broader
set of achievements in the early nineteenth century: the dramatic
expansion in the size of the territory it controlled; the rapid surveying and settlement of these lands and their speedy transformation into equal, rights-bearing states; and the binding of whites in

these states to American ideals. The federal government appeared to have accomplished its aims.

Yet it had done so only with great difficulty. The deep aversion to a centralized civil bureaucracy and professional military had generated some weaknesses. The federal government repeatedly lost control of the land settlement process to the settlers and the states that represented them, and had to make repeated concessions to them or face a catastrophic rejection of its authority. These concessions typically came in the form of preemptions, which were acts passed by Congress to exempt from prosecution, land confiscation, removal, or imprisonment groups of individuals that squatted on land that was either not owned by the United States or declared off-limits to settlers. That Congress issued nearly one preemption a year between 1799 and 1838 highlights the failings of the General Land Office in exercising its own authority over land distribution and occupation.[77]

This failure was at least partially by design: majorities in Congress during the Jeffersonian era distrusted government bureaucrats, especially those with administrative discretion. These majorities wanted to curtail the ability of such bureaucrats to make decisions about land distribution on their own, independent of Congress. One way of doing this was to starve administrative agencies of personnel and funds. As a result, there never seemed to be enough personnel or talent in the General Land Office. One observer reported to the Senate in 1823 that "it was impossible to obtain the services 'of individuals qualified by their independence of character and discriminating powers of mind, to adjust . . . [land] claims speedily and satisfactorily, unless a more adequate compensation for their services [was] given.'"[78] Because administrative agencies lacked resources and talent, Congress had to devote an inordinate amount of its own time, year after year, to resolving specific land disputes. This was hardly a good use of Congress, and it also meant the land distribution process was vulnerable to political meddling.[79]

Administrative weakness and confusion at the center of government, in turn, frustrated individuals on the territorial peripheries, where questions of land acquisition and cultivation were most intense. Many squatters blamed their own illegal actions on a federal government that never seemed to have enough surveyors or offices where land could be registered and legitimately claimed. And as if to legitimize the squatters' point of view, the central government, more often than not, gave in to their claims and, through the preemption process, conferred legality on them.[80]

The repeated legitimation of squatter claims was consequential for Indian-settler relations. Much of the squatting in the early nineteenth century was on lands that the United States had agreed by treaty to regard as the rightful property of Indian nations and thus not available to its own white settlers. The repeated pouring of American settlers into these lands, the federal government's violation of its Indian treaties in order to recognize these settler claims, and the resultant dispossession of Indians of their land is a well-known story. Less widely known, however, is the strong sentiment felt in significant parts of the American population and government for respecting the nation's treaty obligations with Indian nations and restraining, if not halting altogether, settler expansion.

The respect in portions of government and among private groups of citizens for the integrity of Indian nations and the territory they controlled was in part an expression of geopolitical necessity: the United States needed Indian allies to resist rival European empires, and treaties with Indian nations were thought to cement such alliances. And as Pekka Hämäläinen and others have shown, successful alliances with powerful Indian nations could yield substantial geopolitical gains.[81] In part this respect reflected, too, the universalism that underlay revolutionary ideals, imbuing significant numbers of Americans with the belief that at least some Indian tribes could be civilized, made into yeoman farmers, taught to treasure liberty and self-government, and hence eventually brought into the American republic. These pro-Indian attitudes surfaced in the thinking of presidents Washington and John Quincy Adams, Secretary of War Henry Knox, and Chief Justice John Marshall; they were also seen among groups of Federalists (and later Whigs), professional military officers, and missionaries who worked among the Indians. But despite their influence, these individuals and groups had little success encoding their beliefs into national policy, and the smallness of America's central state may bear partial responsibility for their failure.[82]

It was one thing to have this central state undertake the surveying of all land in the public domain. It was another for it to stop settlers from entering territories declared off-limits to them. Stopping illegal settler expansion would have required a far larger standing army than the United States was prepared to tolerate. This army would have had to enforce boundaries of settlement, which would have meant using force against settlers determined to break through those boundaries and dismantling—by coercion, if necessary—illegal settlements that squatters had established on forbidden ground.[83] Enforcing the prohibition of settlement in Indian country also would have required a more professional army, with its members given to understand that their full and unconditional loyalty lay with the central state that employed them. Citizen-soldiers were frequently reluctant to give the central state this kind of loyalty, especially those living with their families in frontier areas and coveting Indian land for themselves. A lieutenant in the regular army that had massed in Illinois in 1831 to fight Black Hawk and his Sac warriors described his citizen-soldier militia allies in these terms: "[The militia camp was a] multitude of citizen volunteers, who were as active as a swarming hive; catching horses, electioneering, drawing rations, asking questions, shooting at marks, electing officers, mustering in, issuing orders, disobeying orders, galloping about, 'cussing and discussing' the war, and the rumors thereof."[84] If the central government acted against these unruly militiamen, as it sometimes did, these men might abandon their military duty altogether, or they might draw on their political sophistication—evident in this account's report of the interest of these men in electing their own officers and electioneering more generally—to counterpose their own authority as rights-bearing citizens against that of the federal government. Alternatively, they might give their first loyalty to their state governments rather than to Washington, DC, on the grounds that the federalism of the Constitution gave the states greater and prior power to determine the course of Indian-settler relations. And many states, such as

Georgia, were eager to put themselves at the disposal of those citizens who were hungry for Indian land.[85]

The federal government, in other words, lacked the kind of large and professional military that might have enabled it to restrain the expansion of white settlers into Indian lands. Dependent on citizen-soldiers for muscle, the US state had to tolerate their loose discipline, visceral hatred of Indians, and deep emotional connection to many of the settlers whose landgrabbing habits they were expected to restrain. These citizen-soldiers sometimes drove the United States into Indian wars it did not seek, and then acted in such a way so as to drive up the financial and psychological costs of the wars themselves. This was the case, for example, with the Black Hawk War in Illinois from 1830 to 1832, which resulted from white squatters illegally seizing land from the Sac Indians, thereby dooming the federal government's attempt to resolve the differences between the settlers and Indians through negotiation. The United States would win that war, but only after enduring massacres along with an outbreak of Asian cholera in the ranks of a new force of five thousand regular troops and militiamen that it had been compelled to raise. In short, the cost of winning was high.[86]

Similar weaknesses showed up in the country's efforts to subdue Indians in Florida, in what is known as the Second Seminole War (1835–41), which cost fifteen hundred American soldiers their lives, and to control the Canadian border in 1837 during a revolt by Canadian settlers against British rule.[87] Commenting on the Second Seminole War in 1840, John Quincy Adams wrote that "it depresses the spirits and humiliates the soul to think that this war is now running into its fifth year, has cost thirty million dollars, [and] has successfully baffled all our chief military generals."[88] Part of what drove generals to distraction was the need to work with a jerry-built and constantly changing constellation of militias. In multiple Indian wars, this need required a level of political and social skills that most individual commanders simply did not possess. Jackson had these skills, but even he had been rendered vulnerable at times by misbehaving militias. In early 1814, for instance, on the eve of Jackson's decisive attack on the Red Sticks in Alabama, thousands of his militiamen abandoned him, shrinking his force virtually overnight from two thousand to fewer than two hundred. Had the Red Sticks had this information and attacked Jackson at this moment of grave numerical weakness, they might easily have routed his now-tiny army, and killed or captured Jackson himself, thereby reducing Old Hickory's status to a mere footnote in American history. But they did not know about Jackson's weakness, and soon a new force of Tennessee militiamen came to his rescue. Jackson quickly fashioned these new men into the formidable army that defeated the Red Sticks at Horseshoe Bend and then the British in New Orleans. His skills in effecting this transformation, however, should not obscure just how decentralized and ad hoc was the militia system with which he had to contend, or lessen our appreciation of how his mission against the Red Sticks in Alabama could have easily failed in the hands of other, more ordinary generals.[89] The central government for which Jackson worked, with its aversion to large and professional military, was sometimes dependent for its battlefield success on both extraordinary individual commanders and plain, dumb luck.

It also depended on a potent ideological mix of liberal-democratic and racial supremacist beliefs that motivated citizen-soldiers to come to their country's defense. From the central government's point of view, one positive feature of the militia system was the elasticity of its manpower reservoirs. In general, Jackson and other commanders were able to quickly replenish their armies at moments when masses of existing militiamen decided they had had enough and wanted to go home. Why? Recruitment almost always worked among settlers in frontier states who believed that they were fighting for their way of life. This way of life was one that both enshrined liberal self-interest, promising to put an abundance of cheap land within the reach of ordinary people, and celebrated popular sovereignty, putting these same people in charge of their own individual and collective destinies. Protecting this way of life almost always entailed war against the Indians and Indian removal, both to gain access to the land tracts that Indians controlled and then to secure this land—and the family homesteads and self-governing communities that arose on them—from Indian reprisal.

And when the Indians refused to go peacefully and struck at white settlers with a ferocity designed to scare them away, wars against the Indians acquired a racial dimension: these peoples, the settlers came to believe, were savages who were by nature incapable of civilization or democratic self-rule.

The specter of a savage Other who could, at a moment's notice, wipe out the republican families and communities taking root in the American wilderness became indispensable as a motivating ideology among white settlers. The settlers' experiment in liberty coupled with their ability to construct a nation that put liberal-democratic principles at its core required the destruction of these racial inferiors. Hence Jackson's appeal: he was a man who did not hesitate to attack and kill Indians, and often in the most ruthless possible manner. Hence, too, Jackson's ability and that of other like-minded commanders to replenish depleted armies with fresh waves of citizen-soldiers. In these circumstances, popular sovereignty took on a deep racial cast, defined as a system that only certain peoples, distinguished by the social and political quality of their racial inheritance, could sustain. This sentiment surfaced everywhere in the young republic, from the urbane halls of Congress, where a determination was made in 1790 that only white immigrants could become citizens, to the most distant outposts on the frontier. The frontier nourished the most extreme versions of this attitude, for there savage war became a substitute for the kinds of civil negotiations and enforceable treaties that a federal government with a more powerful presence might have been able to sustain.[90]

Negotiating difference while keeping the peace between peoples as different as Indians and white Americans tends toward administrative complexity. Enforcing the treaties with the Indians would have taken far larger and more centralized governmental apparatuses—both civilian and military—than anything that the Jeffersonians, and later the Jacksonians, were willing to contemplate. The strongest supporters for building such a large state in America were to be found in the ranks of the Federalists and later the Whigs. They were also the groups most ready to use the power of the central state to restrain settler expansion for the sake of peaceful relations with the Indians. But they were on the wrong side of the democracy revolution that the Jeffersonian-Jacksonians had unleashed. Federalist-Whig skepticism about the political capacities of the common man and the desire to see the American republic governed by enlightened elites pushed electoral success— and the opportunity to build a large centralized state that electoral success might have conferred—ever further from their grasp.[91] The political failure to build a more capacious state, one might argue, heightened the importance of race as a sinew of sovereignty in this new nation. This sinew may have helped to stabilize the heady but fragile mix of liberal-democratic sentiments that white settlers carried with them to the frontier.

The limitation of America's liberal central state is not to be found, then, in some inherent weakness that rendered all its initiatives futile. To the contrary, this state enjoyed major successes in the early, critical decades of the republic: distributing land, procuring settlers, protecting its territory, and projecting its sovereignty. But after 1800, the injunction to be lean and nonbureaucratic did put certain policy options out of reach. As a result, this liberal central state was both strong and weak, flexibly creative and rigid— patterns that would reproduce themselves in other areas of governance across nineteenth-century America.

2

THE STATES AND
THEIR POLICE POWER

Few recent accounts of the "American state" know what to do with the
states. One issue is logistics: there are simply too many states, and
few scholars have wanted to spend their research time in dreary
state archives. A more fundamental issue is a conceptual one: European theory has driven studies of the state for most of this subject's history, and that has meant an emphasis on the nature and
activities of the central state, understood to be a unitary institution powerfully directed from a political center. The very term we
use to discuss the phenomenon being analyzed—"the state"—is
indicative of this reliance on concepts developed for polities that
could plausibly be thought to have a unitary institution of this sort.
It is obvious that this singular term does not work well for a polity such as the United States, in which multiple institutions carry
out "state" activities. Nevertheless, more often than not, the states
have fallen out of conversation in discussions about American government, except among social scientists and legal scholars who
study federalism. But this latter group, while advancing our understanding of federalism in major ways, has had only intermittent impact on studies and conceptualizations of the American state.[1]

This chapter may be understood as an effort to "bring the states back in" to that broader conversation.[2] It is vital that we do, for the states operated according to a different governing principle than did the central state. This principle was and is known in judicial circles as the "police power," but is largely unknown outside those circles. A broad portion of the activities of state governments cannot be understood without reference to it. It constituted a second principle of American governance, and one that often stood in contradiction to the liberal principles that structured the activities of the central government.

The point of departure must be what students of federalism have always insisted: that from the start, the United States was a federal republic, meaning that it divided authority between the central government and the governments of its constituent parts, the thirteen states. This division was central to the overriding liberal ambition to prevent any one institution of government from gaining too much power.[3] But America's federal system went beyond a simple division of powers. It organized the two major divisions of government—the central state and the states—around different *theories* of power. A liberal theory, as we have seen in chapter 1, animated and guided the central government. The fundamental principle of this liberal theory was that citizens had rights that no government could take away except under the most extraordinary of circumstances. As a result, the powers of the central government had to be limited in clear and effective ways. The Bill of Rights came to embody this aspiration.

The individual states were not obligated to operate according to this liberal principle. Instead, their power derived from a different political principle—one that held the public good in higher esteem than private right. This principle called for a polity well regulated by government in which, as the legal historian William Novak has written, "no individual right, written or unwritten, natural or absolute," could be permitted to eclipse "the people's safety" or welfare.[4] It resembled in part what scholars writing in the mid- to late twentieth century—figures such as J.C.A. Pocock, Quentin Skinner, Gordon Wood, and Mauricio Viroli—have called the ideology of "republicanism."[5] Like republicanism, this principle of governance put its faith in the ability of responsible, virtuous citizens to determine and agree on the public interest or *salus populi*, the people's welfare. This principle of governance was not indifferent to individual rights. But it insisted that the enjoyment of personal freedom and individual rights depended on the carefully regulated society that government would construct.

This second principle of governance endowed the states with a scope of authority more capacious in many respects than that which inhered in the central government itself. In truth, state governments possessed a staggering freedom of action. They had the power to direct internal transportation improvements; issue controls on capital and labor; build schools, libraries, and other educational facilities; and engage in town planning and supervise public health. They organized moral life. Rules governing marriage, drinking, narcotics, gambling, sexuality, theatergoing and the arts, and a community's disposition to the migrant poor were all subject to the control of the states. The states also held jurisdiction over municipalities in the sense that all city and town governments derived their powers from what the states decided to give to (or take from) them. The powers of the states could be deployed progressively, as, for example, in insisting that capitalist development be subjected to the people's welfare, and regressively, as, for instance, in legislating hierarchies grounded in race or gender into law. The vast majority of laws legitimating slavery from 1789 to 1863 were state laws; so too were the laws buttressing America's system of racial apartheid after the Civil War—a system formally installed in the 1890s that governed all the states of the American South until the middle decades of the twentieth century.

Americans like to celebrate the brilliance of their founding fathers, yet the different theories of governance that came to animate the two levels of government resulted only in part from their grand design. We can see one element of design in the Tenth Amendment, the last of the Bill of Rights, which declares, "The powers not delegated to the United States by the Constitution, nor prohibited by it to the States, are reserved to the States respectively, or to the people." Through this amendment, state governments acquired what legal scholars have labeled "residual powers."[6] There was nothing at all residual about this power, however. From the start, key framers of the Constitution understood that the very refusal to enumerate the powers of state governments might endow them with substantial power. As James Madison himself wrote in the forty-fifth *Federalist*, "The powers reserved to the several States will extend to all the objects which, in the ordinary course of affairs, concern the lives, liberties, and properties of the people, and the internal order, improvement, and prosperity of the State."[7] In 1788, another Federalist, Tench Coxe, spelled out far more specifically what state governments under the Constitution would be able to do:

> Create corporations civil and religious; prohibit or impose duties on the importation of slaves into their own ports; establish seminaries of learning; erect boroughs, cities and counties; promote and establish manufactures; open roads; clear rivers; cut canals; regulate descents and marriages; license taverns; alter the criminal law; constitute new courts and offices; establish ferries; erect public buildings; sell, lease, and appropriate the proceeds and rents of *their lands*, and of every other species of *state property*; establish poor houses, hospitals, and houses of employment; regulate the police; and many other things of the utmost importance to the happiness of their respective citizens.[8]

If part of this system emerged by constitutional design, other parts resulted from messy circumstances and compromises, on the one hand, and what we might call the Tocquevillian law of revolution, on the other. The messy circumstances and compromises arose from the reluctance of the former British colonies coming together to form the United States to subsume themselves under a new central authority. They had rebelled against the central authority of George III, and powerful groups within each colony-cum-state worried that there were those in the new republic who wanted to erect a similar form of authority. Moreover, most of these colonies had developed robust sets of governing institutions across the long period during which they had been under British rule, and many of the leaders of these colonies had come to believe that the very robustness of these institutions gave these colonies a claim on sovereignty. Colonial governing institutions had never been sovereign, of course; this is why the American War of Independence had broken out in the first place. Yet the war for independence had, at the very least, raised the possibility that Virginia, New York, Pennsylvania, and South Carolina, among others, would become their own fully independent entities. The rebels in these colonies knew that they needed each other. No struggle against Britain would have succeeded without such intercolonial cooperation. But lateral relations among the colonies were historically weak. British rule had bound each colony to the metropole more strongly than it had bound the colonies to each other. And in the 1780s and 1790s, there was strong support within the former colonies for the notion that each should keep as much sovereignty as it could. From this perspective, the drive to empower the states arose not from republican principles but rather from the efforts of semisovereign entities with long and independent histories to maintain their autonomy.[9]

What would the content of the power being reserved for the states actually look like? Here is where what I am labeling the Tocquevillian law of revolution comes into play. Alexis de Tocqueville's law of revolution is actually about the difficulty of effecting revolution, of successfully turning the world as one knows it upside down. Tocqueville argued that even in the most revolutionary societies, such as his own France of the 1790s, it was impossible to start everything anew. The prerevolutionary ancien régime therefore came to play a far more important role in the new revolutionary society than anyone could have imagined. In France's case, Tocqueville maintained, the centralization characteristic of French absolutism reappeared in the revolutionary French state.[10] In America's case, I contend, an approach to public law that had deeply shaped governance in early modern England and the colonies influenced everyday governance in the states of the new American republic.

We can clearly see this continuity in the doctrine of the public police that had long been rooted in the king's prerogative in England, and that had worked its way into multiple North American colonial charters, and then into the legal codes and jurisprudence of the new American states. Under England's public police doctrine, the king had not only the right but also the obligation to bring order and welfare into his kingdom. The doctrine rested on the notion that the kingdom constituted a household writ large with the king in the role of paterfamilias. In 1769, William Blackstone, the premier codifier of eighteenth-century English law, defined the "public police" in these terms: "The due regulation and domestic order of the kingdom: whereby the individuals of the state, like members of a well governed family, are bound to conform their general behaviour to the rules of propriety, good neighbourhood, and good manners; and to be decent, industrious, and inoffensive in their respective stations." This doctrine, as Blackstone understood it, did not define the police function precisely or clearly delimit its boundaries. A ruler, like a father obliged to both discipline and "raise up" his subjects, had to be invested with authority that was broad and, in good paternalist fashion, versatile.[11]

The revolutionary generation of Americans repudiated kingship, of course, as they went about creating their republic. But in confronting the problem of bringing order out of revolution, they increasingly drew on the prerevolutionary public police doctrine that Blackstone had identified to shape governance in their new nation. This continuity is first apparent in nomenclature. By the early nineteenth century, American lawmakers and jurists were drawing on Blackstone's *Commentaries* to elaborate a police power doctrine that, they asserted, was fundamental to the authority of each of the American states. The continuity is equally apparent in doctrinal substance. Like the public police, the police power embodied a breadth of activity that exceeds our modern, commonsense notion of what it is police do. Police power certainly entailed the customary tasks that polities of all sorts must undertake and that we associate with policing: the protection of life, property, and public order. However, in nineteenth-century America, as in eighteenth-century Britain, the police power meant much more. In the words of nineteenth-century Massachusetts Supreme Court chief justice Lemuel Shaw, it was the "power vested in the [state] legislature . . . to make, ordain and establish all manner of wholesome and reasonable laws, statutes, and ordinances . . . as they shall judge to be for the good and welfare of the commonwealth."[12]

Shaw's proximate authority for this understanding of the scope of his own state's police power was article 4 of the Massachusetts Constitution.[13] But he both knew and acknowledged that this theory of governance had originated in the public police doctrine of eighteenth-century England. Shaw observed that many powers associated with "the royal prerogative" had been "vested in the commonwealth [of Massachusetts] . . . together with all other royalties, rights of the crown, and powers of regulation, which had at any time previously been held and exercised by the government of England."[14] This theory only survived the American Revolution because its proponents transferred the sovereign authority formerly vested in the king of England to the people of Massachusetts. Massachusetts and other state governments thrust together republican and royal doctrines amid the hopes and chaos unleashed by revolution. The result, overall, was a vastly different political system from that which had existed in the mother country. Yet in one critical respect—and here we see the Tocquevillian law of revolution at work—eighteenth-century English political practice survived: like the authority that inhered in the eighteenth-century English king, the powers held by nineteenth-century American states were broad, capacious, and vaguely defined, as befitting governing institutions charged with bringing order to a polity conceived of as a public household.[15]

Indeed, the authority wielded by Massachusetts and other states was far reaching. The police power authorized state governments not only to act on problems that posed an immediate and physical hazard to the community—for instance, a cow carcass rotting in the street that had to be removed, or a ship full of diseased sailors that needed to be quarantined. It also authorized state governments to act against anybody or any institution thought to offend public order or comity, as determined by democratic majorities. Police power allowed state governments to engage in extensive regulation of the economy, society, and morality, in both progressive and regressive fashions.[16] It underwrote an American theory of governance that was collectivist and majoritarian rather than liberal. In this theory, liberal notions of individual rights played only a secondary role. Shaw understood this theory's illiberal tendencies, acutely observing that it was not easy "to mark" the police power's "boundaries, or prescribe limits to its exercise."[17] We might affix the label "republican" to this theory, in light of republicanism's strong inclination to put public interest ahead of private right, but then we would have to stretch the meaning of republicanism to account for the way its instantiation in the governments of the various states drew on prerevolutionary royalist influences. One could just as easily call this a theory without a name. It lacked a name because it emerged less from a grand design than from the messiness of the historical circumstances surrounding America's political revolution. And it came to be principally lodged not in the central government but rather in the governments of the states.

BROAD AUTHORITY

In the early decades of the nineteenth century, state governments deployed their power across a broad front. In the economic realm, these governments promoted extensive internal economic improvements. Prior to 1860, in fact, state governments' involvement in economic affairs exceeded that of the federal government, both in terms of total funds expended and in the variety of projects undertaken. Antebellum state governments, for example, spent far more on internal improvements ($300 million) than did local governments ($125 million) or the federal government ($7 million).[18] They were also more involved than the federal government in the organization and direction of internal improvement projects. The premier example of this was the Erie Canal, built by the government of New York between 1817 and 1825 to connect the Great Lakes to the Hudson River, and by extension, the Midwest to the Atlantic Ocean. With the building of this canal, New York moved from its earlier disposition to support private enterprise with subsidies and other incentives to "direct funding and operation by the state" itself. This remained the model in New York until the early 1840s, by which time the state had constructed more than six hundred miles of canals at a cost of more than $50 million.[19] Pennsylvania had no one project of size and importance to rival the Erie Canal, but from the 1820s through the 1840s, it did expend more than $100 million on a comprehensive internal improvement program of roads, railroads, and canals.[20] More common than public enterprise in Pennsylvania were mixed enterprises, in which the state partnered with a private bank, transportation company, or manufacturing enterprise, with both partners sitting on a project's board of directors, equally responsible for investing money, hiring workers, and managing the project. By the early 1840s, Pennsylvania had invested over $6 million in more than 150 such enterprises.[21]

Until the right of incorporation became generally available in the 1840s and 1850s, state governments used their chartering rights to direct and control private investment. Entrepreneurs had to petition state governments for the privilege of incorporating themselves, and such governments often attached conditions to the charters they granted. For example, they selected the cities through which a transportation company had to build its railroad; chose the private ventures to which a bank was required to lend or grant its money; and determined the standards manufacturers had to meet in producing their goods.[22] Finally, some state governments passed laws limiting the liabilities and punishment of debtors, and regulating the conditions of workers by curtailing child labor and restricting the hours of adult labor. From his comprehensive study of Pennsylvania, Louis Hartz concluded that state government had "assumed the job of shaping decisively the contours of economic life."[23]

Capacious police power also permitted states to extend their authority beyond economic matters to include education, social welfare, marriage, family life, and morality. Consider this list of the thirty-eight powers that the new city of Chicago, with the approval of the Illinois legislature, arrogated to itself in 1837 for the purpose of achieving a well-regulated society. These included the power to regulate "the place and manner of selling and weighing" commodities traded in the city; the right to compel merchants, manufacturers, and owners of any "unwholesome, nauseous house or place" to clean these properties and dispose of "any unwholesome substance"; the power to "direct the location and management of all slaughterhouses, markets, and houses for storing power"; the responsibility of keeping all public ways—streets, rivers, wharves, ports, and town squares—free of encumbrances ranging from boxes, carts, and carriages to loose herds of "cattle, horses, swine, sheep, goats, and geese" along with large dogs; the power to regulate or prohibit all games of chance and practices of prostitution in the city; the right to ban any show, circus, or theatrical performance, or even innocent games of "playing at ball, or flying of kites" if they were deemed repugnant to the general welfare; the regulation of all buying and selling of liquor through licensing; the power to "abate and remove nuisances" and "restrain and punish vagrants, mendicants, street beggars, [and] common prostitutes"; the establishment and regulation of the city's water supply; and the authority to operate a police force, survey the city's boundaries, license ferries, provide lighting for the city, and "regulate the burial of the dead."[24]

This list is impressive for what it reveals about how far the governing powers of states went beyond the economic.[25] State and local governments not only took it on themselves to regulate commerce, manufacturing, and labor relations, and in the process establish a "public economy"; they also made private (and noneconomic) behavior—drinking, gambling, theatergoing, prostitution, vagrancy, and kite flying—matters of public welfare and regulation.[26] The activities of state and local governments could produce positive consequences in the sense of privileging the public interest over private claims, and could yield pernicious results in suppressing dissent and freedom. In the laws of states and municipalities, those most frequently targeted for surveillance, punishment, and reform were members of suspect groups—single women who lived outside patriarchal families, the poor, blacks, migrants, and immigrants.[27] That the scale of surveillance and punishment seemed to increase as the nineteenth century advanced suggests that it will not do to simply root this social and moral regulation in some Puritan past that was dark but receding. The impetus to regulation did have early modern European roots, as the enlistment of eighteenth-century notions of the public police by American states makes clear.

But this tradition was not just a relic or annex to the main business of government. It was integral to the work that state governments did.[28]

In the Southern states, the police power doctrine was used to legitimate slavery, and to put state governments on the side of slave owners and the world they had made. The Constitution did not speak with one voice about slavery. That it did not explicitly endorse slavery, and nowhere mentioned it by name, as the Constitution of the Confederate States of America would do more than seven decades later, reveals a discomfort with the institution on the part of a substantial portion of delegates to the Constitutional Convention of 1787. Similarly, that these delegates wrote into the Constitution a date, 1808, at which the "Importation of . . . Persons"—a euphemism for the international slave trade—would cease, suggests a diffuse expectation or hope that "in the flow of time," as historian Don E. Fehrenbacher once wrote, "slavery would disappear."[29] Yet the Constitution also countenanced the fact that there were groups ("other Persons") in America who were not free and would count for less than "free Persons" in determining the number of congressional representatives assigned to each state. More significantly, it set forth no mechanism or timetable for pressuring states with slaves to move these individuals from partial to full personhood, from servitude to freedom.[30]

The net effect of the Constitution's obliqueness on the slavery question was to leave decisions about the institution's future in the hands of the states. Within a generation of the Constitution's ratification, states in the North had largely eliminated slavery while Southern states deepened their commitment to it. The latter drew on the police power doctrine to justify their social order, arguing that a well-regulated society and one that served the "people's" welfare had to be one grounded in the enslavement of resident African American populations. Using police power in this way impelled some white Southerners to strip African Americans of their humanity and personhood altogether and exclude them from considerations of the people's welfare. Alternatively, state courts could grant African Americans a childlike personhood status—one that obligated slave owners to look after their slaves' needs in a paternalist fashion while withholding from them the right to have their own say in the people's welfare. The police power doctrine could be employed in either of these ways to give legal sanction to the Southern slave system.[31]

The Constitution did contain one potentially serious challenge to this state-based system of slavery. The ten amendments comprising the Bill of Rights did not reproduce the distinction between "free Persons" and "other Persons" laid out in article 1 of the Constitution, and thus offered none of the implicit acceptance of slavery therein implied. The amendments referred several times to the "right of the people" and to actions that the government could not take against any "persons." Since the Bill of Rights contained no reference to "Other persons" or some other group to which its rights would not apply, what was to stop a black slave in America from claiming that he, as a person, had a right to possess what the Bill of Rights promised to every individual in the United States: to be secure in his person as well as his life, liberty, and property? And what was to stop him from presenting a petition to this effect in court?[32]

The Supreme Court answered this question in the early nineteenth century in the process of establishing its role as arbiter of last resort for what the Constitution had left unclear. In a decision handed down in 1833, the Court ruled that the Bill of Rights applied only to actions that *Congress* could and could not undertake with respect to the people. The First Amendment stipulated that "Congress shall make no law . . . abridging the freedom of speech, or of the press"—language that the Court interpreted narrowly to mean that it applied exclusively to the actions of Congress itself.[33] Congress could pass no law abridging freedom of speech, press, or religion. Congress could pass no law suspending trial by jury, or stripping an alleged lawbreaker of liberty and property without the due process of law. But the First and Fifth amendments said nothing about what *state legislatures* and *city councils* could or could not do in this respect. If Virginia wanted to pass a law abridging the freedom of the press, it could. If Georgia wanted to put into place a slave code stripping blacks of the rights guaranteed by the ten amendments, it could. If the city of Baltimore (under

Maryland's jurisdiction) happened to damage the private property of a wharf owner in the course of improving the city's harbor, it was not bound by the Fifth Amendment's command to offer that owner just compensation.

In writing the decision in the 1833 case (which concerned a lawsuit brought by a wharf owner against the city of Baltimore), Chief Justice John Marshall did not base his decision solely on the language of the first ten amendments, and specifically the repeated references to what Congress could and could not do. He also looked into the intent of those who had framed the Bill of Rights. He stressed that their concern was entirely with the abuse of power by the central government, and not by the states. By 1789, the states already had their constitutions, he noted; several had installed their own bills of rights to protect citizens against the arbitrary exercise of state power. Moreover, Marshall stressed, the states possessed a sound mechanism for addressing majoritarian excess. If the "people of the several states," wrote Marshall, "required additional safeguards to liberty from the apprehended encroachments of their particular [state] governments, the remedy was in their own hands." They had merely to call for a constitutional convention, Marshall observed, and the "required improvement would have been made."[34]

Underlying Marshall's thinking was a conviction that states drifting toward majoritarian tyranny would find ways to make "required improvements," and that such improvements would invariably enhance the people's liberty. The Supreme Court that he led was not particularly troubled by the thought that majorities in state legislatures might move in the opposite direction: they might run roughshod over minority opinion, and constitutional conventions might do the same. More than the central government, state governments were thought of as embodiments of the people, and from this it followed that the people would not ordinarily require protection against themselves. The theory of power on which the authority of the states rested called for the people to be made sovereign; it invested state legislatures, the bodies representing the people, with broad authority to act for the "good and welfare of the commonwealth." This theory did not partake of a liberal insistence that every institution of government, no matter how democratic, had to have limits placed on the exercise of its power. Rather, it sanctioned illiberal policies in the name of the people. The Supreme Court regarded such policies, even when they violated the federal Bill of Rights, as a legitimate way of organizing governance in the states.

Any state, North or South, certainly was free to incorporate its own bill of rights into its constitution, and many had.[35] And every state was also free as well to extend those rights to African Americans residing within its borders, which is what some northern states, such as Massachusetts, had done.[36] States possessed a great deal of latitude in these matters. This had been the intent of the revolutionary generation that had framed the Constitution and Bill of Rights, and Marshall and his fellow justices were determined to honor it. In so doing, the Marshall Court reinforced the exemption of states from the federal Bill of Rights. This exemption would stand as a principle of American governance for another hundred years, from the age of Jackson to the age of Roosevelt.[37]

QUESTIONS OF EFFICACY

The governing efficacy of states did not always match their formal authority. They could not always accomplish in fact what they were statutorily empowered to do. Were they successful in raising funds for their economic ventures and paying back the debts from the borrowing they incurred? Were they able to put skilled administrators in place? Did they deliver on promises to constituents? Could they keep corruption in check? Even a cursory survey of state government actions reveals broad variability in efficacy. Variability came in two forms. The first was internal to each state. Some tasks of government were easier to carry out than others. It was simpler, for example, for a state to regulate marriage than it was to build and manage a mammoth canal. Applications for and issuance of marriage licenses were matters that could be administered rather straightforwardly. And with respect to the surveillance of those already married, a state could easily supplement the work of its own officials with the work of those in civil society who acted as lookouts, spotting those who had cohabited or married illegally, or who had violated marriage vows through adultery or in some other way.[38] Building a canal hundreds of miles long, on the other hand, involved assembling factors of production on a vast scale, and managing large aggregations of capital and labor using skills possessed by few individuals at the time in either public or private life. The opportunities for mismanagement and corruption in grand public works projects were substantial, especially in light of America's privatized election campaign system, to be discussed in chapter 5. As instances of such mismanagement and corruption multiplied in the 1830s and 1840s, ardor for state-run projects of economic development cooled measurably. New York State, for example, ended its program of public works construction in 1842. Such projects were increasingly seen as stretching the tasks of most state governments beyond their capabilities.[39] Indeed, a new reluctance to have governments take on major public works influenced Congress's decision in the 1860s to hand the task of building the transcontinental railroad to private firms. But the passion for policing marriage did not decrease, nor was there ever a sense that this kind of surveillance was beyond the capacity of the states.

The second form of variability was one manifested in differences *among* the states. States could and did pursue diametrically opposed policies: one state might allow its citizens to drink, while another one might outlaw the sale and consumption of alcohol; one might authorize divorce, even as another might prohibit it; one might sanction slavery, while another might abolish it. That states could make such profound decisions about how their citizens lived testifies to the scope of their power. Yet the variability in the strength and focus of coercive regimes served as a constraint on the power of the states. States could not, after all, control movements into and out of their territory.[40] Only the federal government could control migration, and it generally patrolled only national borders, not those separating New York from New Jersey or Ohio from Kentucky.

Because states were frequently in competition with each other for laborers, industry, investment, immigrants, and settlers, some sought to draw the desired people and commodities by instituting what they understood to be attractive laws. New Jersey and Delaware, for instance, would seek to draw industry by making public incorporation easier in their states than in others. A number of states, beginning with Connecticut in the nineteenth century, made it easier than in most other states for unhappy couples to secure a divorce. Trans-Mississippi western states in the late nineteenth century hoped to draw women by giving them the vote earlier than they gained it elsewhere as well as by increasing the rights of women in both the public and private spheres. Those suffering from their state's prohibition laws could choose to live close to another state that allowed them legally to quench their alcoholic thirst. The point should be clear: sometimes Americans could escape the police power regulatory regimes of their states by pulling up stakes.[41] Indeed, it may be that the patchwork nature of this system of state rule encouraged the high levels of geographic mobility for which Americans have long been known. It may be, too, that the toleration by Americans of powerful and intrusive state governments rested on their conviction that an individual could always find a way to escape their clutches. Mobility, voting with one's feet, expressing one's political views through "exit," to use Albert Hirschman's phrase, arguably became a way of life in America.[42] If states individually were illiberal polities, one might contend that collectively, they sustained an imperfect but nevertheless recognizably liberal and pluralist order. As long as one could choose one's state, one could live as one wished.

This is a plausible interpretation up to a point, even as we must acknowledge that whatever pluralism a polity of multiple states offered was limited. There was no nineteenth-century state that legalized homosexuality, and only a few gave women substantial rights within and beyond marriage. Such a view also underestimates Americans' attachment to place, most often defined by region; New England, the Midwest, the South, and the West each developed a specific regional consciousness that anchored its inhabitants in important ways. Still, the reality of open borders among the states, and the freedom to leave one state for another did constrain police power regimes in significant ways.

On many issues, states could do nothing to keep residents who wanted to live elsewhere. But on one issue, they had to do something. That issue was slavery. Because the Constitution, as we have seen, permitted slavery but did not mandate it, the various states were free to make their own decisions about whether or not to sustain it. Sustaining it required writing the slave system and the mechanisms for enforcing it into law. By the 1820s, the Southern states had done so while the Northern states had largely eliminated the institution. Those latter states, which would become known as the free states, came to pose a mortal challenge to the slave states in two ways. First, if the free states were to outnumber the slave states in quantity and population, which appeared likely in light of how many were emerging from the Louisiana Purchase, their representatives in Congress might persuade that sovereign legislature to pass laws that would weaken slavery to the point of collapse. The slave states thus fought hard, through the Missouri Compromise and subsequent legislation, to maintain a rough balance between slave and free states, and to preserve the slight but decisive advantage they possessed in the US Senate.[43]

The second way in which the free states posed a challenge to the slave states was their function as a destination for runaway slaves. What was to stop massive numbers of slaves from fleeing north and west? If enough took flight, the edifice of slavery in the South would crumble. Southern slave owners had always understood the seriousness of this problem, which is why they had won adoption at the 1787 Constitutional Convention of a clause, article 4, section 2, stipulating that any person "held to Service or Labour in one State, under the Laws thereof, escaping into another," must be returned to his or her rightful owner. This fugitive slave clause, reinforced by the Fugitive Slave Act of 1793, was meant to solve the problem of open borders between states by making it impossible for slaves to escape their servitude through flight.[44]

These constitutional and legislative sanctions did not put federal authorities directly on the trail of fugitive slaves. Instead when petitioned by slave catchers who had seized fugitives, they compelled state magistrates in free states to permit catchers to leave the state with their "bounty."[45] Hence, for example, judges in Ohio would be obligated by federal law to allow slave catchers from Kentucky to leave Ohio with the slaves they had seized and return them to the Bluegrass State plantations from which they had fled.

This system worked for a time, but broke down in the 1830s and 1840s. Increasingly, abolition-minded Northern magistrates refused to approve the removal of captured slaves, even when proper legal procedures had been followed.[46] Alarmed by such refusals, Southerners pushed a new fugitive slave law through Congress as part of the Compromise of 1850, which dramatically increased the power of the central government in the rendition process, taking it out of the hands of Northern state magistrates and putting it in the hands of a federal commissioner, his deputies, and federal circuit judges.[47]

Most Southerners regarded the new Fugitive Slave Act as a triumph. The deeper thinkers in their ranks, however, understood that it posed a problem for their conception of states' rights. After all, relying on the federal government for enforcement showed that the Southern states, on their own, could not protect an institution that they held dear. The *Dred Scott* decision of 1857 further underscored this weakness. On the surface, this decision too seemed like a major victory for slave owners. It declared that the Constitution barred blacks from ever becoming citizens of the United States, which meant they might never have access to the rights of citizenship, including the rights to marry, vote, sit on juries, enter contracts, and sue for breach of contract. But in making this ruling, the Supreme Court had strengthened the priority of national citizenship over state citizenship. As such, even as it declared slavery to be perfectly compatible with the federal Constitution, the Court had adopted a jurisprudence that in the long run, threatened to weaken the power of the states to shape membership of the national community of which they were, so they claimed, the primary parts.[48]

The repeated recourse by the Southern states to the federal government—securing the passage of fugitive slave laws from Congress and persuading the Supreme Court that African Americans could never be citizens of the United States—was evidence of the central state's complicity in maintaining the institution of slavery.[49] Does it follow from this that the notion of different theories of power inhering in the central government and the states loses its significance as a tool for explaining political development in the United States? Why not assert that the two levels of government were moving in the same direction, with their movement shaped not by political theory—either liberal or coercive—but rather by raw power, here understood as the slave owners' influence in national *and* state politics?

John C. Calhoun, one of the antebellum South's leading politicians and thinkers, reflected at length on this question, concluding that if the South were to ignore the distinction between the power that inhered, respectively, in the federal government and in the states, it would imperil the survival of slavery. Calhoun argued that the vital interests of the South required that it use its raw power to bend the federal government to its will. But he insisted that this be done in ways that would make federal intervention efficacious without granting the national government authority in the form of a federal police power that it might someday use to destroy the police powers of the states along with the slave regimes that those powers authorized and protected.

Calhoun articulated this position in the 1830s, as he and other Southerners debated how to deal with the inundation of antislavery literature from the North in the wake of Nat Turner's rebellion. An angry Andrew Jackson wanted to ban such mailings outright, viewing them as a deliberate strategy adopted by Northern abolitionists to stir up further insurrection in the South. Yet Calhoun feared that any national censorship law would amplify the federal government's authority to regulate interstate commerce, and that such expanded authority might one day be used to regulate—and perhaps ban—the interstate slave trade. Calhoun's sentiments, buoyed by First Amendment concerns, carried the day, and Congress declined to pass a federal censorship law. Calhoun did not get exactly what he wanted, which was a law requiring the federal government to enforce state censorship laws. Congress instead demanded that Southern post offices accept all mail, even abolitionist mail, carried to them by Northern mail carriers. What Calhoun could not achieve legislatively, however, he achieved through a sort of executive action: his ally Amos Kendall, President Jackson's postmaster general, informed Southern postmasters that it was within their power to refuse to deliver the abolitionist literature arriving in their offices. Postmasters could simply lock it away in a vault or basement so that its contents would never reach the eyes of the Southerners, white and black, to whom it was addressed. Federal censorship would succeed without having to rely on the passage of a new federal law.[50]

Calhoun believed that this strategy offered a model for the South to draw on federal power without increasing federal authority. It was inherently unstable, however; the election of a Whig or, later, Republican president might result in the appointment of a postmaster general who would not abide by the "Kendall rule." As such, it was incumbent on Southerners to look for other strategies for making the federal government, in Fehrenbacher's words, "an agent of state sovereignty and not its master."[51] The Supreme Court, under Chief Justice Roger B. Taney, thought that its *Dred Scott* decision could serve Southern interests in this way. That intervention was clumsy, however. Jurisprudentially, it failed to protect states' rights; politically, it deepened divisions over slavery in the country as a whole, hastening the rush toward war and the destruction of the slave system that the decision was meant to protect. But even as the *Dred Scott* decision failed to achieve its aim, the Calhoun strategy of conscripting an agency of the federal government—in this case, the Supreme Court—to support the distinctive theory of governance that inhered in the states stayed alive. Indeed, as we will see, the strategy of turning to an institution of the central state—in particular the Supreme Court—to preserve the powers of the states would give the police power doctrine nearly another century of life.[52]

RECONSTRUCTION AND RESTORATION

The Civil War is often thought to mark a transition in the history of governance in America, with the victory of the North ensuring both the triumph of central over state authority and the transformation in conceptions of the scope and uses of central government power. The Thirteenth and Fourteenth amendments to the Constitution directly challenged prevailing conceptions of states' rights, not only by rendering all state laws protecting slavery unconstitutional, but also by transferring the power to grant citizenship and enforce its rights from the states to the central government. Moreover, the exigencies of war impelled the Union to take on tasks that it had previously considered to be beyond the scope of the national government's power: employing millions in its army, centralizing banking functions, and directing manufacturers and merchants to serve the government's need for food, ammunition, uniforms, artillery, guns, and munitions. This centralization and expansion of federal power may also be discerned in the wartime introduction of national systems of taxation and paper currency, expenditures on scientific research and public universities, the building of the transcontinental railroad, and the distribution of federal lands to ordinary agricultural settlers through the Homestead Act of 1862. This growth in federal government power carried over into Reconstruction, nowhere more so than in the Freedman's Bureau, a federal initiative to integrate emancipated slaves into the South's economic, social, and political life on terms of equality with whites. As well, Congress in the 1860s put into place a generous pension system for disabled veterans and the widows of dead soldiers that by 1875, was paying benefits to more than a hundred thousand claimants. Though this pension system was temporary, in the sense that it would expire when the last of the Civil War veterans and their widows died, it nonetheless can be construed to have been, as Theda Skocpol has argued, the first mass welfare system in the industrializing world.[53] The Freedmen's Bureau and the veterans' "welfare state" appeared to exemplify the sort of work that a powerful federal government could do.[54]

We must be careful, however, not to assume that the powers and activities assumed by the central government during war and Reconstruction simply continued into the post-Reconstruction period. In some arenas, and especially through laws pertaining to corporations, the power of the central government continued to grow.

But in others, such as laws governing marriage, sexuality, morals, race, free speech, and social welfare, the power of the central state was rolled back and the authority of the states restored. Even corporations sometimes found themselves enmeshed in networks of state regulatory laws. In delineating the new lines between the central government and states, the Supreme Court would once again play a decisive role.

Nowhere was the display of post-Reconstruction central government power more impressive than in affirmative steps taken to free private corporations from public regulation. Much of the control that governments had exercised over corporations across the first seven decades of American history had come from individual states using the expansive police power doctrine at their disposal. The post–Civil War Supreme Court increasingly invoked two new doctrines to limit that control. Both doctrines drew on a clause in the Fourteenth Amendment declaring that no state shall "deprive any person of life, liberty, or property, without due process of law."[55] The first doctrine, which came to be known as substantive due process, allowed the Court to expansively define the meaning of Fourteenth Amendment liberty. Liberty, in this view, included not only the freedoms enumerated in the Bill of Rights—freedom of speech, assembly, religion, and so on—but also new freedoms that Americans, in the context of a rapidly changing world, had begun to perceive as fundamental aspects of their personhood. "Liberty of contract" was one of the new freedoms elaborated by the postbellum Court. It meant that individuals possessed the freedom to enter any commercial or employment transaction unencumbered by government restraint or regulation. It incarnated the late eighteenth-century liberal dream of allowing buyers and sellers of commodities and labor to come together to strike deals of their own choosing and on terms that they embraced. It gave rise to a new judicial philosophy known as laissez-faire constitutionalism.[56]

The second new postbellum doctrine, which the Court quietly adopted in 1886, was to declare that corporations were persons in the eyes of the law. The Court took this step in order to argue that corporations themselves possessed a liberty of contract given to persons by the Fourteenth Amendment.[57]

The advent of laissez-faire jurisprudence, as important as it was, should not cause us to presume that its triumph in American economic life was by the 1880s or 1890s assured, nor should it cause us to overlook important policy areas where the shift in power to the central government that was set in motion by the Civil War either weakened after Reconstruction or was reversed altogether. In their rush to proclaim the triumph of the federal government in post-bellum America, scholars have often ignored the states. And thus many have overlooked a critical development: the resurgence of the states after 1877. State legislatures passed thousands of laws during this time to challenge laissez-faire. These laws sought to regulate all kinds of economic activities: the hours per week that men working in dangerous occupations as well as women and children in general would be allowed to labor; rates that railroads and grain storage facilities could charge their customers; and where employers would be allowed to set up their businesses (and for which portions of the day) and where they would not. States also passed numerous laws to set minimal standards for residential dwellings, on the one hand, and regulate "vices"—drinking, gambling, and pornography—on the other. Public health and safety became abiding concerns, as manifest in laws passed to minimize the dangers of disease and injury along with the destruction caused by fire. States established a wide variety of public institutions, ranging from labor bureaus, fish commissions, and liquor licensing agencies to universities, charities, hospitals, insane asylums, and health boards—few of which had existed prior to the Civil War. This institutional expansion also triggered rises in state employment and the professionalization of skilled occupations, such as statisticians, inspectors, and pharmacists, on which state governance was coming to depend. The laws passed by the states were not always effectively enforced, and the quality of the work done by the new agencies varied greatly from state to state. But this should not cause us to ignore the breadth and intensity of government campaigns undertaken by the states.[58]

Supreme Court justices legitimated this late nineteenth-century surge in the scope and vigor of state governance by reinvigorating the police power doctrine for a postbellum age. Even those Supreme

Court justices thought to be the advocates of laissez-faire constitutionalism wrote opinions in the 1880s that protected the police
powers of the states in remarkably generous terms. As laissez-faire's
key architect, Associate Justice Stephen Field, argued in 1885,

> Neither the Fourteenth amendment, broad and comprehensive
> as it is, nor any other amendment, was designed to interfere with
> the power of a State, sometimes termed its police power, to pre-
> scribe regulations to promote the health, peace, morals, educa-
> tion, and good order of the people, and to legislate so as to in-
> crease the industries of the State, develop its resources, and add
> to its wealth and prosperity.[59]

Indeed, as legal historian Christopher Tomlins has noted, Field
construed his advocacy of laissez-faire as "a very narrow path of
inquiry," confined to matters of economic freedom and regulation,
and one that eschewed a "critique of the state's powers of moral
and criminal police."[60] Even within the area of economic regulation, Field was willing to acknowledge that the police power doctrine could still hold sway, and he looked favorably on states that
passed legislation to limit the maximum hours of work and offer
compensation to those workers engaged in hazardous jobs.[61] In
the Supreme Court's willingness to rehabilitate the states' police
power doctrine in the 1880s and 1890s, we can discern the role
that Calhoun had envisioned for the federal government in the
1830s: that it would become an agent of state sovereignty without
becoming its master. To an impressive extent, the Court succeeded
in restoring the boundary between federal and state power that the
Civil War had obliterated, and in protecting the authority exercised
by the states along with the police power doctrine thought to un-
derlie it.

The Court's determination to restore considerable power to the
states helps us to understand what we have long known and yet have
had difficulty assimilating into our analysis of the history of government power in the United States: the explosion in the late nineteenth century of *state* legislation regulating race, sexuality, and

morality in a society supposedly consecrated to laissez-faire and individual freedom. From the late nineteenth century through the first quarter of the twentieth—the supposed high point of America's laissez-faire regime—many states exercised what in other societies would be regarded as sweeping forms of control over individual behavior: the prohibition of the sale and consumption of alcohol, the forced separation of the "colored" and white populations, and the banning of interracial marriage, polygamy, prostitution, and contraception.[62] The federal government participated in and encouraged this regulatory regime, outlawing polygamy in 1862, banning birth control materials from the US mail in 1873, and prohibiting the transport of women across state lines for sexual purposes in 1910. But even as the federal government expanded its ability to regulate morality during this time, the power to legislate moral life remained largely within the province of the states. And the Supreme Court repeatedly upheld the states in their rights to exercise their power in this way.[63]

Segregation offers one of the most interesting examples of the Supreme Court's decision to defend an expansive conception of police power. Virtually every student of American history sees *Plessy v. Ferguson* (1896) as a landmark constitutional decision—one that legitimated a system of racial apartheid in the southern states for more than fifty years.[64] There will be no dissent from that point of view here. What remains unclear about this case is how the Supreme Court justified its decision to circumscribe the movement of African Americans and their ability to interact with whites at a time when the Court was purportedly enshrining laissez-faire as the key principle of economic affairs. Less than ten years after *Plessy*, the Court issued its *Lochner v. New York* decision, declaring that New York State had no right to pass a law limiting the number of hours that employees in bakeries could work per day. No state, the Court insisted in *Lochner*, possessed the right to interfere with the freedom of workers to enter into employment contracts of their own choosing.[65] If this liberty of contract philosophy was so important to the Court, how could it have denied this very freedom to African Americans living in conditions of segregation?

Was not one of the principles of *Plessy* that state governments possessed the right to deny African Americans freedom of assembly, movement, and contract?

The explanation for this apparent contradiction is that the principle of laissez-faire was not yet, in the 1890s, an all-powerful constitutional principle.[66] When, in the late nineteenth century, laissez-faire conflicted with the doctrine of police power, the Court was still willing to set laissez-faire aside. In a series of civil rights cases culminating in *Plessy*, the Court not only ruled that states could deny African Americans freedom of movement but that they could also deny corporations the freedom to do business as they pleased. The segregationist transportation laws passed by states such as Louisiana in the 1880s and 1890s were directed as much at regulating corporate behavior as at separating the races. These laws not only stipulated that the black and white races had to be separated on all railroad passenger cars. They also required railroad corporations to provide separate carriages on every train running through the states in question.

Prior to *Plessy*, railroad corporations had determined for themselves whether or not to offer separate railroad coaches for blacks and whites. The Interstate Commerce Commission had begun ruling in the 1880s that if railroads chose to segregate black and white passengers, they had to provide the former with accommodations that were substantially equal to those they were offering whites. But the Interstate Commerce Commission did not require railroads to segregate passengers by car. Thus, the racial seating policies adopted by railroads varied depending on the train route, numbers of white and black travelers on a particular train, and other business considerations. On routes traveled by few black passengers, for example, railroads did not provide separate cars, preferring to accommodate the occasional African American individual by means of informal segregationist arrangements within single cars. State segregationist ordinances in Louisiana and elsewhere in the 1890s deprived railroad corporations of this flexibility. The freedom of corporations to make decisions that were in their own profit-maximizing interests had succumbed to what legal historian Barbara Young Welke has described as the "expanded police power of the state to legislate on behalf of the health, safety, and welfare of its citizens." This impulse to put the people's welfare ahead of corporate privilege was the same one, Welke maintained, that would soon animate Progressivism. Significantly, the states were the original architects of Progressivism, not the federal government, and they drew their justification at least in part from a reinvigorated conception of the states' police power.[67]

The persistence of the states' police power can be discerned equally well in matters pertaining to interracial marriage. The regulation of marriage had always been regarded as the province of the states. In the early to mid-nineteenth century, movements arose to enhance the freedom of individuals to choose marriage partners, which meant treating marriage as a contract freely undertaken by two individuals and not as a civic act in which government, on behalf of the people of that state, took an interest. This tendency marked the increasing sway of laissez-faire principles in personal life. It is not accidental that this tendency became more pronounced as the federal government sought to increase its power vis-à-vis the states during the period of the Civil War and Reconstruction. But a reaction against this liberal approach gathered force in the last third of the nineteenth century amid growing fears that emancipation, urbanization, and immigration were creating general social disorder, too many worrisome sexual and marital unions, and too many mixed-blood offspring.[68]

Nowhere was this reaction more apparent than in the strengthening of state laws outlawing interracial marriage. These laws were not new in the second half of the nineteenth century, as colonial and state governments had been regulating interracial unions almost from the time that African slaves first had been brought to North American shores. Emancipation and Reconstruction had temporarily created a more favorable climate for legalizing interracial romance and marriage. By 1882, though, the Alabama Supreme Court declared that "the higher interests of society and government" permitted a state to exercise its police power to regulate both sexuality and marriage as it saw fit.[69]

Between the 1880s and 1920s, more than twenty states and territories strengthened their bans on interracial sex and marriage, or added new ones. The most comprehensive and repressive such law came in 1924, in Virginia, with a statute that one historian has labeled "the most draconian miscegenation law in American history."[70] These laws appeared not only in southern states but in northern and western ones as well, meaning that elements of the segregationist order should be seen as national and not simply sectional. Many states extended the prohibition on intermarriage from whites and blacks, to whites and Asians as well as whites and Native Americans. This is what the 1924 Virginia law had done.[71]

The Supreme Court showed a similar deference to states in the case of the First Amendment and its guarantees regarding freedom of speech. The federal government could not curtail this freedom, except in the most extreme and temporary of circumstances, usually as defined by war. But states could, and when they did, the Supreme Court did not object. Indeed, as political historian William Leuchtenberg has observed, during the years when the Court was developing its liberty of contract jurisprudence, "it did not perceive freedom of expression to be an aspect of 'liberty.'" Those justices who were willing to dissent from this view, such as John Marshall Harlan, were in the minority. A few others, such as Oliver Wendell Holmes, were beginning to express discomfort with the states' disregard of First Amendment rights. Although one can discern in this discomfort the genesis of a free speech position for which Holmes would later be celebrated, he was still two decades away from asserting this position vigorously in Court debates. Thus, Holmes voted with a large Supreme Court majority in 1907 to uphold the sentence of a Denver editor who had been convicted of contempt in state court for his editorials criticizing the rulings of Colorado's judiciary. Harlan issued a sharp dissent, defending freedom of the press as fundamental and burnishing his reputation as the Court's leading civil libertarian before that term was even being used. Yet his was a lonely position on the early twentieth-century Court.[72]

Only in the 1920s did the Supreme Court start to get serious about drawing limits on state government interference with the rights of American citizens to free speech and to carve out a sphere of private life that no government could touch. A new regard for the individual and for his or her integrity and privacy had been slowly taking shape in late nineteenth- and early twentieth-century America. A reform-minded Boston lawyer, Louis Brandeis, was a pioneering figure in this respect. The indiscriminate violation of personal liberties that defined World War I for the United States on its home front inclined many Americans to join Brandeis in rethinking the relationship between the individual and his or her governments.[73] The American Civil Liberties Union (ACLU) was born during this moment, and the phrase "civil liberties" gained prominence in American politics.

This cultural sea change penetrated the walls of America's premier hall of justice and began to influence the justices' deliberations, in part because Brandeis himself now sat on the Supreme Court. But conservative justices had also started to develop a more robust commitment to civil liberties and to question whether the Court had gone too far in deferring to the states' police power.[74] That change was in the air first became apparent in a 1923 case in which the Court articulated a new commitment to the principle of individual rights. Every individual, the Court declared in this decision, should have the right "to contract, to engage in any of the common occupations of life, to acquire useful knowledge, to marry, establish a home and bring up children, [and] to worship God according to the dictates of his own conscience."[75] In 1925, the Court declared in another case that "freedom of speech and of the press—which are protected by the First Amendment from abridgment by Congress—are among the fundamental personal rights and 'liberties' protected by the due process clause of the Fourteenth Amendment from impairment by the States."[76]

This 1925 declaration that the states could not "impair" the Fourteenth Amendment did not much help the man, Benjamin Gitlow, whose case the Supreme Court was then reviewing. Gitlow was a left-wing socialist imprisoned in 1920 for writing a revolutionary manifesto calling for the destruction of the "parliamentary state." Even as the Supreme Court went on record supporting freedom of speech as a fundamental right, it declined to reverse Gitlow's conviction (five to ten years in jail). Historic change did come in 1931, however, when the Court overturned two convictions in state courts—one of a left-wing camp counselor in California who had her charges singing the praises of Communism while raising the Soviet flag every morning, and another of a right-wing Minnesota newspaper editor who filled his paper with anti-Semitic diatribes. No matter how offensive other Americans might find these examples of speech, these two individuals, declared the Court, could not be punished by state censorship laws. "It is no longer open to doubt," wrote the new chief justice, Charles Evans Hughes, "that the liberty of the press, and of speech is within the liberty safeguarded by the due process clause of the fourteenth amendment."[77]

Even this 1931 victory was partial, however, for the Court was not yet ready to put aspects of personal life other than speech under the protection of the Bill of Rights and Fourteenth Amendment. Thus, for another thirty-six years after this 1931 ruling, the Supreme Court upheld state laws banning racial intermarriage, thereby refusing to implement its 1923 declaration that the freedom to marry a spouse of one's own choosing was a fundamental right that no state government could abrogate. Until 1967, the power to ban racial intermarriage was deemed to lie well within the power of state governments to regulate society in the people's interest. Until that almost precise moment as well, this power was interpreted by the courts to mean that state governments possessed the right to control women's bodies and reproduction by banning contraception and abortion.[78] State legislatures likewise possessed the right to criminalize homosexuality and a variety of other so-called unnatural sexual acts.[79] If the Supreme Court had bestowed a fundamental charter of liberties on artificial persons—the corporations—in the late nineteenth century, it still granted no such charter of freedoms to actual living and breathing individuals. In the most personal decisions regarding how to live one's life—for example, whom to choose as a marriage partner—real individuals remained subject to the police power doctrine of the states for a hundred years after the Civil War's conclusion.

Despite the Court's footdragging, it is nevertheless plausible to contend that the two 1931 free speech decisions inaugurated a critical transition extending through the 1960s, during which the courts unevenly and hesitantly yet steadily carved out a sphere of individual rights that no government, state or federal, could touch. Legal scholars refer to this longer process of change and adaptation as one of incorporation, through which the federal government compelled the states to recognize the primacy of individual rights set forth in the Constitution, Bill of Rights, and Fourteenth Amendment. In the process, the central government diminished and then largely vanquished the police powers of the states. In fact, we can say—and chapter 9 will make this argument—that events in the 1960s decisively broke the states' power.[80] But what impresses one about this story is how long it took to create a sphere of inviolate rights and autonomy, and how long state governments and the federal courts were resistant to its claims. It took the Supreme Court 142 years (1789–1931) after the ratification of the Constitution to put its full power behind what were arguably the two most important rights in the Bill of Rights: freedom of speech and the press. And it took this Court 178 years to declare that individuals could not be barred for reasons of race from marrying others of their own choosing.

Historically, legal scholars tended to be nonchalant about how agonizingly slow the process of incorporation really was. This posture can be seen even in the work of scholars who have written incisively about it. Thus William Leuchtenberg refers to the freedoms secured for individual Americans in the 1960s as America's Second Bill of Rights.[81] However, this 1960s' moment was not about a Second Bill of Rights. Rather, it was about securing America's first Bill of Rights, more than 170 years after it had supposedly become the law of the land.

Those Americans who have taken the stirring message of the Declaration of Independence to heart may be forgiven for thinking that possessing inalienable rights meant that no government could legitimately take those rights away. Yet under the police power doctrine, it turns out, state governments could regulate and even ignore several of these rights for much of American history, from the beginning of the nation until the eve of its bicentennial. As we will see, the liberal doctrine of governance enshrined in the national

Bill of Rights did eventually defeat the illiberal doctrine that animated politics in the states. But for three-quarters of American history it mostly did not. Until that moment of conquest, America was neither liberal nor illiberal. Instead—and paradoxically—it was both. A polity that promised individuals great freedom also encased them in systems of coercion. An examination of the states and their police power helps us to explain how this paradox became institutionalized in law and jurisprudence across so much of American history.

PART II
Improvisations, 1860s–1920s

3

STRATEGIES OF LIBERAL RULE

Unlike the states, the federal government possessed no national police power to act for the "good and welfare" of the country. Delegates to the Constitutional Convention of 1787 had discussed several such clauses, including one by Gunning Bedford Jr., to give Congress the power "to legislate in all cases for the general interests of the Union." But they were rejected as having no place in the Constitution that was emerging from deliberations.[1] Two references to the "general welfare" did slip into the Constitution: first in the preamble, and then in article 1, section 8. The preamble itself, however, was not understood as granting any power to the national government, and the reference to general welfare in article 1, section 8, was preceded and followed by discussions of Congress's power to tax. This placement inclined the courts to interpret it, the general welfare, as pertaining largely to the enumerated power of taxation itself.

Still, the power to tax was substantial, as were the other powers expressly given to the central state, such as the authority to raise an army and make war, regulate international and domestic commerce, control the country's finances, supervise the mails, administer immigration and naturalization, and acquire and distribute land, including that belonging to the Indians. These powers brought the central government far more authority than its predecessor had possessed under the Articles of Confederation. As Alexander Hamilton and his Federalist supporters saw it, the federal government was now poised to become a major force, perhaps the preeminent one, in promoting the nation's prosperity, welfare, and power.

Yet few could deny for long the limits within which the central government had to operate. It possessed only those powers explicitly named in the Constitution. These did not include a broad right, as the states possessed, to act for the good and welfare of the commonwealth. Moreover, the critical Tenth Amendment, which reserved all undelegated powers to the states, was repeatedly deployed to undercut arguments that the central government possessed a host of implied and as yet unspecified powers simply waiting to be discovered. The other nine amendments of the Bill of Rights further restricted what the central government could do by enumerating individual rights that no congressional, executive, or judicial action could touch. The central state, in other words, found its powers hemmed in on three sides: by the absence of an enumerated power permitting it to act for the general welfare, by the decision to reserve all unenumerated powers to the states, and by a Bill of Rights explicitly naming rights inherent in persons living in the United States that no central government could abrogate, except under the most extraordinary of circumstances. The powers of the central state were indeed bounded, rendering it a liberal institution in the classical sense of that term. In the 1830s and 1840s, these formal constitutional limits gave rise to a popular antistatist ideology whose adherents, most of them marching under the banner of Jacksonianism, sought to cast suspicion on federal government initiatives and workers. Ideological antipathy to the growth of the federal government thus became yet another factor constraining central state power.[2]

So we return to the question posed in chapter 1: How did this liberal state get its work done, and do so while operating within constitutional parameters? In the sixty-year period following the Civil War, this question became even more urgent than it had been during the antebellum years as America made itself over into an urban and industrial nation, and found itself afflicted with problems that this transformation generated wherever it emerged in the nineteenth-century world: the growing inequality of incomes and economic power; vast concentrations of people living in urban circumstances of poor health and limited opportunity; the influx of laborers from abroad carrying with them foreign cultures and religions that threatened prevailing conceptions of nationhood; mounting moral problems, including those involving prostitution, drug use, and crime; and finally, an intensifying conflict with other powers abroad, as rival nations sought remedies for their domestic troubles in the profits of foreign markets and the glory of imperial conquest.

Canonical historical accounts typically center on the revolutionary effects of the Civil War on the American nation and its state. The defeat of the Confederacy interred states' rights and concentrated power in the central government to an unprecedented degree. This central state, this "Yankee Leviathan," in the words of Richard Bensel, first focused on creating a legal and political environment in which capitalism could flourish. In the hands of the Populists and Progressives, this same central state then developed the political resolve and administrative capacity to remedy the multiple ills that an unbounded capitalism had generated. By the time of the New Deal, big government, conceived in the tradition of European social democracy, had tamed big capitalism.[3]

What this account leaves out is the influence of the postbellum counterrevolution on state building in America. Historians have had little trouble identifying this counterrevolution in respect to African American life. It is a staple of historical understanding that the revolutionary hopes unleashed by emancipation and Reconstruction were crushed when Union troops left the South after 1877, and when whites in the South were permitted to reestablish their supremacy over blacks in economics, politics, and culture. But historians have had more difficulty seeing how this same counterrevolution influenced both the conception and deployment of government power between 1877 and 1920.[4] The last chapter demonstrated how the states and their police power resurged after 1877, and how this resurgence gave southern legislatures the authority needed to encode white supremacy into law and political and social life. This chapter asks how this counterrevolution shaped the powers of the central state. A quick answer would stress that the radically centralizing energies unleashed by the Civil War were contained, and that classically liberal limits on the scope of central government power were reaffirmed. A deeper answer, and the one that structures this chapter, would emphasize the creativity of a constrained central state in circumventing the formal limits on its power.

To grasp this creativity, we must move away from a story organized around the Civil War, and around narratives of revolution and transformation, and toward a *longue durée* periodization that will illuminate the various strategies state builders adopted when they came up against the constitutionally affirmed limits placed on the central state. These strategies emerged not in a flash or in a burst of revolutionary fervor but rather slowly and unevenly. Their shape was ultimately not determined by inspiring manifestos that were discovered by American sojourners while in Europe and brought back to educate backward Americans. Rather, these strategies took shape on American soil. Though they emerged independently of each other, each sought to address the same circumstance: that the formal limits on the central state's power were too severe and had to be circumvented if the United States was to solve its problems and realize its promise. By the early twentieth century, these strategies had become staples of central state building in America. They still are.

Three strategies in particular command our attention. The first one, exemption, refers to activities in which the central government freed itself from constitutional constraints. These activities usually involved matters lying beyond the polity's formal borders, such as war, international trade, colonial administration, and immigration. As we will see, these "foreign" affairs often had major domestic consequences. The second strategy, surrogacy, refers to attempts by the federal government to use one of its enumerated powers—principally, the power to regulate commerce, supervise the postal system, and levy taxes—to achieve unenumerated policy goals. Thus, for example, the federal government had no specified constitutional right to pass a law to protect the morals of the American people. But if it could construct morals legislation in such a way so as to make it part of its power to regulate commerce or the mails, then that legislation was likely to pass constitutional muster. Those who wanted to increase the size and influence of the federal government therefore busied themselves with the project of turning the commerce, postal, and taxation clauses of the Constitution into surrogate general welfare clauses.

The last strategy, privatization, refers to initiatives undertaken by the central state to persuade private groups in American society to do work that it, the federal government, was not authorized or willing to take on itself. In field after field of governing endeavor in the decades following the Civil War, we can see the federal state seeking to achieve public ambitions by enlisting the energies, skills, and organizations of private individuals and groups. The US government, for instance, turned to the private sector when it wanted to build a transcontinental railroad, "civilize" Indians, Americanize immigrants, engage in diplomacy, raise moral standards, and squash dissent. Through this strategy, the central state hoped to circumvent constitutional limitations on the scope of its regulatory authority and draw support for its initiatives from those ideologically opposed to the growth of central government power.

Each of these three strategies has attracted attention from students of American government. Rarely have they been considered as an ensemble, as constituting a repertoire of techniques that America's liberal central state used extensively across the six decades of the country's industrialization and emergence onto the world stage. The argument of this chapter is twofold: through the deployment of these three strategies, America's liberal central state proved energetic, creative, and improvisational in its attempts to meet the governing challenges of the industrial age. And yet these three strategies were insufficient, both individually and together, for solving the problems of an industrial age.

EXEMPTION

Exemption refers to those areas of central government activity freed from strict constitutional scrutiny. Prominent among them were policies toward nations, territories, and peoples that could be defined as standing outside America's formal polity. Foreign relations, by definition, lay outside the polity and its constitutional strictures, as did America's conduct of war. Policies in these areas did require some kind of congressional approval: Senate ratification of commercial and peace treaties with other nations, and House and Senate approval of the executive's desire to go to war. But the actual content of the treaties with foreign nations or indigenous Indian nations were not usually subject to constitutional review. In these areas, the executive, in combination with Congress, was exercising plenary power—a power that the courts defined as lying largely beyond the reach of the Constitution. The courts, too, gave the executive and Congress a wide berth during times of war, believing such latitude to be in the national interest. The courts had confidence that they could rein in or eliminate "exempted" activities once hostilities ceased. Thus, for example, the courts raised no serious objection to Abraham Lincoln's suspension of the writ of habeas corpus during the Civil War, nor did they contest violations of civil liberties authorized by the Espionage and Sedition acts during World War I. This system of temporary wartime exemption worked reasonably at moments and in areas where America was fighting wars that had clear beginnings and ends; in other words, after the wars' ends, the courts did succeed in clawing back from the executive much of the power ceded to it. Yet this system worked far less well in the case of the Indian Wars of the nineteenth century and Cold War of the twentieth—wars that had no declared beginning and, for decades, no clear end. As such, the exemption from close legal scrutiny in these latter instances lasted far longer and generated damaging consequences to the notion of a central state limited in its powers.[5]

The United States could choose to import liberal principles into relations with foreign and Indian nations and into its conduct of war, much as the individual states of the United States could choose to accentuate a liberal orientation by writing a bill of rights into their own constitutions. Sometimes it did just that. But the United States was not obligated to bring its conduct of foreign relations and war into accord with liberal principles any more than an individual state was obligated to hold itself accountable to the national Bill of Rights. Thus, the face that the US government showed to the world and Indian nations, or that it showed to its enemies in war, was not first and foremost a liberal one. Certainly most Indian nations and foreign adversaries of the United States did not experience American power in this way.[6]

In the decades after the Civil War, the US government, furthermore, strove to increase the areas of activities exempt from constitutional review. This initiative is especially apparent in the central government's success in enlarging its freedom of action in administering land formally designated as territories. The central government had, on the one hand, always enjoyed broad latitude of action in its territories. On the other hand, precedents laid down in the original territorial legislation, the Northwest Ordinances of 1785 and 1787, circumscribed that latitude for a century. The second ordinance, passed initially by the Confederation Congress and reaffirmed by the first US Congress, prohibited slavery and guaranteed freedom of religion in the designated territories. It also defined land in the Northwest Territory as "incorporated territory"—a legal status granting the settlers who lived in it the right to petition the central government for a rapid transition to statehood. Every new state was to receive the same broad authority that the Tenth Amendment and police power doctrine had conferred on every existing state. Territorial incorporation also made the people living in these lands—or rather the white majority among them—full American citizens. This commitment to endowing new states with the same powers as the old ones ensured that the expansion of the United States would not make America an empire in the traditional mold, with those residing in the imperial core enjoying rights and privileges denied to those living on the colonial periphery. The policy of expansion, with the commitment to carving powerful states out of federal territiories, acted as a check on the power of the central government.[7]

This policy began to weaken during the Civil War era with respect to three territories that the United States had organized out of the land taken from Mexico during the Mexican-American War (1846–48). Two of those territories, Arizona and New Mexico, contained large numbers of Indians and Mexicans, suspect races whom many Americans thought could not handle the responsibilities of republican statehood and citizenship. A third territory, Utah, was home to a Mormon majority that wanted to write its polygamous practices into its state constitution. Each of these territories eventually gained statehood, but not before the process had stalled for decades (and not before Mormons in Utah formally relinquished the right to practice polygamy). The long period of time in which these territories were kept in limbo encouraged the Court to invent a new exemption from constitutional rule—the "unincorporated territory"—that freed the central government from the obligation to put newly acquired land on the road to statehood. This new legal category gave the US government the power to establish colonies— polities that it could rule indefinitely, and without having to worry about representation, rights, due process, and other liberal/democratic imperatives imposed on it by the Constitution. Arizona, New Mexico, and Utah escaped this unincorporated designation, but the land that America acquired as a result of the Spanish-American War—Puerto Rico, Samoa, and the Philippines—did not. By the early twentieth century, the US central government had acquired what it had not hitherto possessed: a legal mechanism for pursuing formal empire. In this respect, the central government had secured a permanent exemption, increasing its authority in the process. The United States deployed a similar rationale with regard to overseas military bases, such as Guantanamo Bay, Cuba, that it built on land leased from foreign countries. Although these bases were not colonies, they, too, were spaces largely beyond the reach of the Constitution.[8]

The federal government also dramatically increased its power across the nineteenth century to regulate immigration. Prior to the Civil War, the federal government had shared control of this matter with the states. In the postbellum years, the federal government asserted exclusive jurisdiction. The Supreme Court also made immigration regulation a plenary power, meaning that it released federal government policy on this matter from strict constitutional scrutiny. The Court justified this exemption by arguing that the regulation of immigration was an element of foreign policy, an area of governance in which the courts had long given the executive and Congress a free hand.[9]

Prior to the 1880s, the central government adhered to an open immigration policy. America possessed a rapidly expanding economy that was chronically short of labor. As a result, the government allowed almost anyone from any part of the world to enter the United States and stay for as long as he or she wished. In the forty-year period from the 1880s to 1920s, however, Congress and the executive branch replaced this open borders policy with a "closed border" one. Approximately a million immigrants entered the United States annually in the early years of the twentieth century. By the 1920s, the US government had shrunk this total by 80 percent, to fewer than two hundred thousand a year. It had the authority to do so.[10]

It also possessed the authority to achieve these reductions through racial exclusions. Congress banned immigration of Chinese laborers in 1882, and President Roosevelt ended immigration of Japanese laborers in 1907. Congress prohibited all immigration from East and South Asia in 1917. In 1924, Congress extended its ban on immigration from East Asia to most of the world. And for the first time it struck at Europe, and particularly groups from southern and eastern Europe who were also thought to be racially inferior, and hence damaging to America's "Anglo-Saxon" or "Nordic" stock.[11]

Frankly racist justifications underlay such discriminatory practices. Restrictionists argued that the Chinese and Japanese were so primitive, so different from Americans of European origin, that they could never be civilized or acculturated. Here is Congressman Fred S. Purnell of Indiana describing eastern and southern European immigrants to his House colleagues in 1924: "There is little or no similarity," he declared, "between the clear-thinking, self-governing stocks that sired the American people and this stream of irresponsible and broken wreckage that is pouring into the lifeblood of America the social and political diseases of the Old World."[12] The legislation excluding southern and eastern Europeans passed both houses of Congress by overwhelming margins. No one could challenge this legislation in court. Because the right to control immigration was a plenary power, the actions of the central state were not held to the nondiscrimination standards laid out in the Fourteenth Amendment. If the United States wanted to bar specific groups from entering the United States on the basis of race or nationality, it was free to do so.[13]

Naturalization policy likewise lay beyond the reach of the Constitution. The 1790 naturalization law described in chapter 1 as affirming American liberal principles also created a racial test for citizenship. An immigrant had to be free and white in order to qualify for inclusion in the American nation. This law was revised during Reconstruction to exempt immigrants of African descent from its exclusions, but the law itself remained on the books for another eighty years, preventing virtually all immigrants from East and South Asia from becoming citizens of the United States. Once again, few of these individuals could find a remedy in the federal courts.[14]

Unrestricted control of immigration and naturalization gave the federal government the power to profoundly shape the composition of the American population and polity. Still, it would be wrong to conclude from an examination of this area of exemption that liberal governing principles had ceased to matter altogether. Even as the central government was making full use of the free hand it possessed in designing immigration and naturalization laws, it also came up against a new constitutional limit on its power. That limit was contained in what came to be known as the birthright citizenship clause of the Fourteenth Amendment.

The clause declared in deceptively ordinary words that "all persons born or naturalized in the United States, and subject to the jurisdiction thereof, are citizens of the United States." These words actually constituted a ringing endorsement of the principle of equality first articulated in the Declaration of Independence. Anyone born on American soil automatically became a citizen at birth. That individual's race, ethnicity, religion, and gender were irrelevant; so, too, was the nationality (or "blood") of that person's parents. The immediate purpose of this clause was to offer African Americans an ironclad citizenship guarantee. It was meant to— and in fact did—deny future courts or any state within the Union the ability to do what the Taney Court had done in *Dred Scott*: strip the citizenship of American-born people of African descent.[15]

From the start, the supporters of this constitutional amendment made known their belief that the clause's protections extended to other groups whose color and/or culture had rendered them sus- pect populations in the United States. Chief among these groups in the 1860s were the Chinese who, since the San Francisco gold rush, had begun coming to California in large numbers. Senator Lyman Trumbull of Illinois, a Fourteenth Amendment architect, declared on the floor of Congress in 1866 that under the proposed amendment's terms, "the child of an Asiatic is just as much a citi- zen as the child of a European."[16] Trumbull gave the same answer when queried about the "Gypsies" of Pennsylvania. No one in Con- gress seemed to know whether Gypsies actually then resided in the Keystone State, or whether this group existed only in the imagina- tion of Fourteenth Amendment opponents, conjured up as a cat- egory of perpetually footloose, strange, and dangerous foreigners that no society had ever successfully incorporated. Certainly Gypsy children born on US soil should never be admitted to American citi- zenship declared Fourteenth Amendment adversary Senator Edgar Cowan of Pennsylvania. To which Trumbull calmly but firmly re- plied: of course they should.[17]

Trumbull and his allies clearly intended to construe birthright citizenship broadly. The words of section 1 of the Fourteenth Amendment accurately expressed their intent, which is why the Supreme Court, in *United States v. Wong Kim Ark* (1898), affirmed that even children born on US soil to immigrant parents barred from citizenship (for reasons of race) were themselves American citizens at birth. As part of Reconstruction, Trumbull and other Fourteenth Amendment supporters gave the United States the strongest system of birthright citizenship then extant in the world.[18]

The decision to do so had significant long-term consequences. Specifically, it prevented the transformation of East and South

Asian populations into an American version of the untouchables—hereditary castes barred from citizenship and economic opportunity across generations. Both Chinese and Japanese communities in the United States understood the practical importance of birthright citizenship. Japanese immigrants purchased land in the names of their children, thereby circumventing the state laws that barred the Issei from acquiring land themselves. Chinese communities, in turn, used birthright citizenship as a way of gaining entry into the United States for sons, both real and fictive, who could make a convincing case for having been born on US soil. Birthright citizenship also carried great symbolic weight in these communities. Parents hoped that their children, as American citizens, would gain what they had been denied: membership, political voice, and economic opportunity. Through the birthright citizenship clause, the central government sowed the seeds for destroying the racial nation it had so intricately designed and sustained with its plenary power to regulate immigration and naturalization. Thus did the central state affirm its liberal character even during a period in which it was actively trying to circumvent the constitutional limitations on the exercise of its power that had given this state its liberal character in the first place.[19]

SURROGACY

Efforts by the central state to surmount its constitutional limitations can be discerned as well in the strategy of surrogacy: using a power explicitly authorized by the Constitution to pursue a policy aim not otherwise sanctioned. The efforts to do so multiplied in the late nineteenth and early twentieth centuries as Americans confronted the effects of industrialization, chiefly in the form of a society that increasingly seemed dangerously unregulated in both its morals and economy.[20]

The Constitution gave the central government virtually no authority to legislate on moral issues. This was a policy area where the absence of a police power clause, which would have empowered

the central state to act for the "good and welfare of the commonwealth," was acutely felt. By the late nineteenth century, more and
more Americans wanted Congress to address what they perceived
as moral problems. Many feared that pornography, prostitution,
and drug use were surging. State regimes of control appeared inadequate.[21] But how could Congress act in ways that would pass
constitutional muster? The answer became to deploy a surrogacy
strategy.

The first step in this strategy was to identify what one scholar
during the Progressive era called a "definite constitutional peg": a
power explicitly enumerated in the Constitution and given to Congress. The second step was to hang on that peg a policy not clearly
sanctioned by the Constitution. For example, the central government had no power to outlaw or regulate prostitution. But if the
regulation of prostitution could be construed as the regulation of
commerce, it might pass constitutional muster. This is what the
Mann Act of 1910 set out to do. This law did not outlaw prostitution per se, but it did outlaw transporting women across state lines
for such purposes. Prostitution rings that crossed states lines were
a form of interstate commerce, and thus subject to federal regulation. Because interstate prostitution polluted interstate commerce,
proponents of the Mann Act contended, the federal government
had the authority to stop it. The Supreme Court agreed, and upheld the Mann Act in 1913. A similar kind of reasoning influenced
the Court's decision to uphold congressional acts that kept fake
medicines and diseased meat out of interstate commerce. A parallel logic also informed the Harrison Narcotics Act of 1914. Though
the central government did not issue an outright ban on drugs—an
act thought to be beyond its authority—Congress had found a way
to use its taxing authority to control drug distribution and use.[22]

In addition to the commerce and tax clauses of the Constitution,
surrogacy rested in the late nineteenth and early twentieth centuries on a third constitutional peg: the power to establish and operate a postal system. That this power was invoked from the 1860s
forward to establish the federal government's right to control and
even nationalize the emerging telegraph system is not so surprising.

The purpose of telegraphs, after all, was the same as that of the post: to circulate important information quickly and cheaply to citizens in every part of the republic.[23] But the fact that the power to regulate the mails would be invoked as justification for an anti-obscenity campaign undertaken by the federal government does reveal how far this power was being stretched beyond its original purpose.

In the 1870s, Anthony Comstock, a hitherto-unknown dry goods clerk in Connecticut, became America's leading anti-obscenity crusader. Comstock and his supporters defined obscenity broadly to include not only pornography but also all publications discussing or advertising contraception, abortion, and indeed anything else that could be construed as being "intended or adapted for any indecent or immoral use of nature." Absent an explicit constitutional sanction to act on behalf of the people's morals and welfare, the Comstock-led moral reformers needed a peg on which to hang constitutional justification for what they urgently desired: a sweeping antiobscenity law. They found that peg in the power given by the Constitution to the federal government to establish and regulate a national postal service. Comstock moralists asserted that the central government had the right to remove all "obscene" literature from the mail as part of its power to regulate the post. In 1873, Congress passed a law, known as the Comstock law, which empowered the post office to do just that. The Supreme Court upheld the law as lying within the central state's authority to regulate the mails.[24]

Shortly after the law's passage, the post office actually hired Comstock as a special agent and placed him in charge of its obscenity work. In this capacity, he widened the scope of moral surveillance beyond sexual and reproductive matters to include the banning of materials that had anything to do with gambling, drink, or drugs. Comstock's coalition of supporters broadened, too, to include the Women's Christian Temperance Union, the Anti-Saloon League, and the American Medical Association. This phalanx of private groups, working through the post office, succeeded in using the latter's authority to restrict the circulation of obscenity literature through the mails. Moral crusaders had made the post office into the Trojan horse of morals regulation in America.[25]

From one perspective, private reform groups were using the post office for their own moral agenda. From another perspective, the post office used its new "moral" authority as well as the prestige that went with it to expand its appropriations, employees, and services. Some of its new services, such as rural free delivery (regular and cheap mail service to every domicile in the continental United States, no matter how remote and isolated), were well within the post office's original constitutional charge. So too was its introduction of parcel post, which made the post office a player in package delivery, a branch of the mail then in the hands of private services (the Federal Express outfits of their day). But one of the post office's new services, postage savings plans, seemed to dramatically expand the post office's jurisdiction into the realm of finance and social welfare. Such plans made post offices into de facto banks for small depositors—a reliable and cheap financial option for the nation's working poor. These postal savings plans were popular, especially in the North.

By adding financial services to its portfolio, the post office carried surrogacy to new heights. In the process, it gained the loyalty of ever more diverse constituencies, from the most isolated farmer to the fresh-off-the-boat immigrant who found in postal savings plans a convenient, cheap, and trustworthy public banking mechanism. The number of employees working for the post office more than doubled between 1892 and 1912. With 214,770 employees, it was six times the size it had been when Comstock's obscenity-inspired expansion had begun in the 1870s.[26]

The leadership of the post office was brilliantly entrepreneurial, exhibiting both an innovative spirit and shrewdness in adding new services desired by many different kinds of Americans (thus ensuring enduring support and round after round of robust congressional appropriations). It had been that way since the earliest days of the republic, making it one of the most dynamic centers of federal government initiative and growth. Nevertheless, questions about its late nineteenth-century expansion abound: Was it appropriate for the federal government to allow part of itself to be so deeply influenced in the 1870s and 1880s by a relatively small group of moral crusaders? Was it appropriate to introduce morals legislation through this technique of surrogacy, which can also be seen as a way of circumventing constitutional limitations on the control that a central government could exercise over personal behavior? And even if one admires the creativity of postmaster generals and their staffs, was their agency the best site for a new form of public banking to take root? Did this pattern of innovation and growth not risk the possibility of the central state taking on a jerry-built quality, lacking central coordination and rationality, with strange beehives of activity in some places and equally strange absences of activity in others?

The strangest absence in federal state regulatory activity during these years was in manufacturing and in the failure to address the employer-employee relation that lay at its core. Rapid, uncontrolled growth characterized industrialization in the late nineteenth century. Busts followed booms with alarming frequency and intensity. Many of the working poor found themselves unable to secure a living wage because they were paid too little or because the firms they worked for were vulnerable to collapse at any time. Capitalists themselves were disturbed by the pell-mell nature of growth, and by the vulnerability of their enterprises to reversals and even destruction. Congress began to address these economic problems in the 1880s and 1890s, especially in the area of commerce, which the Constitution had unambiguously empowered it to regulate. In 1887, it passed the Interstate Commerce Act and in 1890 the Sherman Antitrust Act, both expressions of that regulatory power. But at this same time, the Court started to rule that the commerce clause did not entitle the federal government to regulate manufacturing, or relations between managers and workers at factories and other workplaces. These activities, the Court held, did not constitute commerce. The distance between commerce and manufacturing was arguably smaller and logically much easier to cross than the distance between delivering the mail and regulating morality, yet the Court rarely allowed legislators to hang the regulation of labor or conditions of production on the peg of commerce.[27]

Not only did the federal courts largely exclude the central government from regulating employer-employee relations; on several occasions, they also invalidated state laws that sought to accomplish this aim. Most famously (or infamously) in *Lochner v. New York*, the Supreme Court in 1905 overturned a New York State law limiting the hours that bakers worked to ten a day.[28] The Court ruled that this law had improperly infringed on the liberty of contract: the freedom of workers to enter voluntarily into employment contracts and determine for themselves the wages, hours, and working conditions under which they were going to labor. Here was an instance in which the Supreme Court enforced its laissez-faire constitutionalism on American industry. The Court did allow the states and central government to rein in laissez-faire in multiple situations: for the sake of racial segregation, as we have seen; in workplaces such as underground mines, where questions of health and safety were paramount; and in cases involving women and child laborers who, for reasons of gender and age, were thought to lack the maturity and independent mindedness necessary to negotiate a proper employment contract on their own behalf.[29] But even here, progress was uneven, as evident in the Court's 1918 decision to invalidate a law, the Keating-Owen Labor Law, which prohibited child labor. The law hung its ban of child labor on the Constitution's commerce peg. Specifically, it prohibited the introduction into interstate commerce of commodities that, within thirty days of crossing state boundaries, had been manufactured with the aid of child labor. Such commodities, Congress declared, constituted a misuse of commerce. The Supreme Court disagreed.[30]

The ruling revealed the reluctance of the Supreme Court to uphold laws regulating employer-employee relations in American factories. As a result, manufacturing districts throughout this period remained lightly regulated spaces, often dangerously so, characterized by high rates of injury and exploitation, and a tendency to resolve disputes through strikes and violence. Congress had the will but not the authority to bring a sufficient measure of order, rationality, and justice into this critical area of economic and social life.

That the central government successfully expanded morals and banking initiatives via the post office while failing to solve industrial relations problems speaks to the uneven impact of the surrogacy strategy. Among the advocates of surrogacy were talented lobbyists, legislators, and jurists who designed clever, sometimes brilliant schemes for enlarging the powers of the central government beyond what the Constitution had granted. The post office offers an example of bureaucratic ingenuity and entrepreneurialism. But this ingenuity did not yield nearly enough in the way of regulation to address the problems that American society faced.

We might explore the broader consequences of stretching the meaning of the Constitution through surrogacy. One of the most enthusiastic advocates of this strategy was Robert Dean Cushman, a political scientist and Progressive at the University of Minnesota. Cushman had convinced himself that the powers of surrogacy gained by the federal government during the first two decades of the new century were so substantial that they amounted to nothing less than a national police power. A number of Progressives, including Chicago Law School's Ernst Freund, shared this view.[31] Yet even Cushman had to admit that this new power, one he greatly admired, rested on "indirection" and the ability of the central state to "cloak its good works" in instruments created for other purposes. He was worried that the use of indirection and cloaking would not be enough "to protect the nation" from "dangerous and much more numerous evils."[32] Surrogacy was at best a remedial tool, and one that could break apart from overuse. The tool that the central state really needed, Cushman conceded, was a constitutional amendment transferring to the federal government a healthy portion of the police powers that resided in the states.[33]

Such an amendment, though, even if passed by Congress, was unlikely ever to be ratified. A national police power amendment would have demanded from three-quarters of the states a willingness to cede a major portion of their power to the central government. States would never agree to jettison such a substantial part of their authority. And so those who wanted to increase the regulatory authority of the central government had no choice but to continue with their strategy of surrogacy, hoping to render more and more problems susceptible to regulation by adept use of this tool.[34]

PRIVATIZATION

Given the uneven results yielded by surrogacy, the central state needed another tool in its workbox. It found one in privatization, a strategy of persuading private groups to do the work of the federal government—work for which it lacked either the authority or capacity to act on its own.[35] We have focused thus far on questions of authority: What were the activities that a central state could legitimately undertake? But we must also examine questions of capacity: Did the state have the agencies, resources, and personnel necessary to achieve its more ambitious goals? For much of the nineteenth century, the central state was not only limited in its powers but also short on institutional reach and sophistication. Initiatives in areas where the central state was exempt from constitutional restraint—foreign relations, immigration, and naturalization—did not require a large bureaucracy for much of the nineteenth century. War did, but war was then understood as anomalous. Majorities in Congress believed that whatever had been scaled up for war easily could be scaled back down once hostilities ceased. The central government pulled off this feat between the 1860s and 1890s by shrinking the multimillion-person Union Army that fought in the Civil War to a force numbering only about twenty-five thousand men.

In contrast, peacetime central government projects that required large expenditures of funds and organizational sophistication posed acute problems. This was especially true of major internal improvements, such as railroads, dams, and highways, and large-scale assistance programs to farmers, poor mothers, and other groups perceived to be at risk. In some cases, the federal government turned to the states for assistance: the former would design the programs, ask the states for funds to match, and then leave much of the program administration in the hands of state and local governments. This approach made sense, particularly at a time when the need exceeded what the federal government could provide and when the states were surging as vigorous political entities. But this embrace of federal-state cooperation was hardly enough to sustain the ambitions of the federal government. The states, with their police power intact, could do as much to stymie as to assist federal state initiatives, so the federal government increasingly turned to the private sector, asking a broad range of groups within it to "volunteer" to do all or part of the work that the government wanted done. Involving private groups in government projects could release remarkable and transformative economic energies, but it could also generate problems, especially in terms of giving privileged groups too much access to the wealth and power of the federal government. The building of the transcontinental railroad illustrates both the positive and negative tendencies embedded in the strategy of privatization.

By the 1850s, substantial cross sections of the American people saw in the transcontinental railroad an opportunity for the United States to realize its potential as a mighty, prosperous, and continent-spanning nation. Build the railroad, California senator William M. Gwin declared in 1858, and from "the Atlantic to the Pacific the great arterial industrial current would flow, and the great central valley of the Mississippi, the heart of the nation, would pulsate from ocean to ocean with renewed power." A transcontinental railroad, Gwin added, would establish the United States as a world power: "We would command the institutions of the world— not like the colonies of Rome, by the sword and vassalage, but by the irresistible moral power which would . . . carry our institutions with our commerce throughout the sphere we inhabit."[36] The federal government might have built this railroad itself, acting within its powers to provide the country with an adequate infrastructure for delivering the mails. Yet what had once been a considerable constituency supporting public works of this sort at both the federal and state levels had dwindled. A new consensus deemed the building of the railroad to be a complex undertaking best placed in the hands of private organizations. Congress believed that it could put enough controls on these private organizations to compel them to build a road that in terms of cost, safety, and reliability, would serve the public interest.

The Pacific Railway Act that Congress passed in 1862 set the terms under which the federal government asked private railroad companies to do its work. The incentives and subsidies of the 1862 legislation are the better-known part of the transcontinental legislative package. The railroad companies were to receive large land grants and other generous subsidies in the form of bonds payable back to the government after thirty years with 6 percent interest. Eventually, these provisions would make available to the Union Pacific Railroad twenty million acres of land and $60,000,000 in US bonds—amounts, Robert Fogel has written, that "easily eclipsed any previous public aid and which was not approached [again in scale] until the beginning of the twentieth century."[37]

The government also created a private corporation, the Union Pacific Railroad Company, to handle the work, authorizing it to break ground in Omaha and Council Bluffs and work westward (another corporation, the Central Pacific Railroad of California, had won the government contract to build a road eastward from Sacramento). To capitalize the Union Pacific, the government appointed 163 commissioners to sell 10,000 shares of company stock to investors at $1,000 per share. Once 2,000 shares had been subscribed, the commissioners would replace themselves with a corporate board of directors, in the process shifting control of the corporation from public to private hands.[38]

The federal government combined this effort to jump-start private enterprise with an attempt to put the enterprise it unleashed under public controls. Patents to land that the railroad company had "earned" would be distributed only after forty-mile sections of track had been completed. The same compensation rule governed the issuance of bonds, with the additional proviso that government assessors had to certify each forty-mile section of work before bonds would be transferred. Even then, 15 to 25 percent of the value of the bonds was to be withheld until it could be determined whether the Union Pacific "had complied with all . . . [government] provisions," including using only American-manufactured iron, paying for railroad maintenance, and treating whatever mineral deposits were discovered in land granted to the railroads as government property. Congress also reserved the right to reduce rates, and amend the act governing the terms of government–Union Pacific relations whenever and however it wished. Finally, if the Union

Pacific did not finish its road by July 1, 1874, it would forfeit the company (and the railroad) to the government.[39]

This admirable 1862 attempt to place private railroad enterprise under strict public regulation failed. Deeming the incentives too small and public regulation too stringent, capitalists refused to come aboard.[40] A panicky Congress thus passed a second railroad law in 1864 with provisions far more favorable to investors: the land grant was doubled, and the Union Pacific was given coal and iron rights to the land. The federal government would issue bonds and land patents after twenty-mile sections rather than the previously proposed forty-mile sections of the road had been built. Individual investors could now acquire shares for only $100 apiece, instead of $1,000. And the central state diluted its influence on the board of directors.[41]

Though intrigued by these concessions, capitalists still did not invest their resources. Railroad construction only took off in 1866 once a clever group of railroad promoters figured out how to receive federal government benefits while evading most of the remaining public controls. The key innovation was the decision made by eight Union Pacific directors led by Thomas C. Durant to establish a dummy corporation, the Crédit Mobilier, to replace the central government as the principal capitalization agent for the railroad. The purpose of the Crédit Mobilier was to give capitalists an earlier and larger return on their investments than what Congress had allowed. The Crédit Mobilier billed the Union Pacific for construction, and the Union Pacific then went to the federal government for the money to pay the Crédit Mobilier. The Crédit Mobilier inflated construction costs from the top to bottom of the supply chain, and the Union Pacific persuaded the central government to pay everything that the Crédit Mobilier charged. Private money now poured into the railroad.

The Crédit Mobilier was actually a device invented to allow a handful of promoters and congressmen to pull the levers on the entire operation, escaping public supervision in the process. The Union Pacific and Crédit Mobilier shared board members, and their presidents were brothers and business partners. The man chosen to oversee the Union Pacific on behalf of the federal government was Secretary of the Interior John P. Usher, a friend of the company's promoters and stockholder in one of the Union Pacific's subsidiaries. The list of stockholders in the Union Pacific and Crédit Mobilier also included future president James Garfield, Vice President Schuyler Colfax, and Speaker of the House James G. Blaine. The Union Pacific, Steve Fraser has written, represented "America's first full immersion in the political culture of crony capitalism."[42]

As the sense of economic opportunity increased, the brothers Oliver and Oakes Ames challenged Durant for control of the Crédit Mobilier. The Ameses, based in New England, belonged to a network of railroad entrepreneurs and financiers; among them were Jay Gould, Cornelius Vanderbilt, and John Murray Forbes. This network interwove itself both with centers of finance in Boston and New York and with the federal government in Washington. Oakes Ames was himself a member of Congress, well positioned to buy off government officials either directly through bribes or by permitting these officials to purchase large amounts of stock in the Union Pacific for little money.[43]

The Crédit Mobilier machinations came to light in 1872, engulfing the transcontinental railroad in scandal. In 1873, the speculative bubble that these and other episodes of insider dealing and fanciful investment had generated burst, triggering the first of several painful depressions that would convulse the American economy from the 1870s to the 1890s. And yet despite this economic turmoil, the Crédit Mobilier and Union Pacific built their assigned road with impressive speed, laying an astonishing 1,032 miles in only three years, and completing the first transcontinental in 1869 when their road met up at Promontory Summit, Utah, with the one that had been built west to east by the Central Pacific during that same period.[44] The 1870s' crash barely sated the hunger for railroad construction, and the federal government supported the building of several more transcontinental lines.[45]

Laying down these western roads had a significant impact on the nation. In 1870, only 2 million non-Indians lived in states situated all or partially west of the Missouri River. By 1890, this number had more than quintupled to 10.4 million. With respect to the size and rapidity of this mass movement, Richard White has observed,

"It had taken Anglo-Americans roughly two and a half centuries to secure the continent up to the Missouri River. They used the railroads to control the remainder in a generation."[46]

This westward movement was partially a matter of individuals seizing opportunities for what they imagined would be a better life. It was also, as White's words suggest, about nation building. From the start, part of the appeal to Congress about building a transcontinental road was to imprint the sovereignty, laws, and cultures of the American republic on the trans-Mississippi Territory that was only nominally under the nation's control. From the country's earliest days, white settlers imbued with republican ideals had been crucial to this process of imprinting. Their role continued in the trans-Mississippi West. With the settlers came towns and then states, with constitutions that reproduced patterns of republican rule and law that had been established in the East. With the settlers, too, came the mails, carried by the railroad, and the new telegraph lines that everywhere hugged railroad routes, both vital mechanisms for turning the entire continental United States into a single imagined community.[47] With the railroads, finally, came federal troops, who could now be sent to most destinations in the vast area in a matter of days.

No group felt the impact of the railroad and the national muscle it embodied—even if it had been privately built—more than Indian inhabitants of the region. Railroad building impelled the federal government to seize Indian land, and in the process to violate numerous US-Indian treaties, so that this territory could be parceled out to railroad companies as land grants. Railroad building also rendered most Indian military resistance futile, as the US government, through its ability to move around troops with dispatch, could now quickly counter Indian insurrection. Indeed, the only Indians to escape the powerful reach of the federal government in the 1870s and 1880s lived in areas largely untouched by the railroad.[48] By the 1890s, railroads had made America's conquest of the Indian lands complete.

Canada and Mexico also felt the effects of railroad building and the surge in national power it effected, experiencing the increase as a threat to their abilities to project sovereignty throughout sparsely inhabited regions of their own nations. So did California, where the transcontinental railroads put an end to discussions about the Bear Flag Republic going its own way, or being reintegrated in part or in its entirety into Mexico. By the 1880s, the United States was no longer imaginable apart from California. The railroads shifted the major axis of the American nation from North–South to East–West, with the country increasingly defining itself as stretching from the Atlantic to the Pacific. This process of national refashioning had unfolded at lightning-fast speed, and had done so at both the elite and popular level. A bourgeoisie, national in scope, had emerged from the extensive networks that the Sacramento entrepreneurs who built the Central Pacific—Collis Huntington, Charles and Edwin Crocker, Leland Stanford, and Mark Hopkins—had forged with federal government officials in Washington, DC, and financiers in New York and Boston.[49]

Meanwhile, the California gold rush of 1849 had generated an image of California as a place where any American could go to seek a fortune. California's status as the repository of the nation's greatest hopes and fantasies would not crest until the twentieth century. But the railroads made America's most alluring western destination accessible to everyone, and in this way powerfully served the interests of a central state intent on expanding the efficacy and glamour of its sovereignty. Because central state incentives had made possible the building of the transcontinental railroad, the central government could take credit for the sovereignty benefits that flowed its way as a result. This represented a major achievement for the federal state.[50]

The economic impact of the transcontinental railroads was also substantial. Railroads in general were critical components of America's nineteenth-century economic growth and industrialization. Between 1865 and 1916, the period during which the railroads became a coordinated national system, the annual value of manufactured products increased seventeenfold. Advances in the speed, cheapness, and predictability of transport pioneered by the railroads had made it possible to bring many new American goods to markets both throughout the United States and abroad. Railroads triggered an expansion of western silver and copper mining and of

other extractive industries. They did the same for the major industries of the East and Midwest, including iron and steel, engineering, and machine tools, by creating demand for rails, locomotives,
train cars, and the machines required to build them. Railroads encouraged rapid growth in cities that were handling this expanded
economic activity, and thus could take partial credit for the building booms that enveloped these urban centers in the Gilded Age.
Railroads also spurred technological change, the development of
mass-production techniques, and innovation in financial markets
and managerial practices. More than any other single industry,
they were responsible for defining the contours and character of the
modern corporation.[51]

The specific contribution of the transcontinentals to this
railroad-inspired boom is not as clear as it once was. The federal
government authorized the building of too many transcontinental lines between the 1860s and 1890s, and significant portions of
them remained underutilized. Several of the economic sectors they
stimulated—agriculture west of the hundredth meridian, cattle
and sheep farming, and silver mining—proved to be of uncertain
economic value, and yielded less growth and fewer profits than anticipated. The greatest gains in economic growth during the first
twenty years of the transcontinental era, in both agriculture and
industry, occurred in the Midwest and within California, and these
areas were in fact well served by regional railroad networks that
had received nowhere near the level of central government assistance and incentives bestowed on the transcontinentals. The latter
had been built ahead of demand in the expectation that they would
generate economic growth. In some cases, these transcontinental
roads stimulated the kind of dense settlement in the West that had
been anticipated, but in other cases they did not. The corporations
that owned the transcontinentals thus often found themselves competing for insufficient business, leaving them perpetually in or on
the edge of financial trouble. This predicament prompted them,
in turn, to engage in questionable financial practices—watering
down their stock, practicing fraudulent accounting, and taking on
unsustainable levels of debt—in order to survive or at least make
themselves appear to the central government as though they were

too important to the economy to be allowed to fail. And more often than not, the federal government stepped in to keep these entities afloat and preserve the private wealth that their owners had amassed.[52]

Richard White's assessment of the cost of keeping these transcontinentals afloat led him to conclude that the American economy and people would have been better off if these roads had been built two or three decades later, and if the huge resources that the central government and private investors had sunk into them had gone into sounder ventures in the interim. Writing fifty years earlier than White, Robert Fogel came to a different conclusion about the economic health of the transcontinentals. While acknowledging their weaknesses, Fogel judged them to have been, on balance, viable economic enterprises that delivered an essential service. He deemed the high rates of return that private capitalists earned justifiable in light of the amount of risk that they had taken on.[53] But when Fogel turned from economics to politics, his analysis emphasized the costs more than benefits of the railroads, and in so doing, took up a position that anticipated White's critique. Fogel and White both argued that putting the building of the transcontinentals into private hands weakened the democratic nature of the US central state by allowing private corporations to penetrate it, control portions of it, and then to use such control to advance their own agendas.

The federal government was especially vulnerable to this kind of takeover in part because of the dependence of elected officials on private sources of money for their electoral contests. By the time the first transcontinental was built, America had the biggest and most labor-intensive electoral system in the world, if measured by the number of people voting (universal white manhood suffrage), the number of offices that were subject to the will of the electorate, and the frequency of elections. This system was not only large but also costly: the founding fathers had made no provision to fund it or even to ensure that the electoral process would not be overwhelmed by private money. The political parties that arose to get their members elected and make public policy also became money-gathering machines. The story of money, politics, and government is so important that it will be explored at length in a subsequent chapter. Yet part of it is relevant here, for in many cases, the private organizations and individuals to which the central government turned for assistance in accomplishing its railroad-building aims were the same ones in a position to supply funds for congressmen and senators in need of reelection. And the promise of delivering such funds—or the threat of withholding funds or giving them to a rival candidate—profoundly affected the process through which Congress awarded contracts (i.e., which companies would get them) as well as the content of the contracts themselves (i.e., how lavishly these companies would be rewarded for their willingness to do the federal government's work). These are the circumstances in which the Ames brothers and their circles of investors and government officials amassed their wealth, and in which the central state ceded a portion of its authority to the private corporations asked to do the government's work.

The cession of authority was most obvious in Congress, where railroad lobbies exercised remarkable power in the 1870s and 1880s. But it also affected the executive and judicial branches of the federal government. In 1893, for example, President Grover Cleveland appointed Richard Olney, a railroad lawyer and general counsel to the Chicago, Burlington, and Quincy Railroad, to the position of attorney general. Olney stayed on the payroll of the Burlington Railroad while serving as the highest law enforcement official in the nation, and in that double capacity, led the federal government's campaign to defeat the nationwide railroad workers' strike of 1894.[54] During that same stretch of time, the Supreme Court justice, Stephen Field, was pushing the Court to issue rulings that enhanced the rights of corporations and limited the ability of labor organizations and other anticorporate groups to challenge them. Field had already played a pivotal role in ruling that corporations were persons under the Fourteenth Amendment (and that their rights could not be abrogated or regulated without due process), and that labor unions undertaking strikes and boycotts against their employers could be designated as illegal combinations in restraint of trade under terms of the 1890 Sherman Antitrust Act. Field had begun his career as a railroad lawyer in San Francisco, and maintained a lifelong association with the owners of the Central Pacific. The interests and well-being of the railroads remained dear to him throughout his judicial career.[55]

One way in which the overbearing railroad lobby might have been kept at bay, Fogel suggested, was for the federal government to have built the first transcontinental railroad itself. The transcontinentals in the 1860s and 1870s, Fogel argued, were so "premature" in terms of what the US market could sustain that they required extensive levels of government support simply to survive. In light of this, Fogel argued, it would have been better for the federal government to have built and managed its own road until the American economy in the West had grown to the point where a transcontinental could have become self-sustaining. Then the central government could have turned over its public road to private companies with the confidence that the latter could now go it alone. Had the federal government done so, Fogel maintained, the central state could have achieved its aims without granting private corporations extravagant subsidies and excessive power.[56]

Fogel was aware that his preferred option of a publicly built road was never under serious consideration in the 1860s. "The spirit and aim" of the railroad legislation of the 1860s, noted Collis Huntington, the leading figure in the consortium building the Central Pacific, "was to establish . . . railroad communication" in America "without the direct agency of the nation."[57] The American central state could undertake steps to stimulate internal improvements by the private sector, but not the work itself. The story of railroad building, then, became one of the federal government using what we might call its "indirect agency"—the distribution of incentives and subsidies to the private sector—in order to achieve its aims. This indirect agency points to an essential dimension of the privatization strategy deployed by a liberal central state to promote economic development. It was not sufficient to appeal to the higher instincts of private organizations to do their bit for the nation. Privatization also entailed transferring public monies and subsidies to corporations to make it profitable for them to do the work that the central government wanted done. Well-deployed privatization strategies, we have seen, could trigger economic growth and enhance the sovereignty of the US state. But the costs were high, nowhere more so than in the damage done to the integrity of the country's democratic political system. The story of privatization as manifested in the transcontinentals is simultaneously about government strength and weakness, of Congress exerting its will and at the same time seeing it compromised. Across the next hundred years and in a variety of endeavors, the central state would find, again and again, its ambitions both supported and undercut by its decision to invite private corporations to do its work.

VOLUNTARY ORGANIZATIONS

The liberal central state's vulnerability to corruption explains a second important form of privatization that emerged in the nineteenth century: the federal government's desire to press private watchdog groups into its service in the belief that they would bring into public affairs the morality and virtue that were missing in the activities of the profit seekers, entrepreneurs, speculators, and con men who had discovered that Congress could be turned into a cash machine. Among the groups to which the government turned to for moral backbone were religious organizations whose members were expected to offer the state a superior kind of service. The impulse to moralize a political culture seen as veering toward corruption came not just from the central government itself but also from voluntary organizations that were springing up everywhere in American society in the mid-nineteenth century. In addition to religious institutions, such as churches and missionary and bible societies, these associations included temperance and antislavery organizations; women's groups advocating for women's suffrage, education, charity, and moral purity; and various kinds of nationalist and nativist groups. The ubiquity, variety, and vigor of these voluntary associations impressed Tocqueville more than any other facet of US society or politics. "At the head of any new undertaking," Tocqueville wrote, "where in France you would find the government or in England some territorial magnate, in the United States you are sure to find an association."[58] These organizations, in Tocqueville's eyes, cultivated the "morals and intelligence" of Americans and improved the quality of their civilization. They enabled the individual to overcome the twin dangers of a democratic society: the weakness and isolation of a citizen when forced to act on his or her own, and the possibility that a government with tyrannical ambitions might prey on this weakness by offering such a citizen false camaraderie in organizations initiated and controlled by the government itself.[59]

Once this Tocquevillian perspective was marshaled in the mid-twentieth century to critique totalitarianism (and demonstrate America's invulnerability to totalitarianism's seductions), American commentators began to emphasize this voluntary sector's independence from the central state and its ability to serve as a counterweight against government attempts to take over private life, and extinguish political and social freedoms.[60] In fact, however, in the nineteenth century many of these voluntary associations were thoroughly interwoven with both the political realm and with the central state itself, which Tocqueville had understood quite well. As James M. Banner Jr. notes, "Voluntary association flourishes best where no rigid distinction is drawn between what is considered public and private activity." By their very nature, he adds, "voluntary associations designed for peaceful ends are quasi-public, composed of private citizens acting in behalf of group or public needs and seeking to accomplish legitimate purposes for one reason or another considered outside the competence or power of public authority."[61] The American central state proved to be fertile ground for the flourishing of voluntary initiatives.[62]

As Banner correctly observed, many nineteenth-century voluntary associations harbored political ambitions: to "civilize" Indians, eliminate slavery, give women the vote, humanize prisons, cure drunkenness, and end government corruption. And so they sought to influence politics. For some organizations that meant striving to become deliberately political in their associational character. Internally they constituted themselves as miniature republics that operated, as Arthur M. Schlesinger once wrote, "on the basis of a constitution or charter," with "elected and appointed officials, prescribe[d] standards of conduct," and "taxation in the guise of dues and assessments."[63] Organizationally, as Theda Skocpol has shown, that meant developing a federal form of association—local chapters assembled into state federations that in turn streamed into a single national society—that mirrored the decentralized character of American politics, and thus could exercise sufficient influence in multiple local and statewide elections so as to shape public policy on every level.[64]

From one perspective, these groups wanted to keep their distance from the day-to-day grime of American politics. Many envisioned themselves as morally superior, and the maintenance of such superiority required a formal separation from the political sphere. Women's organizations were exemplary in this respect. Female associations were formally "outside" the political realm as women could not vote, sit on juries, or hold political office. Some groups of women agitated to end their exclusion. But this did not stop them from embracing parts of the outsider role that had been forced on them. Women, they argued, possessed a purity and virtue that men lacked precisely because they could not become full players in the political sphere. As such, the hurly-burly amoral character of American politics required female input and vigilance.[65]

And yet many voluntary organizations, including women's organizations, yearned to go beyond influencing policy from a distance and become part of the central government itself. They longed for the day when they would be officially authorized to do the government's business. For significant stretches of time, then, these associations formed into what the nineteenth-century political commentator William Ellery Channing called "a kind of irregular government created within our constitutional government."[66] Voluntary associations had a model at hand for such service in the form of the republican militia, which called on ordinary private citizens to volunteer for military service when asked by their government to defend their nation. Until the early twentieth century, this militia tradition remained an important component of the nation's approach to mobilizing troops for war.[67] Many private associations saw themselves as civilian counterparts to the militia, with fulfillment coming when they could volunteer for, or allow themselves to be pressed into, national service.

The US Sanitary Commission formed in the Civil War was pioneering in this regard. Born out of female benevolent societies in New York City and then expanding to include hundreds of similar groups throughout the country, the commission assembled a budget in cash and supplies of $25 million and a corps of five hundred personnel to look after the health of Union soldiers and sanitation of the Union Army's camps.[68] Initially, the Sanitary Commission had to overcome suspicion from the Union military and Lincoln government, which it did in part by putting well-connected men in charge of this largely female organization, and by emphasizing the professionalism, efficiency, and efficacy of its work. By the war's end, the federal government had come to view the Sanitary Commission as indispensable to its military efforts, and gave its imprimatur to the Sanitary Commission's successor, the American Red Cross, when it was established in 1881.[69] In these areas, the use of private organizations and energies for public welfare was judged to be a major success.

The opportunity for this kind of government service was not limited to wartime. From the late nineteenth century through the 1930s, governments repeatedly turned to private groups to enforce racial, sexual, or financial order, and to impose industrial "peace" on rebellious workers. These groups imagined themselves as vigilant citizens joining together into "protective" and "loyalty" leagues to preserve their (and the American) way of life. A private committee of prominent citizens in New York City, calling itself the Committee of Fourteen and closely allied with Comstock's New York Society for the Suppression of Vice, played a major role in monitoring the morals of New York City's population, reporting offenses to police and developing policies to strengthen moral practices and moral living. These and related committees also took on the aim of exposing corruption in public institutions—the police, political parties, and municipal governments.[70] Frequently the activities of these groups crossed the line from vigilance to vigilantism, as members of these organizations appropriated the powers of arrest and punishment that were by law exclusively vested in such public institutions as the police and the courts.[71]

Such vigilantism became something of an embarrassment especially as the United States made its bid in the late nineteenth and early twentieth centuries as a player on the world stage. Anti-Japanese riots in San Francisco in 1907 were one example of how local vigilantism could give the United States a black eye in world affairs. The rioters objected to both the immigration of Japanese laborers to the United States and the presence of Japanese children in the public schools that white children also attended. They wanted to ban the entry of Japanese laborers, just as the Chinese laborers had been banned, and wanted the segregationist practices of the southern states to be deployed against Asians in California schools. These demands angered President Roosevelt, who was then engaged in delicate negotiations with Japan, itself just emerging onto the world stage. Roosevelt managed to come up with a face-saving agreement with the Japanese government that forestalled racial segregation in San Francisco schools and preserved US relations with Japan, but he long remained furious at the vigilantes and what he called "their criminal stupidity" for interfering so clumsily and dangerously with affairs of state.[72]

A similar kind of frustration was building with respect to initiatives launched by better-behaved groups of private citizens. Roosevelt and members of his team, for instance, were increasingly irritated by what they perceived as the amateurism of voluntary organizations, with the members of these groups now perceived as individuals who lacked the training to carry out the tasks of public administration they were so eager to take on. What the federal government needed for this new century were not enthusiastic do-gooders from private life but civil servants trained to a high standard, and able to inject their expertise, efficiency, and professionalism into public affairs. Adding civil servants meant expanding the federal government and having this enlarged central state appropriate many tasks formerly given to private groups.

This growing disenchantment with a reliance on private citizens to do public work occurred alongside the rising popularity of surrogacy as a strategy of rule. At its heart, surrogacy was a way for the central state to expand its regulatory area of authority beyond what the Constitution officially allowed. To the extent it succeeded, the federal government would be able to expand its size and orbit of action—and take over many of the tasks formerly done by private groups. But as we have seen, the obstacles to expanding the sway of surrogacy were themselves formidable. Given this limitation, no broad shift from privatization to surrogacy was imminent. The central state would perforce continue to rely on a mix of strategies to get its work done. Exemption continued to be indispensable to key affairs of state. The many Progressives who supported surrogacy believed that the future belonged to them, and many were tireless in plotting surrogacy's advance. The advocates for privatization and voluntarism were also busy, determined to reinvent their strategy to make it relevant to the needs of a modern and complex nation. In many ways they would succeed, and in the process, make the repeated predictions of their imminent eclipse look more and more like false prophecies. This late nineteenth-century repertoire of strategies for building the central state endured well into the twentieth and even the twenty-first century—testimony to the continuing power of the liberal inheritance in shaping the contours and actions of America's federal government.

4

LESSONS OF
TOTAL WAR

Many contemporaries saw World War I as the moment when the United States could abandon its "archaic" government structure, consisting of states that were overly powerful coupled with a central state that had too little authority and capacity, and build a streamlined and integrated edifice adequate to the industrial and world power the nation had become. This aspiration was strongest among Progressives, who had been making arguments for expanding the central state for years prior to 1914. Frustrated by the fragmented world of American governance, many in their ranks saw war as their deliverance. The demands of war would require authorities to put quaint objections to the growth of federal government power aside and build the kind of central state that could win the war. Moreover, reformers were hopeful they could retire the convoluted process of broadening the regulatory reach of the central state by means of surrogacy. The imperatives of wartime administration would allow reformers to show the American people what a strong, unbounded central state could do to bring order, opportunity, and justice into civil society, and thus improve life for most Americans. Even many who opposed the war saw in it the opportunity to bring a powerful and just central state into existence.

Some World War I era conservatives, such as J. Edgar Hoover, also saw potential benefits in the growth of government not as a means of regulating capitalism or expanding individual opportunity but rather as a way of extinguishing what they saw as the unruly, anarchic, and politically radical features of the nation's industrial and urban turn. The long-term twentieth-century future would belong to these liberal-left and conservative forces. But neither triumphed in the 1920s. Instead, a progressive Republicanism centered on the indefatigable Herbert Hoover carried the day. Emerging from the war as a celebrated figure for his administration of food relief in World War I, Hoover saw himself as an advocate of government, but one who worked within the tradition of nineteenth-century American statecraft. Hoover believed that the private-public strategies that he and other wartime government officials had deployed in their agencies had won the war. His consuming passion in the 1920s, as secretary of commerce and then as president, lay in applying the lessons of war to peace. That meant reinvigorating and reworking America's nineteenth-century central state for a modern age. And even as the firestorm of the Great Depression destroyed Hoover's reputation, the work that he and his supporters had done to refurbish this central state endured, making the patterns of governance that were established in the nineteenth century a greater part of America's twentieth-century state than is generally recognized. Not for the first or last time were predictions of the death of the nineteenth-century American governing system greatly exaggerated.

TOTAL WAR

World War I was the world's first total war, meaning that combatant nations had to devote virtually all their resources, military and civilian, to the fight. The scale of the armies, with tens of millions of young men conscripted into battle, had no precedent in Western warfare, nor did the numbers of killed and wounded. War had become industrialized on both the field of battle and on the home front. Victory now turned as much on a country's ability to harness its economy for the war effort and arouse patriotic ardor among its population as on the skill of its generals and soldiers. Leaders in combatant nations welcomed these home front challenges; this was an age in which many believed passionately in the power of governments to direct human energies and mold minds. The Great War, they argued, was an opportunity to show what national states could do. Many in the United States, especially in the ranks of reformers, also embraced this test, and saw in war a fulfillment of the central state's destiny.[1] But for others, the impulse to unleash government energy ran up against the venerated ideological injunction to keep the central state fragmented.

Apart from ideological considerations, the US government faced the practical problem of how to fight a total war with the limited institutional infrastructure that it possessed. In the year after it declared war on Germany in 1917, the United States increased the size of its army from a mere one hundred thousand to a five-million-man force. That was challenge enough, but the federal government also had to provision this force with arms, ships, uniforms, and food. It had to persuade industrialists to reorient their production to war materiel and workers to give up the right to protest exploitative working conditions at a time when wartime labor shortages made such actions advantageous. To pay for this mobilization, the central government deployed a new weapon in its arsenal—the income tax, made possible by the Sixteenth Amendment—while asking every citizen to "volunteer" to purchase large numbers of "liberty" bonds.[2]

On paper it looked as though the United States, in the nineteen months that it was at war, had seized the opportunity to build an entirely new federal state. Everywhere one looked, new agencies were being established at an astonishing rate. The federal government launched the Selective Service to prepare millions of young men for conscription. It created the War Industries Board, National War Labor Board (NWLB), Aircraft Production Board, US Railroad Administration, Emergency Fleet Corporation, Fuel Administration, and Food Administration to direct economic activity across a wide array of sectors. It launched the Committee on Public Information, and asked it to mold public opinion on the goodness of the war across America's fault lines of class, ethnicity, and race.[3]

Large sectors of this new federal government, however, were a mirage, much like the White City that Chicago constructed for its 1893 World's Fair: vast, gleaming, and imposing, but meant to be temporary like the World's Fair, to be dismantled after the world conflagration ended. A few of America's new governing institutions were genuinely powerful, and had acquired the coercive power to enforce their will. Yet most were not. The hard work that would have been required to imbue these agencies with genuine authority was, by and large, not undertaken. This would have meant either passing a constitutional amendment giving the central state a national police power or turning again to surrogacy. Passing either amendments or effective surrogacy laws was a difficult strategy to deploy, especially under conditions of war. And so the central government turned to the two other arrows in its quiver of strategies: coercion through exemption, on the one hand, and expanding the reach of the federal government through public-private mechanisms, on the other. Using these two strategies in tandem proved to be a powerful though unstable and ultimately unreliable mix.

The strategy of exemption, as we have seen, involved freeing the central government from constitutional limits on its powers either with respect to a specific task or in specific moments, such as war. In 1917 and 1918, Congress passed the Espionage, Sabotage, and Sedition acts—laws that collectively constituted the most drastic restriction on free speech at the national level since the enactment of the Alien and Sedition acts in 1798. The Espionage and Sabotage acts set severe punishments for spying for the enemy, or interfering with processes of industrial and personnel mobilization in ways that no government could be expected to tolerate during war. The Sedition Act was the most troubling of the three because in drafting it Congress had overreached: it defined sedition broadly to apply to any statement that could be construed as profaning the flag, the Constitution, or the military. This law, in other words, gave the federal government the right to brand as seditious almost any form of dissent. Under its banner, the leader of the Socialist

Party, Eugene V. Debs, was sent to jail for ten years merely for giving a speech criticizing the government for taking America to war.[4]

The passage of such a broad sedition measure reflected congressional worries about the social and political divisions in American society. Socialists and syndicalists had become a political force, and most opposed the war. The growth in labor militancy and increasing frequency of strikes appeared to point to the spread of socialist sentiments among the working masses. Protestant churches had rising numbers of pacifist-minded ministers and congregants in their midst. Millions of immigrants in the United States had been born in Germany or the Austro-Hungarian Empire, and many among them were suspected of harboring sympathies for America's enemies. The brutal suppression by the British of the Easter Rising in Ireland in 1916 convinced many Irish Americans, an ethnic group second in size only to German Americans, that the best hope for Irish independence lay in the defeat of the entente side that America had joined.[5]

The existence of such broad and varied streams of dissent, and the possibility that they could coalesce into a movement that would sap America's will to fight, worried US policymakers. They resolved to place broad sections of the US population under surveillance in the hope that such scrutiny would expose plots against the government and resistance to its military effort before any actual damage occurred. For the duration of the war, the American courts agreed to go along. The sedition law, along with the Espionage and Sabotage acts, represented an extraordinary extension of central government authority, and one against which there could be almost no appeal.[6]

That the central government increased its repressive powers in so dramatic a way inclined contemporaries to think that it extended its powers with equal force in other directions as well. In some respects, the central state followed this path. It did so in establishing the Selective Service in 1917. By war's end, local Selective Service boards had compelled twenty-four million young men age eighteen and older to register for the draft, and had conscripted nearly three million of them into the military. The US Railroad Administration was equally strong, having been granted the authority to take over the nation's private rail system and manage it in the public's interest for the duration of the war.[7]

But in most of its other activities, the central government lacked the power to impose its authority directly on individual Americans, groups, or states. In 1916, Congress had passed the Federal Highway Act, appropriating $5 million a year (a large sum for the time) to distribute to states willing to match federal contributions dollar for dollar. Although at the time this act was seen as a major step forward in the nationalization of the road system, it in fact left most of the important decisions about levels of funding and about the location, building, and administration of the roads to the states themselves. The weakness of the federal government became manifest when Woodrow Wilson took America to war in 1917, and the nation urgently needed a major expansion of its road system to move soldiers, workers, and materiel quickly and efficiently from one place to another. The federal government appealed to the states to get to work, but few complied, either because they lacked the infrastructure and expertise, or because their state legislators and bureaucrats got bogged down in disputes over what kinds of roads to build and where. The federal government lacked the power and administrative capacity to break these deadlocks.[8]

For many of its infrastructural and economic aims, the government therefore resorted to programs of persuasion and incentives. Consider, for example, the War Industries Board, an administrative body established by President Wilson in July 1917 to harness the might of manufacturing to the needs of a government at war. The board floundered for the first nine months of its existence, as it lacked the statutory authority to force manufacturers to adopt its plans. The appointment of Wall Street investment banker Bernard Baruch as chair in March 1918 turned the agency around. Rather than attempting to force manufacturers to do the federal government's bidding, Baruch "persuaded" industrialists to go along by allowing them to charge high prices for their products, thus significantly increasing their profits. He won exemptions from antitrust laws for corporations that complied with his requests, thereby strengthening their economic power. And he filled the War Industries Board with investment bankers and corporate lawyers from Wall Street—experienced capitalists whom manufacturers would instinctively trust. War production increased substantially, and manufacturers discovered the financial benefits of cooperation between the public and private sectors. The cost of Baruch's persuasion was high, however, as evident in the money that the federal government had to borrow to pay for the lucrative contracts it had given corporations and in the privileges they now enjoyed in the corridors of public power.[9]

Securing cooperation from the private sector proved easier for the central government to attain when the states and big corporations were not involved. This was especially true of the private organizations to which it turned to supply noncombat services to the millions of soldiers under arms. The leading such organization was the Red Cross, which by 1918 boasted almost four thousand chapters, thirty-one thousand branches, and more than twenty million members.[10] The Red Cross built warehouses, hospital centers, and homes for army nurses. It provided volunteers to army and navy hospitals and established aid organizations to tend to the needs of soldiers' families. It delivered kits to soldiers, set up canteens at train stations and ports, and encouraged its members to form knitting committees. Overseas, Red Cross volunteers set up canteens for Entente soldiers, and supplied food, hospital, and construction services to civilians. It did most of this work with privately raised money; its twenty million members paid yearly dues. Many also made supplementary donations and went door-to-door to raise additional funds. The Red Cross collected $181,000,000 in spring 1918 alone, "the most stupendous fund-raising effort by a voluntary relief society," quipped one observer, "that the country had ever known."[11] The Red Cross made itself into the most successful mass philanthropy organization of its era.[12]

While not as large an organization as the Red Cross, the Young Men's Christian Association (YMCA) also became a ubiquitous presence in army camps in both the United States and Europe, where its chapters ministered to the needs, morale, and morals of American servicemen. On the eve of war, the YMCA was already running nearly two thousand centers in American towns and cities. During the war, it built an additional four thousand centers, dubbed "Y-huts," in army and navy training camps and ports in the United States and abroad. These chapters offered millions of soldiers recreational facilities and activities, taught illiterate soldiers how to read, and instructed servicemen in health and hygiene. YMCA representatives, or secretaries as they were called, worked hard to educate servicemen about venereal disease, because the disease both reduced American soldiers' ability to fight and provided distressing evidence of soldiers' promiscuity. YMCA chapters also addressed the needs of the servicemen's families and the communities that rose alongside military bases. Servicemen frequented fifteen hundred canteens operated by the Y where they could purchase the necessities and small pleasures of daily life, such as candy and cigarettes. And the US military readily accepted the recreational, educational, counseling, and commercial services that the organization provided.[13]

The General Federation of Women's Clubs, three million members strong by 1917, also pressed itself into national service. Hundreds of thousands of federation members went door-to-door on behalf of the US Food Administration, persuading fourteen million households to sign pledges to conserve food, which meant both minimizing waste and curtailing purchases of foodstuffs most needed in war theaters, such as beef and wheat. While the efforts of these clubwomen appeared not to make much difference to the quantities of food that America actually conserved (much more important were the financial incentives given to farmers by the Food Administration to increase their production), they did a great deal to enhance the stature of the Food Administration and, more generally, the humanitarian dimension of President Wilson's war policy.[14]

Coercive pressures laced themselves through the appeals made by these voluntary organizations. Homemakers who refused to sign a food conservation pledge risked moral opprobrium and social ostracism. The same was true of those who resisted requests by groups hawking war bonds. Refusing to join America's army of civilian volunteers might not seem that consequential a decision. Yet it is important to remember that the central government had acquired emergency powers to silence and punish dissenters. By 1918, the number and size of the populations that the government had placed under some kind of surveillance had rippled outward at an alarming rate. The roster of these suspect populations included socialists, syndicalists, and groups of militant workers who believed that capitalists were using them to enrich themselves; Germans and immigrants from the Austro-Hungarian Empire who were thought to be soft on the Central Powers; Irish Americans who seemed too eager to see England, the enemy of Ireland, roughed up; any immigrant who dared to protest "one hundred percent Americanism," the demand that individuals pledge themselves to extinguish every last ember of their Old World culture; and native-born Protestants who stood up on behalf of pacifist principles.[15] Cumulatively, those groups regarded as suspicious numbered in the millions.

Homemakers with connections to one or more of these groups may well have felt that displaying a reluctance to join their local woman's club might indeed subject them and their families to suspicion. The central government, with the critical assistance proffered by private groups, did foster a climate in which individuals feared being singled out as not doing enough for their country in its hour of peril.

But this central government was still limited in its powers. If this state was successful in engendering fear among its citizenry, it lacked the capacity on its own to put millions of people under effective surveillance. On the eve of war, the central government's chief enforcement agency, the Department of Justice, was minuscule to the point of invisibility. In 1914, the Bureau of Investigation—the forerunner of the Federal Bureau of Investigation (FBI)—employed a mere 234 investigative agents on its staff. And even after the Espionage, Sabotage, and Sedition acts enormously expanded the scope of national police work, the Department of Justice had trouble finding sufficient numbers of trained and skilled agents to execute this necessary task. It had no alternative in the short term but to turn to hundreds of thousands of private citizens for assistance. These individuals were enthusiastic and energetic, but they were not trained for the jobs they took on. Their work was often shoddy and of questionable legality. In several high-profile initiatives, the activities of such volunteers embarrassed the government, exposing it to ridicule and calling into question the legitimacy of its home front campaign. Limited capacity remained the core problem of this central state, still rooted in its nineteenth-century structures.

Consider the case of the American Protective Association (APL). Founded in March 1917 by a group of Chicago businessmen, the APL quickly amassed a membership of a quarter million, most of them businessmen, professionals, shopkeepers, and white-collar workers organized in city and town chapters across the nation. "What saves a country in its need?" asked an APL partisan. "What reinforces an army called on for sudden enlargement? Its volunteers." America "always has had Volunteers" ready to do their part for God and country.[16] Armed with this historic sense of mission, APL members threw themselves into battle. They spied on fellow workers and neighbors, and broke into homes and workplaces whose occupants were thought to threaten national security. They opened mail (with the post office's permission), tapped phones, and otherwise harassed those suspected of disloyalty. They were especially eager to expose and arrest radicals, labor militants, and German sympathizers.[17]

Attorney General Thomas Gregory welcomed the APL as a partner. He legitimated the league's expansive sense of its power by authorizing it to imprint this message on its letterhead: "Organized with the Approval and Operating under the Direction of the United States Department of Justice, Bureau of Investigation."[18] Gregory also sanctioned an APL request to distribute identification badges to its members that made them appear to be public law enforcement officials. For all intents and purposes, the Department of Justice had deputized APL members to do the government's work. In 1917, the two organizations launched their first joint operation, raiding the offices of the Industrial Workers of the World in twenty-four cities. This public-private police force smashed furniture and carried off the records it found. During the war, the federal government succeeded in breaking the power of the radical Industrial Workers of the World; the APL provided indispensable assistance to this campaign.[19]

But other campaigns in which the APL played an important role revealed not the strength but rather the limitations of a campaign grounded in a mix of public and private coercion. The "slacker raids" of 1918 made this startlingly clear. The APL convinced law enforcement officials that hundreds of thousands and maybe millions of young men were slackers, the World War I term for draft evaders. The APL further believed that the slackers would be easy to identify in light of the Selective Service requirement that men of draftable age carry their draft registration and classification cards with them at all times. To expose these slackers, APL chapters joined forces with local and federal officials as well as groups of US soldiers and sailors on leave. The goal in city after city was to assemble an inspection force large enough to stop and interrogate every man of draftable age present in parts of a city that slackers were known to frequent. Anyone without proper papers would be whisked off to jail or an improvised holding facility, and detained there until his true status could be ascertained. In large cities, the scale of this work was breathtaking. For example, in Chicago in July 1918, a force of 10,000 interrogated 150,000 young men at baseball stadia, movie theaters, and train stations. Over the next two months, similar raids were staged in urban centers along the Atlantic, Pacific, and Gulf coasts.[20] The largest took place in New York City in September when a private-public law enforcement army estimated at 20,000 to 25,000 fanned out across the five boroughs, and over the course of three days, stopped somewhere between 300,000 and 500,000 men. More than 60,000 were arrested and taken to makeshift jails set up in the city's armories and other facilities.

In New York, the APL had overreached. Of the 60,000 men arrested, only 199—amounting to one-third of 1 percent—were eventually determined to have been draft dodgers. One of those arrested was a seventy-plus-year-old man on crutches.[21] Protests against the APL offensive began immediately as legions of New York City women stormed armories demanding that their husbands and sons be released. Legislators in both parties in Washington, DC, were now embarrassed that these raids had been carried out in the federal government's name. Many saw them as nothing but mass vigilantism—thousands of private citizens taking the law into their own hands—and were appalled by the complete disregard for due process that had sanctioned them. Senator George Chamberlain of Oregon, chairman of the Military Affairs Committee and a strong supporter of the war, declared, "There is not a man in the Senate or in the country who despises a man who undertakes to evade his military duty as much as I do." But he added, "These men who are slackers ought to be reached by due process of law."[22] In Chamberlain's eyes, that meant getting voluntary organizations, which were really nothing more than collections of eager but untrained amateurs, out of the business of making arrests. Only the federal government possessed that authority. It had to guard it jealously and refuse to share it with private citizens.

The Department of Justice reversed itself in reaction to these protests, declaring that the APL had no authority to make arrests. The post office backpedaled as well, announcing that it would refuse all further APL requests to inspect the letters of suspected subversives. In October 1918, officials at the Department of the Treasury won a long-running battle to strip APL members of the right to wear their coveted government badges. By December the APL was in steep decline, finally folding on February 1, 1919.[23]

The excesses of war persisted into the postwar era. Even as the central government quickly disassembled most of the institutions it had established to fight and radically downsized the army from several million to fewer than two hundred thousand, it found itself enmeshed in another vast surveillance project: monitoring the drinking habits of a hundred million Americans. It was obligated to do so as a result of the Eighteenth Amendment to the Constitution, which became law in 1920. With only one thousand Prohibition agents, the government once again lacked the capacity to impose its will and was forced to rely on armies of private citizens. The newly formed American Legion provided many of the Prohibition regiments. Its members could point to their own "extensive" government training—their military service, that is—as evidence of their ability to handle this new task of domestic policing. The legion's involvement followed the pattern set by the APL, resulting in another spectacular governing failure. Various states, New York among them, attempted to supplement federal law with enforcement mechanisms of their own, but these measures quickly overwhelmed state and local police resources. The magnitude of this administrative failure prompted Congress in 1933 to pass a new constitutional amendment, the Twenty-First, solely to undo the ill effects wrought by a previous constitutional amendment—and one that was only fourteen years old. The Prohibition fiasco was not an example of the kind of careful and deliberative government that the founding fathers thought their constitutional design had bequeathed to subsequent generations of Americans.[24]

J. EDGAR HOOVER'S DISTRESS

Anger at and frustration with how the government had managed the home front during the war and its aftermath drove some Americans to reexamine the question of how the United States should best be governed, and what rights individuals should possess vis-à-vis their governments. A small but vigorous group opposing the deployment of coercive government power in any form founded the American Civil Liberties Union (ACLU) in 1920. The campaigns led by the ACLU and its allies played a significant role in generating new respect for the rights of individuals, and in creating pressure to constrain the power of the government at both the federal and state levels. The agitation that it generated was one factor influencing the Supreme Court finally to discern in the Bill of Rights barriers against the abuse of individuals that no government at any level could be allowed to circumvent.[25]

Others argued, however, that the proper solution to the problem of government misbehavior was not to limit the power of the central state but to increase it instead. They located the misdeeds of the central government in its chronically inadequate capacity and resultant need to turn to squads of untrained volunteers to accomplish its goals. A central state with institutional capacity equal to its responsibilities would no longer need to turn to the private sector for assistance. A federal government with ample resources also would be able to demand expertise and professionalism from its employees—qualities that would improve the government's work, and thus enhance the reputation of public servants and the legitimacy of the central state as a whole.

We customarily locate the critics calling for more and better government on the Left of American politics, among those who believed that a strong federal government was necessary to manage the business cycle and constrain the power of capital. Their ranks had grown substantially in numbers. They had first surfaced in the Populist and Socialist movements, and then in Progressivism, with figures such as Herbert Croly, Robert La Follette, Theodore Roosevelt, Florence Kelley, Jane Addams, Charles Beard, and John Dewey prominent in their ranks. They attributed the failures of World War I not to the overreach of federal government power but rather to a too-heavy reliance on private groups to execute the government's business. They believed that the nation, in order to function well, required new and powerful instruments of *public* governance. Some were drawn to nationalization programs undertaken by Communists in Russia, and others to the Fabian ideas for reform that dominated much of the British Labour Party in the 1920s. Employed in universities and in government agencies, they devised schemes for expanding the power of the central state's power over economic life, and for bringing stability, order, and justice into industrial and social relations. They dreamed of establishing a comprehensive social welfare state in America. In the 1930s, they guided a near revolution in state building at the federal level that would be known as the New Deal. But in the 1920s, they lacked both access to Republican-dominated administrations and the constitutional authority necessary to expand the scope and power of the central state.[26]

A smaller coterie of conservatives energized by dreams of building a national security state rather than a national welfare state was similarly frustrated in the 1920s. The most important figure in their ranks was J. Edgar Hoover, a rising star in the Bureau of Investigation who became its director in 1924. During the first decade of his tenure, Hoover fashioned the FBI into an agency radically different than what it had been during the war. But during this time, Hoover could not get from Congress what he most wanted: a broad charter of authority that would allow him unlimited power to identify and prosecute dissenters.

Born in Washington, DC, in 1895, Hoover was raised in a family of government employees. His grandfather and father both worked for the US Coast and Geodetic Survey, and an older brother served as inspector general of the US Steamboat Inspection Service. As an undergraduate and then law student at George Washington University, Hoover worked at the Library of Congress, rising from messenger to cataloger, and finally to clerk. He was impressed with the Library of Congress's new system for cataloging books, and later modeled the FBI's central files and general indexes on it. Equally significant, he developed a respect for the work that professionals in government could do.

On his graduation from law school in 1917, Hoover landed jobs with the Bureau of Investigation, first in the War Emergency Division and then in the Alien Enemy Bureau. He rose quickly through the ranks to become head of the Alien Office and then head of the Radical Division in 1919, becoming deputy director in 1921, and director in 1924—a job that he would hold for nearly half a century, until his death in 1972. During his tenure as director, he made the FBI into a formidable government institution.[27]

As a junior officer in the bureau, Hoover had played a role in directing the slacker raids of 1918, and then the antiradical (Palmer) raids of 1919 and 1920. He had no qualms about using federal power against slackers or radicals, but he was distressed by the bureau's amateurism, evident in its many patronage appointments and in its reliance on unskilled volunteers to carry out both investigative and arrest functions. When Hoover became director in 1924, his first objective was to professionalize the FBI, and to make bureau employees answerable solely to his authority. He fired two-thirds of the bureau's agents within months of his appointment and instituted stiff new hiring requirements. Prospective federal agents had to be between twenty-five and thirty-five years of age, hold a degree in law or accounting, pass rigorous mental and physical exams, and submit to a three-month course in weapons training and crime-fighting techniques. Once hired, agents had to subscribe to a strict dress code and high standards of conduct. They were also required to stay abreast of the state-of-the-art intelligence gathering and sorting techniques that Hoover introduced. By the mid-1930s, Hoover's agents were among the most highly trained and visible civilian employees of the federal government. They were known as government men, or G-men, recognizable everywhere by their dress and demeanor. Their comportment set them apart from the state and municipal police officers Hoover disdained as mired in webs of patronage and cronyism. Hoover's FBI would do away with all of that.[28]

Hoover held himself to the same high standards of training, dress, and demeanor that he expected of his agents. He was an impeccable dresser, with a sharp eye for detail, and he had a flair for organizing and navigating his way through complex information systems. But the institutional revolution he brought to the bureau was about more than personal taste and talent. Hoover was building the FBI into an entity quite different from those that still dominated the federal government during World War I. His was to be populated by professionals rather than amateurs, by experts rather than enthusiasts. As he saw it, creating a successful organization required centralization of authority in the government agencies and, more specifically, in the hands of their directors, who were to be insulated from patronage, electoral considerations, and other forms of political pressure, including those brought to bear on the central government by individual states.

Hoover, in other words, had fashioned the FBI into an institution led by powerful technocrats with a bureaucracy full of highly trained professionals at its disposal. The FBI that he built broke sharply with America's eighteenth-century vision of a liberal central state that was limited in its authority and resources and with the nineteenth-century practice of compensating for the central state's weakness by enlisting private organizations as government auxiliaries. World War I, with its reliance on armies of private citizens, had shown Hoover that America's existing central state was inadequate to the demands of modern governance. The United States, Hoover believed, now needed a strong federal government with an expansive sense of its own power and large numbers of skilled civil servants at its disposal.

But while Hoover was transforming the internal workings of the FBI, his efforts to empower his national police force were still stymied by the narrow constitutional authority under which he had to operate for much of the 1920s. This limitation became painfully clear in the Palmer Raids of 1919 to 1920. The raids themselves were bold: on January 2, 1920, for example, the Department of Justice broke into the homes of more than 4,000 suspected radicals in thirty-three cities spread across twenty-three states. Those arrested were jailed for weeks and in some cases months without being charged with a crime, and often under harsh conditions. Of these, 591 would be deported by spring 1920.[29]

The ferocity of the raids disguised a constraint from which they suffered. They targeted only alien radicals because, once the war ended, the central government lacked the statutory power to arrest their native-born counterparts. Hoover had possessed the authority to arrest and deport foreign-born radicals; the nineteenth-century jurisprudential decision to make immigration a plenary power largely exempt from constitutional scrutiny was the source of his expansive authority over immigrants. The Bureau of Investigation did not possess this power with respect to American citizens, however, whether native born or naturalized. Hoover desperately wanted to pursue native-born radicals on his subversives' list, which by the early postwar years contained the names of 450,000 Americans. Yet he could not. The wartime sedition law expired soon after the war ended. Congress would have had to extend the sedition law or pass a new one to allow Hoover to arrest and prosecute native-born radicals. But Congress was not ready to give Hoover the peacetime sedition law he wanted, neither in 1920 nor for the rest of the decade. To the contrary, Congress acted to end the broad exemption that the central government had enjoyed during 1917 and 1918, putting the largest part of the radical community in the United States beyond Hoover's reach.[30] To prosecute native-born or naturalized radicals, Hoover required a national police power of the sort that the central government assumed only in wartime. The constant campaign that Hoover wanted to wage against radicals was possible only in an era of permanent war. Hoover would get his chance to experience a war without end during the Cold War and he would use that experience to amass emergency powers for the FBI on an enduring basis. Since such a war did not exist in the 1920s, Hoover could not get what he so dearly wanted. His FBI had acquired the capacity—but not the authority—to root radicals out of American life.

HERBERT HOOVER'S ASCENT

J. Edgar Hoover's frustration in the 1920s helps us make sense of the popularity of another Hoover in the 1920s: Herbert Hoover. Because he failed as president (1929–33) to relieve the economic and social distress of the Great Depression, this Hoover is today remembered (if he is remembered at all) as a stiff, clueless, and unimaginative public servant. But prior to the crash, he was regarded as one of the most talented and creative men of his generation. His experience in World War I had convinced him that public-private modes of governance had propelled America to victory, and if adapted to circumstances of peace and modernity, would elevate the United States to world leadership in the 1920s and beyond. Designing that adaptation became his consuming passion and road to the White House.

An Iowa orphan, Hoover graduated from Stanford University with a degree in geology in 1897, and embarked on a career as a mining engineer for the world's largest international firms. He worked in Australia, China, and London, quickly making himself a millionaire several times over by World War I. His success rested not on the entrepreneurialism that defined the railroad moguls of the late nineteenth century but rather on his skillful management of large, diverse, and complex organizations. Raised a Quaker, Hoover had a strong commitment to public service. Progressives such as Theodore Roosevelt inspired him, especially with their desire to regulate capitalism in the public interest. Hoover's opportunity to enter public life came with World War I. While living in London in

1914, Hoover took charge of an effort to secure safe passage home for the many Americans stranded in that city. Then he launched the Committee for the Relief of Belgium, persuading both national governments and private entities to contribute funds and food to support this campaign to save the Belgian and French people from starvation. When America entered the war in 1917, Woodrow Wilson appointed Hoover head of the US Food Administration, and charged him with organizing the production and distribution of American foodstuffs to millions of Entente soldiers and European civilians. He performed this task brilliantly, continuing his food distribution efforts into the postwar period.[31]

Hoover excelled at bringing together private and public entities in common projects. The Committee for the Relief of Belgium, a private organization, raised hundreds of millions of dollars from both public and private sources. Hoover moved into the public realm when he became head of the Food Administration, but his public funds and authority were both limited. His success therefore depended on his and others' abilities to persuade millions of American farmers and consumers to do the right thing: in the case of farmers, to expand their acreage under cultivation and grow the crops most needed in Europe; and in the case of consumers, to curtail their purchases of scarce foodstuffs and donate money to European food relief. To make his case, Hoover turned to the three million members of the General Federation of Women's Clubs, thinking that the door-to-door work of this army of persuaders would yield the necessary results.[32]

Hoover believed that the intimate person-to-person encounters undertaken by the federation and other private groups would reinvigorate nineteenth-century traditions of voluntarism, localism, and individualism. Moreover, these encounters would yield better results than similar ones in the past because they were now under the direction of a national agency skilled at education and coordination. At the center of that agency was Hoover himself, the master engineer and facilitator, able to instruct voluntary organizations on how to enhance their effectiveness and draw the energies from such enhancement to the central state itself. Historian Olivier Zunz has written that Hoover's method was "an idiosyncratic synthesis of authoritarianism—in its will to subordinate citizens' organizations to executive authority—and voluntarism—[with] its claiming merely to channel the flow of voluntary energies to the collective good."[33] What Zunz sees as idiosyncratic Hoover regarded as ingenious, a means of giving centralized and cooperative direction to the diverse activities of thousands of local and voluntary organizations. Here was a way to thread the modern (sophisticated methods of management) through the traditional (local habits of voluntary service), thereby adapting America's nineteenth-century state to meet the challenges of the twentieth. Because he was wielding executive authority that was long on exhortatory energy and short on statutory power, Hoover believed that he was preserving the essence of the liberal central state.

When Hoover became secretary of commerce in 1921, he set about adapting his wartime model of public-private governance to peacetime America. He was relentless in his efforts to have various groups—businessmen, public policymakers, think tank researchers, private philanthropists, and government officials—meet among themselves and with each other, sponsoring 250 meetings in his eight years as secretary. He believed that such meetings would impart both a keener sense of self-interest and appreciation for the benefits of intergroup cooperation. "Each group," Hoover wrote in 1922, "is a realization of a greater mutuality of interest, each contains some element of public service and each is a school of public responsibility."[34] Hoover was once again using the bully pulpit of government to enhance the spirit of voluntarism and qualities associated with it: service, cooperation, and social harmony.[35]

The Mississippi River flood of 1927 gave Hoover his best opportunity to show Americans what his brand of government could do. The river overflowed its banks on April 16, killing 246 people and rendering 700,000 homeless. At the flood's peak, the river formed a lake sixty-miles wide, submerging substantial stretches of land across seven southern states. Placed in charge of recovery efforts, Hoover first assembled available resources from government agencies—civilian and military, federal and local. As he had done so effectively in World War I, he then turned to the private sector: local citizens' committees, the American Legion, local charities, regional banks and credit associations, national relief organizations, and private foundations. At his behest, the Red Cross mobilized an army of 34,000 volunteer relief workers to rescue victims in flooded areas, provide them with medical care and shelter, and start them on the road to recovery. Local Red Cross chapters expected to be reimbursed for the costs of their operations, and Hoover was at the center of the campaign to raise funds, alternately imploring and browbeating foundations, regional banks, and local charities to do their part. He largely succeeded, and received credit for a relief effort that was impressive in its speed, size, and efficiency. The honor and fame that came his way as a result both enhanced the prestige of his modernized public-private mode of governance and made him the front-runner for the Republican nomination in 1928.[36]

The 1927 relief effort also exposed serious limitations to Hoover's approach to governance that are especially apparent in his failure to address the problems of racial inequality that flood relief efforts exposed. Almost half the people displaced by the flood were African American, many of them poor sharecroppers living in low-lying areas close to the Mississippi. In the flood's aftermath, they were segregated into black relief camps in which conditions were significantly worse than in white camps. Though they were offered less, African Americans were nevertheless expected to provide a disproportionate amount of the labor required to clean up towns and cities, and rebuild the levees after the waters receded. With no homes and little relief, and subjected to regimes of hard labor, a significant number of black flood victims tried to leave the South on trains heading north. But National Guard troops called up to aid in the relief effort were positioned at train stations to stop them from doing so.[37]

The discrimination and harassment suffered by African American flood victims resulted directly from the federal government's dependence on local and private groups to organize the relief effort. In most instances, these local groups sat at the top of their town's or state's racial hierarchies. They were middle and upper class, and exclusively white, and consisted of bankers, philanthropists, heads of Red Cross chapters, and community leaders who would not allow flood relief work to challenge Jim Crow. Hoover liked to think of himself as a liberal on race, however, and commissioned a report on racial tensions in the relief camps once he learned of them. When the report provided evidence of racialized poverty and discrimination, Hoover devised a bold and perhaps naive plan to attack both problems. The boldness of the plan lay in his desire to buy up property owned by wealthy white landowners in flooded areas and break up these "plantations" into small farms on which displaced blacks could be settled as tenants. If the income of these tenants proved robust enough, they could look forward to someday owning the land they worked. In its broadest ambitions, Hoover's plan was similar to the "forty acres and a mule" proposal for land redistribution that Radical Republicans in Congress had proposed at the high tide of Reconstruction sixty years before.[38] Rather than have public authorities handle the land transfers and associated costs, however, Hoover wanted the work to be done by a consortium of private entities and interests—banks, corporations, and philanthropists.

Hoover's naïveté was manifest in his expectation that private groups would be willing to undertake such an expensive and politically explosive project of social transformation. In fact, none of the private bankers, relief organizations, or philanthropists he approached would have anything to do with his scheme of racial redress, not even his good friend Julius Rosenwald, the Sears, Roebuck and Company philanthropist who had already devoted millions of dollars to improving the education, health, and economic opportunity of African Americans in the South. Rosenwald believed that the scale of Hoover's proposed project was simply too vast to be addressed by private philanthropy. He may also have feared that violence might ensue if northerners were perceived to be once again interfering with southern racial hierarchies. In 1929, Rosenwald wrote Hoover that any effort to solve the economic dimensions of the race problem in America had to involve public and not private funds, stating that "private groups can do little in the fundamental matter of employment and economic well-being."[39]

How ironic that one of the nation's most successful capitalists and leading philanthropists delivered the message to the newly elected president that private groups could not solve all of America's problems. Of course, as the case of the transcontinental railroads had shown, private capital had a long history of turning to the government for assistance. Yet Rosenwald not only wanted the federal government to facilitate a southern reconstruction undertaken by private organizations. He also wanted it to own that reconstruction. Rosenwald thought the world of Hoover. "I know of no man at present in public life," he declared to a nationwide radio audience in 1928, "who has displayed such extraordinary vision in dealing with many stupendous and wholly novel problems" that were "crucially affecting human welfare."[40] However, when confronting certain particular challenges such as race and capitalism's later collapse, Rosenwald was clear that there was no substitute for a resource-rich federal government capable of forcing change among groups in civil society.[41]

Rosenwald's objections did not sway Hoover. If the latter's plan for a public-private reconstruction of southern agriculture was not going to work, then he would propose no other. As president, Hoover would take the same approach in responding to the crisis in American capitalism. He could not envision a category or scale of problem that his preferred public-private mode of governance could not solve. Hoover's refusal to adapt or experiment in the face of widespread suffering resulted in his becoming one of the most reviled men in America in the 1930s. But the tradition that he so fervently strove to adapt to the modern politics of the 1920s did not die. It would resurface in various places and times, woven most notably into government even as the New Dealers were proclaiming the death of Hooverism and the triumph of a new kind of bureaucratic and regulatory American state. Such was the durability of the eighteenth-century idea that America's central state ought to be limited in the scope and coercive authority of its powers.

5

PARTIES, MONEY, CORRUPTION

The United States required a system of representation to realize its aspi-ration to be a republic in which the people ruled. The Constitution designed such a system for the federal government, with Congress at its core. A lower house, the House of Representatives, would be a body of members apportioned by population, one for every thirty thousand people living in a state, and elected for two-year terms by the state's eligible voters. An upper house, the Senate, would draw two members from each state; state legislatures rather than voters would select these representatives, and for terms of six years rather than two. The Constitution said nothing about representative systems that the individual states were to put into place, leaving such matters, in good federalist fashion, to the states themselves. The framers expected that the state systems of representation would be roughly similar to the national system. With respect to territories desirous of becoming states, Congress had the power to require a republican system of representation as the price of statehood.

The Constitution offered strong guidance on systems of representation, but little instruction on procedures for electing representatives to office. Elections received only this brief, inconclusive mention in article 1, section 4: "The Times, Places and Manner of holding Elections" should be left to the legislatures of each state, except that "Congress may at any time by Law make or alter such Regulations."[1] In other words, for the most part the states would be the architects of the election system, with the central government standing on the sidelines, setting broad parameters but only occasionally altering the laws. The Constitution made no mention of state and local election systems at all; thus, by the terms of the Tenth Amendment, the control of these, too, would reside with the individual states.

On the one hand, it seems to make sense that a Constitution emphasizing federalism left so many matters regarding the conduct of elections to the states. On the other hand, it seems strange, given what we now know about the scope and complexity of electioneering, and how easily election fraud and corruption can undo democratic systems, that the Constitution had so little to say about how elections in the United States ought to be conducted. Consider this list of important matters on which the Constitution was silent: which people within the polity would be eligible to vote; how many positions within state and local governments would be elective as opposed to appointive; how electoral boundaries for the House of Representatives and state legislative districts would be drawn; when elections would occur; who would organize elections, and issue and count ballots; and who would pay the costs of electioneering. These matters could be construed as details too minor to occupy the attention of the Constitution's framers, who were grappling with the weightiest matters of governance, and had only eighteenth-century models of electoral design available to them. Still, we now know that the quality of any democracy often depends on getting these details right.

The framers' reluctance to specify the rules of the election system reflected more than their insistence that the work be done by individual state governments. It also reflected uncertainty and anxiety about how fully to commit the new republic to the principle of popular sovereignty. It was one thing to proclaim that the people should rule. It was quite another to give actual people direct access to the levers of government. Failure had dogged republicanism, beginning with ancient Greece and Rome, and the framers knew this history well. Sometimes republican failure was manifest in the rise of monarchy or aristocracy, and at other times in the rise of democracy—then understood as the rule of the mob. As such, democracy could be as great a threat to liberty as a Caesar or George III. Anxiety about ordinary people getting out of control, letting their passions get the best of them and taking down a noble experiment in republican liberty runs like a red thread through the Constitution. It explains, for example, why the Constitution stipulated that the highest elected officials in the national government—the senators and president—were not to be elected directly by the people themselves but instead by elites who were to interpret and act on behalf of the popular will: state legislatures in the case of the senators, and electors, soon to be known as the electoral college, in the case of the president.[2]

The wise, disinterested, and economically secure individuals who made up these elites would handle important decisions with virtue and public mindedness, via state legislatures, the Senate, and the electoral college. The people would be allowed to directly elect many lower-level representatives in their towns and states, and in Congress itself. The wise elites would take note of these elections, and the democratic aspirations that they reflected, and work them into deliberations about what would be best for the nation. Perhaps because the framers saw elections as only a part of the architecture of American republicanism, they did not regard specifying detailed rules to protect their integrity as critical.

The framers could not have anticipated the electoral revolution that exploded in the United States across the fifty-year period after the Constitution's ratification. That revolution can be said to have started with the election of Jefferson in 1800 and matured during Jackson's two terms in office, from 1829 to 1837. By 1840, the United States had established a republic unrivaled in history in terms of the breadth and intensity of the electoral process. By that year, the number of electoral districts and elective offices in the United States, the number and frequency of elections, the breadth of suffrage, and the number of new people constantly seeking office had broken all records. Elections became America's strongest claim to being a society in which the people ruled, and they have kept this status ever since. Indeed, American history is punctuated by democratic electoral uprisings that stand out as being among the most powerful and eloquent demonstrations of the people's will: Jacksonianism, populism, Progressivism, the New Deal, and Reaganism.

Once this kind of democracy took hold in the United States in the 1820s and 1830s, the lack of rules, funds, and mechanisms for running elections became a serious problem. Private groups developed the institutions, resources, and procedures to render elections a manageable and effective enterprise, once again stepping forward when government declined to take the lead. The critical institution was a newly invented organization that came to be known as a political party. Originating in the 1820s and 1830s, such organizations had evolved by the late nineteenth century into the largest and most sophisticated enterprises, public or private, on American soil, rivaled in size and complexity only by the biggest economic corporations. Parties were remarkably inventive and improvisational institutions—qualities they needed to survive the broad changes in American economics and society across the long nineteenth century. In the process of organizing American democracy, they made themselves not only critical to the political process but also central to the affairs of state. Their role was extraconstitutional: they received no mention in the founding document, and yet they became a crucial element of public governance in America.

Five features of American democracy proved especially challenging, eliciting the innovation embodied in the rise of the political party: vast size, decentralized nature, density, labor intensity, and costliness. By the 1830s, the United States had become the largest republic in history, measured both by physical scale and by the absolute numbers of voters. Decentralization took two forms: first, in states and municipalities holding their own elections separate from the national ones, and second, in the resolutely local nature of virtually every election contest. Consider the case of a state granted ten slots in the House of Representatives. The state in question would divide its territory into ten election districts, and authorize each district to stage an autonomous election among two or three candidates, with one winner from each district going to Congress. This state, in other words, would host ten separate elections to the House, thus placing a premium on the local nature of contests. An alternative and more efficient way of organizing these elections would have been to stage one statewide election to the House. Every eligible voter in the state could cast a ballot for one candidate (or several), with the top ten vote getters moving on to Congress.

This alternative system, common in parliamentary systems across the world today, never took root in America in which local elections came to signify the highest form of democracy. These contests compelled candidates to engage in frequent face-to-face contact with their constituents. At the same time, however, this emphasis on the autonomy of each election built powerful centrifugal forces into the system, with disorder an ever-present danger unless skillful organizations stepped in to weave local contests into a broader electoral struggle.

American democracy's third feature, its electoral density, compounded the problem of decentralization. The ratio of elective to appointive offices was high—a development especially visible at the municipal and town levels. Every local official, from the mayor to the municipal judge to the dogcatcher, seemed to be running for office. And terms of office were short. Elections were thus occurring all the time, requiring a bottomless supply of candidates and funds.

No other known republic developed a system of voting as broad, decentralized, and dense as America's. The system affirmed the democratic character of the republic, for it allowed many ordinary people to have a substantial voice in determining their own affairs. But it also imparted to American democracy, and to the parties that took on the task of organizing it, a fourth and fifth feature: labor intensity and costliness. The labor-intensive nature of the system was manifest in the large number of campaign workers required to seek out candidates, monitor elections, and get out the vote. Parties could mobilize enough labor power if they paid these workers for their efforts. Solving this labor problem, however, made electioneering expensive, and often extravagantly so.

Where would the parties find the necessary funds? The Constitution made no provision for funding elections, and states were reluctant to put up their own funds for electoral purposes. Without access to public monies, political parties began turning to private sources for funds and to selling access to government through patronage and graft. In the process, parties gave private interests substantial opportunities to penetrate governing institutions. The parties that did such an extraordinary job organizing the complex democracy that took root in America also repeatedly put that democracy at risk by opening it to monied influence. The selling of government power to the highest bidder that became routine in the building of the transcontinental railroad was hardly a unique case. To the contrary, it was a systemic feature of American governance, made necessary by the emergence of an electoral system that was huge, dense, decentralized, labor intensive, and expensive, and for which the Constitution had authorized no public funds.

This chapter reconstructs the story of how political parties in the nineteenth century raised and spent money; how they established links with groups with which they wished to curry favor; how they built enterprises that rivaled the biggest corporations in America; and how they so interwove these enterprises with municipal, state, and federal governments that they (the enterprises) in effect became an arm of public administration—without ever losing their private status. I also ask why, in the late nineteenth and early twentieth centuries, it proved so hard to reform the electoral system that these parties had created and to narrow the influence of monied interests on American democracy.

It is worth stressing the dual public-private character of the American political party. Parties became public institutions in the sense that their leaders represented political constituencies, sat in public assemblies, and made public policy. The parties, as the political scientist Stephen Skowronek has written, also played a key role in binding "together a radically decentralized state and faction-ridden nation."[3] Along with the federal courts, they were the only political institutions to span all levels of American government. Parties developed brilliant mechanisms for containing the centrifugal forces unleashed by American federalism. They brought groups from every part of the country together in omnibus and national organizations. They allowed and even encouraged the circulation of party officials, supporters, and ideas through the different levels of government, thereby bringing individuals who worked in the diverse state and federal systems into frequent contact. In so doing, the parties performed a vital public and governing service. They became, in essence, an indispensable fourth branch of government.

But the political party was also private in the sense that it was an organization that mobilized followers to claim as large a share of government "spoils" as they could, and in the process increase the wealth and power of its members and supporters.[4] The dual internal hierarchies that emerged in America's nineteenth-century parties— one consisting of the party's official leaders who, if elected, would hold the highest offices in federal and state governments, and the other consisting of party bosses who controlled the flow of patronage and graft—are indicative of this institution's hybrid status. A close examination of the way in which this institution functioned offers one more demonstration of the importance of private-public interpenetration as a mode of governance in America.

THE MOST COMPLEX ELECTION MACHINERY IN THE WORLD

Studies of suffrage over the course of the last generation have rightly emphasized the large number of Americans who were excluded from voting: women, African Americans (slave and free), and newly arrived immigrants.[5] Yet this should not allow us to lose sight of how inclusive and democratically convulsive the US polity had become by the 1820s and 1830s. Almost two-thirds of American states had property requirements for voting in 1800. By 1830, the percentage of such states had fallen to one-third. By the 1850s, all but two states had embraced universal white manhood suffrage.[6] States also committed themselves to frequent and decentralized elections;

the terms of office were short almost everywhere. Virtually every incorporated polity from the state to the smallest village or town began insisting on running its own elections, with the election dates and candidates themselves chosen locally. At the same time, many local and state government positions that had been appointive became elective. These developments signaled a significant departure from what the founding fathers had intended. The men who had framed the Constitution had not wanted to create a republic with this breadth of suffrage, volume of elected officials, frequency of elections, and degree of popular control. Most expected the country to be governed in the classical republican way: by wise, disinterested, and economically secure individuals who would handle the country's business with virtue and public mindedness.

For some time, it seemed as though the new republic would indeed be able to operate according to these classical republican principles. The Federalists who dominated politics in the early years of the republic limited the franchise to propertied white men, kept the ratio of elective offices to appointive ones relatively low, and reserved most important decisions for America's "best men"—the merchants, plantation owners, lawyers, former generals, and others of substance who sat in Congress and would be called on to resolve differences through face-to-face relationships and by applying virtue and wisdom to the country's affairs. Plebeian Americans were expected to fall into line with congressional decisions and play their secondary part in a political system still permeated by the deference that was a powerful legacy of British colonial rule. The preeminence of Congress's best men is evident in the congressional caucus that controlled nominations for the presidency and other national offices from 1800 through 1824, and in the designation of Congress as an electoral college of last resort, as it became in the election of 1800. Similarly small caucuses operating in the states often decided who would stand for state office and the critical positions of presidential electors. Most of these caucuses drew their candidates from their states' social and political elite. An elite also came to dominate the federal bureaucracy; many of its members expected to serve indefinitely. In fact, only seventy-four employees were removed from office in the nearly four decades between the ratification of the Constitution in 1789 and Jackson's victory in 1828.[7]

Americans today are still living with vestiges of this best men system of republican rule. We can see an example of it in the Senate's cloture rule, which allows a minority of senators to ignore the will of electoral majorities in the alleged "best interests" of the nation. But there have also been significant challenges to this original system, with many groups of Americans attempting to establish a republic in which the people actually ruled, such as they believed the Constitution had authorized. The initial attempts to render the American system a government "by the people" arose in the aftermath of the election of 1800, as democratic enthusiasm spread quickly through the ranks of a population eager to exercise its sovereignty.[8] The politics of deference withered as states liberalized rules governing the franchise, expanded the number of elected (as opposed to appointive) offices, and staged more frequent elections. Since the Constitution said little about when elections were to occur, states and towns made their own decisions about when to hold them. By the 1820s, it seemed as though elections were going on all the time, and they were.[9]

That an electoral democracy of this breadth and intensity had emerged is exemplary of what Gordon Wood has called the radicalism of the American Revolution, a radicalism that unleashed ideological forces of equality and democracy that transformed over the course of two generations the ways in which Americans thought about and conducted their politics.[10] The process of creating a broad, decentralized, and frequently mobilized electorate was unruly, as were the elections that were often boisterous, and whose male participants indulged in drinking, rude behavior, and occasionally violence. Some observers were disturbed enough by the electoral process to wonder whether it was really serving democracy or simply unleashing the passions of the mob.[11] The smashup at the White House that followed Jackson's 1829 inauguration seemed to presage what was to come through the early years of the twentieth century. One early student of political parties, Moisei Ostrogorski, pieced together the tale of the mob that invaded Jackson's new residence in this way:

The crowd broke into the White House, filled all the rooms in a twinkling, pell-mell with the high dignitaries of the Republic and the members of the corps diplomatique; in the great reception hall men of the lower orders standing with their muddy boots on the damask-covered chairs were a sort of living image of the taking possession of power by the new master. When refreshments were handed round . . . a tremendous scramble ensued, crockery, cups, and glasses were smashed to pieces, rough hands intercepted all the ices, so much so that nothing was left for the ladies. . . . The fury with which the people flung itself on the refreshments was destined very soon to become highly symbolic.[12]

Even as they acknowledged that elections had become an opportunity for drunken white men to riot, many Americans still believed that this electoral system fulfilled the revolution's democratic promise. Still others would find inspiration in the way Jacksonian democracy opened American politics to groups of poorer Americans who had been on the margins. Their ranks included antislavery forces of the 1840s and 1850s; supporters of Henry George and his campaign for the mayoralty of New York City in 1886; the People's Party campaigns of 1892 and 1896; Progressives who coalesced out of electoral struggles in America's municipalities and states in the early years of the twentieth century to take back America from the "interests" and return it to the "people"; FDR's Democratic Party, which mobilized many sorts of poor people, urban and rural, Catholic, Protestant, and Jewish, white and black, to build an enduring New Deal Order; and Reagan's Republican Party, which deployed a populist conservatism to throw the last New Dealers out of office and create a new electoral majority committed to market capitalism, individualism, and evangelicalism.

Momentous electoral uprisings are only part of the story of electoral democracy in the United States, however. The other part centers on how the broadly based democratic system that the founding fathers had not anticipated, and for which they had made few procedural provisions, would be managed. The Constitution offered almost no guidance on organizational issues regarding elections.

"The founders of the American Republic," wrote Ostrogorski in 1902, "had not, it would appear, bestowed a moment's thought on the question as to how the electors should be set in motion" or given the tools to be able to put their mandate into effect.[13] The founding fathers also made no provision for funding an enterprise that by the 1830s, involved hundreds of thousands of people, consumed huge amounts of time, and cost millions of dollars.[14]

Political parties emerged in the 1820s and 1830s to bring order and resources to this experiment in electoral democracy. The parties recruited candidates, and then nominated them, raised money for them, campaigned for them, and turned out the vote for them. They began to regularize elections, confining them to a more limited span of days. They invented new institutions, such as the state delegate convention, the function of which was to satisfy the voracious need for nominees for state offices and also to choose delegates to attend the national party convention—an institution introduced by the Jacksonian Democrats in 1832 to select the national party's presidential nominee and extract pledges from party members to support him. By the 1840s, when the Whigs adopted these Jacksonian techniques, political parties had taken over the election system, making themselves central to the operation of government.[15] Writing about this party system when it was at its peak at the turn of the twentieth century, the English political analyst James Bryce noted that "it has now grown to be the second ruling force in the country, in some respects fully as powerful as the official administration which the Constitution of the Nation and of the several States have established." In a development that Bryce and other European observers found stunning, the parties constituted "a second and parallel government" that had arisen entirely unanticipated by the Constitution yet "directing that which the Constitution creates."[16]

That this "second and parallel government" had emerged reflected in the first instance the maddeningly complex, decentralized nature of politics in America. Party organizations had to follow the federalist model, as all electoral contests took place within the boundaries of individual states. This was true even of presidential elections, whose outcome was determined not by national vote totals but rather by the votes of electoral college delegations from each state. Thus, in order to be nationally competitive, a party had to field a large and effectively autonomous organization in virtually every state. State party leaders, along with those from America's largest cities, became the most important figures in a political party's firmament. These leaders had to find a way to somehow knit together a national party from its constituent state and big city units. Matthew Josephson, a 1930s' student of nineteenth-century politics, observed that party government acquired the form of a "colossal elective pyramid, a vast mechanical structure of primaries, conventions, committees, whose workings, wheel within wheel, whose numerous details, committee business, advance arrangements, were far too complex to remain subject to the casual will or decision of the masses of busy workaday citizens."[17] Josephson's sentence is as dizzyingly complex as the phenomenon he was trying to describe.

That this party system grew into the "parallel government" portrayed by Bryce and Josephson also reflected the reluctance of the country's "official administration" to extend its own direct dominion over the electoral system developing under party auspices. In a polity vigilant about dispersing government power and limiting its formal scope, it seemed reasonable to hand off responsibility for elections to groups in civil society that wanted to make their voices heard. Such privatization, as we have seen, was one of the most important strategies through which America's nineteenth-century central state governed. But who would ensure that a system developed under private auspices would be made to serve public purposes? And if the federal government declined to assume responsibility for funding what Josephson depicted as the "colossal . . . pyramid" of electoral machinery, who would do so? In the 1830s and 1840s, the second question was more pressing than the first. Increasingly the answer focused on a new type of politician, known in the nineteenth century as the "professional politician" to some, and the "party boss" to others. We may also usefully describe him as a political entrepreneur and, later in the century, a CEO.

These professional politicians devoted themselves to looking after the affairs of the party full time. They developed elaborate organizations that reached down to individuals in the smallest electoral unit in their municipality or state. They sponsored partisan newspapers to get out favorable notices about their candidates running for office; they raised money; and they printed and distributed ballots, the expense of which, for much of the nineteenth century, had to be borne by the parties themselves. If they lived in immigrant areas, they facilitated the naturalization of large numbers of the foreign born, often the moment they got off the boat. They turned out numerous supporters in public venues to celebrate and then vote for their candidates—occasions that became ever more spectacular and carnivalesque as parties dueled with each other for electoral supremacy. By the mid-nineteenth century, no campaign in a major urban area could conclude without an elaborate and hugely expensive torchlight parade involving thousands, and even tens of thousands, of party supporters. Rural areas would host giant barbecues, eagerly serving up what the *Nation* in the late nineteenth century characterized as an "unlimited supply of roast ox for the multitude."[18]

Bosses also flooded election sites with ballot distributors to press their party's ballot into the hands of willing voters. Other party representatives carried large sums of monies in their pockets to purchase the votes of "floaters," individual citizens who were more interested in being paid for their vote than in casting a ballot on the basis of ideology or partisan loyalty. So many of these floaters sought to cast their votes twice (and thus be paid double) that they became known as "repeaters" in the parlance of nineteenth-century election professionals. The going rate per vote for much of the nineteenth century was $5, with rates sometimes escalating to $7 or $10, and occasionally reaching the stratospheric level of $20 or $30.[19] Still other party workers scrutinized polling places, making sure that individual voters cast the right ballot, and that the ballots were deposited and then counted correctly. Electoral success became the obsession of the party bosses and the measure by which they expected to be judged.

Party bosses and their staffs made the party their life and politics their livelihood. This meant finding ways to generate sources of income more robust and more secure than what the elected positions themselves provided. Most professional politicians were not gentlemen or gentry; rather, their origins lay in the lower and middling orders. Many, like New York's Martin Van Buren—the paradigmatic professional politician—conformed to the profile of the classic American outsider who gains power and influence not through education, apprenticeship, or marriage but rather through energy, smarts, single-mindedness, boldness, and if necessary, ruthlessness. Party bosses needed to generate income not just for themselves but also for the armies of political operatives on whom their electoral ambitions depended. Elections were labor-intensive operations, requiring the deployment of huge numbers of workers.[20]

Because cash for party workers was often in short supply, the Jacksonians invented the spoils system in which the victorious party declared its right to fill appointive positions it controlled with party members. Originally a noncash way of paying off those who had worked on the party's behalf, it became a mechanism for generating new streams of cash for the party. As early as the late 1830s, a House of Representatives committee reported a "regular taxation of public officers . . . for the support of party elections at the New York customs house."[21] By the end of the Civil War, party bosses had extended this mode of taxation, now known as "assessments," to most individuals holding local, state, or federal patronage jobs. This constituted an extralegal system through which patronage appointees deposited a portion of their annual salary, usually estimated at between 2 and 6 percent, in party coffers.[22] In 1882, the Republican Party of Pennsylvania sent the following slightly menacing letter to public employees who had failed to pay their assessments: "An important canvass like the one now being made in an important State like Pennsylvania requires a great outlay of money, and we look to you as one of the Federal beneficiaries to help bear the burden. Two per cent. of your salary is _____. Please remit promptly. At the close of the campaign we shall place a list of those who have not paid in the hands of the head of the department you are in."[23] Such aggressive assessment of public employees in Pennsylvania continued well into the twentieth century, especially in Philadelphia.[24]

Party bosses also began charging a substantial fee to individuals who received plum patronage positions or nominations for those positions. In New York City in the 1880s, individuals paid anywhere from $10,000 to $15,000 for the right to run for aldermanic and sheriff posts and for superior and common pleas court judgeships. Nominations to state senatorships, state judgeships, the US Congress, and county clerk and registrar positions began at $20,000 to $25,000 and rose from there.[25]

Paying fees for the right to run for elective office made sense because one could generate cash from officeholding itself. Revenue flowed in a variety of streams. Prominently placed individuals in municipal public works departments demanded kickbacks from contractors chosen to do city work. Police officers extracted protection money from vice entrepreneurs operating in their precincts. Federal supervisors of the Internal Revenue, based in Department of Treasury field offices, enjoyed especially lucrative opportunities as they went about collecting excise taxes on whiskey and other hard liquors. In one notorious case, General John A. McDonald, supervisor of Internal Revenue for Missouri, conspired with distillers and government inspectors in the early 1870s to report only 25 percent of the whiskey being produced in the five-state region over which his office exercised jurisdiction. As a result, distillers paid taxes on only 25 percent of their total product, plus handsome fees to McDonald and other officials for allowing the rest of their booze to enter the marketplace tax free.[26]

For party men working at the federal level, imports constituted an even greater source of funds than whiskey. In the nineteenth century, the federal government taxed virtually all imports, and the resulting tariffs constituted the principal source of federal revenues. Three-quarters of the imports entering the United States annually came through the Custom House in New York City. More than a thousand federal officials worked there under the direction of the collector of the Port of New York.[27] A large majority of these employees paid an assessment on their salary, making the Custom House the single-greatest source of party patronage in the country. Moreover, a significant number of employees generated additional revenue through the goods inspection process. They conspired with importing merchants to underreport the value of goods coming in, or conversely, levied fines on merchants for misrepresenting the size and value of their cargoes. When an inspector caught one importer lying about a large shipment in the 1870s, the Custom House charged the importer more than $250,000 in fines to be paid to four employees, including Chester A. Arthur, then the Port of New York collector. It is little wonder that the future president became a wealthy man during his eight-year tenure (1871–78) in this position.[28]

The extraction of these sums from manufacturers and merchants cannot be understood simply in terms of the personal venality of spoilsmen. Arthur knew that he had to pass along to the state and national Republican parties a portion of the assessments and payoffs he collected. At each state Republican convention, he reserved a hotel suite at his "own" expense, and filled it with food, drink, and cigars for the Republican nabobs gathered to plot party strategy. So, too, did Republican Party bosses regularly call on McDonald, the head of the St. Louis Whiskey Ring, to infuse cash into critical electoral struggles. "Faced with a hot campaign," wrote Josephson about the role of whiskey in 1870s' electoral politics, "a great Senator would telegraph to McDonald's headquarters for new levies upon the distillers, so that a congressional district would not be 'lost' or so that even a State might be 'saved.' "[29] In the 1872 campaign, McDonald alleged that the Republican Party boss of Indiana, Senator Oliver Morton, traveled to St. Louis to personally call on McDonald. The aged and infirm senator slowly climbed the stairs to McDonald's second-floor office on his crutches for the purpose of soliciting whiskey funds to stop Indiana from tipping over into the Democratic column.[30] Political parties, in other words, had come to depend on an extensive system of extralegal and sometimes illegal financing to fund their activities. The origins of this system lay in the vast and decentralized system of electioneering that the framers of the Constitution had not anticipated, and for which they had designed no mechanism for funding. Political parties arose to bring coherence to this lawless system, and to raise the large sums of money required to make it work.

We do not often pause to ponder the costs and labor requirements of this entrepreneurial electoral system. Ostrogorski estimated that by the 1890s, "the regular and permanent machinery" of party organizations involved as many as eight hundred thousand to a million individuals actively working on the parties' behalf out of a total electorate of fifteen to sixteen million. At election time, this one million swelled to four million, or "one militant . . . to every four or five electors."[31] This is a stunning statistic.

In New York State, a Republican machine run by Thomas Platt employed an estimated ten to thirteen thousand regulars at a cost of almost $20 million per year.[32] The Republican Party machine in neighboring Pennsylvania counted twenty thousand state citizens on its rolls, including those who held patronage positions in Pennsylvania government as well as nongovernment workers whom the machine paid to get out the vote. The size of the Pennsylvania Republican Party workforce was larger than those of most US corporations at the time, and two-thirds the size of the workforce of the Pennsylvania Railroad, then the largest corporation in the world. Maintaining this army of party workers cost its boss, Matt Quay, an estimated $24 million annually.[33] Quay raised these millions in a variety of ways: assessments levied on state patronage employees; "fees" assessed on banks for the privilege of holding state funds; profits from state funds that Quay directed banks to invest in securities; kickbacks from construction firms and utilities awarded city or state contracts; contributions from candidates desirous of securing their party's nomination; and "frying all the fat" (a phrase that Quay made famous) out of manufacturers operating in the state and dependent on it for favorable legislation.[34] The buying and selling of privileged access to government resources that dominated the process of building the railroads was found at every level of American politics.

New York City's Tammany Hall was an even more extravagant operation than Quay's Pennsylvania machine. In the late 1880s, Tammany controlled about ten thousand patronage city jobs in New York City alone. At election time, an estimated twenty to twenty-five thousand Tammany workers swarmed over New York City's 812 election districts. Their job was to corral Tammany voters, place the party's own privately printed ballot in their hands, and "persuade" them to deposit it in the polling box. This army of electoral workers also labored to peel voters away from other parties when possible, carefully monitor the casting and counting of ballots, and harass the opposition. Their efforts were contested by a smaller but still-large army of fifteen to twenty thousand election workers employed by the Republicans and other parties, or deputized by the city and federal governments to act as "neutral" observers at polling places. New York City's election districts were small (numbering only 250 to 400 voters each), and so for significant stretches of Election Day, detachments from the rival armies of election workers outnumbered the unattached citizens who came to the polls to vote. This heavy party presence magnified the opportunities for intimidation, as did the fact that voting often took place at saloons awash in free-flowing liquor for all. Opposing masses of election workers frequently dueled with each other, jousting verbally, pushing and shoving, and sometimes fighting.[35] Already in the nineteenth century, elections constituted America's greatest theater.

Few election workers were laboring or fighting for free. Most expected to be paid either with wages or a party patronage position (especially one that could generate graft income), or both. Providing large numbers of patronage positions was challenging for political machines, but worth the cost in light of the benefits that flowed from winning electoral contests.

Tammany bosses relied on the same kinds of revenue sources that Quay developed for Pennsylvania—patronage assessments, "fees" businessmen paid for securing lucrative city contracts, and surpluses generated by contracts beyond the real cost of the work and then siphoned into party coffers. One notorious New York City case of inflated contracts was the so-called Tweed Court House, commissioned by the city in 1858 for $250,000 and completed fourteen years and a staggering $12.5 million in city funds later. By then, Boss William Marcy Tweed's brazen ways of steering graft his way had brought him down, although not before he had deposited an estimated $45 to $60 million in Tammany coffers.[36]

Tammany also made money on the rich stream of revenue flowing through the city's seven-thousand-strong municipal police force.

One scholar has estimated that the New York City machine charged each new patrolman $250 to $500 for the privilege of joining the force. Those elevated to the highest positions on the force were expected to pay $10,000 to $15,000 for their promotions. Ordinary patrolmen levied fees on both the legal and illegal parts of New York's commercial sector for the privilege of doing business in the city. One 1890s' investigation of the New York City police force revealed that officers charged the following monthly fees to merchants in their precincts: $5 to $25 to licensed liquor dealers, $60 to pushcart vendors, $50 to $100 to brothel owners, and $250 or more to unlicensed saloons.[37] These fees, multiplied by the number of such merchants, dealers, and vice entrepreneurs in New York City, generated sizable sums of money. One estimate put the annual yield in police "fees" at $7 million in 1894, and another at $25 million in 1912.[38] J. Edgar Hoover and other law enforcement professionals of the 1920s and 1930s would come to regard the graft that suffused local police work as posing as big a threat to the integrity of their mission as the amateur enforcers of loyalty and Prohibition during World War I and its aftermath.

We cannot know, of course, how much money collected through bribes and kickbacks went into the pockets of individual policemen, and how much made it up the chain of command and into the hands of Tammany bosses. Some evidence suggests that Tammany permitted individual policemen to keep fees they had collected from prostitution and saloons while demanding that they turn over revenue gathered from gambling operations.[39] We do know that Tammany regarded the police as integral to its political operation, not simply because of the revenue they generated, but also because the department, through its Bureau of Elections, administered the elections that sustained Tammany's power. The bureau drew electoral districts, kept records, chose polling sites, selected inspectors and poll clerks, and oversaw vote counting.[40] Though it was nominally a neutral, nonpartisan body, Tammany exercised influence on the bureau by virtue of its control over the police. The Irish American identity shared by so many New Yorkers who populated both organizations also served to strengthen the connections between the two. In effect, Tammany made the Bureau of Elections an adjunct of the machine. The thickness of Tammany–police department relations, then, enhanced Tammany's ability to win elections and widened the stream of extralegal and illegal revenues.[41]

The systems developed by urban machines to administer their wide-ranging and complex operations could be as sophisticated as those of the country's most impressive private corporations. Indeed, the biggest Gilded Age political machines rivaled the great corporate entities in size and influence. The machines were business entities, obsessed with inputs and outputs. The inputs were the voters; the task was to ensure that the flow of this "raw material" was steady and its "quality" was reliable. The outputs were the spoils of elections: patronage jobs, contracts, franchises, city services, and graft. The inputs—the voters—cost money. Output brought in money. Party managers were the CEOs of political enterprises, spending their time balancing inputs and outputs, investments and revenues, in the interest not so much of profit maximization as of staying in power. Their work was political economy of the truest sort.

At the top of each machine stood the boss himself, customarily a man of entrepreneurial and managerial ability who ruled with an iron fist and sought to extend his power wherever his political organization had set down roots. Quay of Pennsylvania controlled those appointed to top positions in state government departments, and through them he managed the distribution of state funds to state hospitals, schools, prisons, charities, and asylums. He made it clear to state legislators that he would withhold money from these institutions if they did not give him what he believed the state of Pennsylvania wanted and needed.[42]

Quay placed state legislators under close scrutiny to keep them in line. He kept a card for every legislator on which he recorded that individual's voting record and whatever favors and services he had been given as well as information about his personal life. These cards came to be known as "Quay's coffins" because they often contained the kind of embarrassing information that, if released, could end a legislator's career. When the state legislature was in session or when the state Republicans were holding a convention, Quay would often rent a hotel suite near the statehouse or convention site, with two suites' rooms connected by a bathroom in which he installed his card files. He would call in Republican legislators one by one, always with a card in hand. After meeting in the first room, he would retire to the bathroom, where he would collect a card for his next meeting in the second room. Back and forth he went, using his vast knowledge about politics, policy, and the lives of legislators to flatter, cajole, and threaten. Controlling individual legislators in this way, he was at the same time centralizing state powers of patronage, policy, and sweetheart deals in his own hands. Corporations valued this centralization, which allowed them to cut their deals with one politician in Pennsylvania rather than scurrying after and trying to secure the support of scores of unreliable legislators with their divergent and often-petty concerns.[43]

Quay was an innovator. His attention to organization and detail and his appreciation of the uses to which information could be put in political struggles gave him important advantages over his competitors—a model that later generations of political operatives from Marcus Hanna to Tom DeLay, Karl Rove, and David Plouffe would seek to emulate.[44] Particularly imaginative in this regard was Quay's decision as head of the national Republican committee to elect Benjamin Harrison in 1888 to conduct two private censuses of New York City. One identified the adult men in the city and their places of residence in order to determine who was an eligible voter and who was not. Another identified all vacant apartments and homes in the city so that Quay's operatives could pinpoint where Tammany might be stashing Democratic voters brought illegally across city or state lines. Quay challenged enough Democratic votes in the 1888 election to carry New York for Harrison.[45]

Tweed had undertaken a similar kind of centralization of Tammany in New York City in the 1860s, establishing a pattern of boss rule that would persist across fifty years, through the "administrations" of John Kelly (1874–84), Richard Croker (1886–1901), and Charles Murphy (1902–24). A clique of one to six "sachems" and "commissioners" sat at the Tammany boss's right hand, and with him made the most important decisions. Below them stood twenty-four district leaders, formerly called ward bosses, one for each of New York City's state assembly districts.[46] These assembly district leaders appointed more than eight hundred captains, one for each of New York City's electoral districts.[47] Each captain, in turn, collected information about the needs, opinions, and aspirations of voters in his election district, put out services, and solved social and political problems. Captains developed particularly close relations with five to ten individuals in their districts. Sometimes these individuals would occupy "formal" positions in the district organization as block captains (for city blocks) or house captains (for apartment buildings); at other times, these individuals would simply be embedded in strategically important neighborhoods. In either case, they would become the assembly district leader's and election district captain's eyes and ears.[48] These "lieutenants" added another four to eight thousand individuals to the core of the Tammany machine, giving it a cadre of five to ten thousand individuals distributed across the entirety of New York City. Their numbers included only a fraction of Tammany's patronage workforce of ten thousand, which constituted a second reserve army to be deployed for electioneering purposes. Tammany was indeed an extensive and deep organization that had drilled its way down to the neighborhoods, the bedrock of New York City politics.[49]

Sustaining an organization of this scale was expensive. Machines raised money through assessments on both patronage appointments and those who sought nominations for choice electoral offices. The graft collected by the police provided another important and dependable stream of revenue. Indirect revenue came from a machine's ability to place a significant number of its operatives in salaried municipal jobs and to have the city in effect pay these individuals to do the machine's work. But the size and reach of the machines also depended critically on their ability to draw revenues from the great infrastructural expansion of the late nineteenth and early twentieth centuries—the building of the roads, aqueducts, sewers, street railways, and gas and electric lines that undergirded America's physical and economic transformation. Machines played a central role in facilitating, directing, and often compromising the quality of this transformation.

The practices engaged in by the transcontinental railroads and their allies in Congress in the 1860s and 1870s became common throughout American states and municipalities across the next thirty years. Political machines proved indispensable to this monied politics. Like the Crédit Mobilier, political machines inflated the cost of contracts for public works that were being charged against city and state accounts. They collected private money by requiring corporate bidders for city construction contracts to "grease" the machine. In New York in 1900, the Board of Public Works was the most important institution of city government, accounting for 60 percent of the city's total expenditures of $100 million. The mayor nominally appointed the commissioners of this board, but in reality they had been chosen by the Tammany boss, Richard Croker, from the ranks of Tammany Hall assembly district leaders. The allegiance of these commissioners, argued New York City alderman P. Tecumseh Sherman, was not to the mayor but instead "to the boss and to their district organizations." Sherman conceded that these Tammany appointees were "all men of considerable ability," but he loathed them for focusing their talents largely on promoting Tammany welfare: winning elections, compelling contractors who wanted contracts to make contributions to the Tammany campaign fund, and demanding that these same contractors fill the unskilled positions on their projects with Tammany loyalists.[50] In years when the Democrats controlled not just New York City but also the entire state by holding the governorship and majorities in both houses of the Albany legislature, the Tammany assessments on corporations operating in New York City rose to particularly steep levels. One journalist reported that the biggest corporations (those with capitalizations exceeding $25 million) were being assessed $50,000 apiece while the smaller ones were paying $10,000 to $15,000 each. With as many as two thousand New York City corporations subject to this kind of assessment, Tammany could have easily raised $10 to $20 million in years when its control of city and state politics verged on the complete.[51] Private corporations acceded to this shakedown only because they, like the transcontinental railroads, trusted that the return on their "investments" would be great.

Whether Tammany operatives were as single-mindedly selfish as Sherman thought them to be is an open question. It is possible that Tammany commissioners chose superior contractors to do the city's public works and distributed unskilled jobs under their control to deserving New York City citizens. Indeed, until the scale of his theft became known in the early 1870s, Boss Tweed was hailed by many New Yorkers for the vigor and vision that he brought to street and landscape improvements in the city.[52] Tammany could bend to pressures from both middle- and working-class reformers; at times the machine played a crucial role in defusing class conflicts in the city.[53] The machine's malleability makes it difficult to say where its function as an institution of government shaded into its ambition as a private entity intent on amassing riches and power. We should not try to fix that point too precisely because it changed over time, as did the mixture of public and private imperatives shaping party and machine behavior. At the same time, we need to recognize that parties never overcame their dual, public-private nature. Succeeding in American politics always required parties to devote considerable energy not just to developing public policy but to raising the private funds that enabled them to win elections.

This dedication to fund-raising does not mean that political parties can be understood simply as beholden to the "monied interest." Parties were complex political organizations whose origins predated the full-fledged development of capitalism in the United States, and whose purposes and functions remained independent of those governing private corporations. In fact, one vector of late-nineteenth-century reform was fueled by the frustration of business leaders who felt unable to make government by machine conform sufficiently to their needs.[54] Nevertheless, the machines' incessant search for money widened the access of private interests to public funds, public policy, and public power. This access helps us to understand why late-nineteenth-century foreign observers of American politics were frequently shocked by what Daniel Rodgers has called the "porosity" of urban governments to private influence.[55] The roots of this porosity lie not in the moral deficiencies of individual men but rather in the deficiencies of a Constitution that had made no provision for funding what had become an extraordinarily expensive and decentralized system of elections. The vulnerability of the American democratic system to graft was chronic and even systemic.

THE PERSISTENT FAILURE OF REFORM

Graft and corruption became the obsession of reform-minded groups that lived through the era of machine politics. Other than the Civil War and industrialization itself, there was arguably no more pressing issue in late-nineteenth-century US politics than the corruption of public institutions by the allied force of party machines and private economic interests. The political passion of many groups of reformers, from the Mugwumps, Grangers, and Populists through the Progressives and beyond, was to institute reforms that would wall the government off from society. Just to glance at a list of anticorruption measures enacted into law sometime between the 1870s and 1920s is to appreciate the extraordinary energy devoted to this task. These reforms include the following: the creation of a federal civil service in which merit rather than patronage would guide hiring decisions; introduction of the Australian, or secret, ballot to prevent parties from unduly influencing the votes of individual citizens; assumption by governments of the task of printing and distributing ballots along with other costs associated with voting; limiting the size of campaign contributions that candidates and corporations could make to political parties; embracing the initiative, referendum, recall, and direct election of US senators as mechanisms to strengthen the citizen-government relation while diminishing the influence of political parties on policy and public appointments; mass disenfranchisement of "suspect" voters—a movement epitomized by stripping the vote away from the vast majority of African Americans in the South and a sizable number of immigrants in the North; embracing women's suffrage in the hope that it would inject "womanly virtue" into a system corroded by "male corruption"; reorganizing municipal and state systems of taxation and expenditure to make them more transparent and accountable, and less vulnerable to exploitation by political machines; and substitution of an appointed officialdom of "disinterested" public servants for corrupt elected officials who were deemed to be too beholden to party bosses.[56]

These reforms and the groups of reformers who stood behind them exerted great pressure on the political parties and political machines. Consider the toll exacted by reform assaults on Tammany. Middle- and upper-class reformers brought down Tammany boss Fernando Wood in 1857 and his successor Tweed in 1872. The working-class reformer George and his Independent Labor Party failed in 1886 to defeat the Tammany candidate, Abraham Hewitt, for the New York mayoralty, but not before George frightened Tammany by taking 31 percent of the total vote, and doing even better than that among the poor, working-class, and immigrant constituencies that Tammany thought it owned.[57] New groups of elite reformers put the anti-Tammany candidates William R. Strong and Seth Low in the mayor's office in 1894 and 1901, respectively. A political coalition bringing elite reformers together with municipal populists elected yet another anti-Tammany mayor, the young and vigorous John Purroy Mitchel, in 1913.[58]

Tammany survived these and other challenges, repeatedly returning itself to power. But doing so required that it be willing to adapt and change. In response to the attacks of elite reformers in the 1880s and 1890s, it became more fiscally prudent and less likely than Tweed had been to run up debt on city accounts. Reacting to the George challenge in 1886, Tammany quickly built the comprehensive, neighborhood-based party organization described earlier in this chapter.[59] Tammany, then, submitted to both a financial discipline from above and democratic discipline from below, and both made a difference in its behavior. Machines, it appeared, could be reformed and made to serve the public purpose.

In the process of adapting, machine leaders demonstrated how clever they were in discerning and channeling reform sentiments. Thus, Tammany pushed its political program in a populist direction as it came to understand that the crucial challenges to its power had shifted by the second decade of the twentieth century from elite reformers (among whom fiscal concerns were paramount) to working-class groups whose primary concern was improved city services (better roads, sewers, schools, and transportation as well as a more plentiful supply of jobs and social welfare benefits). By the 1910s, Tammany was using the new fiscal systems that elite reformers had put in place (which were generating new sources of municipal revenue) to take on new debt to fund projects that would generate jobs and municipal improvements.[60] In so doing, machines like Tammany assembled a program of extensive municipal government outlays for infrastructure, jobs, and welfare that political scientist Steven Erie has called "primitive Keynesianism." During the years from 1900 through 1930, New York's payroll ballooned from 54,000 to 148,000, accounting for 10 percent of the city's job growth.[61] Tammany's adaptability underscores the truth of political scientist James C. Scott's observation that machines were "pragmatic, opportunistic" institutions "that could accommodate new groups and leaders in highly dynamic situations."[62] And it helps us understand how Tammany was still flourishing in the 1910s, despite forty years of sustained assaults on its practices and existence. In this period, it actually raised the number and proportion of its patronage employees to the highest levels in its history. In the 1910s, one out of three Democratic voters in New York City held a Tammany patronage job.[63]

What made Tammany and other political machines so resilient in the face of unrelenting attacks on their existence and way of raising money and campaigning? Tammany's adaptability and resourcefulness is certainly an important factor. But more significant is just how complex a task limiting the influence of money on elections proved to be. Major reforms of the political process did not always yield the anticipated results. Consider, for example, the public authorities' assumption of the costs of printing ballots and managing elections. This reform accompanied the move to the secret ballot almost everywhere in the 1880s and 1890s, and was expected to reduce political corruption by relieving political parties of the need to raise large amounts of private money to print ballots and hire their own people as poll watchers. Yet this anticipated effect did not materialize. The publicly produced ballots often strengthened the privileged status of the Democratic and Republican parties, and raised the cash value of becoming a mainstream party nominee. Under the new government supported and administered election system, the public boards charged with running elections automatically placed candidates from the Republican and Democratic parties on every ballot they produced. Third parties, meanwhile, discovered that their access to elections had narrowed: now they could only secure places on ballots through lengthy and technically complicated petition drives. Such discriminatory treatment of third parties made new party challenges more difficult to generate while also rendering Republican and Democratic nominations more coveted.[64] In places such as New York City where party machines were strong, Republican and Democratic officials actually raised the prices that they charged to individuals who wanted to secure their party's nominations.[65] Meanwhile, election campaigns quickly gobbled up whatever money the parties saved when relieved of the costs of printing and distributing ballots, especially as media innovations raised campaign expenses and political reforms such as the direct election of US senators (1913) and women's suffrage (1920) increased the price of campaigning by expanding the number of voters that parties had to mobilize.[66]

Civil service reform provides another illustration of the difficulty of compelling parties to shake themselves free of the money tree. Advances in civil service reform at the federal level in the 1880s did deprive the parties of their customary number of patronage appointments and thus reduced the flow of assessment taxes into party coffers.[67] The parties, as a result, sought to replace these lost tax incomes with contributions solicited directly from wealthy individuals and large corporations.[68] The 1890s was an important decade of transition in this regard, marked by the emergence of national party bosses such as businessman Hanna of Cleveland, who managed Republican William McKinley's successful run for the presidency in 1896. Hanna raised and spent an unprecedented level of corporate and private donor money in the 1896 election—a pattern of Republican Party activity that continued into the new century.[69]

While Hanna's personal influence on elections was waning by the 1900s, organized corporate influence on political campaigns continued to grow. Indeed, parties had become even more solicitous of corporate funds as civil service reform in some places curtailed the income from party patronage appointments. Opponents of corporate influence, in turn, began to mobilize to bar corporations from making contributions to political parties. They achieved their first successes in several states where the Populists had done well (Nebraska, Missouri, Tennessee, and Florida), and then achieved additional successes through the Progressive movement that was cohering in these and other states during the first decade of the new century. Progressives in Congress in 1907 passed the Tillman Act—named after South Carolina senator Ben Tillman—which prohibited national corporations and banks from contributing funds directly to political campaigns, and required committees organized to raise money for candidates running for the US Senate and House to disclose the dollars they had collected and spent in the general elections. In 1911, Congress limited campaign spending for a Senate seat to $10,000 per candidate and a House seat to $5,000 per candidate, and strengthened the disclosure requirements by compelling senatorial and congressional candidates to reveal how much they had raised and spent in their primary campaigns.[70] These same congresses also eased constraints on patronage appointments by exempting from civil service restrictions a steadily increasing number of federal jobs. By the second decade of the twentieth century, systems of patronage assessments had been given new life. Money in campaigns was like a pool of water, able to force its way through any hole or structural weakness in the dam that reformers were building to prevent private funds from swamping democratic practice.[71]

Few reformers in the late nineteenth and early twentieth centuries seemed willing or able to contemplate the radical measure of drying up this pool completely by insisting that the government pay for all campaign expenditures. George appeared to be heading in that direction when he observed in 1883 that the "great sums for election purposes" required by political parties threatened democracy itself. He wanted America to become a place in which "any citizen may run for office without expense."[72] This logic might have pushed George toward an idea as bold and as simple as the "single tax" notion that had already brought him fame: that government itself bear the entire cost of elections.[73] But George's proposed remedies were limited. He believed that the government's assumption of the costs of election machinery would cancel one major set of expenditures, and that the government could greatly reduce the expenses of the second set (campaigning) by banning a few pricey practices: torchlight processions, candidates treating all saloon customers to a round of drinks, and halls charging fees for political meetings.[74]

Was a completely publicly financed system of elections simply too radical a measure for George or anyone else to contemplate? Was the sheer number of electoral units in the American republic and the frequency of elections within each of those units just too great to permit anyone to imagine how government could possibly pay for and administer every electoral contest? Or would government's entry into this area of politics have involved such extensive controls on what could be spent, or such arbitrary distinctions about who would be eligible for government money and who would not so as to violate constitutional rights to free speech and equal protection? In searching through political debates during the Progressive era, we can find a politician here and there—sometimes even a prominent one—willing to declare that private financing of campaigns ought to be eliminated altogether. But this idea never gained traction. No one took seriously the 1904 call by Tammany lieutenant William Bourke Cockran for the federal government to pay for campaign expenses and thereby "do away with any excuse for soliciting large subscriptions of money."[75] Nor did President Theodore Roosevelt's 1907 request to Congress to provide "an appropriation for the proper and legitimate expenses of each of the great national parties" fare any better among those who had dedicated themselves to the cause of campaign finance reform.[76] Indeed, one such reformer, Perry Belmont, dismissed Roosevelt's "radical measure" as a ploy to distract Congress from passing campaign disclosure laws that were likely to embarrass this antitrust president by revealing his own dependence in the 1904 election on big contributions from a small number of corporate donors.[77]

In 1909, the state of Colorado actually did pass a law declaring that the "expenses of conducting campaigns to elect State, district and county officers at general elections shall be paid only by the State and by the candidates themselves." The contributions of the candidates were to be sharply limited to 25 to 40 percent of the salary for the office for which they were running.[78] This measure never took effect, however, as the state Supreme Court declared it unconstitutional. Not even from the ranks of labor or the Left was there a call to ban private money in elections. Leftists focused instead on creating socialist or labor parties that by definition would be free (or so it was believed) of the taint of capitalist money, and on working for a future in which a broad redistribution of wealth would render controls on campaign expenditures superfluous.[79] In the here and now, the Left offered no panacea for the problem of money in politics, as the reformer William Ivins had pointed out in 1887. For a third party to remain competitive with the Democrats and Republicans across a series of elections, Ivins had argued, it was necessary for it "to have a very complex Machine, and frequently a very expensive one."[80] This insight eluded the socialist William Weyl, who in 1913 rejected a proposal for government-funded campaigns in favor of one that the Socialist Party had already instituted: raising campaign funds through subscription fees levied on party members.[81] How fees from a hundred-thousand-odd (and mostly poor) socialists could counter the millions of dollars that a score of robber barons could throw at elections was a question that Weyl left unexplored.[82]

In place of complete bans on private funds, reformers hoped that a combination of partial bans and transparency requirements would significantly reduce the influence of money on elections. Like the founding fathers themselves, Progressives had great faith in the power of information. If disclosure laws revealed the extent of private and corporate underwriting of electoral campaigns, the American people (Progressives believed) would rise up and throw out of office politicians who had allowed themselves to be bought in this way. The vigor and honesty of American politics thereby would be restored. Reformers were confident that the 1910–11 disclosure amendments to the 1907 Tillman Act would have precisely this effect. The Corrupt Practices Act passed by Congress in 1925 ostensibly consolidated and strengthened these earlier laws, and appeared to give the country a comprehensive and effective system for limiting the influence of money on elections.[83]

A close inspection of these laws, however, reveals how narrow they were in conception. They did not apply to expenditures on presidential campaigns (which by 1928 had more than doubled from 1920), or on state and local contests. They also did not apply to money spent by congressional and senatorial candidates on primary elections, which a 1921 Supreme Court decision had exempted from congressional oversight, or money spent in general elections by advocacy organizations, which because they were officially independent of political parties, succeeded in defining their activities as nonpolitical. Moreover, the reporting requirements of these laws were often easy to evade for so-called nonpolitical organizations. The mechanisms for enforcing the provisions of these statutes on political parties and the candidates themselves were weak. For all these reasons, the passage of the 1925 law did little to curtail the influence of money on elections.[84] "The fact is," wrote political observer Frank R. Kent on the eve of that law's passage in the 1920s, "that nowhere in the country has there been devised a legal method of effectually limiting the amount of money that may be spent in political fights. No law has yet been enacted through which the politicians cannot drive a four-horse team."[85]

Louise Overacker, an interwar political scientist who devoted her career to studying money and elections in the United States, judged the effects of the 1925 Corrupt Practices Act somewhat more positively, especially in its tightening up campaign expenditure reporting requirements for congressional elections and generating more government investigations of corrupt political practices. But turning her attention from the nation to the states, where most of the electioneering in the United States took place and most of the campaign money was spent, she delivered a harsh verdict: "Limitations upon expenditures and contributions," she wrote in 1932, "have proved a farce. Enforcement machinery has been hopelessly ineffective. Little or no attempt has been made to solve the problem of the candidate who is handicapped financially. . . . [T]he publicity features themselves, have proved to be mere *papier mache*."[86]

The failure of efforts to curtail the influence of money on elections helps to explain something important about the democratic upheaval that was beginning to take shape at the very moment when Overacker wrote these words and that, through a political movement of poor Americans coalescing around Franklin Roosevelt in the 1930s, would shake up the world of American politics as deeply as Jacksonianism had done a century earlier. The participants in this democratic upheaval expressed little interest in continuing the fight for campaign finance reform. Rather than attempting to staunch the flow of private money into political parties, its advocates set out to neutralize what had been a corporate, Republican advantage in elections by mobilizing hundreds of thousands of poor workers to contribute their money to Roosevelt's reelection in 1936. It was a fateful choice. Although it brought the Democrats short-term gain in terms of putting Roosevelt in the White House for a second term, it bound the Democratic Party ever more closely to the privatized system of electioneering and to the private money that was its lifeblood. As a result, the Democratic Party would become nearly as dependent as the Republican Party on the support of wealthy individuals and corporations.

The sprawling, decentralized electoral system that emerged in America in the 1830s was a remarkable development. So, too, were the political parties that arose to manage it. Their leaders improvised brilliantly to provide the country with effective electoral machinery. But no one had anticipated the gargantuan costs of this machinery. Even after these costs became apparent, the central government lacked the will and wherewithal to address the issue by either limiting the costs of elections or by providing subsidies to candidates. Despite concerted efforts at reform, American democracy became chronically vulnerable to private monied influence on government. Even during the Great Depression, elites were never far from power. Their money was still required to make the machinery of democracy—elections—work.

PART III

Compromises, 1920s–1940s

6

AGRARIAN PROTEST
AND THE NEW
LIBERAL STATE

Since the 1880s, many Americans had been looking for ways to increase the reach and power of the central state. Multiple groups of plebeian Americans, including farmers and workers, came to see in an expanded central state the best chance of managing capitalism and enhancing their own economic security and opportunity. Middle-class reformers joined forces with farmers and workers to build a state of this sort as well as one that would restore moral order in a society unhinged by industrialization and urbanization. But these forces had to contend with both powerful corporate groups that were unwilling to be regulated in the public interest and a Constitution that constrained the size and reach of the federal government. Thus, through the 1920s, the power and resources of the central state would remain piecemeal and only sporadically effective except in times of war and in areas of policy, mostly related to foreign affairs, that the courts exempted from constitutional restraints.

The Great Depression that began in 1929 broke through this resistance in ways it had never before been breached in peacetime.

President Franklin D. Roosevelt confronted a bleak situation when he assumed office in March 1933. Thousands of banks had closed their doors, and tens of billions of dollars of wealth had vanished. New investments in the economy approached zero, and unemployment had soared to 25 percent. With the private economy in shambles, the government appeared to be the only institution with the capacity and will to act. Heir to the Progressive government-building traditions in both the Democratic and Republican parties, Roosevelt grasped the significance of his moment. "The time has come," he declared in his 1935 State of the Union address, "for action by the national government." In Roosevelt's view, the economic crisis demanded a dramatic increase in the powers of government to provide relief and temporary employment, to revive the sectors of the American economy—mining, manufacturing, farming, and banking—that seemed crushed, and to restore security and opportunity to the American people. "The Federal Government is the only governmental body with sufficient power and credit to meet this situation," Roosevelt declared. "We have assumed this task and we shall not shrink from it in the future."[1]

Roosevelt intended for this new central state to be large not small, and expansive rather than narrow in its ambitions. He wanted it to have regulatory rather than exhortatory power, and to be supported by a professional corps of government civil servants and panoply of new administrative agencies rather than relying on private organizations and volunteers. He understood that his vision for enlarging the role of the central state put him at the cusp of a revolution in American governance that would dramatically change the contours of federal power. FDR also grasped that his ambition to expand the central state in so rapid and daring a fashion would find resistance in a society that was committed to keeping it small and bounded, even in the emergency circumstances of the Great Depression. And so he hedged his embrace of this new vision of government, and took pains to emphasize that his proposed changes would not veer from but adhere to America's most important political traditions. "We have undertaken a new order of things," Roosevelt conceded in 1935, but "we progress to it under the framework and in the spirit and intent of the American

Constitution."[2] As if to underscore the traditional ambitions of this new state, Roosevelt increasingly took to calling it "liberal," even though what he had in mind differed substantially from the original, classically liberal structure of America's central state.

Roosevelt's appropriation of the term "liberal" infuriated Herbert Hoover, members of the Liberty League, and for a time, a majority of justices on the Supreme Court, all of whom saw in it the theft and defiling of America's most distinguished political tradition. Roosevelt saw himself less as an opportunist or revolutionary than as a broker seeking to bring a new central state into existence while remaining respectful of American traditions and institutions. If we move beyond political rhetoric to consider political practice in the 1930s, we see Roosevelt and his New Dealers repeatedly trying to balance these conflicting pressures. On the one side, they had to contend with plebeian, frequently radical pressures to give the new central state the powers necessary to place the New Deal squarely on the side of America's poor and marginalized and to stimulate a full economic recovery in the process. These pressures were particularly acute in 1934 and 1935, when an incipient economic recovery faltered and mass mobilizations from below put FDR's reelection in 1936 in jeopardy and threatened to jolt American politics in a leftward direction.[3] On the other side, Roosevelt and the New Dealers had to contend with instruments of governance they did not fully control, even when the New Deal was at its zenith. Roosevelt had only limited authority over the state and local governments whose cooperation he needed to deliver New Deal services. Similarly, he had to get his government-building legislation through a Congress where disproportionate power lay with long-serving southern congressman and senators who would not tolerate challenges to the racial and class hierarchies of their region.[4] How would Roosevelt balance these conflicting pressures? And how would his resulting program shape the new central state that the New Deal was bringing into being?

This and the following chapter explore these questions. We begin, perhaps a bit unexpectedly, by looking at agriculture, a critical component of the New Deal regulatory state. Before the New Deal, the federal government had developed an exceptionally strong bureaucratic apparatus for addressing farmers' needs. This made it possible for agricultural reformers in the 1930s to take the lead in building a new central state, with the result that agriculture became the focus of some of the New Deal's earliest and most sweeping experiments. The crown jewel of agricultural reform was the 1933 Agricultural Adjustment Act, a comprehensive plan for managing and stabilizing American agriculture. This program and its successors transformed a long-distressed economic sector into one of enduring prosperity and stability. They constituted one of the New Deal state's most lasting achievements. At the same time, the freedom of New Deal agricultural reformers was severely constrained by a range of state and local institutions as well as by a lobbying organization of prosperous farmers. For this reason, reformers failed in their efforts to redistribute resources from rich to poor farmers, and from the landed to the landless. Instead, New Deal reform actually accelerated the flight of the poor out of agriculture, and the benefits from the federal government's new programs went disproportionately to larger farms and more prosperous farmers. In agricultural policy, then, regulatory initiatives demonstrated how the new liberal state could be turned away from its goal of redistribution, and toward the maintenance and reinforcement of privilege.

In the country's larger industrial sector, New Dealers proved more successful in redistributing economic resources and political power from the rich to the poor. Still, the agricultural economy was in the vanguard of New Deal reform, and that is where an analysis of 1930s' changes in governance must start.

POPULIST ANGER AND THE RISE OF AN AGRICULTURAL STATE

Examining the arc of agrarian protest and government responses from the 1880s on will help us grasp both the possibilities and limits reformers faced in the 1930s. The waves of agrarian protests that culminated in the Populist challenge of the 1890s had posed acute challenges to the established economic and political order. While Populism as a formal organized protest failed, the fears it generated compelled government authorities to find ways to ameliorate the conditions of farmers, if only to forestall another mass agrarian uprising. These are the circumstances that spurred one of the most surprising developments in the history of American government: the transformation of a bureaucratic backwater, the United States Department of Agriculture (USDA), into an innovative and capacious institution of domestic governance in the first three decades of the twentieth century.

Mass agrarian protest began with 750,000 farmers who joined one of the 19,000 chapters of the Grange in the 1870s, and culminated in the millions in the South and Midwest who joined the Farmers' Alliance and then the People's Party in the 1890s. Corporate power of many sorts disturbed the agrarians, but none as much as that exercised by the railroads, with their outsized influence on legislative bodies and their ability to charge discriminatory shipping rates to small and isolated farmers who were served by only one railroad. The railroads, it was commonly charged, constituted a "monopoly," and were using the privileges granted to them by the government to abuse the public good.[5]

As agrarians took their protests into politics, they initially thought that putting forward their own candidates to run against the railroad candidates for Congress and statehouses would be enough to achieve their goals. When this proved insufficient, they attempted to reform politics by minimizing opportunities for backroom dealing, chiefly by proposing laws to make elections more honest and the links between individual voters and their representatives more direct. Several of the most important political reforms of the late nineteenth and early twentieth centuries emerged from the ranks of agrarian protesters. These included the adoption of the Australian (secret) ballot, direct election of US senators (1913), and the initiative and referendum. Already in the 1890s, however, it had become clear that these reforms were insufficient to end the reign of capital. The Populists began calling on the central government to expand its reach and intervene in the economy on the farmers' behalf.[6] The campaign to put "the people" in charge of the US government lay at the heart of the People's Party insurgencies of 1892 and 1896. "We believe," declared their 1892 platform, "that the power of government—in other words, of the people— shall be expanded" so that "oppression, injustice, and poverty shall eventually cease in the land."[7] The platform called for the central state to take over the railroads and telegraph lines, and to operate them in the people's interests. It also called on the federal government to combat the vicissitudes of the agricultural and currency markets by building and operating a vast loan and crop storage system that would sell crops at opportune moments (as measured by movements in world crop prices), and extend credit to farmers who would be without income until those crops could be sold.[8] The Populists somewhat clumsily labeled this system the "sub-treasury plan." But they were hardly clumsy in declaring their intention to build a central state large and powerful enough to manage the transportation, communication, and agricultural sectors of the American economy in the public interest. The need to contain the power of the corporations, defuse social conflict, and stabilize the economy, the Populists argued, demanded nothing less.[9]

Though they were defeated in 1896, the issues the Populists had put on the table did not go away. Throughout the era of Progressive reform (1900–20), political scientist Elizabeth Sanders reminds us, farmers were "the most numerous constituents for expanded public power in the southern and Midwestern states."[10] Many of the most important achievements of the Progressives—including improvements in the regulation of the railroads and finance, reductions in the tariff, the breaking up of monopolies, and the establishment of an income tax—had been part of the Populist agenda. Several of the most visionary of Progressive leaders, such as Robert La Follette of Wisconsin, had close connections to the agrarian insurgency of the 1890s.[11] And finally, the USDA became one of the largest sectors of the federal state during the Progressive Era, as officials sought to make it an instrument for addressing farmer needs and demands. By the 1920s, the USDA had built an apparatus for mobilizing constituents and regulating economic activity unmatched by any other agency of the national state. This infrastructure, in combination with the department's capacity for innovation and reform, made farmers a force in Washington politics.

Understanding the vanguard role of agricultural reformers in the New Deal necessitates taking a closer look at the agricultural state that emerged in the first thirty years of the twentieth century and the manner in which its powers were deployed to relieve agricultural distress. The USDA had been founded in 1862 at the same time that Congress gave federal lands to states to establish their own universities. The USDA was authorized to both attend to the practical needs of farmers and assist the new public universities with their agricultural research. In its first twenty-five years, it was a minor institution engaged in little more than distributing seeds for new crops to farmers every year. Only in the 1880s and 1890s did the USDA draw attention, as various individuals and groups hoped that it might be made into a useful instrument for relieving or at least channeling farmers' discontent. In 1887, the federal government passed the Hatch Experiment Station Act, authorizing federal monies to support the establishment of agricultural research stations in the states. These stations would develop new crops, or new strands of existing crops, and new techniques for growing them. The USDA, which acquired Cabinet status in 1889, would support these efforts by establishing agricultural labs of its own in which new strains of crops would be developed and then sent to the various experiment stations for trials. The USDA expected to collect data from these experiments, and then disseminate news of what worked and what did not through the ranks of American farmers across the country.[12]

Crucially, the federal government hoped to achieve its goals of agricultural improvement by working with rather than circumventing the states. Most of the Hatch stations were closely connected to state colleges and universities, many of which had been made possible by federal land grants. By the 1890s, these institutions of higher learning were entirely administered and largely supported by state governments. Federal Hatch funds thus came directly to state governments, which funneled them either into agricultural centers that were part of state colleges and universities, or to other state agencies overseeing agricultural development within their jurisdiction.

The Hatch experiments were one of the earliest examples of what political scientist Kimberley S. Johnson has called the "new federalism." This federalism made central government monies available to the states for public programs that Congress deemed essential—agricultural innovation, highway construction, and later, maternal and child health care services—but called for the actual distribution of funds and administration of programs to be left in the hands of the states. Its purpose was to enlarge central government influence over public policy without diminishing the powers of the states. For a long time, the new federalism would succeed in advancing these dual aims. Success required deference on the part of the federal government toward the states or groups controlling agricultural politics within the states. For the first three decades of the twentieth century, the central government was content with this role. It advised farmers on crop-growing techniques and facilitated their coalescence into a formidable interest group that for a time had no peer. It did not yet attempt to compel farmers and allies in their statehouses to bow to federal imperatives. The supporters of the new federalism understood that the states were powerful entities, and that the federal government had to accommodate itself to their interests.[13]

That the new federalism could yield major benefits became apparent in the USDA's establishing itself as the country's premier center for agricultural research and in its readiness to share that research with public universities and groups of farmers throughout the forty-plus states. Across the first two decades of the century, the USDA developed new strains of crops, explored novel growing practices, created conservation techniques that would assure the nation of adequate reserves of timber, and took steps to protect the country's food and drug supply from contamination and fraud. The USDA's standing drew top natural scientists to it. Many worked there for long periods, flourishing in a university-like environment supportive of research, innovation, and autonomous inquiry. That this scientific and intellectual culture took root in this government agency helps to explain why some of the country's most imaginative political leaders and policymakers, from Gifford

Pinchot to Rexford Tugwell to Henry Wallace, found their homes in the USDA during the first third of the twentieth century.[14]

The flourishing of the USDA as a knowledge center also spurred improvements in research at land grant universities that it was charged with supporting. The flow of both knowledge and personnel between the USDA and state universities increased substantially in the first three decades of the twentieth century. Initially, knowledge production had been entirely focused on the natural sciences, and on improvements in crop strains and growing techniques. But in 1922, the USDA established the Bureau of Agricultural Economics, which expanded the department's research agenda to include social science. As the nation struggled with the postwar recession in agriculture, the USDA concentrated its research as much on economic questions, such as balancing production and consumption and bringing long-term stability to the agricultural sector, as on improving crops and cultivation techniques. The bureau would serve as an incubator for ideas that would prove indispensable to New Deal reform in the 1930s.[15]

Political scientist Daniel Carpenter sees a triumph of "bureaucratic autonomy" in the USDA's early twentieth-century achievements—a triumph made possible by exceptional leadership that was both bold in its vision and strategic in its ability to assemble a wide-ranging political coalition, extending well beyond the ranks of farmers themselves, to turn its vision into policy.[16] In the first five years of the new century alone, the USDA added six new bureaus and successfully battled the Department of the Interior for control over the Forest Service. In 1906, it was a major force in pushing Theodore Roosevelt's Food and Drug Act through Congress and then making itself the law's enforcer.[17]

The USDA certainly made the most of its opportunities. But those opportunities resulted from more than the vision and clever maneuverings of its leaders. Memories of the "days of Populist wrath," to use Grant McConnell's phrase, were still fresh in the early twentieth century, prompting multiple groups in American society, both inside and outside the government, to seek ways of addressing farmers' concerns while steering this agrarian constituency away from Populist radicalism.[18] A dynamic and responsive USDA able to direct farmer discontent into "constructive" channels was envisioned as a bulwark against a Populist resurgence.

To this end, the USDA developed a remarkable "county agent" system both for soliciting input from the agrarian grass roots and establishing federal authority in every agricultural region of the country. This system originated as an effort to help individual farmers secure their prosperity by disseminating among them the latest crops and cultivation techniques emerging from USDA labs. To make it work, the USDA hoped to appoint one farmer in every agricultural county, with the expectation that each would serve as a technical adviser to area cultivators. Farmers who became USDA county agents agreed to offer their farms as experiment stations on which to demonstrate the latest crops and cultivation techniques developed by USDA scientists. In cases where the demonstration worked, the agents were asked to spread news of the success to farmers in their area and encourage them to make similar improvements with their land. More broadly, county agents were called on to serve as a conduit through which Washington could spread its knowledge, funds, and it hoped, influence.[19]

Originally, pragmatic considerations had driven the USDA to involve local farmers in disseminating its influence. The government had discovered that farmers would try new crops or cultivation techniques only at the behest of someone in good standing with the local fraternity of cultivators. In the first years of the twentieth century, agricultural reformer Seaman Knapp, a physician and former president of Iowa Agricultural College, had shown in Texas what a difference local input and leadership could make to the spread of new agricultural practices—in this case, those that Knapp had developed to combat the boll weevil that was then devastating southern cotton.[20] Both the USDA and private philanthropies (including Rockefeller's General Education Board) took note of Knapp's Texas success, and began spreading this cooperative demonstration idea to multiple counties in different regions of the country. The federal government gave this plan a boost in 1914 by passing the Smith-Lever Act, which made federal matching funds available to states that extended the county agent system. States responded positively to this offer of federal funds, and by the 1920s, the USDA employed more than twenty-two hundred county agents, representing three-fourths of the agricultural counties in the United States.[21]

By that time, too, the county agent system had become much more than a mechanism for dispensing technical advice to farmers. With an outpost in a large majority of agricultural counties, the USDA had established a presence more comprehensive than any other institution of the central state except for the post office and, in World War I, the Selective Service. By World War I, the USDA was the third-largest nonmilitary branch of the federal government (bested only by the post office and treasury), and it maintained that status while growing substantially between World War I and the 1930s.[22] Ambitious central state builders within the USDA understood that the county agent system gave their department a capacity to project power and influence in ways available to almost no other public institution in the country.

This dramatic assertion of central government power found easy acceptance because it respected American traditions of local autonomy. In fact, the county agent system's model of governance, which embodied both centralized direction and local control, seemed made to order for a polity groping its ways to a stronger central state without being ready to relinquish the classical liberal limits on the concentration of power. The county agents were not scientists or bureaucrats sent from some distant university or national training center. Rather they were local farmers who were respected in their communities and possessed extensive local knowledge. And they worked through advice and persuasion, not regulation or coercion.[23]

In selecting these agents, Knapp told Congress, "we aim to get the best farmers in their own section, men whom their neighbors believe in, and they will listen to. . . . We find that these men are more influential than if they knew ten times as much about science, as they know what the farmer considers the best science in the world—and that is the science of winning out, of making a good crop and making money on the farm."[24] Significantly, these agents were under the direction not of the federal government but of the state in which they resided, and specifically the state's agricultural extension service, usually headquartered at the state's principal agricultural college or university. The expansion of this federal government program, then, often worked to further empower the states. Moreover, the county agents could use the administrative grid of which they were a part not simply to receive instructions from Washington and their statehouses but to increase the volume of information and intensity of demands flowing toward the nation's capital.[25]

By the early 1920s, county agents were doing just that, having formed themselves into a national lobbying organization, the American Farm Bureau Federation (AFBF). With the support of the USDA headquarters in Washington, DC, county agents had begun in the 1910s to establish local farm bureaus—organizations that area farmers joined to swap stories and techniques, and to formulate plans for reforming and improving agriculture in their locales. By war's end, thousands of these local farm bureaus had sprouted up, and by 1919, had federated themselves nationally into the AFBF. The AFBF had close to a million members in 1921 spread out across hundreds of local chapters. These chapters fed into state federations and then the national one. Through this federation, farmers had found a way not only to effectively disseminate technical information about farming but also to flex their political muscle.[26]

Having created and sustained the farm bureaus, the USDA expected to control them. That the county agents themselves frequently became heads of the local bureaus seemed to indicate that the USDA was in charge. But reality was more complicated. The state and national AFBF organizations were independent of the USDA, and largely supported by membership fees. They hired their own lobbyist, Gray Silver, whose job was not to serve USDA interests but instead to press Congress to pass legislation favorable to AFBF members. Under Silver's leadership, the AFBF started to think of itself as a private, voluntary organization and to conceive of its purpose not to serve the central state but rather to petition it on behalf of its members.[27] We have already seen how much energy the federal government expended in the early decades of the twentieth century to enlist already-existing private groups in its projects. In the case of agriculture, the reverse was the case: the federal government encouraged a publicly sponsored organization—the county agent system—to go private. That the federal government was working the public-private divide in both directions underscores yet again the centrality of public-private interpenetration as a mode of governance.

Farm bureau members everywhere began lobbying government officials about their projects. They proposed legislation and sometimes wrote it. They got their people appointed to government agencies deemed important to agricultural interests, including the USDA. The bureaus developed special relationships with and influence over key congressman and senators. They were acquiring power in Washington that fifty years earlier only the railroads possessed. While most private groups had to work for years to place their representatives or lobbyists in positions of influence, the AFBF was handed its influence on a silver platter: the heads of their county bureaus were already employed by the central state as county agents, meaning that the lobbying network that most groups had to laboriously create from scratch was already in place for farmers, courtesy of a federal government program. The comprehensiveness of this network and its ready access to levers of government power help to explain why, for many observers of and participants in American politics, the AFBF became the model pressure group.[28]

The coalescing of farmers into a strong interest group occurred amid renewed agricultural hardship. The war years had been bountiful ones for American agriculture. Farmers had been called on not only to support an all-out war effort at home but also to sustain a multimillion-man army in the field as well as countless European civilians whose sources of food had been consumed by soldiers or destroyed by war. Challenged by Herbert Hoover and others to become Europe's granary, and offered high prices for their crops, America's farmers responded with dramatic increases in production. The acreage devoted to wheat production alone increased by more than 60 percent between 1915 and 1919, from 48 to 78 million acres.[29] The reputation of American agriculture soared, as US farmers both earned record incomes and received credit for saving millions of Europeans from starvation. The postwar crash in agriculture, however, was as harrowing as the wartime ascent had been heady. Not only did European agriculture quickly recover, but American producers also confronted a global market in agricultural commodities more integrated and efficient than before the war. By 1921, agricultural prices had plummeted 85 percent from their 1919 highs.[30] The extra acres that US farmers had acquired and planted during the war were now a crushing burden.

The AFBF was one of several groups to take shape in this moment of crisis, and it was one of the more conservative ones: its ranks included many larger and commercial farmers whose goal was to restore their own prosperity, not to upend the social order. Private bankers, big agricultural processors, and businessmen were eager supporters of the AFBF, especially as it became clear that other, more radical organizations were challenging the AFBF for the right to represent the American farmer.[31] One such organization, the Nonpartisan League, emerged in North Dakota in 1915 and expanded into Iowa, Wisconsin, South Dakota, Montana, and other midwestern and western states during the war. Radical in its critique of government's subservience to corporate influence, the league focused its efforts on removing this influence by getting its people elected to state governments. Another such organization, the Farmers Union, had existed since 1902, but reached the height of its influence during the postwar agricultural crisis. It abjured the political approach of the Nonpartisan League, choosing to concentrate its efforts instead on establishing farmer-owned and farmer-operated cooperatives for storing grain, shipping livestock, and purchasing farm necessities. Through such programs, farmers affiliated with the union hoped to liberate themselves from the mercantile middlemen—and perhaps the tyranny of the market itself—whom they held responsible for many of the farmers' ills. The Farmers Union loathed the AFBF, which it viewed as a privileged group of corporate-influenced farmers who did not have the best interests of most cultivators at heart.[32]

By 1922, farmer disaffection had spread far and deep enough to persuade the stalwart Progressive Robert La Follette to launch another major reform effort from an agrarian base. Drawing inspiration from the contemporaneous success of the Labour Party in replacing the Liberals as Britain's second major party, La Follette and his supporters got sixty Progressives elected to the US House of Representatives in 1922.[33] Emboldened by this success, La Follette ran for president in 1924 as a representative of a newly formed third party, the Farmer Labor Party. He would not be successful in terms of electoral votes (he carried only his native Wisconsin), but the five million ballots that he did receive—five times the number that the socialist Debs had ever gained in a presidential election— testified to the depths of farmer anger and disaffection.[34] The various agrarian challenges culminating in the La Follette campaign worried Washington, now firmly in the hands of conservative Republicans. These challenges put pressure on the AFBF, USDA, and their allies in Congress. Already in 1922, the president of the AFBF had warned Congress that "at this time, in this Nation, the farmers are sorely pressed. They are almost ready for bolshevistic movement."[35] The specter not just of Bolshevism but also populism still haunted the land. AFBF leaders argued that the country needed their organization to thwart a radical turn.

Politically, the AFBF sought power by forming an alliance with the USDA and a group of Capitol Hill legislators who were concentrated in the Senate and known as the "farm bloc." In policy terms, the AFBF began calling on the government to grant agriculture "equality" or "parity" with industry. These terms both upheld a general principle and became labels for specific packages of economic reforms. The general principle was that government ought to bestow on agriculture privileges "equal to" or "on par with" what it had already granted industry. Chief among industry's privileges was a strong tariff wall that had long relieved American manufacturers of the burden of competing against foreign goods in the US market. More generally, the AFBF viewed Congress as having repeatedly taken steps to protect manufacturers through subsidies and shaping markets in ways that maximized the latter's opportunities to succeed. The AFBF wanted similar or equal protection for farmers. This thinking had advanced the furthest in the "industrialized" sectors of American agriculture: among the syndicates that owned the large fruit and vegetable farms in California; with the managers who ran the Montana Farming Corporation, which had amassed ninety-five thousand acres for wheat growing in that northern Plains state; and in the growing number of Americans who purchased agricultural land for investment rather than as a place to settle their families.[36] But family farmers, still the largest sector of American agriculture (as measured by the number of farm units), were also drawn to this campaign to compel the federal government to equalize the economic benefits it bestowed.[37]

The specific package of reforms pursued by the AFBF in the 1920s revolved around the concept of "price parity." Agricultural economists had begun to identify the years from 1910 to 1914 as the period of time when agricultural prices had been on par with industrial prices. This meant, first, that farmers earned high enough prices for their produce to make a profit and purchase a strong share of manufactured goods for themselves; second, that industry was itself prospering, with the wages of its workers rising; and third, that urban consumers could afford both the food and manufactured goods that they needed or desired. This price parity, or "fair exchange value" between industrial and agricultural goods, had vanished in the 1920s, impoverishing farmers even as manufacturers were raking in profits. The AFBF and other groups of agriculturalists now called on the federal government to take steps to restore the parity between agriculture and industry that had prevailed in the years prior to the war.[38]

Agricultural policy debates through the interwar period centered on how best to achieve parity. A three-part plan that came to be called McNary-Haugen—after sponsors of the congressional legislation—dominated the 1920s. McNary-Haugen called first for tariffs on foreign agricultural produce to support a "fair" price for US crops in the domestic market. Second, it advocated that the central government commit itself to selling domestic agricultural surpluses in foreign markets for whatever price this produce would command. Third, McNary-Haugen mandated that the government compensate farmers whose sales in the international market did not cover production costs. This compensation was to be paid for with a federal government tax on agricultural commodity processing.[39]

As the details of McNary-Haugen make clear, the terms that dominated agricultural politics in the 1920s had narrowed since the days of the Populists. The farmers who supported McNary-Haugen did not talk, as the Populists had, about ending oppression and injustice. Many no longer identified with a foundational principle of agrarian democracy as understood by the Populists: that farmers had an obligation to make US political institutions open and responsive not just to farmers but also to all American citizens. Rather, McNary-Haugen supporters increasingly thought of themselves as an interest group that above all wanted a corporate-size slice of government privilege for itself. Yet even after taking into consideration the narrower bounds in which agricultural politics now operated, McNary-Haugen still challenged the status quo. If it had passed, McNary-Haugen would have required the federal government to substantially expand its regulatory apparatus. The social scientists in the USDA, whose tracking of agricultural prices had yielded the "discovery" of the 1910–14 moment of parity, were now claiming that the central state possessed the knowledge and capacity not only to restore parity but to maintain it indefinitely as well. They wanted the central government to expand its powers accordingly. Those further to the Left, both inside and outside the USDA, recognized in McNary-Haugen an opening to the kind of comprehensive social democratic planning that the Left in Europe had begun to undertake.[40]

President Calvin Coolidge vetoed McNary-Haugen not once but twice in 1927 and 1928, precisely because he saw it as a substantial expansion of the regulatory reach of the federal government. To mollify angry farmers and their representatives in Congress, he and Herbert Hoover, his secretary of commerce, supported alternative legislation to expand subsidies to farmers for cooperative grain storage and marketing ventures. Hoover had gotten Coolidge to support his preferred mode of government action: the central state acting as a facilitator of collective organization in the private sector rather than undertaking regulatory activities itself. Hoover's plan might have worked, as it had in other spheres of governing in the 1920s, including the challenges posed by the Mississippi River flood of 1927. But the Great Depression hit the United States in October 1929, only six months after Hoover succeeded Coolidge as president, causing an economic crisis too big even for the indefatigable and inventive Hoover to handle, and exposing his private-public model of governance as inadequate. The chaos of capitalism and the misery of America's farmers had shaken up the political balance sufficiently enough to give the supporters of an expanded agricultural state their chance. The Democrat Roosevelt took office in March 1933. A regulatory program to overhaul American agriculture would be among the earliest and most enduring of Roosevelt's New Deal initiatives.[41]

THE SUCCESS AND FAILURE OF THE NEW DEAL'S FARM PROGRAM

The centerpiece of the New Deal's farm program was the Agricultural Adjustment Act, passed in 1933 during Roosevelt's first hundred days in office. This act was an omnibus bill that gave the USDA the power to attack agricultural problems on multiple fronts: through inflationary monetary policies, marketing agreements, trade treaties, and extensions of farm credit. But most important was its novel approach to eliminating crop surpluses. Instead of authorizing the federal government to dispose of these surpluses in international markets and compensate farmers who had had to sell below cost (the McNary-Haugen plan), this legislation instructed the central state to pay individual farmers to reduce the acreage they put under the plow. Agricultural production would decline as a result, bringing supply into closer correspondence with demand and thus exerting upward pressure on prices. This farm law established the Agricultural Adjustment Administration (AAA) to implement the new programs. AAA supporters claimed that farmers would end up earning more money for each bushel harvested. The income earned from those sales, in combination with federal payments for acreage left untilled, would hopefully bring farmers more enduring economic security than most had ever known.[42]

The scope of this crop reduction program was vast; so, too, were the number of government employees and associations of farmers needed to make it work. The AAA required the secretary of agriculture to identify each year the percentage of acres to be removed from cultivation for each of the major crops and determine how much the federal government would pay for each bushel not produced. Setting those figures was actually the easier part of this governing challenge, and the Bureau of Agricultural Economics embraced it. The hard part was writing individual contracts for each of the millions of farm owners whom the AAA hoped to involve in this venture. Those contracts were to stipulate the acreage that farmers were to leave untilled, the number of unplanted bushels for which they were to receive compensation, and the total subsidy that the federal government was to pay them. The contracts were also to extract pledges from farmers not to exceed their allotments, and authorize the central state to take action against those who did.[43]

If some farmers were initially reluctant to allow the federal state to intrude so deeply into their economic lives, most embraced this program once they understood that the central government was in effect offering to pay them to work less. Quickly, the central state found itself confronted with the need to write hundreds of thousands and then millions of individual contracts. By 1934, AAA officials had issued more than a million contracts among cotton farmers in the South alone, and most contracts had to be rewritten or renewed on an annual basis. Here was an instance of the central state reaching down to millions of citizens and involving each of them individually in a grand plan to stabilize American agriculture.[44]

The federal government's only chance of executing this daunting task was to draw on the formidable apparatus it already possessed: the county agent and farm bureau network that had grown vinelike inside as well as around the USDA in the previous twenty years. In many cases, the central government simply drafted county agents and farm bureau directors to head up the new production control units that the AAA established in each agricultural county in 1933 and 1934.[45] These production control units had several responsibilities. First, they either computed the unplanted acreage and bushel targets for each farmer in their jurisdiction, within parameters that the USDA headquarters had set, or assisted agricultural experts in the region's land grant university with this task. Second, they educated individual farmers on the content, privileges, and responsibilities of their contracts. Third, they visually examined farms in their jurisdiction to make sure that none of the farmers with AAA contracts had exceeded their allotments or violated contracts in other ways.[46] Where no county agents or farm bureaus existed, the AAA either built county production units from scratch or asked the AFBF to do so.

From the earliest days, then, the AFBF and AAA production control units became almost indistinguishable from each other, and both were deeply enmeshed with land grant colleges operated by the states along with their agricultural experts and administrators.[47] By the end of 1934, only eighteen months after the legislation had passed, the AAA had put forty-two hundred production control units in operation, and was training more than seventy thousand local farmers to be AAA officials and facilitators.[48] By 1934, the AAA had also taken to the air to deliver both information and inspiration to the nation's farming millions. Through both the personal visits of country agents and centralized media campaigns, the AAA, claimed sociologist Paul H. Landis, reached every farm family.[49]

The monies that the AAA began handing over to farmers were substantial. Each participating farmer in Haskell, Kansas, a dust bowl Great Plains county, received $812 on average from the federal government in 1936. As historian Donald Worster has written, this "was a tidy sum of money for not doing a thing—more money, in fact, than millions of Americans could scrape together to live on each year, more money than a Haskell schoolteacher or minister might make."[50] And this sum was only a portion of the Haskell farmers' income, with the rest coming from the crops that they actually did raise and then sold in agricultural markets. Given the heft of these subsidies, it is not surprising that the AAA program was immensely popular, drawing participation rates in many counties in excess of 90 percent. Farmers quickly began to think of federal government subsidies as a constitutional right.[51] When the Supreme Court struck down the AAA in 1935 for illegally restraining trade, Congress and the president were quick to pass new legislation that made soil conservation rather than restrictions on production the rationale for paying farmers to pull portions of their land out of cultivation. And in 1938 (after the makeup of the Supreme Court changed in ways that benefited the New Deal), the federal government replaced the social conservation program with yet another AAA, this one authorized to buy up agricultural surpluses from farmers so as to place agricultural prices on par with industrial ones. The 1938 act gave the central state the power to release these surpluses into the domestic market in years of low yields in pursuit of what came to be called the "ever normal granary."[52] Later, the federal government would start distributing these surpluses abroad for humanitarian ends and strategic foreign policy aims. At home, it began donating portions of these surpluses to public schools with large populations of poor children in what would become formalized as the National School Lunch Program in 1946, and in the postwar years would grow into one of the federal government's largest and most popular social welfare programs.[53] The United States had launched a portion of its welfare state through the USDA.

By the late 1930s, the New Deal system regulating agriculture looked a great deal like the ambitious subtreasury plan that the Populists had called for in the early 1890s. And true to the Populists' prediction, the vastly augmented regulatory role for the central government brought unprecedented stability and security to America's agricultural sector. Stability did not come cheaply. In 1940, the American central state spent $1.4 billion on agriculture, more than it did on any other single item in its budget. The South Building addition to the USDA headquarters in Washington, DC, became, on its completion in 1936, the largest office building in the world. Measuring almost three football fields long, and one and a half football fields wide, the "addition" housed forty-five hundred rooms in its seven floors.[54] The monumentality of this structure and the funds necessary to sustain a government enterprise of this scale seemed to be worth it, however. American agriculturalists would never again experience the devastating depressions of the 1880s to 1890s or the 1920s to 1930s. Moreover, the gap in income between rural and urban America, which had reached extreme proportions in the 1920s and 1930s, narrowed steadily in the

1940s and 1950s.[55] Federal government policy brought consumers a steady supply of food and provided farmers a dependably decent income. These were major accomplishments for America's central state. The New Deal, FDR boasted in 1936, had "laid the basis for a permanent plenty," and gotten "for the farmer his fair share in the comforts, the advantages, the wider interests and the deeper satisfactions which go to make the good life for himself and for his children."[56]

New Dealers were wise to focus so much energy on getting agriculture right. Stabilizing agriculture would legitimate the New Deal state. Many still gauged the welfare of America by the welfare of its farmers, thought to be the citizens who most fully embodied the country's republican ideals: independence, virtue, and love of liberty. The continuing high stature of America's farmers helps to explain why the New Deal lavished so much of its attention and funds on rural America at a time when the country had in fact made itself over into an industrial and urban society. In the New Deal, Worster has written, "saving the American farmer was, to many officials, the key to saving the entire society from Depression and injustice—'agricultural fundamentalism,' the stance was termed, meaning help the farmers first and everyone would be better off."[57] Few images of urban workers could evoke the broad popular sympathy that Dorothea Lange's portrait of the migrant mother did when it began to circulate in 1935. The New Deal could deliver no more powerful message that the American people were in trouble. An emphasis on the plight of the farmer could justify efforts to build a new kind of federal state in ways that a focus on the predicament of the urban worker could not. In this way, a preoccupation with farmers gave the New Deal a kind of cover as it went about building a central state far different than the classically liberal one of nineteenth-century America.

And yet the emphasis that Roosevelt placed on helping the American farmer was more than a mechanism for legitimating the policies of his new central state. In claiming that the AAA had gained for the farmer not just prosperity but also his fair share of the good life, Roosevelt was subtly but significantly reworking the meaning of liberty and liberalism. Traditionally, liberals had defined liberty in negative terms, as the protection of individuals from a government intent on limiting their freedom. The Bill of Rights embodied this negative conception of liberty, identifying the government as the chief source of tyranny. But during the twentieth century, many reformers, Roosevelt included, believed that the enjoyment of freedom required more than protection from the central state. It also required assistance from this state in the form of education and economic security, so that individuals would be able to enjoy and make good use of the liberty afforded them. In the 1950s, English political philosopher Isaiah Berlin would term this second conception of liberty positive liberty, designating a regime in which government took affirmative actions to make the experience of liberty broadly and meaningfully accessible. New Dealers had no such label but were, in fact, advocates of positive liberty avant la lettre. They held that the federal government had a critical role to play in helping individuals to enhance their security, education, and culture. If policies of this sort were put into place, both in agriculture and beyond, then Americans would find their experience of freedom dramatically enhanced.[58]

The biggest shortcoming of the AAA was its failure to adequately address deepening stratification within the agricultural economy, and the problems that such stratification posed to a fair distribution of federal government resources across a varied farm population. On the one side of the farm economy stood the large landowners whose operations resembled corporations far more than they did family farms. In 1939, Carey McWilliams would label these "factories in the field."[59] Whether these corporate outfits needed federal government subsidies at all was open to question, as was the issue of whether there ought to have been a cap on the number of unplanted acres for which a cultivator could receive compensation so as to prevent the corporate farms from receiving the lion's share of AAA subsidies. Even in drought-stricken Haskell County, where the gap between rich and poor farmers was relatively modest, the inequalities in federal subsidies could become extreme. Hence, for example, the president of a bank in Haskell County who had invested in local land received $4,270 from the AAA in 1933 while a Mennonite farmer living on 160 acres received only $23.[60]

On the other side stood the substantial and growing numbers of individuals who worked in agriculture but owned no land at all, and had few prospects of getting any. These agriculturalists fell into three main groups—tenants, sharecroppers, and laborers—who together constituted at least 4.4 million, or 35 percent, of the 1930 cultivator population of 12.5 million.[61] AAA architects had made no subsidy provision for laborers, migrant or otherwise, so their legislation brought this sizable group no relief. But the AAA did call on farm owners to make every effort to preserve access to land for tenants and sharecroppers even in those circumstances in which the demand for agricultural labor was in decline owing to the cutbacks in cultivation that farm owners were being asked to undertake. As such, for instance, the standard cotton contract of 1933 included a section 7 asking the farm owner signatory to "endeavor in good faith to bring about the reduction of acreage . . . in such manner as to cause the least possible amount of labor, economic and social disturbance." A later clause was even more specific, calling on the signatory to maintain on his land "in so far as possible . . . the normal number of tenants and other employees."[62] The intent of this language was, on the one hand, clear—landowners receiving federal funds were to take the needs of their tenants and sharecroppers into account—and, on the other hand, ambiguous: Did planters have an obligation to the landless beyond "endeavoring" to keep them working on the plots of land they had long tilled?

AAA administrators quarreled bitterly over this issue. The AAA's Legal Division, based in Washington, argued that section 7 obligated planters to keep every one of their existing sharecroppers and tenants on the land and in the houses where, as of 1933, they had resided. The AAA's Cotton Section, by contrast, contended that the language of section 7 stipulated only that planters make a good faith effort to address the needs of sharecroppers and tenants, not that they maintain the landless in the same patterns of land tenure that had prevailed prior to 1933.[63]

Profound political and cultural differences between these two branches of the AAA bureaucracy underlay this policy split. Jerome Frank, a brilliant University of Chicago Law School graduate and favorite of Harvard Law Professor and Roosevelt adviser Felix Frankfurter, headed up the Legal Division. Frank wanted to help both blacks and whites at the bottom of the South's agricultural pyramid. He staffed his division with northern liberals and radical attorneys like himself, including those such as Lee Pressman, Alger Hiss, Nathan Witt, and John Abt who (unbeknownst to Frank) formed a secret cell of Communists.[64] Frank had the support of Rexford Tugwell, a Columbia University economist with close ties to Roosevelt, who by 1934 had ascended to the second-highest position in the USDA, subordinate only to the secretary, Henry Wallace. Through most of 1934, Tugwell and, by extension, Frank's Legal Division whiz kids had Wallace's support. They were allied, too, with the AAA's Consumer's Counsel Division, led by the venerable reformer Frederic Howe, who had personally assembled a cadre of progressive AAA administrators, including the young Gardner Jackson. Adolf Berle Jr. and Abe Fortas were among the other young insurgents hoping to turn the AAA into the New Deal's liberal phalanx. Unabashed in their activism, these northerners supported the efforts of southern tenant farmers and sharecroppers in 1933 and 1934 to organize themselves into an agricultural union, the Southern Tenant Farmers' Union, and to bargain with farm owners in the South over crop shares, crop prices, rents, and the distribution of AAA benefits. The Frank group constituted a formidable bureaucratic power center within the AAA.[65]

The men of the Cotton Section could not have been more different. Their leader was Cully A. Cobb, a Tennessee preacher's son who had graduated from Mississippi A&M and had used the South's agricultural extension service to rise in USDA ranks. If the group led by Frank had achieved power in the AAA's Washington bureaucracy, Cobb possessed the capacity to strike back with an army of AAA field and Democratic Party operatives—a force that was particularly strong in southern statehouses. The directors of farm bureau chapters in the South sided with him, as did the USDA's network of county agents and the agricultural colleges located in the region's land grant universities. The heads of these agricultural colleges, who usually doubled as directors of the USDA's extension service in their respective states, owed their appointments to state and national Democratic Party leaders. To be a southern Democrat in good standing required a commitment to the maintenance of white supremacy and a one-party South. Any support for policies that might upend the region's economic, racial, or political hierarchies would not be tolerated. These were Cobb's people, and he sided with them against the largely black sharecropper class, opposing the latter's efforts to both form a union and find a more equitable manner to distribute AAA benefits across the South's entire agricultural population.[66]

The dispute between the radical Legal Division and conservative Cotton Section came to a head in 1935. Responding to numerous complaints from sharecroppers about the way in which landlords in the South were using the AAA to throw them off the land, Frank's Legal Division summarily ordered AAA-participating landlords to desist from all evictions. This order caused an uproar among the planters, prompting Cobb to mobilize his USDA–farm bureau constituency and flood Washington with protests. Within days, Cobb's army, with its ready access to political power in southern statehouses and Congress, had prevailed. Frank and four of his associates were fired. Their replacements in the Legal Division immediately overturned the radicals' prosharecropper ruling. Tugwell, who had been recuperating from pneumonia in Florida, rushed back to Washington and pleaded with Roosevelt to restore his people to power. Roosevelt refused, knowing that nothing from his New Deal would survive if he alienated the Democratic Party barons in the South. As consolation, Roosevelt threw Tugwell the directorship of the Resettlement Administration, a new agency created to resettle those who on account of drought, poverty, or federal policy had lost access to agricultural land. Ever the good Roosevelt man, Tugwell poured his intellect and passion into the Resettlement Administration and later into its successor, the Farm Security Administration, in both places establishing pioneering programs to aid the rural poor. But Tugwell understood that these agencies would never have the resources or clout that the AAA enjoyed.[67] The AAA, meanwhile, increasingly catered to the more prosperous farmers and big agricultural processors. The liberals' best opportunity to restructure the social basis of American agriculture had slipped from their grasp; they would not get a second chance. By 1943, the Resettlement and Farm Security administrations were both gone, too. The ramifications of Tugwell's defeat would extend beyond agriculture as well. The radical insurgency within the AAA undertaken in Tugwell's name sought to end the deference of the central government toward the states. In its place, the insurgents insisted on the primacy of the federal government and its authority. That they failed in this endeavor signaled that deference toward the states would continue to play an important role in portions of the New Deal. The new central state that the New Dealers were forging remained deeply tied to the old one. The New Deal was as much about compromise as about transformation.

In agriculture, the result was a significant dispossession of the landless and a corresponding concentration of land and benefits in the middle to upper echelons of this economic sector. The farm tenant population declined by almost half between 1930 and 1950, from 2.7 to 1.4 million.[68] A significant portion of this decline emerged directly from government policy: farm owners removing land from cultivation in response to the AAA, and the AAA declining to direct enough subsidies to farm tenants who wished to remain on the land. Another part of the decline was the unintentional effect of federal policy. Farm owners using AAA subsidies to introduce capital improvements to the land they were allowed to cultivate—purchasing more equipment, using more fertilizer, and applying more pesticides—resulted in a declining need for farm labor.[69] Capital improvements increased the productivity of these government-subsidized farmers, making it ever more difficult for the marginal agricultural producers to compete. Even the most resolute agrarians among these marginal producers found themselves without a future in the South. More and more pulled up stakes, migrating to northern and western urban centers in the 1940s where the US government had stimulated the creation of millions of new jobs as it mobilized the economy for war. In ways intentional and unintentional, then, central state planning accelerated the flight from the land, especially in the South, Southwest, and Plains states—a migration that broadened into a movement of millions in the 1940s and 1950s.[70] Meanwhile, the average size of the American farm shot up by more than 35 percent in the 1930s and 1940s, and again by more than 35 percent in the 1950s—a sign of both the growing significance of corporate farms and the ability of the more prosperous family farmers to solidify their economic status as a result of the New Deal.[71]

Rationalization of the agricultural sector may have been inevitable and desirable, New Deal policies notwithstanding. The numbers attempting to live off the land were, in fact, too large. And it may have made sense to sacrifice marginal producers in the interest of ensuring for those who remained on the land economic lives of greater security and prosperity than what millions in American agriculture had hitherto enjoyed. But what of the federal government's obligation to those who had been forced off the land? And what was to be the central state's role once the agricultural sector was deemed to have achieved stability and prosperity?

The central government appropriated few funds to assist the agriculturally dispossessed, and once the Resettlement and Farm Security administrations were terminated in the 1940s, it did next to nothing for them. The agricultural poor either scraped by in desperately poor conditions in the South or West, or joined vast migration streams heading to urban areas in the North and West. Either way, they were on their own. Most were excluded from Social Security benefits and the rights to collective bargaining that the National Labor Relations Act would grant to industrial workers. The needs of sharecroppers and migrant workers would largely go unaddressed until the 1960s, when the children of black sharecroppers began creating turmoil in America's cities, and when Mexican migrant workers in the West formed a union, the United Farm Workers, that drew national attention and sympathy.[72]

Those in the protected sector of American agriculture, meanwhile, became more of an ordinary interest group than apostles of agrarian democracy. The farm bureaus were largely in the hands of local and regional elites, whose connections to both the agricultural colleges and USDA gave them exceptional access to political power in the states as well as federal government. Farm bureaus increasingly deployed that power behind closed doors in negotiations with clusters of senators and representatives who were beholden to powerful agricultural interests. Thus, important deliberations and decisions regarding US agricultural policy were increasingly inaccessible to the public and impervious to democratic processes. The agricultural lobby would come to be regarded as the first of what political scientists began calling "iron triangles," governing arrangements in which a private interest group—in this case, farmers—captured a government bureaucracy (the USDA) and a group of senators (the farm bloc), and made policy in behind-the-scenes ways that subverted democratic ideals of transparency, debate, and accountability.[73] These arrangements had first arisen in the Gilded Age in the relationships between railroad corporations and Congress. New Dealers envisioned themselves instituting regimes of public regulation that would eliminate the spaces in which such arrangements could operate. But this was not to be the case in agriculture.

American agriculture underwent a stunning transformation in the fifty-year period from the Populist revolt through World War II, moving from chronic crisis to security, privilege, and even oligarchy. America's central state was critical to this, generating new ideas in the Bureau of Agricultural Economics and elsewhere, demonstrating impressive will in bending the actions of private economic actors to its wishes, and constructing a remarkable federal and public-private infrastructure that secured the participation of millions of individual producers in the economic reforms mandated by Washington. This transformation saw the American central state distance itself from the classically liberal foundation of circumscribed power and limited bureaucracy on which it had long rested. The agricultural reformers of the 1930s laid the foundation for a new central state endowed with broad powers and impressive bureaucratic capacity. And this new central state lifted the agricultural economy from the distress that had afflicted rural producers across the previous fifty years: year-to-year uncertainties about yields, wild periods of acreage expansion leading to ruinous

overproduction, and the chronic susceptibility of individual producers to exploitation by powerful agricultural merchants and
transporters. The AAA and its allied programs removed much of
the anguish and distress from American agriculture. This was a
major achievement of the American central state, and its implications extended well beyond agriculture.

This feat was accompanied by much handwringing at the time
and thereafter. The agricultural settlement sacrificed the agricultural landless, who found themselves "rationalized" out of rural
existence. It also damaged the agrarian democratic ideal, which
proclaimed that farmers were battling not just for themselves but
also for the rights of all Americans to enjoy the fruits of positive liberty. By the 1940s and 1950s, many farmers were simply too comfortable and affluent to press that claim. Additionally, the agricultural settlement of the 1930s was costly in a literal sense. Managing
America's agricultural markets for the sake of stability turned out
to be an expensive undertaking. The industrialization of food manufacture that it encouraged and the overproduction of calories that
it yielded would in subsequent decades become factors associated
with the nation's obesity epidemic. Finally, concern spread that the
agricultural settlement of the 1930s was corrupting American politics by allowing economic groups with narrow and self-serving interests to take over portions of the central state apparatus and, for
all intents and purposes, exempt them from democratic oversight.
The iron triangle began to look more like a new form of government tyranny than the fulfillment of democratic ideals.[74]

There is a temptation to treat the triumph of this iron triangle
as the inevitable result of interest group politics intersecting with a
rapidly growing government bureaucracy—a manifestation of the
"iron law of oligarchy" first articulated in the early years of the
twentieth century by German sociologist Robert Michels. Michels
formulated this law while writing about the decline of the German
Social Democratic Party, which evolved from a movement embody-
ing robust socialist ideals into a conventional political party dedicated to maintaining the perks of its parliamentary officeholders.[75] Michels's law might appear relevant to American agricultural

reform, which also witnessed a narrowing of political aims from the radical democratic vision of the Populists to the interest group maneuvering of the AFBF during the New Deal. Yet for at least two reasons, his argument that every political organization invariably turns oligarchic is too simple an explanation for the American case. First, the equality that many farmers sought from the 1920s on did not involve improving the lot of every poor American but rather was driven by the aim of putting agriculture on par with industry, which meant granting farmers government privileges similar to what manufacturers had long received. For this sector of agricultural America, then, the fashioning of farmers into a strong interest group was not a perversion of the agrarian political quest but its fulfillment. The case of the farmers underscores how much the pursuit of government privileges by advantaged or relatively advantaged economic groups fueled the growth of government power in America, even during the headiest days of the New Deal.

Michels's contention is also problematic because it misinterprets the bureaucratic story in agriculture. The sharecroppers and tenants in the South lost out in the 1930s and 1940s not because of some iron law of bureaucracy or oligarchy but because their advocates within the new bureaucracy lost their struggle against the supporters of the larger farmers. The central state, in this instance, reproduced within its own structures the inequality in power relations that had prevailed between planters and sharecroppers in civil society. It may be that a central state bureaucracy always favors the more powerful; this indeed is what radical agrarians had asserted in the 1870s and 1880s when they were passing detailed statutory laws to obviate (or so they thought) the need for bureaucracies of government regulators. It is premature to conclude from this study of agriculture, however, that bureaucracies invariably ratify rather than challenge or moderate the power relations prevailing in civil society. Such a conclusion takes no cognizance of a major factor shaping the outcome of policy in agriculture: that two sets of bureaucratic structures were in play—one located in Washington, DC, and the other in the capitals of the major agricultural states. As the struggle between the Frank and Cobb groups reveals, these two structures were themselves at odds, animated by different visions of whom the primary beneficiaries of federal agricultural policy should be. We have to explore whether other economic policies of the New Deal state also ratified existing power relations—in both civil society and federal-state interactions—or whether they challenged them. If such is the latter, we must also inquire into the reasons for the divergence. To pursue this line of questioning, we will look at another instance of central state intervention into social relations in 1930s' America—this one concerned with relations between workers and employers. Here, the central state went much further than it had gone in agriculture to restructure rather than reproduce the balance of power between the haves and have-nots in American society.

7

RECONFIGURING LABOR-CAPITAL RELATIONS

Labor's role in the rise of the new state of positive liberty both paralleled and diverged from that of farmers. The tumultuous capitalist development that gave rise to populism in the late nineteenth century also generated widespread working-class unrest and mobilization, and demands by labor on government to rein in the corporations. Like farmers, workers suffered shattering political defeats in the 1890s. But while the central state pursued a policy of accommodation vis-à-vis farmers in the early decades of the twentieth century, it dealt with labor primarily through repression, judicial and military. Organized labor was as a result less a political force than were farmers, and its ability to press its demands was in consequence weaker.

When the crisis of the Great Depression hit, however, labor's weakness ironically proved an advantage. Lacking an administrative machinery of the sort it had constructed in the agricultural sector, the central state was largely unable to moderate or control the emerging labor insurgency. In consequence, poor and marginal groups of workers were better able than farmers to advance their agendas and elicit advantageous responses from the federal government. Some of what they achieved was remarkable and enduring. Prolabor interventions on the part of the New Deal state lifted millions of workers out of poverty and gave them unprecedented economic security. Indeed, prior to the 1930s, the affluence that would come to characterize broad sections of the working class by the 1950s was unimaginable, and it would not have taken place without central state intervention.

Industrialists' responses to labor's advance were fierce. While they could not dismantle the central state agencies that facilitated labor's rise, they successfully hemmed them in, and in the process restored much of their own influence and halted labor's further advance. By the 1950s, organized labor, like organized agriculture, was a relatively privileged interest group within the broader economic sector it inhabited. Labor leaders fought much harder than did agricultural leaders to break out of this privileged position and pursue policies on behalf of the working class as a whole. The new central state, however, had not entirely shed the ways of the old. In particular, it continued to rely on privatization as a strategy of governance, and in so doing, allowed corporations and other monied interests to reestablish their influence on public policy. As a result, organized labor's most ambitious goals were compromised.

THE ROOTS OF WORKING-CLASS PROTEST

A labor challenge crystallized in the late nineteenth century for the same reasons as the agrarian challenge: chaotic and often-ruinous capitalism. The industrial economy was expanding rapidly during these years, and in a wildly uneven manner. Periods of rapid growth alternated with periods of severe contraction. During the latter, employers with declining revenues laid off large numbers of workers. Employees remaining on the job frequently found their wages cut and hours lengthened. Corporations were also revolutionizing the means of production, often replacing artisans and skilled workers with low-waged and unskilled laborers. Many found their traditional ways of working disrupted; others despaired of finding a way to live securely and with dignity. Turning to politics, workers supported candidates and parties that promised to rein in the power of the corporations. At their workplaces, they began organizing unions and labor assemblies in the belief that such displays of working-class power could compel employers to improve working conditions and raise wages. Their ultimate weapon was the strike, which was intended to force employers to renegotiate the terms of employment. Numerous local strikes broke out across the last third of the nineteenth century, with some of the larger ones riveting the nation's attention. As in agriculture, the railroads were the flash point.[1]

The risky economic practices in which railroads engaged—building lines of questionable value, borrowing large sums in expectation of future revenues that often did not materialize, and watering down their stock—made these corporations vulnerable to economic reversals. They were quick to pass on the costs of these reversals to their employees, in the process stretching workforces to the breaking point and sometimes triggering revolt. In 1877, during the fourth year of depression, the B&O Railroad imposed a third round of wage cuts, prompting employees in Martinsburg, West Virginia, to walk off their jobs. On hearing news of this strike, railroad workers in other locales also walked out, determined to shut down the nation's rail traffic until wages were raised.

Railroad executives were just as determined to keep their trains running, frequently turning to hastily hired and inadequately skilled replacements. Confrontations, often violent, between strikers and replacement workers ensued. Railroad corporations pleaded with the governors of the states to call out the National Guard to protect the trains and the engineers running them, only to discover that in many cases, National Guardsmen were either outdueled by the strikers or in sympathy with them. When the Pennsylvania state militia fired on strikers in Pittsburgh in 1877, killing twenty and wounding twenty-nine, an enraged mob routed the militiamen and set fire to the local headquarters of the Pennsylvania Railroad, destroying thirty-nine buildings as well as more than a hundred locomotives and twelve hundred train cars. President Rutherford B. Hayes called in federal troops to subdue the insurrection there and elsewhere. Elites saw the strike as evidence that the radicalism of the Paris Commune had spread to America and hastened to build armories in their cities to defend their property against an anticipated class war.[2]

Another battle in that war broke out in 1894 when George Pullman, the Chicago-based manufacturer of the eponymous passenger train car, cut his workers' wages, prompting them to walk out. The newly formed American Railway Union (ARU), an industrial union of railroad workers, rushed to the Pullman workers' aid, refusing to move any train carrying Pullman cars. Once again, rail traffic across the country came to a standstill, and confrontations between workers and corporations turned violent. And once again a president of the United States, this time Grover Cleveland, sent in federal troops to break the strike.[3]

As conflict in railroad workplaces and other industries mounted, workers developed ambitious political programs to elect supporters at every level of government—city, state, and federal—in the hope that they would direct public policy in a prolabor direction. Like farmers, workers envisioned themselves not as an interest group but as defenders of the republic, and of the independence and welfare of its citizenry. They sought to improve the hours and conditions of labor, and to require employers to meet minimum standards in factories, workshops, and mines. They wanted to regulate and even abolish private banking, garner public subsidies for worker cooperatives, establish greater legislative control over large industry, and if necessary, nationalize corporations. The more radical of the two labor federations that emerged at this time, the Knights of Labor, looked forward to the "abolition of the wages system." This political agenda required dramatic increases in government clout. By the early 1890s, the radicalism of the labor movement mirrored that of the Populists. Significant groups in both movements had committed themselves to building a large central state to regulate private capital and thereby reclaim the American republic for its citizens.[4]

After the mid-1890s, the politics of labor veered in a different direction. The labor movement had to contend with the federal courts, an arm of the central state hostile to organized labor. As we have seen, the courts in the late nineteenth century developed a laissez-faire jurisprudence meant to limit the ability of governments, federal and state, to regulate employer-employee relations. The courts' core argument was that such regulation undermined the liberty of both employers and workers. Employers had to be guaranteed the liberty to use their property as they saw fit, and workers had to be given the liberty to enter into employment agreements of their own choosing. No government should interfere with such choices. This liberty of contract discourse, which drew on both classical liberalism and the Fourteenth Amendment, rested on a double fiction: first, that corporations were individuals who brought no more resources to a negotiation than did employees; and second, that workers "chose" to work in sweated trades for long hours—twelve hours a day, six days a week. But corporations were not individuals, and workers who acquiesced to laboring in oppressive conditions did so not from choice but from necessity. Only rarely did employment contracts emerge from circumstances of market equality between buyers and sellers of labor. Liberty of contract discourse underwrote a regime of labor relations that generally favored employers over employees.[5]

With the Supreme Court's laissez-faire jurisprudence gaining traction in the 1890s, labor leaders began to question the value of political action. Adolph Strasser of the Cigarmakers Union argued in 1894 that broad changes in the "constitution of the United States and the constitution of every State in the Union" were necessary before Congress or a state legislature would pass a general law restricting hours of work to eight per day. He did not want to expend his union's time and resources fighting for legislation that faced such impossible odds. Strasser was in part mistaken; state legislatures could and did pass general hours laws—lots of them, in fact. But he was spot-on in recognizing that fewer and fewer of these laws would pass constitutional muster, especially those that denied the "best" citizens—male, mature, and able-bodied—the freedom to enter employment contracts of their own choosing. By the mid-1890s, Strasser and his chief disciple, Samuel Gompers, were repudiating labor's campaign for public regulation of the workplace and calling for an embrace of "private regulation" instead. By private regulation they meant, first, organizing strong unions, and next, compelling employers to enter collective bargaining agreements with those unions over wages, hours, patterns of hiring, and other issues pertinent to workplace organization. Once signed, these agreements would gain a protected status that the courts bestowed on all contracts. A party seeking to escape its agreement would face a lawsuit and a court willing to impose heavy penalties on it. The two parties in question, of course, had to have entered their contract freely. This emphasis on free choice prompted the American Federation of Labor (AFL) to apply the term "voluntarism" to its strategy of private regulation.[6]

Labor's voluntarism was in some respects a clever adaptation to the repressive circumstances in which American working-class movements found themselves by 1900. It held the potential to empower craft workers, whose skills made them prized employees. If such workers quit or went on strike, employers would face serious disruptions in production, sales, revenues, and profits. These were risks most employers did not want to take. Thus, the AFL was able to use its voluntarist approach to persuade employers to sign collective bargaining contracts with several million craft workers in the early decades of the twentieth century. This strategy should not have worked nearly as well for unskilled workers, who were more easily replaced. But the labor movement discovered in the secondary strike and product boycott potent weapons for augmenting the power of the unskilled.

The secondary strike or boycott worked as follows. A relatively weak group of workers at one workplace would go on strike. Other groups of workers in the same or related industries would then also go on strike or organize a boycott of the goods produced by the manufacturer whose labor policies had triggered the first strike. In undertaking this kind of support strike or boycott, these secondary groups of workers supplied the primary group—those whose strike had precipitated the conflict—with the kind of economic muscle they themselves lacked.[7]

The power of this strategy is well illustrated by the Pullman Strike of 1894. The conflict originated as a local one between Pullman and his workers, whose wages he had slashed. The Pullman workers did not have sufficient power on their own to win this strike. But they gained leverage in their struggle once the ARU, a union with skilled workers in its ranks, declared that it would not move any train carrying a Pullman car. The ARU, in other words, had committed itself to a secondary boycott. Passenger rail traffic ground to a halt. A local strike had gone national, giving labor the upper hand. Everyone involved in the conflict understood that the strike's outcome would have major implications for the balance of power between capital and labor throughout industrializing America.

The railroad corporations implored the courts to issue an injunction against the ARU, declaring its secondary strike and boycott to be illegal and ordering its members to return to work. The courts complied, citing the Sherman Antitrust Act's prohibition on collusion among economic actors to restrain trade. Although the original purpose of this 1890 act had been to prevent corporations from working with each other to set shipping rates or prices for their goods in ways that obstructed competition, the courts now ruled that it applied with equal force to labor unions that had allegedly conspired with each other to restrain trade. The injunction rendered the ARU's action illegal; its leaders including railwayman Eugene V. Debs were fined and jailed. The federal government now had legal justification for sending troops to break the strike, which it did.[8]

The ARU challenged the injunction, and the case, *In re Debs*, went to the Supreme Court, which upheld the injunctions issued by the lower courts. The decision and related ones over the next decade legitimated the broad use of injunctions to break strikes, and crippled strategies of labor solidarity that were intended to transcend divisions of skill, industry, and locale among workers. All such efforts were now vulnerable to being outlawed as conspiracies in the restraint of trade.[9] Union leaders persisting in such actions risked imprisonment and fines as well as confrontation with the armed might of the central state. US courts issued thousands of such injunctions between the 1890s and 1920s, and governments deployed state or federal troops on hundreds of occasions to break strikes. Repression became the chief weapon in the government's industrial relations arsenal, proving particularly effective against secondary strikes and sympathy boycotts. It drew on exemption, a strategy of liberal governance that had become important in the late nineteenth century. From the Supreme Court's point of view, labor unions engaging in secondary boycotts had placed themselves beyond the law. The federal government was thus justified in treating union leaders as outlaws who had forfeited their claim to rights of free speech and assembly guaranteed them by the Bill of Rights. That these workers had forfeited these rights exempted the central government from the constitutional restraints that otherwise would have applied to its actions.[10]

American workers did not stop protesting as a result. New labor organizations and movements arose, demanding better wages, hours, and working conditions, and sometimes seeking either nationalization or a democratic reorganization of private industry. America's corporations, however, resisted sharing their power with workers or with the central state. Given corporate opposition, unskilled workers found labor organization difficult. The AFL flourished largely because it limited its membership to those for whom voluntarism really worked—craft workers whose privileged labor market power allowed them to enforce regimes of private workplace regulation on their employers. A minority of workers carved out a secure and well-remunerated place for themselves, while the vast majority of the working class remained unorganized and underpaid, forced to labor in poor, insecure circumstances. On the eve of the Great Depression, fewer than 10 percent of American workers belonged to unions.[11]

There are two reasons why the central state's approach to workers in the early decades of the twentieth century was dominated by judicial and military repression rather than by the accommodation it displayed in dealings with farmers. First, working-class demands challenged the propertied prerogatives of corporations in ways that most agrarian demands did not. Workers were present *inside* corporations; most farmers in the early twentieth century were not. Labor union demands for higher wages, better hours, and a restructuring of authority within firms directly challenged the right of corporations to control their property. Agrarian demands for the regulation of shipping rates and warehouse fees did not test the power of individual corporations in the same direct way. Moreover, most farmers aspired to be property owners themselves, giving them an investment in a set of proprietary values that in some respects mirrored that of corporations. When propertied agrarians were confronted on their own farms by laborers, tenants, sharecroppers, and other kinds of employees, they often proved to be as repressive in their labor policies as were corporate heads in dealing with union activity among their workers.

The second reason why the central state tended to be more accommodating of farmers than of workers had to do with the greater political clout farmers wielded. Even as workers came to outnumber farmers in the nation, the former remained concentrated in a band of industrial states largely confined to the northeastern quadrant of the country: Massachusetts, Connecticut, Rhode Island, New York, New Jersey, Delaware, Pennsylvania, Ohio, Michigan, Wisconsin, and Illinois. The restricted geographic location of industrial workers was a source of chronic weakness for labor in America's federalist system, which prized the representation of states as much as—if not more than—the representation of the people who lived in them. Labor's weakness was agrarian America's strength: large numbers of farmers lived in a greater number of states, which made them a potentially much more formidable force in the nation's politics. In addition, systems of representation in many states were disproportionately weighted toward agrarian and nonurban areas. Agrarian political movements could bring greater pressure to bear on statehouses and Washington than could labor movements, making the need for some kind of accommodation to agrarian pressures more urgent.[12]

Labor's demands, then, were more threatening to individual corporations than those of farmers, on the one hand, and less threatening to the political system, on the other. Central state responses to labor thus alternated between repression and an indifference to meaningful programs of accommodation. In these circumstances, central government efforts to manage industrial relations peacefully usually faltered. Only in 1913 had the Department of Labor become a freestanding, Cabinet-level branch of the federal government, and it drew none of the resources and nurtured little of the creativity that by then had become hallmarks of the US Department of Agriculture (USDA). World War I held the promise of a new departure, with the need for industrial manpower inclining the federal government to bring organized labor into policymaking. President Woodrow Wilson established the National War Labor Board (NWLB) in 1918, endowed it with legitimacy by installing a former president of the United States, William Howard Taft, as co-chair alongside Gompers, and granted it substantial powers. The AFL might have abandoned its voluntarist approach in favor of entwining itself with the central state—a strategy that would have paralleled what the American Farm Bureau Federation was successfully pursuing in the USDA. But the NWLB had existed for barely a year when Wilson mothballed it and the rest of the central state's wartime labor machinery. In the 1920s, employers resorted to the injunction with an even greater frequency than before. Meanwhile, the central government's postwar abandonment of labor once again demonstrated to union leaders that only a voluntarist approach was viable over the long term. Herbert Hoover welcomed trade unions to join his associational commonwealth, but was unwilling, either as secretary of commerce or president, to push for a law that recognized the right of unskilled workers to form labor unions and compelled employers to negotiate with them. As the Great Depression loomed, organized labor enjoyed few rights and government possessed little machinery other than its judiciary and military for managing industrial relations.[13]

The central state's determination to repress labor and refuse it the kind of accommodation offered to agriculture rendered workers politically weaker than farmers. Yet, in one way, workers may have been advantaged by the absence of a federal apparatus for handling labor disputes. Upheavals in labor relations during the Great Depression were more intense than any protests in the agricultural sector, and proved more difficult for the federal government to resolve. Unlike the AFBF, which skillfully negotiated its way into directing federal agriculture policy (and in the process, excluded the poorest groups of agricultural workers from government benefits), the AFL found itself shoved aside by new and more radical unions representing some of the most underprivileged groups of workers. By 1945, these new unions had compelled the New Deal state to reconfigure the balance of power between capital and labor.

NEW DEAL BREAKTHROUGH

The New Deal rolled out a plan for industrial transformation in 1933 as ambitious in scope as was the Agricultural Adjustment Act. The National Industrial Recovery Act (NIRA) established the National Recovery Administration (NRA) and charged it with organizing the largest producers in every sector of manufacturing into groups, or conferences. Each conference was expected to develop a code of fair competition to govern prices, wages, and hours in its industry and to set overall production ceilings both in the aggregate and for each firm. The NRA shared with the AAA the aims of curtailing and stabilizing overall production in the hope of encouraging prices and revenues to rise.[14]

The federal government had little means, however, by which to implement this ambitious program. It had no infrastructure of "industry agents," like the nationwide system of county agents that already existed in agriculture, and it had no mechanism for compelling compliance, either through coercion or payouts of the sort offered to individual farmers by the Agricultural Adjustment Administration (AAA). The size and complexity of the industrial sector might have rendered the prospect of issuing hundreds of thousands of individual contracts to manufacturers along AAA lines impossible. In any case, the lack of an infrastructure meant that the federal government could only advise, cajole, and implore groups of industrialists to do the right thing, much as Hoover had done in the 1920s while running the Department of Commerce. Hoover operated in a prosperous time, however, and could pick and choose his targets. He was not confronting a national economy in ruins.[15]

NRA administrators nevertheless embraced their advising role with gusto. For a time, industrialists cooperated, drawing up the requested codes of fair competition and living by their terms. In a variety of sectors, the indexes measuring economic health began to rise. Yet in winter and spring 1934, economic indicators plunged downward once again, and manufacturers started to evade code provisions. The NRA lacked the power to levy penalties or embargo the goods of companies violating their industry's code. Roosevelt and his advisers were prepared to abandon the faltering NRA even before the Supreme Court declared it unconstitutional in 1935.[16]

The NRA was dead, but the working-class insurgency that it had unintentionally sparked was not. Section 7(a) of the authorizing NIRA legislation declared that "employees shall have the right to organize and bargain collectively through representatives of their own choosing, and shall be free from the interference, restraint, or coercion of employers of labor, or their agents."[17] Few Americans gave this section much thought at the time of the NIRA's passage, and organized labor itself had not lobbied hard for it. Roosevelt's advisers had agreed to it as a way of forestalling consideration of a prolabor bill that senators Hugo Black of Alabama and Robert Wagner of New York were pushing in Congress. Section 7(a) worried some employers, but most regarded it simply as a nuisance. Their indifference was a major miscalculation. This obscure clause triggered one of the largest working-class insurgencies in American history. It did not begin to abate until 1937, by which time five million new workers had flooded into labor unions and the central state had been compelled to establish machinery for managing industrial relations that was far more favorable to labor than anything previously built.[18]

The demands that workers initially put before their bosses in 1933 and 1934 were modest: they wanted employers to recognize their unions and observe the wage and hour provisions of the NRA codes. Few employers were willing, however, to accept these demands. Workers, as a result, inundated Washington with letters protesting employer violations of the NRA codes. FDR then realized that the NIRA had not authorized a government agency to adjudicate the disputes that these letters were bringing to light, and belatedly established a National Labor Board with three representatives from labor, three from business, and one to represent the public. But the board possessed no satisfactory mechanism of enforcement. As the impotence of the NRA and National Labor Board became clear, frustrated workers began to take matters into their own hands. In 1934 alone, they staged two thousand strikes, some of which escalated into armed confrontations between workers and police that drew national attention. In May, ten thousand workers surrounded the Electric Auto-Lite plant in Toledo, Ohio, declaring that they would block exits and entrances until the company agreed to shut down operations and negotiate a union contract. Two strikers were killed in an exchange of gunfire. In Minneapolis, unionized truck drivers and warehousemen fought police, private security forces, and the National Guard in a series of street battles from May through July that left four dead and hundreds wounded. In July, skirmishes between longshoremen and employers in San Francisco killed two and wounded scores of strikers. This violence provoked a general strike in San Francisco that shut down the city's transportation, construction, and service industries for two weeks. In September, four hundred thousand textile workers at mills from Maine to Alabama walked off their jobs. Attempts by employers to bring in replacement workers triggered violent confrontations that caused several deaths, hundreds of injuries, and millions of dollars in property damages.[19]

Working-class anger spilled over into the 1934 election, as Democrats won 70 percent of the contested seats in the Senate and House, and increased their majority from 60 to 69 (out of 96) in the upper chamber and from 310 to 319 (out of 432) in the lower one. No majority party had ever done so well in an off-year election, prompting the *New York Times* to declare that "the President and his New Deal . . . won the most overwhelming victory in the history of American politics."[20]

As FDR basked in this big Democratic win, he had reason to worry. Included in this seventy-fourth Congress was the largest contingent of radicals ever sent to Washington. Meanwhile, radical third parties were busily organizing in a variety of states— the Farmer Labor Party in Minnesota, Progressive Party in Wisconsin, Commonwealth Builders in Washington, and End Poverty in California—and were ready to abandon their alliance with the Democratic Party if Roosevelt proved too timid in his response to working-class demands. A good deal of working-class anger also focused on the AFL, now seen by many as too slow to respond to the organizing and political opportunities opened up by the 1934 insurgency. John L. Lewis, president of the United Mine Workers, grasped the significance of the moment. In 1935, his union and six other unions bolted from the AFL to form a new labor federation, the Committee on Industrial Organization (CIO), to give the working-class revolt the leadership and resources it needed.[21]

In the face of so much insurgency, Roosevelt himself turned leftward, castigating the wealthy for their profligate ways, and calling for new programs to aid the poor. To back up his rhetoric, he worked with the heavily Democratic Congress on a Second New Deal, this one directed more to the needs of ordinary citizens than to the needs of big business. From labor's perspective, the most important piece of new legislation was the National Labor Relations Act (NLRA), also called the Wagner Act after its Senate sponsor, Robert Wagner of New York. This act offered workers the strong collective bargaining that they had long sought. It guaranteed every worker covered by the act the right to join a union of his or her own choosing. The act obligated employers to bargain with unions in good faith. It labeled common employer techniques for breaking up unions as "unfair labor practices," and prohibited employers from deploying them. Perhaps most important, it set up a new government regulatory body, the National Labor Relations Board (NLRB), and endowed it with broad investigatory and enforcement powers. The labor movement hailed the NLRA as its charter of freedom, its Magna Carta. This legislation significantly expanded the federal government's regulatory role. The central state would soon use that expansion to encroach on corporate power and privilege in unprecedented ways.[22]

The NLRB would be composed of three members appointed by the president. The national board would have twenty-two regional boards operating under its direction, all empowered to conduct elections for union representation at workplaces in their jurisdictions and to certify the results. These results were reviewable by the national board in Washington, DC, which would issue the final findings, and either confer or deny collective bargaining rights on the unions involved. The NLRB also had the power to determine the contours of bargaining units, rule on the scope of issues subject to collective bargaining, and find employers "guilty" of a variety of offenses. If charges were brought against an employer, the NLRB had the right to investigate, subpoena evidence and oral testimony from the parties to the dispute, and punish those who had violated the law. Its remedies ranged from imposing monetary fines to ordering employers to reinstate workers fired for their union organizing activity. The architects of the NLRB took pains to insulate the agency from what they believed was the undue influence of corporations both within workplaces and in Congress and the executive branch of government. Thus, NLRB rulings were subject to review only by the federal appeals courts and the Supreme Court itself. Not even the president, as head of the government's executive branch, could interfere with NLRB rulings.[23]

Once the NLRB developed a body of labor rules, Senator Wagner and other NLRA architects argued, workplaces would come to resemble miniature republics governed by laws rather than by arbitrary power. Workers would now meet with their employers, or representatives of their employers, in workplace "parliaments" to determine wages, hours, and working conditions. Disputes would be solved through discussion, negotiation, and arbitration rather than by an employer's unilateral decree. As the industrial world adapted to this new constitutional order, Wagner believed, workers would put aside the strike, and employers would no longer resort to armed force. Industrial relations would finally come to be characterized by peace not war, with dividends that would redound not just to labor and capital but also to the general public.[24]

Most employers rejected the NLRA's dream of peaceful industrial relations for two reasons—one practical, and the other jurisprudential. First, even if the NLRA's long-term goal was to create an industrial relations regime in which both sides felt secure in their rights, the short-term goal was to expand the rights of labor and shrink those of industry. NLRA architects believed that such a rebalancing act was critical if "industrial democracy" were to have any chance of success. Corporations, however, did not like being asked by the central government to curtail their power in this way. Second, the NLRA was seen by industry as a betrayal of the laissez-faire jurisprudence that the Supreme Court had championed across the previous sixty years. This jurisprudence had made it clear that the federal government's power to regulate interstate commerce did not confer on it a right to regulate industry or interfere with an employer's right to administer his property as he saw fit. Thus, the federal government's denial of the employer's "right" to say whatever he wished in the battle for the hearts and minds of his workers in union representation elections, or ability to compel an employer to rehire workers whose union activity had interfered with production, constituted deep and intolerable affronts to the way in which corporate America was accustomed to doing business.[25]

Industrialists were so sure that the Supreme Court would overturn the NLRA that they by and large refused to comply with its provisions. Roosevelt wanted political balance on the three-member NLRB, but no captain, lieutenant, or even corporal of industry agreed to come aboard. To participate was to be complicit in a re-ordering of industry that was not only loathsome to corporations but would also soon be declared unconstitutional. Those seeking to join the business-government policymaking elite saw service on the NLRB as a dead end and quite possibly a career killer.

For the chairmanship of the NLRB, Roosevelt settled on Joseph Madden, an obscure University of Pittsburgh economist thought to have moderately conservative views. But Madden turned out to be an advocate for "fairness" in industry, which in the mid- and late 1930s meant ruling more often than not on labor's behalf. A second member of the NLRB, Donald Wakefield Smith, owed his appointment entirely to his marriage into a powerful Pennsylvania political family. Lacking qualifications and aware of his limitations, he followed Madden's lead in almost every instance. The third NLRB member, Edwin S. Smith, had been involved in mediating industry-labor disputes since the days of the NRA. Politically he had moved steadily to the Left, becoming a firm supporter of the CIO, industrial unionism, and by the mid-1930s, the Communist Party's Popular Front.[26]

Edwin Smith wanted to use the NLRB to effect a far-reaching reconstruction of American industry. He formed an alliance with Nathan Witt, another of Felix Frankfurter's leftist Harvard law students, who in 1935 became the first assistant general counsel for the NLRB. Responsible for hiring, Witt populated the board's ranks with ardent New Dealers and leftists who did not mind the low pay and job insecurity that characterized employment at the NLRB at this time. Witt also attracted talented Jewish attorneys, who were often shut out of prestigious positions in private practice. By 1937, Witt had become the NLRB's secretary, and the most powerful force at the agency. Like his close friend Lee Pressman at the AAA, Witt assembled the young talent he hired into a leftist power center within the NLRB (Witt, like Pressman, was a member of the Communist Party). But while Pressman's group was purged in 1935 by a conservative group led by AFBF leader Curly Cobb, Witt's group elicited no serious conservative opposition in the NLRB's early years.[27] Though the NLRB established regional offices across the country, individual states were given no jurisdiction over them. Local elites and regional interests groups thus found it difficult to take them over. Much more than in agriculture, New Deal labor policy had broken with federalist principles.

FDR's decision to focus his 1936 reelection campaign on the needs of ordinary Americans and, in the process, critique the behavior of America's economic elites further fired up the labor insurgency that been roiling the country since 1934. In summer 1936 the CIO unveiled a powerful new weapon, the sit-down strike. Employees would no longer simply petition employers for union recognition. They would also occupy employer property, rendering normal manufacturing impossible until the employer agreed to recognize the union and bargain with it in good faith. Almost three hundred sit-downs occurred between August 1936 and March 1937. The most decisive took place in late December 1936, when the workers at a General Motors (GM) plant in Flint, Michigan, began an occupation of their factory that lasted for six weeks.

The GM strike mattered because the corporation was then the largest and, in the estimation of many, the most powerful in the world. GM management immediately secured the customary

injunctions ordering the workers to leave the premises, but neither the new Democratic governor of Michigan, Frank Murphy,
nor the newly reelected Democratic president, Roosevelt, was willing to send in the National Guard or federal troops to evict the
strikers. Sit-down tactics spread to more than twenty GM plants
as it became apparent that the federal state was declining to deploy
its armed might to defeat the strikers. On February 5, 1937, FDR
opened up another front in this industrial struggle by threatening
to restructure the Supreme Court if the Court's justices dared to invalidate the NLRA or Social Security Act, the signature legislation
of Roosevelt's Second New Deal. Specifically, Roosevelt proposed
legislation to Congress that would allow him to appoint a new justice for every sitting justice who had reached seventy years of age.[28]

Roosevelt's threat to "pack" the Court increased the pressure
on both GM and the justices to do Roosevelt's bidding. Within a
matter of days, GM capitulated to the sit-down strikers and agreed
to recognize the United Automobile Workers (UAW) as the lawful
representative of GM workers in Flint and in the scores of plants
that the company operated across Michigan and the Midwest. Less
than a month later, on March 2, US Steel, a second industrial titan
and, since the days of Andrew Carnegie, a bastion of antiunion-
ism, capitulated to another CIO union, the Steel Workers' Organizing Committee. A month later, in April 1937, the Supreme Court's
stunning five-to-four decision decreed that the federal government,
under powers given to it by the Constitution to regulate interstate
commerce, had the right to manage industrial relations in ways
consonant with what the NLRA had set forth. FDR's proposed legislation to alter the makeup of the Court may well have persuaded
a Supreme Court justice, Owen Roberts, to switch his vote on the
NLRA from a negative to positive, thereby giving the Court's New
Deal supporters their five-to-four majority. More generally, the justices were wrestling with the NLRA case across months of intense
industrial and political upheaval. Arguments for continuing the age
of constitutional laissez-faire had lost cogency.

The Supreme Court's NLRA decision was a victory for those
who had been arguing for decades that the commerce clause, which
gave the central state the right to regulate trade between the states,

also gave the federal government the right to regulate all manufacturing enterprises whose goods entered the interstate commerce stream. It was a logical and defensible decision. Regulating manufacturing through the central state's power to control commerce was a much better and more legitimate use of the surrogacy principle than the other uses of this tool that the Court had already legitimated: the regulation of prostitution through the commerce clause, obscenity through the post office clause, and narcotics through the taxation clause. As we have seen, the idea of hanging the regulation of manufacturing on the peg of commerce had been so fiercely resisted, not because of the illogic of the connection between the two, but instead because accepting this form of surrogacy would have vastly increased the central state's ability to regulate corporate property and power. As some legal scholars have maintained, the Court had been trying for years to reason itself into the position of justifying the regulation of manufacturing through the commerce clause. But the notion of industry being exempt from government control was still so powerful and so woven into legal precedent that it took a nine-month wave of sit-down strikes, an overwhelming second term victory by a leftward-leaning FDR, and a direct assault by FDR on the integrity of the Court to "persuade" the Supreme Court to tear down the wall separating commercial from manufacturing regulation. The Supreme Court's 1937 decision enshrined surrogacy as the principal strategy for expanding the regulatory reach of the central state. In the coming decades, the Supreme Court would return to the commerce clause again and again to justify the expanding power of the federal government.[29]

LABOR AT HIGH TIDE

Workers and employers brought more than ten thousand cases before the NLRB in 1937 alone, a sevenfold increase over 1936. Its staff almost tripled in size between June 1937 and June 1938, from about 250 to 700 employees.[30] The NLRB conducted almost four thousand elections involving millions of workers between 1935 and 1940, with most of those elections coming after April 1937.[31]

It ruled on a range of questions about workplace regulation that the NLRA authorizing legislation had left ambiguous. The duty of employers to bargain with a victorious union on questions of wages and hours appeared straightforward. But what did the duty to bargain on "working conditions" encompass? Workloads, work distribution, occupational safety and health, promotions, layoffs, hirings, firings, and technological and organizational changes in the production process were all matters that could affect working conditions. Which of these matters would be subject to collective bargaining, and which would be exempt, constituting an area of managerial prerogative that neither workers nor their union representatives could touch? And what mechanisms other than a strike or lockout could unions and employers generate to resolve disputes?

It fell to the NLRB to answer these questions, and in the process, to construct a coherent body of industrial relations law, subject of course to judicial review. Industrialists and conservatives who had been so confident that the Supreme Court would dissolve the NLRA now confronted in the NLRB a public agency that had staked its reputation on a fundamental reordering of the relations between capital and labor. As historian James A. Gross has written, "The NLRB represented a new national power being exerted by the federal government in the economic affairs of the country. . . . The Board had met the most powerful employers in the country head-on," and in many cases, emerged victorious.[32]

As the reality of the NLRB's prolabor orientation became clear in 1937 and 1938, supporters of corporations unleashed a furious counteroffensive. In 1939, Congressman Howard W. Smith of Virginia launched a hostile investigation of the NLRB with the goal of overhauling its mission and powers, or eliminating it altogether. As this high-profile investigation unfolded, an increasingly nervous Roosevelt began replacing the prolabor advocates on the NLRB with appointees who were either genuinely neutral or sympathetic to business. By 1940, two members of the 1938 board, Madden and Donald Smith, were gone, as was Witt, the powerful NLRB secretary. By 1941, the radical Edwin Smith was gone too.[33] Meanwhile, industrialists were appealing NLRB decisions to the court of appeals and Supreme Court, now sympathetic to the argument that the NLRB had tilted too far in labor's direction.[34]

This conservative counterattack was poised to deliver a powerful blow to CIO labor and the New Deal when the Japanese attacked Pearl Harbor in late 1941, bringing America into World War II. The challenge of sending millions of soldiers to three military theaters—Europe, North Africa, and the Pacific—and developing the economic capacity to get these soldiers to their destinations with the food, supplies, and the arms they needed broadened the federal government's management of industry and labor. In 1942, Roosevelt gave the National War Labor Board (NWLB), first established in 1918, new life, and for the duration of the Second World War, shifted much of the NLRB's power to it. The NWLB built on the foundation laid by the NLRB. It treated unions as an indispensable partner in production and in establishing workplace regimes in which both workers and employers had rights, and in which disputes would be resolved through peaceful and negotiated means. To this end, the NWLB supported the spread of unions through more and more of American industry, and required employers to reach agreements with them.

The NWLB helped unions stabilize their membership by compelling workers who joined unions to remain members through the life of a contract. It enhanced organized labor's financial stability by supporting dues checkoff mechanisms, through which employers automatically deducted union dues from employee paychecks and turned them over to union treasuries. Recognizing that limitations on wage increases for the war's duration would frustrate workers, NWLB administrators encouraged employers to increase workers' income by other means, including paid vacations, sick leave, pensions, and employer-sponsored health care plans.[35] Finally, the NWLB lent its support to CIO demands for the simplification and equalization of pay rates in the mass-production industries—a policy that by the war's end had significantly raised the wages paid to the lowest-skilled sectors of the factory labor force.

These steps made labor organizations ever more popular, triggering a second surge in union membership. On the eve of war in

1941, about nine million workers belonged to labor unions, up from four million in 1934. The war brought another six million workers into unions, raising the total unionized workforce to fifteen million by 1945, or about 35 percent of the nonagricultural workforce—its all-time high in the United States.[36] The principle underlying this union surge—that workers were industrial citizens, entitled to certain rights at their workplaces that employers had to respect—sank deeply into the fabric of American industrial relations.

Real wages doubled during the era of peak union strength—a period of twenty-plus years that began in World War II and ended in the late 1960s. Union power was not the only factor to propel wage gains, to be sure; productivity advances made a difference, as did the US economy's ascent to a position of unassailable global hegemony in the postwar period. But the willingness of employers to pass on a significant portion of their profits to their workers in the form of wage increases would never have happened without the pressure that unions were able to exert on employers and the state.[37] Moreover, as a result of labor's rise, the United States became an economically more equal society in a double sense. First, the share of wealth going to the top 1 percent of income earners fell significantly during the first decade of peak union strength, 1946 to 1957. Second, unions reduced the differentials that existed within the working class, between the skilled and unskilled working class, by disproportionately raising the wages of the unskilled.[38] For example, wage differentials in the auto industry fell a staggering 60 percent between World War II and 1960.[39] A substantial portion of wage inequality turned on divisions of race, ethnicity, and gender. Narrowed wage differentials thus shrank the economic distance between black workers and white ones, Old European and New European, and male and female, enabling many more Americans to imagine a country that might finally deliver on its promise that "all men are created equal."[40] While individual unions were often slow to move against racial and gender discrimination in their own ranks and workplaces, the work they did to level wage rates strengthened the principle of equality within the labor movement while emboldening women and minority militants to put forward their claims.

The working-class surge toward economic security and, in some cases, prosperity occurred as a result of the central state's determination to bring industrial relations policy under its control, with an eye toward leveling the playing field between employers and employees. The NWLB was not as prolabor as the original NLRB had been, and its officials strove to be evenhanded in their rulings. Thus, if the NWLB favored labor by insisting that virtually every employer under its jurisdiction grant recognition to the union that had won a representation election on its premises, it favored employers by barring unions from going on strike for the duration of the war. In most unionized workplaces, the NWLB further established its neutrality by insisting that all disputes not settled through negotiation be submitted to an impartial arbitrator whose decision would be final and binding on both parties. The NWLB's vision was in line with the industrial jurisprudence that the architects of the Wagner Act had in mind when they passed this law in 1935. But evenhandedness had not been the modus operandi of the NLRB during its radical, 1935–40 phase. Its implementation during the war and its incorporation into the approach of the postwar NLRB therefore signified an important departure from earlier practices. It should be understood as a partial retreat from the prolabor orientation that the CIO had forced on the central state during the height of its 1930s' insurgency.[41]

There was no serious talk in the 1940s, however, of returning to the older era of capital-labor relations. The force of laissez-faire constitutionalism had been broken, and the principle of surrogacy had been enhanced to the point where it now possessed the potential to underwrite a vast expansion of the central state's regulatory power.[42] A decisively and enduringly reordered industrial relations landscape that substantially reduced the power differentials between capital and labor was the most immediate and consequential result of this jurisprudential earthquake. Moreover, the benefits of this reorientation reached more than just privileged groups of workers, in contrast to the agricultural reorientation supervised by the AAA. They flowed equally to the millions who labored in some of the most exploited portions of the mass-production workforce.

Still, by the mid-1940s, organized labor found itself confronting a dilemma that organized agriculture faced: becoming a privileged interest by virtue of its special access to central state power. In labor's case, the predicament arose in relation to the substantial portions of the working class that remained uncovered by the NLRA. The act had extended none of its collective bargaining provisions to agricultural laborers, which meant that large groups of workers, ranging from sharecroppers in the South to migrant laborers in California and Texas, enjoyed no collective bargaining rights. In addition, occupations located outside the mass-production sector and largely populated by female workers, most notably waitresses and domestic servants, also had no access to collective bargaining rights.[43] Unions, furthermore, were less effective in small rather than large manufacturing or business enterprises, which meant that workers who labored in these small companies, while not formally excluded from the terms of the Wagner Act, had difficulty accessing its benefits. Thus, in the 1940s, the rise of an organized sector of the working class threatened to introduce in new form an old division in the working population: between those with the good wages and benefits that collective bargaining had made available, and those with limited access to the advantages conferred by government-regulated bargaining.

The leaders of the CIO were alert to this possibility. They had been critics of the working-class divide resulting from the AFL's success in garnering a privileged status for itself. They embraced a political strategy meant to advance the interests of all workers, union and nonunion. This strategy was on display in their support of Social Security, legislation passed in 1935 that guaranteed most working Americans a pension on retirement, irrespective of union membership.[44] It also surfaced in the CIO's support for national health insurance in the 1940s. Some of the most creative CIO leaders, such as Walter Reuther of the UAW, wanted to go further still, by introducing corporatist-style management to the economy. In Reuther's vision, representatives of the major economic blocs in society—business, labor, agriculture, and the public—would meet on a regular basis to direct federal government investments in the economy, develop manpower and income policies, set guidelines for profits and prices, and determine the level of government funds to be deposited into welfare programs. In these meetings, Reuther expected labor leaders to press the case for benefits for all workers, not simply for union members.[45]

During World War II, the federal government brought union representatives into enough of these corporatist-style arrangements to stoke Reuther's belief that this kind of national planning was attainable in the postwar period. But the dream evaporated within a year of the war's end, as the central government pulled back sharply from these corporatist arrangements. Reuther was determined to continue being an advocate not just for his own union but for all workers. But to succeed in this quest, he needed the federal government's support. When that support was not forthcoming, he attempted to fashion a UAW strike against GM into a weapon that would advance his and his union's corporatist principles. Once that strike failed in 1946, Reuther had little choice but to scale back his ambitions and work for more conventional goals, in this case improving the working and living conditions of UAW members.[46]

The UAW's campaign to upgrade member wages, benefits, and job security in the 1940s and 1950s yielded stunning results. The 1950 contract with GM, known as the Treaty of Detroit, is especially notable for its largesse, apparent in its five-year duration, 20 percent wage increase, and guarantee of generous old-age pensions and health insurance. As a result of the success in procuring these contracts with GM and other automobile manufacturers, the UAW opened a door for a million-plus autoworkers to enter the middle class. Other unions followed the UAW's lead, sufficiently widening that opening to allow their members to walk through it as well.[47]

But these achievements came at a price, and it was the one that Reuther had feared: that the UAW and its fellow unions had privileged one sector of the working class at the expense of the rest. In public, the UAW still supported campaigns for the expansion of public pensions (in the form of increased Social Security benefits) and universal provision of health insurance. But UAW members were now getting these benefits privately, through negotiations with their employers. As a result, America's "welfare state" took a decisive turn toward becoming a public-private system. An individual aspiring to a "good life" in the United States was now expected to supplement government Social Security benefits with a private pension and receive private health insurance through one's employer—not through the federal state. This public-private system served unionized workers well. By the 1960s it was also working quite well for millions of nonunion workers, especially in white-collar industries, where employers had concluded that keeping their firms union free and competitive with their rivals for the best workers required that they, too, offer their employees generous pension and health insurance packages. And the private insurance companies, which had long ago discerned the opportunities that labor's quest for economic security might generate for them, were ready with alluring pension and health care products for employers and unions alike. The government facilitated this surge of private welfare by exempting employer contributions to pensions and health care from corporate taxes, and by declining to treat the benefits conferred on recipients as taxable income. These were the first instances of what would later be called "tax expenditures," the government's use of tax credits to influence the behavior of corporations and individuals in the private sector. Tax expenditures became a key government technique for spurring the expansion of a government-incentivized private welfare system.[48]

This government-encouraged private welfare system left substantial numbers of Americans in the cold, including those who did not have jobs or worked in small businesses, or whose lack of skills forced them to take jobs with employers who saw no need to supplement wages with pension or health care benefits. And so by the 1960s, organized labor had become something of a privileged group itself, with access to collective bargaining rights, union representation, and well-endowed pension and health care plans that millions of people in America did not have. Reuther and others would continue to seek to break out of the districts of working-class privilege. In 1963 and 1964, for example, the UAW was in the forefront of groups offering their support to the civil rights movement and developing the antipoverty policies and health care programs for the aged and poor that congealed into the Great Society.

But these activities by union leaders often strained their relations with their own members, among whom the imperative of reaching out to less fortunate groups of workers was no longer so urgently felt a matter as it had been in the years of the Great Depression and world war. In such ways were the largest ambitions of the labor movement compromised. Defeat dogged its victories.

OLD PRACTICES AND THE NEW LIBERAL STATE

The expanded regulatory apparatus that the New Deal brought forth did not completely emancipate the new liberal state from the old. Two persistent features of this old system of government particularly constrained the New Deal: first, its federalist character, and second, an electoral system still dependent on private sources of money.

Though American industry had expanded into the South and West Coast during the 1930s and 1940s, the working class remained a disproportionately regional formation with its members concentrated in the Northeast, from Massachusetts in the East to Illinois in the West to the Ohio River in the South. This unbalanced distribution made it difficult for organized labor to generate support for its initiatives in the southern and western states, and thus weakened its influence in the Senate, where politicians from nonunion states, especially southern ones, wielded extraordinary power. The labor movement made two attempts in 1937 and 1946 to penetrate the South, organize the region's workers, and improve its political clout there, but failed on both occasions. In 1946, labor's opponents in Congress, led by southern senators and congressmen, struck back by passing the Taft-Hartley Act, legislation that permitted individual states to pass "right to work" laws that stripped unions of powers that the NRLA had conferred on them. Here was another instance of states using their authority to bend federal legislation to their will. Via the dispensation given to them by Taft-Hartley, southern legislatures found ways to keep their states largely union free for the rest of the twentieth century.[49]

The labor movement was also weakened by an electoral process that remained dependent on private money. Even in its most radical phase, the CIO declined to challenge the legitimacy of the existing electoral system—for instance, by calling for limits to be placed on private contributions made to political parties or for presidential campaigns to be publicly funded. Instead, it persuaded itself that it could beat its opponents at their own game by raising sums of money large enough to enable the Democrats to compete success-fully against the Republican Party, whose coffers had been filled by contributions from America's wealthiest individuals and families. The magnitude of Roosevelt's 1936 victory seemed to confirm the wisdom of this strategy. That year, Labor's Nonpartisan League, a political organization sponsored by the CIO, raised between $500,000 and $800,000 from CIO unions and members, amount-ing to 10 to 15 percent of the Democratic Party's total expendi-tures. Those funds, in combination with the army of Democratic operatives labor put in the field, were enough to make the CIO a major force in Roosevelt's 1936 victory.[50] In 1943, when conser-vatives pushed through Congress the Smith-Connally Act, a law designed to stymie unions by prohibiting them from contributing their funds directly to political parties or candidates, the CIO re-sponded by creating the country's first Political Action Committee, an organization formally independent of the unions but through which unionists could contribute their money to the Democratic Party. Through this PAC and related organizations, the CIO raised approximately $1.3 million for FDR and the Democratic Party in 1944, more than double the amount of money LNPL had assem-bled in 1936. Once again, the CIO was able to play an important role in FDR's reelection, depositing enough money in Democratic Party coffers and putting enough highly motivated election volun-teers in the streets to neutralize the Republican Party's financial advantage.[51]

But as successful as it was in the short term, the CIO strategy was risky in the longer term. The CIO, in effect, acceded to monied plu-ralism as the basis of American politics. In this system, any group could bring its money to the election table and place its bets on the candidates of its own choosing. If a player with smaller pockets played his hand well enough, he could win. In the 1930s and 1940s, and in the highly unusual political circumstances brought on by the Great Depression, the CIO's plan yielded impressive results. But the strategy faced much greater obstacles over the long term, since the funds that the CIO would be able to put into play election after election would likely pale beside those accessible to the corporations and the rich.

New Dealers understood their financial vulnerability all too well. After the Democratic Party raised sums of money in 1928 and 1932 that almost matched what the Republicans had assembled, the money gap widened substantially. In 1936, the Democrats' campaign chest of $5.2 million amounted to less than 60 percent of what the Republicans had raised. The sharply drawn class lines of the 1936 election had prompted a precipitous drop in campaign contributions to the Democratic Party from bankers and Wall Street brokers, who were now giving more than 90 percent of their election money to the Republican Party.[52] As significant as the labor movement was to the 1936 election, the amount of money it raised for Roosevelt amounted to less than what five families—the du Ponts, Mellons, Pews, Rockefellers, and Sloans—contributed to the Republican candidate, Alf Landon.[53] Labor money alone simply could not sustain a campaign, which is why, even during the heyday of the Democratic Party's "class politics" period, Roosevelt and his advisers were open to working with other groups, especially portions of America's business elite, that could bring them additional money, election workers, and votes.

The Democratic Party could not compete across the board with the Republican Party for support of the country's business community, but it did make headway with selected portions of it. Brewers and distillers owed the Democratic Party a debt for the repeal of Prohibition in 1933. Tobacco growers and manufacturers, such as R. J. Reynolds, almost all of which were in the Southeast, appreciated the New Deal's large investments in the region's agricultural and infrastructural development as well as its reluctance to challenge the South's racial hierarchies.[54] Department store owners in the Northeast, such as the Filene, Gimbel, and Straus families, had been persuaded that the future lay with the high-wage, mass-consumption economy that the New Deal was hoping to de-velop. In New York City and State in particular, the New Deal attracted wealthy Catholics and Jews who, despite their eco-nomic achievements, could make little headway in the Protestant-dominated worlds of Wall Street and the Republican Party.[55]

When FDR moved from the governor's mansion in New York to the White House in 1933, he brought the cultural openness of the Empire State's politics with him. This openness drew Wall Street firms with Jewish leadership, such as Lehman Brothers and Gold-man Sachs, more centrally into the Democratic orbit. Roosevelt was similarly attractive to Hollywood's Jewish movie establishment. The Roosevelt administration also garnered support from mem-bers of the Texas business elite. Construction magnates based in the state, such as the Brown Brothers of Brown and Root, received lucrative New Deal contracts to build dams and generate electric power across the Southwest. Texas oilmen believed that New Deal economic policies suited their capital-intensive industry and inter-nationalist orientation.[56]

Roosevelt continued to solicit funds from portions of the na-tion's business elite throughout the period during which rhetori-cally he castigated the wealthy as "money changers" who had be-trayed the country and who had to be jettisoned from the "high seats" they occupied in "the temple" of American civilization.[57] Keeping them in the New Deal coalition meant giving them a role in shaping the liberalism that FDR championed. As a result, the New Deal developed a politics that mixed populist policy and business opportunity, a blend that limited the possibilities for working-class reform. Business interests shaped the politics of the Democratic Party coalition throughout the New Deal era, and did so especially after the conservative counterattacks of 1938 and 1939 checked the working-class insurgency of 1933–37. This influence helps us to un-derstand why the public-private welfare system was the one that came to be associated with the New Deal Order. After all, this was a system that like the Democratic Party of the era, amalgamated popular and corporate interests.

In structural terms, the electoral system of the 1930s should be seen as a survival of America's long nineteenth century, when the central government's scope of action was sharply circumscribed. From the vantage point of the nineteenth century, it was better to put electoral machinery and the responsibility of raising money for it in the hands of private organizations. As other features of the nineteenth-century central state were attacked and overhauled, this one remained intact, and helps to explain the course ultimately taken by the New Deal. That the labor insurgency of the 1930s and 1940s never challenged the monied basis of American politics is a mark of the limitations it perceived in US politics. Given the narrow geographic basis of America's working class, forming an independent labor party was a pipe dream. And advocating for a comprehensive overhaul of the electoral system was to devote energy to what seemed like an unattainable reform. The limitations under which the labor movement operated should not obscure the magnitude of its achievements. Yet a consideration of these limitations allows us to see that the new central state was built on the foundation of the old, with major implications for social policy and state actions in the post–1945 world.

The New Deal state broke decisively from patterns of governance that had been dominant in the nineteenth and early twentieth centuries. Both the capacity and authority of the federal state expanded substantially during the 1930s and 1940s. The startling increases in federal government's regulatory reach brought order and prosperity to economic sectors—agriculture and labor—that for fifty years had been beset by economic chaos and insecurity. The new state of positive liberty demonstrated how effective the federal government could be in bestowing benefits on and improving the lives of its citizens. The divergent impacts of agricultural and labor policy are as interesting as their commonalities. The New Deal stabilized agriculture in ways that ended up privileging one part of the agricultural sector at the cost of the whole. The reconfiguration of industrial relations occurred in a way that benefited far more of America's industrial poor than parallel policies in agriculture had benefited the rural poor. But political struggles over the central state provoked by working-class insurgency also turned back labor's most ambitious proposals and allowed a good deal of the old liberal central state to slip into the new.

A willingness to allow private groups to secure their well-being by widening their access to government privilege was one feature of the old governing system that carried over into the new. In some areas of governance, such as agriculture and social insurance, opportunities for this kind of clientism multiplied, especially as the federal state's power, orbit of activity, and revenues grew. Paradoxically, there were now many more points of entry through which private interest groups could access government privilege. This struggle within the federal state between clientism and what we might label "redistributionism"—central government policies that attempt to shift resources and power from the more to the less privileged—would continue into the postwar era and on enlarged terrain. On the one side, the Cold War would make permanent a large portion of the military establishment that had taken shape during World War II and put the central state at an extraordinary nexus of privilege—what Americans, following Dwight D. Eisenhower, came to call the military-industrial complex. On the other side, a new social movement, civil rights, compelled the American central state to launch its most far-reaching assault on white privilege in a hundred years. Because the individual states had been so implicated in the maintenance of racial privilege, the new liberal state had to attack them at the deepest level, which it did by challenging and then dismantling the constitutional doctrines that had sustained their authority for almost the entire life of the republic. Here was the project that the Civil War and Reconstruction is alleged to have accomplished, but did not. A new politics of redistributionism grew out of this 1960s' assault on the states, as did ferocious battles about the appropriate scope of federal power in America. Meanwhile, in terms of its size and reach, the American central state would begin to resemble a Leviathan.

PART IV

American Leviathan, 1940s–2010s

8

AN ERA OF NEAR-PERMANENT WAR

Since the days of Andrew Jackson, America has proven skilled at mobi-
lizing sufficient resources to fight wars, dramatically expanding
the military and the scope of governmental power. The nation has
proven equally determined, once wars have ended, to reduce both.
The 2-million-man strong Union Army was scaled down to a regular force of little more than 25,000 soldiers by the 1890s. Likewise,
the nearly 3 million soldiers fighting in World War I were trimmed
to a force of only 120,000 by the 1920s.[1] The central state dismantled many other aspects of its wartime apparatus in postwar periods as well. This pattern of disassembling war regimes helps explain
why neither the Civil War nor World War I yielded thoroughgoing
revolutions in governance. Ambitious state-building impulses came
to the fore in each of those wars. But once the wars ended, they and
their supporters came up against enduring commitments to classically liberal principles, particularly the notion that the powers of the
central state should be limited and fragmented, and that the country
ought to possess only the smallest of standing armies.

The experience of World War II was different, not because of
anything inherent in that war itself, but because it was immediately

followed by another war, the Cold War, unlike any that America had fought. The United States confronted a formidable adversary in the Soviet Union that it dared not fight directly, fearing that in an age of nuclear war, a direct showdown would result in the annihilation of both sides. The option of direct confrontation off the table, the two nations instead clashed in a series of conventional, ostensibly limited proxy wars—civil or regional wars in which America supported one side and the Soviet Union backed the other. These wars erupted in Asia, Africa, and Latin America, and threatened to break out in Europe as well. If particular conflagrations had clear ends, for more than forty years the broader conflict did not. The result was that the United States was on a wartime or near-wartime footing for nearly half a century.

The central state in consequence grew into an institution of extraordinary size and reach. It rested on foundations laid by the New Deal, even as war transformed it into an edifice far different from what the New Dealers had imagined themselves constructing. The nation's large standing military, the military-industrial complex required to support it, and the expanded scope of executive power were the most visible manifestations of this wartime state. Less visible but of equal significance were the system of mass taxation that Americans allowed the central state to impose, and the resulting flood of revenue flowing to the federal government. The ambitions of the central state expanded in tandem with its growing size and funds, supporting major investments in infrastructure, education, research, and welfare.

It has become fashionable to argue that much of this spending was contaminated by its connection to military imperatives. Significant portions of it were. But we might just as well see in some of these central state expansions a new form of surrogacy. National security became a fourth constitutional peg to add to the trinity of the commerce, taxation, and post office clauses—one on which to hang expenditures and initiatives that otherwise might not have passed congressional or judicial muster. Among these initiatives were the spatial reorganization of the economy and population, substantial investments made by the central state to improve the nation's infrastructure, and a vast expansion of higher education and federal support for basic research. This new form of surrogacy embold-ened federal policymakers to imagine what a powerful central state might accomplish not only in the fight against Communism abroad but also in building a better society at home. Even the Republican president Dwight D. Eisenhower was affected in this way, develop-ing an interest in reform that is usually associated with the Great Society liberals of the 1960s. A condition of near-permanent war profoundly altered the landscape of possibility and action regard-ing the role of a central state in America.

WARFARE STATE

In the 1940s, the nation entered an era of near-permanent war that would last for more than forty years. Earlier, in the nineteenth cen-tury, the United States fought Indians for an even longer period of time, but this warfare demanded nowhere near the level of re-sources required by World War II and the Cold War.

During World War II, the United States placed 16 million men and women under arms, with the size of the military cresting at 12 million. But for the outbreak of the Cold War in 1946, Congress would likely have dismantled this warfare state as it had done after World War I. Instead, the United States emerged from the 1940s with the first sizable standing military in its history. The United States did not maintain a Cold War military at anything near the World War II levels, but it did sustain a force of 2.5 million, nearly ten times the size of any previous "postwar" military in American history.[2]

This military was supported by an expanded and refashioned central state apparatus. During World War II, expansion either took place in existing institutions of the government, such as the war and navy departments, or occurred in ad hoc ways, as agencies proliferated without a clear design. The jerry-built structure of the war machine was likely the best achievable during the war emer-gency; in any case, everyone assumed it was adequate to fight a war that if all consuming, was expected to be of relatively short dura-tion. Planning for the Cold War was more systematically organized, especially as government leaders came to see that it could be long and grinding. In 1947, Congress passed the National Security Act, an omnibus piece of legislation that created a substantially new infrastructure to assist the country in fighting a long war. It authorized the National Military Establishment with the power to direct all elements of national defense (in 1949, the National Military Establishment would be reorganized as the Cabinet-level Department of Defense). It created the Joint Chiefs of Staff to improve coordination among the various branches of the armed services as well as the National Security Council and Central Intelligence Agency (CIA).[3]

The national security state grew in other ways as well. The FBI expanded significantly in these years, as J. Edgar Hoover finally got the "peacetime" authority and funds he wanted. By 1949, the FBI's annual appropriation exceeded that of its peak World War II levels; ten years later, its annual funding had more than doubled.[4] The Atomic Energy Commission, established in 1946 to oversee nuclear research and weaponry, built a government empire on the back of the Manhattan Project's laboratories, fissionable materials, weapons, and its tens of thousands of employees. By the early 1950s, the commission's facilities and grounds sprawled across huge stretches in multiple states, occupying more territory than Delaware and Rhode Island combined.[5]

Controversy about the shape and reach of the national security state swirled around many developments in the Cold War's early years. Battles were fought over how large the American military should be and how much control it should exercise over foreign policy; whether the United States should adopt universal military training; what level of taxes the American people would tolerate to support this emerging military establishment; the degree to which the central government should own and operate the manufacturing facilities necessary for the war effort as opposed to contracting with private firms to provide those services; and whether atomic energy research should be placed under civilian or military control.[6]

Many Americans, including senators and congressmen, worried that in expanding its war-making capacity for the long term, the United States would metamorphose into what social scientist

Harold Lasswell had identified in the 1930s as a "garrison state."[7] If America became such a state, and in the process curtailed the liberties of its people, then it would lose the Cold War even if it eventually defeated the Soviet Union. Such worries imbued debates about military preparedness in the late 1940s with unusual intensity, and prompted Congress to establish certain bulwarks that would not be breached: the federal government would not compel every able-bodied young male to serve in its armed forces; it would not, by and large, seek to build and operate its own plants for war materiel; and it would not spend infinite amounts on war preparedness. This campaign to restrain the urgency of military imperatives was partly successful. The numbers of civilians working in national defense fell from more than 2.5 million in 1945 to less than 900,000 by 1949. Federal spending on defense declined just as dramatically in those same years, from more than $80 billion annually to less than $20 billion.[8]

In August 1949, hopes that the nation would survive the Cold War without committing itself to support an extensive and expensive warfare bureaucracy vaporized overnight with the Soviet Union's exploding its first atomic bomb and ending the US monopoly on nuclear technology. In October 1949, the Communist forces of Mao Tse-tung vanquished the pro-American Nationalist forces of Chiang Kai-shek in China, establishing the People's Republic of China. And then in 1950, Communist North Korean troops, backed by the Soviet Union, invaded South Korea, triggering the Korean War.[9]

The Soviet Union's acquisition of the bomb and the "loss of China" to the Communists hit the United States particularly hard. Many Americans in government as well as ordinary citizens feared that Communism seemed on the verge of overwhelming Asia. These circumstances were the ones that impelled the National Security Council in 1950 to issue its famous memorandum, NSC-68, which committed the United States to opposing Communism everywhere and in all ways—militarily, economically, and psychologically.[10]

As war fever once again gripped America, the national security state rapidly expanded in size and sway. Of the 5.3 million people working for the federal government by 1955, 4.1 million—

77 percent—were either in the armed forces or civilians employed by the Department of Defense. Federal government expenditures, meanwhile, shot up from less than $20 billion in 1949 to $55 billion in 1953, and remained in that range for the next ten years. Throughout that period, the federal government committed one-half to two-thirds of every federal dollar to national defense. Even in 1960, a time of relative peace in the Cold War, more than seven out of ten federal employees worked in the defense establishment.[11]

The power of this warfare state rested not only on its personnel and resources but on the techniques of coercion it deployed to root out America's enemies at home and abroad. The central state's coercive powers grew rapidly during these years as new laws were passed and older laws reactivated and repurposed. The Central Intelligence Act of 1949 substantially increased executive power. It gave the new spy agency, which had been established in 1947 to manage foreign threats, enormous authority, and stripped Congress of virtually all the mechanisms it customarily used to hold executive agencies to account. This act allowed the CIA to slip free of democratic oversight and accountability.[12]

The FBI, meanwhile, continued to address domestic threats, armed now with legislation expanding its powers. The 1940 Alien Registration Act, also known as the Smith Act (after its sponsor in the Senate), criminalized speech intended to "teach the duty, necessity, desirability, or propriety of overthrowing or destroying any government in the United States by force or violence."[13] In World War II, the FBI used it to identify and prosecute aliens and others who sympathized with one or more Axis powers. By the late 1940s, however, the agency was using the Smith Act to pursue American Communists. In 1948, Communist Party chairman Eugene Dennis and eleven other leaders of the American Communist Party were convicted and jailed for five years under the act's provisions. Dennis and others were not implicated in any actions to overthrow the US government. Evidence of their sedition rested entirely on their fealty to Communist ideology and the Marxist-Leninist principles that underlay it. The prosecution's case depended less on what they had done than on passages in the writings of Karl Marx and Vladimir Lenin from which the American Communists' intention to overthrow the US government by force could (allegedly) be deduced. In upholding the convictions of these men in 1951, the US Supreme Court significantly increased the government's right to restrict the freedom of thought and speech—an expansion in government censorship authority that the Court justified in light of the dangerous nature of the foe confronting the United States at home and abroad.[14]

Executive order 9835, issued by President Harry Truman in 1947, was an equally coercive piece of disciplinary statecraft. It authorized establishment of the Loyalty Review Board to scrutinize and monitor the activities of all federal employees. Hoover's FBI, the board's investigatory arm, embraced its new assignment, reviewing the files of more than two million government employees and conducting full-scale investigations of more than twenty thousand. In the atmosphere of wartime crisis that permeated the late 1940s, the FBI, like the CIA, was permitted to shield its "confidential sources" from independent review and oversight committees. The release of the FBI from standards of accountability was especially troubling in light of the broad definition of disloyalty that governed the Loyalty Review Board's deliberations. As in the *Dennis v. United States* case, evidence of disloyalty could be adduced not simply from actual acts of sabotage and espionage but also from thoughts deemed subversive and affiliations with groups considered suspicious.[15]

The Smith Act and executive order 9835, in combination, were not that different in intent from the 1918 Sedition Act, which had outlawed "disloyal, profane, scurrilous, or abusive language" directed at the US government, flag, or military. If anything, the 1918 law defined sedition somewhat more broadly than did the 1940s' acts. But in 1918, Congress was determined to allow the Sedition Act to remain a law only as long as the United States was at war. It passed this law after issuing a formal declaration of war on the Central Powers in 1917, and it expected to repeal that law as soon as the war and the wartime emergency it had spawned had ended. Congress followed through on this plan, repealing the Sedition Act in 1920, shortly after the warring parties had signed the Peace of Paris Treaty in 1919. This draconian law—and the willingness to exempt the federal government from constitutional injunctions that otherwise would have applied—lasted but two and a half years. Hoover, then a rising star in the FBI, pleaded with Congress to give him a peacetime sedition law to complete his work of rooting out subversives. Congress refused.[16]

The lasting power that evaded Hoover in the 1920s materialized in the 1940s. Congress allowed the 1940 Alien Registration Act to extend beyond the end of World War II. And because Truman's 1947 executive order had not been preceded by a congressional declaration of war against the Soviet Union, it was not in any formal sense a wartime measure. No one had definitive answers to the pressing questions that followed from this. When would the executive order cease to function? When would the permission given to the federal government to limit freedom of speech and assembly end? All that could be said was that the exemption from the Bill of Rights that had been granted the federal government was necessary as long as the Soviet Union and its allies remained a threat. As the Korean War settled into a stalemate, it began to seem that the state of exemption would continue indefinitely.[17]

Under these circumstances, the central state amassed a regular police force greater in size and power than anything the nation had seen before. Between 1939 and 1953, employment at the FBI increased more than sevenfold, from 1,912 to 13,984. The bureau established a network of 109,119 informants across 11,000 defense plants, research centers, bridges, and telephone exchanges. By 1954, it had placed 26,000 Communist Party members and functionaries on its security index. Anyone appearing on this list could be rounded up at any moment. Another 430,000 people and organizations appeared on a list of "slightly less dangerous individuals."[18]

Hoover supplied information on suspicious individuals to relevant agencies in the executive branch and to the House Un-American Activities Committee, the Senate's Internal Security Committee, and Senator Joseph McCarthy's Government Operations Subcommittee. Such information proved indispensable to the congressional crusade, led by McCarthy in the Senate and Congressman Richard Milhous Nixon in the House of Representatives, to rid American government and society of Communists. Mc-

Carthy, Nixon, and many others shared Hoover's conviction that Communists had infiltrated the Department of State, where they were influencing the formulation of American foreign policy; Hollywood, where they were perverting American filmmaking; the labor movement, where they were leading the masses of American workers astray; universities and public schools, where they were corrupting the minds of American youths; and defense industries, from which they had stolen critical secrets and passed them on to the Soviets.

Individuals and groups within each of these sectors felt the heavy hand of repression. The Department of State dismissed many of its best Asian experts because they had allegedly formulated a policy that had allowed China's Communists to seize power. In conjunction with the Department of Defense, it also took the lead in ridding the federal government of thousands of homosexuals, cast as security risks on account of their purported vulnerability to blackmail by Soviet agents. The US Department of Commerce and the Council of Economic Advisers pushed left-leaning economists to the margins, or out of government service altogether. Intimidated by Congress, the heads of Hollywood studios assembled their own blacklist of known and suspected Communists. Any screenwriter, actor, and other film professional appearing on the list suddenly found it almost impossible to get work. The CIO, desperate to resist criminalization charges, ousted eleven Communist-led unions and almost a million unionists from its federation. Universities fired subversive professors and school boards fired Communist teachers. Julius and Ethel Rosenberg were executed for atomic espionage. Alleged subversives—radical dissenters, whether Communist or not—were purged from a range of institutions. The expanded scope and powers of America's national security state had facilitated this repression. Checks that had formerly limited the central government's ability to intrude on the freedom of individuals collapsed.[19]

The national security state expansion took place under Truman, a Democratic president. Virtually every piece of it was in place by the time that Eisenhower, the first Republican to assume the presidency in two decades, took office in January 1953. Even though

Richard Nixon, one of the most fervent anti-Communist crusaders, served as his vice president, Eisenhower prided himself on his capacity to bring the swelling security state under control. Eisenhower initially tolerated McCarthy but then played a role in bringing him down, especially after McCarthy raised questions about the loyalty of General George C. Marshall and accused the army of harboring subversive elements in its ranks. The Senate censured McCarthy in 1954, the year after the Korean War ended, and McCarthy's influence went into rapid decline. By May 1957, he was dead. Just over a month later, the Supreme Court handed down four civil liberties rulings, each of which overturned a conviction that the government had earlier secured against alleged Communist subversives under the Smith Act. The postwar Red Scare was not yet over, but the courts had stepped in to circumscribe the freedom of government agencies to make accusations and prosecute alleged subversives. Though Eisenhower was not directly involved in these deliberations, he did lower tensions arising from the Cold War both at home and abroad, giving Supreme Court justices more room to maneuver.[20]

Eisenhower also played a part in reining in groups in the military that were eager to deploy nuclear weapons. In 1948, General Curtis E. LeMay, America's most accomplished and bellicose airman, assumed control of the Strategic Air Command (SAC), a military branch formed with little fanfare in 1946. LeMay quickly refashioned SAC into a highly autonomous, aggressive military institution charged with planning and, if necessary, executing nuclear attacks. By 1950, LeMay's SAC had a fleet of more than 250 long-range bombers ready to be armed with nuclear payloads at any time. The same year, LeMay oversaw a simulation of an all-out nuclear attack on the Soviet Union. Twice in 1951, his commander in chief, President Truman, authorized the movement of nuclear bombs and bomb parts from the mainland to air force bases in Guam, making them available for use against the North Koreans and their Chinese and Soviet allies. As these weapons passed beyond the borders of the continental United States, they also moved from civilian to air force control.[21]

Eisenhower did not restrain the nuclear military buildup after he entered office. To the contrary, he authorized a dramatic growth in America's nuclear stockpile, from a thousand in 1952 to a staggering eighteen thousand by the time he left office in 1961.[22] But Eisenhower, America's most distinguished and experienced military man, did not allow LeMay and other generals to bully him into using these devices. He instead envisioned the vast nuclear buildup as a strategy of deterrence. His administration embraced a doctrine called mutual assured destruction, which held that an American nuclear arsenal of overwhelming size, which the Soviets would undoubtedly attempt to match, would make devastation from a nuclear conflagration so complete that neither side would dare use any of its weapons. This doctrine was, on the one hand, an imprudent strategy, especially in its unproven assertion that no leader in possession of a nuclear arsenal would actually use it. On the other hand, as it was conceived by Eisenhower, the doctrine was prudential, at least fiscally, for he held that reliance on nuclear weapons would prove much less costly than maintaining conventional forces large enough to match those of the Soviet Union and China. By the end of his presidency, Eisenhower could claim fiscal success for what came to be known as his administration's New Look policy. In the 1960s, the US national security state was smaller than that of the Soviets in its proportion both to population and to share of the gross domestic product. In addition, Eisenhower successfully reduced tensions between the two superpowers well below the boiling point they had neared in 1950 and 1951. And he kept hotheads like LeMay under wraps.[23]

Yet when Eisenhower left office in 1961, these "achievements" gave him little satisfaction. In one of the more remarkable farewell addresses ever given by a president, Eisenhower took the measure of the national security state that had come into being to fight the Cold War. He pointed to the "immense military establishment" that had developed during his presidency and "large arms industry" that had emerged to support it. Both were "new in the American experience." Together they formed a "military-industrial complex" that was full of "grave implications" for the republic, particularly in terms of enlarging "the potential for the disastrous rise of misplaced power." Eisenhower grasped how the condition of near-permanent war had insulated important parts of the central state from democratic review and accountability—thus posing a serious threat to American republican traditions.[24]

RESHAPING "THE VERY STRUCTURE OF OUR SOCIETY"

The secondary effects of this national security state were also of interest to Eisenhower, who feared they were radiating out from the military and military-industrial districts to "every city, every Statehouse, every office of the Federal government." He intuited that this warfare state had started to reshape, in his words, "the very structure of our society."[25] The transformations wrought by national security were indeed momentous, and most visible in three areas: the shifting locations and foci of American industry; dramatic improvements in the nation's infrastructure; and high levels of federal support for research and education.

The most significant of these saw the nation's economic and social landscape fundamentally reconfigured over the forty-plus-year span of the Cold War. From 1946 to 1991, the centers of both population and of industry—especially those necessary to support a large, technologically sophisticated military—shifted from the North and Midwest to the South and West. A new sort of industrial policy is evident in this movement, much of which was driven by federal government decisions about where to locate the various institutions that would make up the military-industrial complex. That the South would be a major beneficiary of this policy is understandable in light of the extensive archipelago of military bases already situated in this region—in part an inheritance from World War II. In the early Cold War years, 40 percent of spending on military installations was dedicated to maintaining these existing bases and, in some cases, to modernizing them, especially those that trained soldiers, seamen, and airmen in new technologies.[26] The prominence of southern senators in the Senate and House as well as their vigilance on national security matters ensured that the South would continue to benefit from military spending. Thus, for example, Senator Richard Russell and Representative Carl Vinson of Georgia, chairmen of the Senate and House Armed Services committees, respectively, had steered fifteen new military installations to their constituents by 1960, making defense-related jobs the largest source of employment in the Peach State.[27]

The military also needed access to a reliable supply of weaponry and other tools of war. Airplanes, missiles, and aerospace electronics loomed increasingly large in the Cold War arsenal. The government ran some facilities itself, such as in the area of atomic weapons research carried out at the Atomic Energy Commission complex in Oak Ridge, Tennessee.[28] For the actual production of weapons and electronic systems necessary to operate them, however, the federal government turned yet again to its venerable privatization strategy. This meant offering hefty contracts to private companies to persuade them to manufacture what the government needed. Production facilities were located disproportionately in the South and West for a variety of reasons including relatively cheap land, clear weather (for air bases), low taxes, weak unions, access to large amounts of cheap energy yielded by infrastructural improvements initiated by the New Deal, and the prominence of southern and western senators on key congressional committees. Democrats Lyndon Johnson and Sam Rayburn, respectively senate majority leader and house speaker for stretches of the 1950s, used their influence to direct sizable percentages of federal government defense funds and facilities to their state of Texas. When the National Aeronautics and Space Administration (NASA) was rushed into well-funded existence in 1958 to enable the United States to catch up with and then overtake the Soviet Union in space exploration, Johnson and Rayburn steered one of NASA's jewels, the Manned Spacecraft Center, to Houston, ensuring that the Lone Star State would become one of the country's most powerful magnets for space research and development.[29]

Only the West would rival the South as home to defense-related industries. Between 1952 and 1962, the government issued $4 billion worth of military contracts to defense sector firms in Southern

California. By 1959, aerospace companies provided employment to three out of every four manufacturing workers in San Diego County. Even in Los Angeles and Orange counties, both of which had somewhat more balanced economies, more than 40 percent of manufacturing served defense needs by the early 1960s. Seattle rivaled Southern California in the scale of its defense industries chiefly because Boeing, one of the country's largest airplane manufacturers, had its corporate and manufacturing headquarters there. Washington senator Henry "Scoop" Jackson was so indefatigable in his efforts to bring federal government contracts to his part of the Northwest that he was commonly referred to as the "senator from Boeing." The federal government invested heavily in defense-related facilities along the southern and western rims of the United States, from South Carolina west to Texas, Arizona, and southern California, and then north to Washington State. These investments triggered a large migration of capital, research, manufacturing jobs, and finally people from the Northeast and Midwest to the South and West. The Cold War, and specifically the regional targeting of defense expenditures, made possible the rise of the Sunbelt and Far West.[30]

That the central government targeted certain industries and regions for its investments signaled that it was engaged in industrial planning, albeit not the sort that Walter Reuther and other pro-labor New Dealers had favored in the 1930s and 1940s. Neither labor nor the public had a seat at the table where decisions about where to build military installations and where to invest in defense-related research and manufacturing were being made. Rather, this industrial policy hewed more closely to the pattern that took shape in agriculture, in which contractors worked closely with powerful committees and committee chairs in Congress, with their deliberations taking place ever more often in iron triangles that were impervious to public scrutiny and accountability. National security provided an unassailable pretext for exempting these economically consequential decisions from the transparency of democratic procedure.

Dramatic improvements in the country's infrastructure, most evident in dams, electric generation, and roads, also facilitated the economic shift from the Northeast to the Southwest. The federal government had launched an extensive project of dam building in the 1930s, primarily in the South and West, both to make water available to agriculture and to generate high enough levels of hydroelectric power to support industrial and population growth in those arid and semiarid areas. By the 1940s and 1950s, such infrastructural investments were yielding impressive results. Water from dams on the Colorado River supplied both water and electricity, carried by thousands of miles of pipelines and electric lines, to Los Angeles and Phoenix, powering the meteoric postwar growth of these cities. Dams on the Columbia River in Washington State, meanwhile, generated the hydroelectricity that fueled Seattle's rapid growth. Dams on the Tennessee River built by the Tennessee Valley Authority generated enough electricity to supply the energy needs both of the nuclear research facilities in Oak Ridge and of numerous towns and small cities located in and around the Tennessee Valley. The initiative for these efforts rested with the federal government, and the Cold War increasingly came to justify their scale and expense.[31]

The federal government supplemented this network of dams, waterways, and electric lines with an equally impressive network of interstate highways authorized by Congress in 1956. Over the next forty years, this project yielded forty-one thousand miles of new, high-speed roads, with almost all the costs paid by federal dollars. The effects of this construction project were evident in the reorganization of the US landscape around a continent-spanning Cartesian grid of east–west and north–south highways—arguably the most comprehensive reorganization of American space since the land surveys launched by the Northwest Ordinances of 1785 and 1787. It was evident as well in the sprawling suburbs that now extended out from major cities as much as sixty miles in multiple directions; in the triumph of automobiles and trucks over railroads as the primary mechanisms of transportation; in the avidity with which Americans took to the road for both business and pleasure; and in the nation's addiction to cheap gasoline. If the effects of this infrastructural initiative were multiple and varied, the causes were ultimately to be found in defense. Congress labeled the road project

"The National System of Interstate and Defense Highways," and justified its expense by reference to the way in which these new roads would facilitate both the quick transfer of military units to parts of the United States under attack and rapid evacuation of people from areas threatened by atomic bombs. The defense-inspired initiatives thus began to transform, in Eisenhower's words, "the very structure" of American society.[32]

The Cold War transformation was equally apparent in the federal government's involvement in research and education. This involvement emerged in the first instance from World War II, which had demonstrated the centrality of scientific research to success on the battlefield. Atomic energy, radar, and penicillin—to name but three critical breakthroughs—all emerged from laboratories in America and Britain that were connected to the war effort. Cold War military planners, quick to grasp that success against the Soviet Union might likewise depend on scientific advances, doubled down on the country's commitment to basic research, channeling most of it through the expanding university system. In the early years of the Cold War, funds for university research came overwhelmingly from the military itself—the army, navy, and air force—or from government agencies, such as the Atomic Energy Commission, closely allied with the military. Between 1946 and 1950, these institutions accounted for 96 percent of federal funds invested in physics and chemistry in the nation's universities. A decade later, NASA began pumping large amounts of money into university-based rocket and orbital science at US universities, lifting out of obscurity an array of public universities in the South, such as those in Alabama, Georgia, and Florida. NASA funds and support almost single-handedly created the University of Alabama at Huntsville in the 1960s, changing what had been a declining textile town into an improbably located high-tech corridor.

The country's other high-tech corridors—Route 128 in Boston, the Research Triangle in North Carolina, and Silicon Valley in Palo Alto—are similarly unimaginable without federal support for research connected to Cold War initiatives. These areas thrived on their connections to universities—Harvard and the Massachusetts Institute of Technology in eastern Massachusetts, Duke and the

University of North Carolina in North Carolina, and Stanford and the University of California at Berkeley in northern California. These universities, in turn, became formidable institutions as a consequence of the vast federal resources flowing into them. In 1940, the federal government had funded less than half of the nation's research and development. By 1960, it was funding two-thirds.[33]

The central state was also funneling large sums to universities through the Servicemen's Readjustment Act of 1944, also known as the GI Bill, which offered millions of World War II servicemen— everyone, in fact, who had served at least ninety days and had not been dishonorably discharged—an impressive array of benefits, including tuition payments and living expenses for those accepted into college or university. In 1950, the US government spent more on the educational benefits of this bill than it did on the vaunted Marshall Plan, the nation's grand and expensive initiative to rebuild Western Europe. By 1956, more than 2 million servicemen had enrolled in colleges and universities under the GI Bill, in the process propelling a major expansion of higher education. Between 1940 and 1960, enrollment in institutions of higher education more than doubled from 1.5 to 3.6 million. The GI Bill had not been conceived as a Cold War measure, but the fact that the peak availability of its educational benefits coincided with the first decade of the Cold War (1946–56), significantly accelerated the growth of higher education in America.[34]

That the federal government was interested in harnessing research to its defense efforts prompted efforts to both shape the nature of the research and police the politics of researchers receiving federal funds. The policing was directed most concertedly at the atomic scientists, and at theoretical physicists in particular, who were at the forefront of nuclear research. These scientists' research was, on the one hand, the most important of all the initiatives that the US government was supporting. On the other hand, crucial sections of this community had been liberal and even left leaning during the 1930s. Though only a very few had attempted to pass on American atomic knowledge to the Soviets, the discovery of spies in their ranks put the entire community under suspicion and increased demands on them to demonstrate their loyalty.

In this climate, arguably legitimate political positions—namely, that atomic energy ought to be placed under the control of civilians in the United States and neutral international agencies abroad— were increasingly deemed to be subversive, even treasonous. Many atomic scientists were subjected repeatedly to loyalty investigations, and some were stripped of the security clearances enabling them to work. The most startling instance of this features Robert Oppenheimer, who headed up the World War II Manhattan Project that gave the United States the bomb. Oppenheimer's brother had been a member of the Communist Party, as had Robert's wife before they were married. Oppenheimer, for a time, had "lots of communist friends," as he freely reported in 1948. But he rejected Soviet overtures to spy on their behalf and received sterling endorsements from such anti-Communist stalwarts as Nixon. None of this was enough to save him from further surveillance and wiretapping, especially once he announced his opposition on humanitarian grounds to US efforts to develop the hydrogen bomb. Although the federal government found no evidence to support the charge that Oppenheimer was a subversive, it nevertheless denied him a security clearance. His place in the firmament of distinguished atomic scientists was taken by Wernher von Braun, the German physicist and rocket expert whose constancy in terms of anti-Communism and support for US Cold War aims was enough to satisfy America's gatekeepers, notwithstanding his well-documented history as a loyal Nazi scientist who knew that slave labor from concentration camps was being used to produce Adolf Hitler's V-1 rockets.[35]

As egregious as these developments were, they should not be construed as evidence of the warfare state's control of all of higher education—a goal beyond the reach of even the most determined Cold Warriors. Higher education was resistant to central state control. Universities were for the most part either private and therefore responsible first and foremost to their boards of trustees, or public institutions answerable to state legislatures. Most had been in existence long before the Cold War—many of them for a period of fifty or a hundred years or more. Many had strong traditions of liberal arts and free inquiry that were core elements of their mission. When pressured by the demands of a central state preoccupied with

war, higher education leaders and their supporters in Congress almost immediately put buffers between the universities and the national security state. One such buffer can be seen in the National
Science Foundation (NSF), an agency established by Congress in
1950 that served as an intermediary between basic research and the
needs of the national security state. Vannevar Bush, an MIT engineer and one of the NSF's strongest advocates, articulated the governing philosophy behind its founding: "Support of basic research
in the public and private colleges, universities, and research institutes must leave the internal control of policy, personnel, and the
method and scope of the research to the institutions themselves."[36]
The imperatives of national security and the small sums initially
appropriated by Congress for the NSF at first limited its significance. But the agency did incubate a critical principle of independence and autonomy that would grow in influence over the next
fifty years.[37]

A second way of protecting higher education from Cold War imperatives was less principled than opportunistic. College and university administrators who wanted to be able to take federal money
without turning their institutions into adjuncts to the warfare state
expansively defined the compass of national security to include liberal arts (educated citizens), so-called area studies (amassing social
science knowledge of regions of the world likely to be lightning
rods for Cold War conflict), and research that addressed domestic
studies in order to demonstrate what a "free society" could accomplish. Scholars have argued that this expanded notion of national
security contaminated and invalidated broad areas of knowledge.
This was so in some cases, but in others universities successfully
deployed national security as a new form of surrogacy: using funds
ostensibly appropriated for one purpose to support another purpose. Just as 1910s' purity crusaders who wanted to increase the
central government's power over moral life turned to the commerce
clause for authority needed to banish prostitution, in the 1950s,
those who wanted to increase federal support for universities looked
to national defense for justification.

The student protests that erupted in the 1960s and 1970s were
ostensibly indicative of the extent to which the priorities of the

national security state had corrupted the universities. Certainly, the student radicals who wanted to banish every trace of the military-industrial complex from their campuses felt this way. That the protests spread so quickly and with such fury might be better interpreted, however, as evidence of the national security state's *limited* power over some of its most important investments and initiatives. By the 1960s, America's colleges and universities were nurturing a profusion of political philosophies and intellectual projects that cannot be understood as extensions of a national security imperative. To the contrary, by the 1960s and 1970s, the nation's universities were devouring federal funds while defying government efforts to force their research and scholarship into narrowly conceived channels.[38]

FROM CLASS TO MASS TAXATION

The responsibilities—foreign and domestic, military and civilian—that the American federal state assumed during these years cost a great deal of money, and were funded primarily by a system of mass and progressive taxation. Before the 1940s, only wealthy Americans—about 4 to 8 percent of the working population—paid any income tax.[39] The Wealth Tax Act of 1935 had made the income tax steeply progressive (those making more than $50,000 paid tax at a rate of 31 percent, and those making more than $5 million paid at a rate of 75 percent), but did not significantly broaden the base of taxpayers.[40]

This class taxation system turned into a system of mass taxation in World War II when the federal government elected to extract revenue from a large percentage of the country's income earners to finance the war. The number of wage earners subject to taxation nearly doubled from 1939 to 1940, and then almost quintupled across the next four years. By 1945, nearly two-thirds of American wage earners were paying income tax in contrast to the single-digit percentage paying taxes in the 1930s. Annual tax receipts, meanwhile, rose twentyfold between 1939 and 1945, from $892 million to $18.4 billion.[41] In 1943 the government adopted a clever new mechanism for collecting these taxes, requiring employers to deduct taxes from their employees' pay and turn the money over directly to the federal government. In a stroke, this system eliminated tax collectors, reviled figures working in hostile circumstances that lessened their effectiveness in raising funds. Replacing tax collectors with a system of employer-authorized deductions greatly enhanced the efficiency of revenue extraction systems.[42]

That this system of mass taxation emerged during World War II is not surprising in light of the revenue demands of total war. More surprising is that the system stayed in place after the war ended. This, as was the case with other aspects of the national security state, generated a good deal of controversy between 1946 and 1950. The Republicans who took control of Congress in 1947 wanted to roll back wartime taxation. In 1948, they engineered a significant tax cut that was envisioned as a first step toward disassembling the entire system. Indeed, the percentage of taxpayers in the working population declined from its World War II peak—from 65 percent in 1945 to 57 percent in 1949.[43] But as the Cold War heated up in 1949–50, and as tensions with the Soviet Union, China, and Korea intensified, the GOP's antitax efforts were thwarted. The United States accelerated its nuclear research and weapons program, and geared up for a major land war in Korea, putting an end to talk of cutting defense expenditures and taxes.

By the 1950s, the Republicans were eager to join a bipartisan coalition committed to a global struggle against Communism. A consensus developed spanning both ends of the political spectrum, from the Left of the Democratic Party to the conservative districts of the Republican Party. It posited that the success of this struggle depended on a system of mass revenue extraction. Wilbur Mills, the conservative southern Democrat who held the chairmanship of the House Ways and Means Committee, was hardly profligate, but appreciated the existing system's necessity: "We live in a complex and dangerous time and there is no use pretending on some happy day very soon we can cut expenditures to the point where we will no longer need large tax revenues," he said in 1959.[44] Most members of Congress on both sides of the aisle shared Mills's sentiment, and serious objections came only from largely irrelevant fringes of the Right.[45]

It would be hard to overestimate the significance of the decision to perpetuate this high-tax system. Never before had such a substantial, regular, and long-lasting stream of revenue come into the central state's coffers. It helped to fundamentally alter the landscape of possibility for federal government activity. Americans inside and outside the federal government began to conceive of it as resource rich and thus capable of major and varied interventions in economic, social, and cultural life. And they started to contemplate harnessing its power to solve problems that were only tangentially related to national security.

Consider Eisenhower's thinking on the question of mass taxation and uses to which these augmented government revenues could be put. Eisenhower made his thoughts public in 1954 as he was steering a complex and comprehensive overhaul of the federal tax code through Congress. The bill was intended to codify the changes in the taxation system that had occurred since 1939 and address the problems that those changes had generated. Eisenhower was especially concerned about tax exemption, a feature of the bill that in his mind, threatened a cherished principle: all working Americans should pay some income tax.

Tax exemption (declaring certain streams of income as wholly or partially tax free) was not in itself a new principle, as universities and religious institutions had been able to exempt their income from taxation for decades. But the 1954 bill was designed to dramatically widen the scope of tax exemption by extending its benefits from institutions to individual taxpayers. Republicans in Congress wanted to confer most of the new exemptions on wealthy Americans as a way of moderating the progressivity of the tax code.[46] Democrats responded with amendments designed to grant working-class Americans exemptions of equal significance. The Democrats' demand for an equality of exemption alarmed Eisenhower, who believed that it would, if encoded into law, fatally compromise the entire mass taxation system. Thus, Eisenhower went on national television and radio on March 15, 1954, to defend the federal income tax.[47]

This system's rationale, Eisenhower told the American people, was simple but powerful: paying income taxes to the federal government had become part of Americans' civic duty. While conceding that paying taxes was a burden, Eisenhower asserted that it was, like military service, one that "every real American is proud to carry." He had seen too many "examples of American pride" and "unassuming but inspiring courage" to believe that "anyone privileged to live in this country wants someone else to pay his own fair and just share of the cost of government."[48]

That a Republican president would choose to defend taxation in such civic terms was itself noteworthy. Equally striking was Eisenhower's vision of the uses to which the revenues could be devoted. Defense, of course, topped his list, consuming "70 cents out of each dollar spent by your government." But Eisenhower dreamed of using tax revenues to do more, to implement a "great program to build a stronger America for all our people." "We want to improve and expand our social security program," he told his national audience. "We want a broader and stronger system of unemployment insurance. We want more and better homes for our people. We want to do away with slums in our cities. We want to foster a much improved health program." Broadened Social Security, better unemployment insurance, urban renewal, and national health care— here, in embryo, was the vision that would animate the Great Society, the ambitious legislative program pushed through Congress by Democratic president Johnson in the 1960s to complete the welfare state that Roosevelt and the New Deal had launched in the 1930s. Already in the 1950s, this liberal vision was being articulated not just by Democrats but rather by a moderate Republican.[49]

Here we can see the coalescence of a liberal consensus, the core of which, as Godfrey Hodgson showed nearly forty years ago, was a belief in the capacity of the federal government to solve economic and social problems. The policy successes in agriculture, industrial relations, and social welfare in the 1930s had led liberal reformers to embrace this belief, and the federal government's 1940s'

successes—winning World War II and resuscitating capitalism—
brought many Republicans on board. If not for the Cold War, this
consensus would have likely crumbled in the midst of the conservative resurgence of the late 1940s. Instead, the crucial Cold War
events of 1949 and 1950 reinvigorated it, and widened assent to the
proposition that a large federal state, armed with a powerful military and efficient mass taxation system, would be a core feature
of American politics for the long term.[50] The new fiscal flushness
of the central state was impelling many citizens and politicians to
contemplate how the federal government might enter more and
more areas of social life, and then engineer solutions for the problems they found there.

One of these areas was civil rights and civil liberties. It was
hardly to be expected that a central state preoccupied with war—
and ready to trample on the liberties of those who opposed its war
aims—should become deeply enmeshed in struggles to defend the
rights of vulnerable groups, most notably racial minorities, religious minorities, and women. But this is what happened in the
1960s. Winning these struggles entailed the federal government
taking on the states, to curtail their freedom to pass laws that dis-
criminated on the basis of race, religion, gender, and sexuality. It
required that the central government strip the states of their police
power—a doctrine that had long given the states unassailable authority on these matters. The New Deal had imparted to this central state the will to do so; the Cold War gave it the resources, legitimacy, and courage to move ahead with this formidable task.

9

BREAKING THE POWER
OF THE STATES

The growth in the size and powers of the central state in the 1940s and
1950s rested on a broad consensus on three vital matters: the threat
of the Soviet Union had to be contained; government could be an
effective tool in managing and even democratizing capitalism; and
the poorest and most vulnerable citizens deserved some level of public support. But there was little consensus in other areas in which
the federal government was flexing its powers, among them the
right of African Americans to live their lives free of discrimination
and with access to the same opportunities as white Americans; the
right of Catholics and Jews to be free of Protestant religion in the
public schools; and the right of individuals of all races and creeds
to make decisions about marriage, sexuality, and reproduction free
of government interference. Management of these contentious issues had traditionally fallen within the purview of the states. In the
1960s, the Supreme Court ruled that the central government would
honor that control on the condition that states bring their laws into
accordance with the Bill of Rights and Fourteenth Amendment.
The long-delayed confrontation between the federal government
and states, between liberal and illiberal conceptions of governance,
was joined.

Once the civil rights movement commenced, this confrontation became inescapable. African Americans had fought for decades for full rights of citizenship. Only in the twenty years following World War II, however, did their efforts coalesce into a mass protest movement drawing tens of thousands, and then hundreds of thousands, black and white protesters. The movement was part of a worldwide insurgency by people of color against Western domination and white supremacy, precipitated in part by the crisis into which the war had thrust European empires. The success of the Japanese in overrunning US and European imperial outposts in East Asia stripped the West of its aura of impregnability. The ensuing collapse of European empires supported the conviction spreading among the colonized nonwhite masses of Asia and Africa that their moment of liberation was at hand. A similar aspiration to end race-based subjugation took root among African Americans.

Added to this was the postwar reckoning with the Nazi racial holocaust, which shook up the complacency with which many whites had long viewed the nation's racial ideologies and practices. Some whites positioned at high levels in the government were motivated less by conscience than by realpolitik. They feared that if the United States did not remedy its racial problem, many of the emerging nations in Asia and Africa, most with majority nonwhite populations, would likely align themselves with the Soviet Union—which claimed to have used Communism to eliminate racial inequality from its midst. The atmosphere of urgency generated by the Cold War helps to explain the timing of the Supreme Court's stunning 1954 decision in *Brown v. Board of Education*, which struck down the segregated system of education that had prevailed throughout the South and in parts of the North for more than half a century. That decision, in turn, added impetus to a civil rights movement already taking shape.

Most aspects of that movement are well known: the mass protests of African Americans in the South, many of them churchgoers or university students, who declared that they no longer would abide by the rules of Jim Crow; the massive, increasingly violent resistance of white southerners determined to defend their way of life and assert the right to govern themselves as they long had, even if it meant defying federal law or federal court orders; the courage of civil rights protesters in the face of such violence and their ability to stir the conscience of the nation, and impel Congress, itself reeling from the violence of John F. Kennedy's 1963 assassination, to pass in 1964 and 1965 the most far-reaching civil and voting rights legislation since the 1860s. This legislation launched a Second Reconstruction as sweepingly ambitious as the first. The legislation not only outlawed Jim Crow in the southern states but also established mechanisms to dismantle it. It gave protesters the tools with which to attack the practices and structures of white supremacy in the North as well as the South. The advance of the civil rights movement, in turn, triggered a broad rights revolution manifesting itself in swelling campaigns for religious, gender, and sexual equality. Individuals and groups increasingly voiced demands to be free of religion in public schools, marry a partner of their choosing, and have control over reproductive choices.[1]

For all that we know about the civil rights movement, that its success required a fundamental change in the relations between the states and federal government has been inadequately explored. Laws governing race, marriage, sexuality, reproduction, and religion were largely the province of the states, written and passed by state legislatures. Upending the existing structure of racial and personal life required not only invalidating laws that supported this structure but also denying states the capacity to pass similar laws in the future. The states, in other words, had to be stripped of their autonomy and police power. The Supreme Court unleashed its assault on states in the 1960s, and would soon be joined by an executive and Congress flush with Cold War revenues and eager to humble the states.

The Cold War gave the central state the confidence to take on the states. That confidence rested on the new fiscal reality created by the mass taxation system established during World War II and maintained during the Cold War: the federal government was now revenue rich. As late as 1938, the states accounted for nearly 60 percent of total government revenues. A mere ten years later, that percentage had been halved, and the share of revenue controlled by the central state had soared to 70 percent of the total.[2]

In only a decade, in other words, the federal government had gone from being the poor cousin in the family of American government to being its wealthiest member. This radical change in the location of public funds silently though profoundly reordered the landscape of federal-state relations. The fiscal power of the federal government put it in the driver's seat of social policy, with the states shunted to the backseat, and more and more compelled to go along for the ride. We should contemplate the irony of this transformation: the same government that would commit itself to the pursuit of individual rights to a degree unprecedented in American history had become a national security Leviathan.

The Supreme Court led the assault on the states in the name of individual rights, deploying two strategies. The first, known as "incorporation," was relatively straightforward. It entailed using the Fourteenth Amendment to require every state to respect liberties mandated by the Bill of Rights. The second strategy, known as "substantive due process," was, as its opaque name implies, anything but straightforward. The Supreme Court used it to identify liberties deserving of constitutional protection even though these liberties had not been mentioned by name either in the Constitution of 1789 or in any of the subsequent amendments. Privacy was the most important such liberty in the eyes of the 1960s Supreme Court, which invoked it to give women the right to use birth control and have abortions. Invoking privacy, the Court also gave women and men the right to marry spouses of their own choosing. In none of these private decisions was government to have a say.

The effort to find a right to privacy in the Constitution was, on the one hand, a commendable attempt to adapt the country's ancient Constitution to the realities of modern life. On the other hand, it raised troubling questions about how far nonelected judges—as opposed to popularly elected legislatures—could go in delineating the content of constitutionally guaranteed rights. As we will see, several of the justices on the Warren Court—the Court that undertook the 1960s' assault on the states—were themselves concerned about the tools they were using to end the control that states had long possessed over private life.

This chapter begins with a glance back to the late nineteenth and early twentieth centuries, when Supreme Court jurists first developed the two strategies—incorporation and substantive due process—that defined the work of the Warren Court. It explains why the federal courts waited until the 1950s and 1960s to deploy these strategies. It then reconstructs the remarkable breadth and intensity of the Court's assault on the states. It concludes with an examination of how President Lyndon Baines Johnson and his Democratic coalition themselves sought to break the power of the states in the course of implementing the Great Society. By the mid-1960s, blows were raining down on the states from multiple federal redoubts. As a consequence, the states emerged from the 1960s the weakest they had been in any period of American history, save for the years of the Civil War itself. Their vaunted power had been corralled and contained.

RIGHTS JURISPRUDENCE AND A LIVING CONSTITUTION

The Bill of Rights, which had articulated the proposition that every individual had basic rights that no government could infringe, had long given civil rights and civil liberties special resonance in the United States. But as we have seen, the eighteenth-century decision to exempt state governments from having to adhere to its provisions circumscribed its reach. As well, the powers of the states were only temporarily eviscerated during the Civil War period. The Court, in a series of decisions in the 1870s and 1880s, restored to the states many of the powers that the war itself and the constitutional amendments that emerged from it had taken away. Thus, even the vaunted Fourteenth Amendment—and its declaration that "no State shall make or enforce any law which shall abridge the privileges or immunities of citizens of the United States . . . [or] deprive any person of life, liberty, or property, without due process of law"—proved to be a surprisingly weak tool for protecting the rights of individual Americans for fifty to seventy-five years after the amendment's 1868 ratification.[3]

Yet the post–Civil War era was not static in terms of jurisprudence and rights thinking. A new "rights jurisprudence" emerged between the 1880s and 1920s; though stalling in the 1930s and 1940s, it would regain its momentum in the 1950s and 1960s, and prove indispensable to 1960s' breakthroughs. One track of this rights jurisprudence actively sought to rehabilitate the Fourteenth Amendment, and specifically, find in its privileges, immunities, and due process clauses sanction for making the Bill of Rights incumbent on the states. In theory, it might have been easy to harness the Fourteenth Amendment for this purpose. A jurist could easily make the argument that imposing federal will on the states had been the amendment's intent all along.[4] But the damage done to the amendment by Supreme Court decisions in the 1870s and 1880s was acute and lasting. Most notably, the Supreme Court ruled in the *Slaughterhouse Cases* that the Fourteenth Amendment protected only a narrow group of individual rights from encroachment by the states. Subsequent rulings—*United States v. Cruikshank*, the *Civil Rights Cases*, and *Hurtado v. California*—reinforced the idea that individuals could not claim that the Fourteenth Amendment gave them protection against state governments that chose not to adhere to the Bill of Rights.[5] It took another war crisis, this one involving the mass violation of civil liberties during World War I, to persuade the federal courts to consider anew the question of whether the Bill of Rights protected individuals from state government intrusion. Responding to these pressures in 1925, the Supreme Court ruled that socialist Benjamin Gitlow had been unfairly jailed by New York State for publishing a radical manifesto in 1919. Freedom of speech and the press, the Court then ruled, were fundamental rights enjoyed by all Americans; no governmental body, federal, state, or municipal, could abrogate them except under emergency circumstances. The Court followed that declaration with a 1931 decision, *Near v. Minnesota*, overturning a state law because it infringed on the freedom of the press. These were among the first occasions in US history in which the Supreme Court ordered states to respect the rights set forth in the First Amendment.[6]

Jurists and legal scholars began to use the term "incorporation" to describe this process of imposing the Bill of Rights on the states.

It would become one of the most consequential judicial doctrines of the twentieth century. The road to incorporation, however, was not straight. Full incorporation could not be accomplished by a single decision. To the contrary, every right enumerated in the Bill of Rights required its own judicial struggle, with plaintiffs coming forward to demand compliance and taking their grievances to court. Multiple judicial challenges were usually required to improve the chances that one would eventually serve as an appropriate test case for the Supreme Court. Even then, victory was not assured. In the 1930s and 1940s, Supreme Court justices were divided on the issue of whether all the rights set forth in the Bill of Rights were to be incorporated under the Fourteenth Amendment or only those deemed to be "fundamental."[7] And all the justices understood that a robust program of incorporation would put the Supreme Court on a collision course with the states, many of which had laws that did not accord with the freedoms and rights set forth in the first ten amendments. The collision with the southern states and the many laws that governed race relations in that region was going to be particularly harsh.[8]

A second track of emerging jurisprudence in the late nineteenth and early twentieth centuries arose from discussions about the meaning of the word "liberty" in the Fourteenth Amendment. Did a person's liberty consist only of freedoms specifically enumerated in the Bill of Rights, such as freedom of speech, assembly, the press, and religion? Or did it entail something broader and deeper— namely, the right to be free of government intrusiveness in all its forms, regardless of whether the founders had enshrined that freedom by name in the Bill of Rights?

The first jurists to answer this last question affirmatively were those who devised laissez-faire constitutionalism in the late nineteenth century. Associate Justice Stephen Field and his partners on the Supreme Court had come to see liberty of contract as an inviolable dimension of personhood. They further held that the Constitution in general and Fourteenth Amendment in particular protected this liberty. Field's heirs saw *Lochner v. New York* (1905), a decision striking down a New York State law that limited the number of hours that employers could require bakers to work, as a triumph for their jurisprudence. In the wake of *Lochner*, individual workers and industrialists gained the liberty to negotiate the terms of employment.[9]

This strategy of locating in the Constitution, specifically in the Fourteenth Amendment, rights that were implied but not specifically enumerated came to be called "substantive due process." This technical and abstruse term should not be allowed to obscure the profound nature of the jurisprudential innovation it embodied. Its proponents had come to see the Constitution as a flexible document whose meaning might change as jurists sought legal solutions to problems arising from economic, social, and cultural developments that the document's framers could not have foreseen. Substantive due process gave Supreme Court judges the ability to both deduce a new constitutional right and, by the terms of the Fourteenth Amendment, compel all governments in America, including states and municipalities, to respect it. As such, substantive due process would function in ways similar to incorporation: it would compel rights enforcement on state governments and whittle away the states' police power.[10]

If laissez-faire constitutionalists such as Field were the first to embrace substantive due process, Progressive jurists such as Louis Brandeis, who joined the Supreme Court in 1916, soon were influenced by it as well. As early as 1890, Brandeis and a collaborator, Samuel Warren, had elaborated a right to privacy that had no explicit standing in the Constitution. At first Brandeis was content to root this right in the common law, and in particular in its recognition that "a man's house" was "his castle, impregnable."[11] But he came to believe that making privacy a robust right required that it be anchored in the Constitution, alongside other core rights. Such anchoring would oblige jurists to conceive of the Constitution not as a set of statutes set in stone whose meaning was immutable but rather as a living document whose principles, Brandeis wrote, could address matters "of which the Fathers could not have dreamed." In applying constitutional principles, Brandeis noted, "our contemplation cannot be only of what has been but of what may be. Under any other rule a constitution would indeed be as easy of application as it would be deficient in efficacy and power," with its principles converted "into impotent and lifeless formulas."[12] Brandeis wanted the US Constitution to be potent and efficacious. To make it so, judges had to adapt its eighteenth-century principles to novel circumstances and, occasionally, discern in those principles as yet unenumerated rights.[13]

Philosophically, Brandeis and his supporters would come close to the laissez-faire constitutionalists who first delineated substantive due process. This helps to explain why Brandeis in 1923 joined a majority of Supreme Court justices, including several laissez-faire supporters, in overturning a 1920 Nebraska law prohibiting the teaching of German in public schools. The justices held that the state law unduly interfered with the rights of parents to determine the content of their children's education. In making this argument, this Court embraced an expansive definition of personal liberty consonant with Brandeis's conception of privacy. Liberty, the Court declared in 1923, included the right of parents to "establish a home and bring up children" in ways that they deemed appropriate. If parents wanted to send their children to a German-speaking school, they had a right to do so. No government could interfere with that right, except in the most exceptional of circumstances. This decision along with a companion one the following year, *Pierce v. Society of Sisters*, were the work of Progressives as much as the laissez-faire camp. These Court rulings would come to be regarded as substantive due process cases equal in import to *Lochner*. They set precedents for future Supreme Court decisions that would seek to dismantle dense webs of state laws governing marriage, sexuality, religion, and morals.[14]

Progressive jurists found common ground with laissez-faire jurists on the question of a living Constitution and the need to articulate rights that the framers had implied but not expressed, but they never formally claimed the doctrine of substantive due process as their own. The *Lochner* decision had appalled them. They regarded the argument that liberty of contract deserved constitutional protection as nothing more than a crude effort by elites to turn the Supreme Court into a supporter of corporate America.

They fought against this liberty whenever possible and in the New Deal era persuaded the Supreme Court to deny it constitutional protection.[15] During their long struggle against *Lochner*, Progressives fashioned themselves as fierce critics of substantive due process. And yet because Progressives—and their liberal successors—wanted the courts to embrace rights not enumerated in the Constitution, such as the right to privacy, they had no choice but to adopt a jurisprudential philosophy similar to that of their laissez-faire antagonists. The Brandeisian camp used substantive due process in fact while opposing it in name—a stance that over the course of the twentieth century, would several times result in legal reasoning that rendered some of its key judicial decisions suspect.

By the 1920s and early 1930s, then, the Supreme Court had two doctrines, incorporation and substantive due process, with which to attack the powers of the states. Yet these doctrines exercised only intermittent influence across the second quarter of the twentieth century. As we saw in the case of agricultural reform, New Dealers were reluctant to attack the states, believing that the latter's legislative and administrative support was crucial to the success of New Deal programs. Conservative Supreme Court justices, anxious to avoid confrontations with the states over the police power, limited their support for incorporation to a small number of rights, such as free speech, that they deemed fundamental. Progressive jurists, meanwhile, were focused on destroying the legacy of *Lochner*, which required them to assail the legitimacy of substantive due process as a strategy. For all of these reasons, the application of the incorporation and substantive due process strategies stalled in the 1930s and 1940s.

THE WARREN COURT TAKES SHAPE

In the 1950s and 1960s, the Supreme Court made these strategies central to its jurisprudence. The Court's turnaround materialized in part because the justices were reckoning with the forces that characterized the historical moment. In a world threatened by totalitarianisms of the Left and Right, and in which protest movements by people of color were moving from the periphery to the center of politics, the pressures on the leaders of America's central state—its Supreme Court justices included—to affirm the rights and dignity of all human beings were steadily increasing. A fundamental makeover in membership between 1937 and 1956 further accelerated the Supreme Court's about-face, as aged justices beholden to older jurisprudential ways died, and younger justices who had come of political age during the New Deal and World War II took their places.

Franklin D. Roosevelt executed much of the overhaul in the Court's membership between 1937 and 1943, appointing eight Supreme Court justices, more than any president other than Washington himself. Dwight D. Eisenhower completed the makeover when he appointed a new chief justice, Earl Warren, in 1953, and a new associate justice, William Brennan, in 1956. The three most important appointments during this nineteen-year stretch were the first, Black, and two of the last three, Warren and Brennan.[16]

Prior to taking a seat on the Supreme Court in 1937, Black had been a US senator from Alabama and a ardent New Dealer. Convinced that the increased power of the central government was legitimate and that states ought to be bound by the Bill of Rights, Black became the Court's strongest advocate of incorporation. That he had emerged from a states' rights background and had been a member of the Alabama Ku Klux Klan in the 1920s made his determination to enforce the Fourteenth Amendment on the states particularly meaningful. Brandeis, who would have been a natural ally, retired from the Court in 1939 (and died in 1941), but Black was able to gather three other Roosevelt appointees, William O. Douglas, Frank Murphy, and Wiley Blount Routledge, into a Bill of Rights–civil libertarian wing of the Court. For a time he was stymied by Felix Frankfurter, another Roosevelt appointee. A Brandeis protégé and onetime New Dealer, Frankfurter had taken a conservative turn in the 1940s, arguing passionately for judicial restraint and for respecting the legislative choices of the states, no matter how politically distasteful. The surprising conservatism of

Frankfurter was matched by the unexpected liberalism of Warren and his closest ally on the Court, Brennan.[17]

Warren had been the first man ever elected three times to the governorship of California.[18] In Warren, Eisenhower saw a Republican in his own mold, a man who occupied the broad center of American life and was comfortable on both sides of the partisan divide. Like Eisenhower, Warren accepted the New Deal expansion of the central government's role in economic life. And like Eisenhower, Warren wanted to make sure that the concentration of power in the federal government did not go too far.[19]

Eisenhower failed, however, to detect that the Bill of Rights had become Warren's North Star. Already in 1938, Warren had called the safeguarding of civil liberties "the most fundamental and important of all our governmental problems."[20] His record as governor of California was uneven in this score, as he presided over the roundup of more than a hundred thousand Japanese immigrants and Japanese Americans in his state and their placement in internment camps. Coming to terms with the evil that Nazism and totalitarianism had unleashed on the world, however, had strengthened his commitment to civil liberties. By the 1950s, he was proclaiming the Bill of Rights "the most precious part of our legal heritage." Moreover, following Brandeis, he argued that the meaning of the Bill of Rights was not fixed in stone but rather required interpretation and adaptation "to changing circumstance." If the rights contained in that precious document "are real," Warren wrote in 1955 soon after becoming chief justice, "they need constant and imaginative application to new situations."[21]

Warren was not a deep thinker, and did not come to the Court possessed of a full-blown theory of incorporation or any other activist theory of jurisprudence. Had he articulated such a theory, Eisenhower likely would not have appointed him. Warren did not imagine that his Court would superintend the most significant assault on states' rights in American history. Still, his reverence for the Bill of Rights and his conviction that the Constitution was a living document in periodic need of adaptation to new social, economic, and political circumstances were firmly established when he joined the Court, both suggestive of the path he would follow as chief justice.

Brennan shared much of Warren's approach to politics and strengthened the latter's resolve to move the Court in a civil libertarian direction. Eisenhower appointed Brennan in the midst of a campaign season, hoping that the choice of an Irish Catholic Democrat from New Jersey would gain him votes in the Northeast states. Eisenhower's attorney general, Herbert Brownell, assured the president that Brennan was a conservative Democrat whose politics dovetailed quite well with Ike's moderate Republicanism. Yet Eisenhower would be surprised, much as he was with Warren, by what turned out to be the robust liberalism of Brennan's jurisprudence. In the 1950s and 1960s, Brennan did not achieve the public reputation of a Black, Frankfurter, or even Douglas, but his closeness to Warren (many came to regard Brennan as Warren's liberal muse) and talent for compromise and coalition building made him a pivotal player in several of the Court's most important 1960s' decisions.[22]

Frankfurter held back the liberal phalanx gathered around Warren, Brennan, and Black for a time, but by 1961 he was besieged and ailing. His retirement the next year cleared the way for Warren and his allies to elevate the significance of the Bill of Rights in American jurisprudence, putting the power of the states in grave peril.

MAKING THE BILL OF RIGHTS THE LAW OF THE LAND

The breadth of the Supreme Court's 1960s' attack on the powers of the states was impressive, stripping them of their long-established autonomy in realms of governance as diverse as criminal justice, electoral districting, marriage, sexuality, education, and religion. A bevy of decisions handed down throughout the decade incorporated state criminal justice systems under the Bill of Rights, which meant it prevailed in cases where state laws contradicted its principles. Criminal law had become a flash point in the struggle for racial equality in the South, as local sheriffs arrested civil rights protesters on spurious charges, violated basic criminal procedures, and condoned vigilante violence. All-white juries, meanwhile, rarely voted to convict whites of crimes committed against blacks.

Led by Black, the Supreme Court boldly waded into the thicket of state laws that had legitimated the actions of southern sheriffs and juries, throwing out many that vitiated protections that the Bill of Rights bestowed on every American citizen. Thus, *Mapp v. Ohio* (1961) barred states on Fourth Amendment grounds from executing unreasonable searches and seizures on individuals. *Gideon v. Wainright* (1963) gave anyone charged with a felony the right to an attorney and ordered states to furnish legal services to those unable to afford them on their own. *Malloy v. Hogan* (1964) ruled that a defendant's Fifth Amendment right against self-incrimination applied to state as well as federal courts, while *Miranda v. Arizona* (1965) declared that court confessions obtained from defendants who had not been informed of their right to an attorney were inadmissible in court. Finally, *Parker v. Gladden* (1966) and *Duncan v. Louisiana* (1968) both insisted that the right to an impartial jury conferred by the Sixth Amendment was fully applicable to any individual being tried in a state court.[23]

These decisions collectively put state judicial systems under unprecedentedly strict constitutional scrutiny. Though the plaintiffs in most of these cases were not black, the decisions were full of racial implications, given the myriad ways in which states, in both the South and North, had woven racial discrimination into their laws, criminal procedures, and judicial institutions. The Supreme Court made it clear that every individual, regardless of race, charged in a criminal justice case possessed rights that no state government could abrogate. State governments thereby lost the freedom they had long exercised to design and operate criminal justice systems that diverged from Bill of Rights principles.

The Supreme Court at the same time stripped states of other powers that had been used to maintain regimes of white supremacy. Determining the boundaries of electoral districts, for example, had always been seen as a power belonging solely to the states. Southern legislatures had used this prerogative to crowd the relatively small number of African American voters whom they had not managed to disenfranchise into a minute number of districts, thereby further limiting their influence in both state legislatures and the House of Representatives in Washington, DC. In states in the South and North, legislatures also had long privileged rural over urban voters, giving agricultural areas more representatives relative to their population than industrial-commercial areas enjoyed, and thus disproportionate power in state politics. In *Baker v. Carr* (1962), the Supreme Court ruled that such procedures violated the "one person, one vote" constitutional principle mandating that the ballot of every citizen should carry the same weight—no more and no less than any other—in state politics. *Baker v. Carr* paved the way for national legislation protecting the right to vote—a move that Congress made in 1965 when it passed the Voting Rights Act. Once again the Supreme Court had asserted the power of the central government over that of the states. Warren came to regard his decision in *Baker v. Carr* as the most important of his tenure as chief justice.[24]

In *Loving v. Virginia*, the Court inserted the Constitution into marriage, another area of law long seen as the province of the states.[25] In 1958, Mildred Jeter, a black woman, married a white man, Richard Loving, in Washington, DC, where interracial unions were legal. Both wanted to return to their native Virginia, but the Virginia Racial Integrity Act of 1924 made it illegal for interracial couples to reside in the state, even if they had been legally married elsewhere. In 1959, the Lovings were promptly arrested on moving to the state and sentenced to a year in jail for violating the 1924 law, with the judge offering to suspend the sentence on the condition that the Lovings leave the state and not come back for twenty-five years. The couple initially complied, returning to Washington to live, but they found the separation from family in Virginia too difficult to sustain. In 1964, they launched a legal challenge to the 1924 law, and in 1967, the Supreme Court handed down a unanimous decision in their favor.[26] Writing for the Court, Warren declared that marriage is one of the "basic civil rights of man," and "fundamental to our very existence and survival." Warren continued: "To deny this fundamental freedom on so unsupportable a basis as the racial classifications embodied in these statutes, classifications so directly subversive of the principle of equality at the heart of the Fourteenth Amendment, is surely to deprive all the State's citizens of liberty without due process of law." In this decision, the Warren Court joined together the notion of Americans possessing fundamental rights beyond the reach of governments with its belief that the Fourteenth Amendment bound individual states to respect those rights. "Under our Constitution," Warren wrote, "the freedom to marry, or not marry, a person of another race resides with the individual and cannot be infringed by the State." Those words rendered null and void the antimiscegenation statutes of all sixteen states that still had them on the books. The once-formidable edifice of antimiscegenation law, built on what had long been regarded as an impregnable police power foundation, came crashing to the ground.[27]

That foundation had begun to crack several years earlier as a result of the Supreme Court's determination not only to delegitimate practices of racial inequality but also to define a realm of privacy possessed by every individual. *Loving v. Virginia* established that marriage belonged to this realm—one in which individuals were to be able to choose their love partners free of government interference. Two years before *Loving*, in *Griswold v. Connecticut*, the Court struck down a Connecticut law banning the sale of contraceptives in the state and outlined what it called a "marital right to privacy.[28]" The decision about whether or not to use contraception rested with individual women, the Court maintained, not with the state. The seven justices who voted to invalidate the Connecticut law were uncertain in 1965, and remained so in 1967, about where to find justification for this right to privacy. At least one justice, John Marshall Harlan II, boldly deployed the substantive due process strategy, both acknowledging that "privacy" was not mentioned in the Constitution as a right and insisting that it was nevertheless implied in the due process clause of the Fourteenth Amendment. Harlan's most eloquent statement on the constitutional right to privacy and its meaning for reproductive freedom had come in a dissenting opinion he had filed in an earlier contraception case, *Poe v. Ullman* (1961). "The full scope of liberty guaranteed by the Due Process Clause," wrote Harlan in *Poe*, "cannot be found in or limited by the precise terms of the specific guarantees elsewhere provided in the Constitution." He continued:

> This "liberty" is not a series of isolated points pricked out in terms of the taking of property; the freedom of speech, press, and religion; the right to keep and bear arms; the freedom from unreasonable searches and seizures; and so on. It is a rational continuum which, broadly speaking, includes a freedom from all substantial arbitrary impositions and purposeless restraints.[29]

As impressive as Harlan's effort was to make the case for privacy as a freedom "on a rational continuum" of liberty, it initially did not draw the support of most other justices on the Warren Court. Some of the Court's staunchest liberals still could not bring themselves to embrace the doctrine of substantive due process because of their continuing antipathy to *Lochner*. Thus Douglas, the justice charged by Warren with writing the majority opinion in *Griswold*, attempted to make the case that the right to privacy was not a new right and that it was therefore not necessary to invoke substantive due process. Rather, Douglas argued, the right to privacy already existed in the "penumbras" and "emanations" in the Bill of Rights. This assertion was vague enough to draw the support of a majority of justices who, like Douglas, were looking for a way to establish a right to privacy without resting it on substantive due process.[30]

Black found the Douglas group's reasoning infuriating, contending that there was no basis on which to make an argument for privacy except under substantive due process. And substantive due process was, in his eyes, an altogether impermissible strategy of constitutional interpretation, for it gave justices the opportunity to make law rather than interpret it. If a right of privacy was going to come into existence, it could only do so by means of a constitutional amendment explicitly adding it to the Constitution. Were that to occur, Black, the Court's most aggressive proponent of incorporation, would make this right incumbent on the states. But he would not join a campaign to force this right into constitutional existence through judicial fiat. Black became one of the two dissenters in *Griswold*.[31]

Although Warren retired in 1969, his spirit continued to shape the Court through the early 1970s. In the new decade, the liberal majority that had voted for *Griswold* abandoned Douglas's argument about penumbras and emanations as unsustainable, and instead embraced the substantive due process argument that Harlan had made in *Poe*. Harlan's *Poe* dissent informed two key 1970s' Court rulings: *Eisenstadt v. Baird* (1972), which extended the right to privacy to unmarried as well as married couples, and *Roe v. Wade* (1973), which put the decision to have an abortion in the hands of the pregnant woman and her doctor.[32]

In Supreme Court decisions about sexuality and reproduction handed down between 1961 and 1973, we can see both a deep commitment to undercutting the power of the states and anxiety about how best to accomplish this. Once Frankfurter retired in 1962, the Warren Court was nearly unanimous in its high regard for incorporation as a mechanism for reining in the states.[33] This had been, in the Court's view, the clear intent of the Fourteenth Amendment, and a majority of justices did all they could to insure that every right enumerated in the Bill of Rights would be made incumbent on the states. There was no unanimity regarding rights not enumerated, however, which is why the right to privacy turned into such a vexatious issue for the Warren Court. A majority came reluctantly to support the idea that substantive due process sanctioned a right to privacy, but several of the liberal justices in the majority's ranks never overcame their fear that engaging this doctrine put them at risk of making rather than interpreting law. This was the charge they had long leveled against the supporters of *Lochner*—a fact that Black had emphasized in his scalding *Griswold* dissent. Black did not draw many of his colleagues to his side; most had already concluded that they had to find some way to grant Americans a right to privacy. Black retired from the Court in 1971 and died the same year. His departure may have facilitated his colleagues' embrace of substantive due process in the 1972 *Eisenstadt* and 1973 *Roe* decisions.

Substantive due process was a clever, even ingenious, strategy for endowing individuals with constitutionally protected freedom in matters of marriage and sexuality that Americans had not previously enjoyed. But deploying it opened the Court to the same kinds of challenges to its legitimacy that Progressives had once leveled at the laissez-faire constitutionalists. Amending the Constitution to guarantee privacy rights might have been a sounder strategy than relying on substantive process, but in the divided nation of the 1960s or 1970s this was a political impossibility. Absent such an amendment, the justices located privacy in the personal liberty guaranteed by the Constitution. If it was the best alternative under the circumstances, it was also a troubled one.

In the 1960s, the Supreme Court had moved against the states in matters of criminal justice, voting, marriage, and sexuality, but it was not finished. In 1962, the Court confronted the states' power to authorize prayer in the public schools—a power that had been theirs to exercise for nearly the entire life of the republic. That year, in *Engel v. Vitale*, the Court ruled that state governments could not mandate prayer in public schools, even if the prayer was voluntary and favored no religion or denomination, invoking only "Almighty God." Taking on the liberal mantle that he would abandon in the privacy cases, Black wrote the near-unanimous decision for the Court, arguing that a prayer of this sort—in this case, authorized by a New York State law—violated the First Amendment stipulation that government could pass no law "respecting an establishment of religion." Courts had traditionally interpreted this First Amendment prohibition as applying only to the laws that Congress had passed. The innovation of the Warren Court was to argue, following Black, that the Fourteenth Amendment had made Bill of Rights prohibitions on Congress binding on state legislatures as well. For Black and his supporters, the doctrine of incorporation clearly prevailed.[34]

In public memory, *Engel v. Vitale* does not have the stature of *Brown v. Board*, *Loving v. Virginia*, or *Roe v. Wade*. But it was a hugely controversial decision. Almost half the states in the country filed amicus curiae briefs to the Court maintaining that a prayer of the sort mandated by the New York State law in question was in fact constitutionally permissible. Millions of evangelical Protestants were aghast at the Supreme Court's decision, unable to comprehend that the highest court of the land would drive God from school. George Wallace, the newly elected governor of Alabama, condemned "a group of men on the Supreme Court," allegedly influenced by Communist ideology, for "forbidding little school children to say a prayer."[35] Preacher Billy James Hargis felt that "this was really the beginning of the end for America, that the country had turned its back on God, and that any country that did that couldn't stand."[36] Many evangelicals saw signs of God's wrath in the nuclear missiles installed by the Soviet Union in Cuba only a few months after the *Engel v. Vitale* decision. A nation that had so brazenly spurned God could not expect to win the Cold War. Religious Protestants resolved to restore God to his rightful place in American life and the classroom. Many evangelicals date their Christian engagement with politics—their devotion to a movement that Jerry Falwell would label the "moral majority" in 1979—to *Engel v. Vitale.*[37]

Some conservatives drew connections between the Supreme Court's decisions against religion in public schools and in favor of racial equality. Representative George W. Andrews, a Democrat from Alabama, declared that "they've put Negros in the schools, and now they've driven God out."[38] But those promoting civil rights were not all secularists; to the contrary, in the 1950s and 1960s, black ministers and churches infused civil rights struggles with religious conviction.[39] No unholy alliance between racial egalitarians and secularists lay behind the Court's decisions on race and religion. Rather, rulings in both domains were informed by an effort to bind the states to the Bill of Rights and Fourteenth Amendment's due process clause. For more than a hundred years, states had exercised autonomy in legislating on matters of race, religion, sexuality, marriage, criminal procedures, and morality. The autonomy was of such long standing and so deeply rooted in mores and jurisprudence that it seemed to many synonymous with the American way. In the 1960s, the Warren Court, in making the Bill of Rights and the Fourteenth Amendment the law of the land, put a decisive end to the states' sovereignty.

When Warren was asked in 1968, on the cusp of his retirement, to reflect on what the Court had accomplished during his tenure, he said, disarmingly, that "most of the Bill of Rights have been applied to the States now."[40] To be sure, the Court had been extending provisions of the Bill of Rights to the states since the 1920s. But Warren's matter-of-fact statement should not obscure the thoroughgoing reversal of the balance of power between the central government and the states that the Court oversaw in a remarkable eleven-year period—starting with *Engel v. Vitale* and *Baker v. Carr* in 1962, continuing with *Loving v. Virginia* and *Duncan v. Louisiana* in 1967 and 1968, and concluding with *Eisenstein v. Baird* and *Roe v. Wade* in 1972 and 1973. In no other period of American history except the Civil War era itself had federal-state relations been so fundamentally transformed. The Warren Court broke the power of the states, a near revolution in American governance.

Only the Supreme Court could have spearheaded this assault. As the only formal institution of American governance to straddle federal and state institutions, it had long arrogated to itself the responsibility of locating and policing the lines dividing the two. The power of the states had been substantially weakened a hundred years earlier, in the aftermath of the Civil War and as a result of the Civil War amendments, but the Court intervened to restore the power and authority of the states in the postbellum period. In this restoration, the states regained a broad array of powers that were maintained through the first half of the twentieth century. Yet what the Supreme Court could give to the states, it could also take away. This is what it did in the 1960s.

Did the Supreme Court have the authority to execute such a profound shift of power away from the states and toward individual citizens, on the one hand, and the central government, on the other? On matters of incorporation it did; the wording of the Fourteenth Amendment—"no State shall make or enforce any law which shall . . . deprive any person of life, liberty, or property, without due process of law"—gave the central government clear authority to impose the Bill of Rights on the states. The doctrine of incorporation, however, could be applied only to rights explicitly enumerated in the Constitution. For rights not so enumerated, such as the right to privacy, Warren Court justices turned to substantive due process. This they did without the confidence that characterized their embrace of incorporation. Douglas was so uncertain about the Court's authority to alter the meaning of liberty to make it relevant to modern America that in the majority opinion he wrote for *Griswold* in 1965, he articulated the questionable proposition that the right to privacy had been in the Constitution all along, unnoticed by all previous generations of jurists unmindful of the document's penumbras and emanations. This argument did not withstand scrutiny for long. Warren Court jurists abandoned it in the early 1970s and instead conscripted substantive due process in defense of the right to privacy.

The constitutional uncertainty that clouded some portions of the Warren Court transformation testified to the magnitude of the undertaking and to the Court's determination to proceed even when legal justifications came up short. Reflecting in 1969 on the "fundamental shift" in "federal-state" relations overseen by the Warren Court, Associate Justice Harlan pointed out that the federal judiciary had come to "distrust in the capabilities of the federal system to meet the needs of American society in these fast-moving times," believing that it had to "spearhead reform" even if that meant sacrificing "circumspect regard for the constitutional limitations upon the manner of its accomplishment." Harlan, one of the more conservative members of the Court, was himself ambivalent about this judicially mediated change. "To those who see our free society as dependent primarily upon a broadening of the constitutional protections afforded to the individual," he observed, "these developments are no doubt considered to be healthy. To those who regard the federal system as one of the mainsprings of our political liberties, this increasing erosion of state authority cannot but be viewed with apprehension."[41]

Harlan's unease about the Warren Court's record, so palpable in these remarks, is understandable in light of the fact that he was the primary architect of the Court's adoption of substantive due process doctrine to define a right to privacy. He had reached the conclusion that the times required judges to interpret individual liberty broadly, locate it where others had not, and make its defense, in all its permutations, the Court's priority. Among Warren Court justices were brilliant thinkers whose legal training had taught them to stretch the Constitution, to tug at its individual clauses to make it serviceable for governance in a society completely transformed since the nation and its Constitution had come into existence. These justices were Brandeis's legatees. Like him, they were confident in their ability to make the Constitution a living document whose core principles would be preserved and enhanced while at the same time rendered useful to continually evolving governing challenges. But their unease with deploying substantive due process—which in their estimation carried the risk that as judges, they would find themselves making rather than interpreting law—reveals a current of constitutional anxiety also evident in Harlan's 1969 remarks. Warren Court justices worried that their innovations had gone too far.[42]

Few took notice of the justices' constitutional anxiety in the America of the 1960s. Other forces were also pushing the nation toward an expanded conception of rights. Multiple social movements were demanding loudly and uncompromisingly that the civil rights of African Americans and other groups subjected to discrimination be respected. The Cold War and threat of nuclear annihilation added urgency to these demands. The United States needed to act quickly to set its house in order. The Supreme Court justices may have been emboldened, perhaps imperceptibly, by the massive shift in fiscal power from the states to the federal government wrought by the Cold War. In establishing a permanent national security apparatus, the central state amassed resources and clout on an unprecedented scale, stealthily but markedly nurturing the ambitions and confidence of federal government officials well beyond the ranks of Supreme Court justices. Members of Congress and the executive branch under President Johnson's leadership were also determined to take on the states.

LBJ, THE GREAT SOCIETY, AND THE HUMBLING OF THE STATES

Johnson and Congress boldly moved against the states as they designed and implemented the Great Society, a comprehensive package of liberal reforms meant to realize the unfulfilled ambitions of

the New Deal. The outlines of the Great Society are visible in proposals circulating within the brain trust of the Kennedy administration between 1961 and 1963, but legislative action gained momentum only in the wake of mounting pressure from civil rights
activists, on the one side, and JFK's assassination in November
1963, on the other. Johnson assumed office determined to take re-
demptive steps after the national trauma of Kennedy's death and
amid growing concerns that racial tensions would explode if Congress failed to address issues that underlay them. Johnson turned
first to JFK's Civil Rights Act, which had been languishing in congressional limbo for months, securing its passage in July 1964,
making it in the process the most important piece of such legislation since Reconstruction.[43] It prohibited discrimination based on
race, color, sex, and national origin in employment, government,
and public accommodations, and gave the federal government new
mechanisms for pursuing those who violated the law. When it became clear that voting rights were inadequately covered by the law,
Congress passed a separate Voting Rights Act in 1965 that empowered the federal government to overturn discriminatory practices
in elections. These two pieces of legislation were among the Great
Society's most important and enduring achievements.

Johnson also envisioned the Great Society completing the work
of the New Deal. For LBJ, for whom FDR was a lifelong hero, this
meant using the power of the central government to eliminate the
disfiguring effects of poverty and to enhance economic security
and opportunity for all Americans. Between 1964 and 1968, Johnson declared a War on Poverty; expanded Social Security benefits;
passed Medicare and Medicaid, the most significant health care
legislation in American history to that point; and immersed the federal government in educational reform and urban redevelopment.
In all, the Great Society was the last of the twentieth century's
grand efforts to transform American society through government
action.[44]

The Great Society fell short of the goals set by the New Deal in
some critical respects. For example, few of its measures intervened
in employment markets to generate jobs or to level the playing field
between capital and labor. Capitalist prerogatives were not chal-

lenged in the 1960s as they had been in the 1930s, and no 1960s' labor movement rivaled the ambition and success of the Depression-era CIO.[45] In other respects, however, the Great Society surpassed the New Deal. This is especially evident in the civil rights arena and in the corollary conviction that the states' freedom to determine their own racial regimes and disregard the Bill of Rights had to be broken.

We have seen how the Supreme Court attacked the states. Johnson and his supporters deployed three strategies of their own to challenge their autonomy: first, they made the states dependent on federal resources to an unprecedented degree; second, they attached strings to the funds they dispersed, requiring states to accept central government agendas as their own; and third, they used the power and resources of the federal government to contest oligarchies controlling state and local governments. Each of these political strategies deserves consideration.

The amount of federal money flowing into states and municipalities in the 1960s and 1970s grew astronomically. In 1950, the federal government, still unsure of how long its war-generated resource abundance would last, contributed a relatively modest $2.3 billion to the states. This figure nearly tripled to $6.3 billion under Eisenhower, who directed substantial sums to highways, education, and welfare. And then the figure tripled to $19.3 billion during the 1960s, and more than tripled again in the 1970s to $61.9 billion. Between 1950 and 1980, in other words, federal government assistance to the states grew by an astounding twenty-seven-fold. Meanwhile, the number of federal grants programs grew from 51 to 530 in the years from 1964 to 1971 alone.[46]

Highways, education, and welfare remained the leading categories of federal expenditure on the states under LBJ as they had been under Eisenhower, although assistance for the last two expanded more rapidly than for road building during the 1960s and 1970s. The Great Society broadened eligibility for Social Security benefits during the 1960s while increasing the size of benefits for the various groups of vulnerable citizens—widows, the disabled, and mothers with dependent children—receiving public assistance. Medicare, the new health insurance program for the elderly, was federally administered and did not involve the states. But Medicaid did, authorizing federal money to be distributed to the states to assist the poor with their medical needs. Meanwhile, the 1965 Elementary and Secondary Education Act significantly increased federal aid to local school districts around the country. The Omnibus Crime Control and Safe Streets Act did the same for state and local police forces in 1968.[47]

There was nothing new in the federal government relying on the states to administer its programs and carry out its policies. The central state had been doing this since the advent of the new federalism in the late nineteenth and early twentieth centuries.[48] New Dealers, too, had relied heavily on the states for both political and administrative reasons. But in the 1960s, the federal government sought not only to involve the states in its programs but also to subdue them by making the flow of federal dollars dependent on the states' acquiescence to Washington-generated policies and standards.

The federal government's deployment of fiscal leverage to control the states emerged first in connection to civil rights. The triumph of racial justice was contingent on undermining states' ability to sustain racially discriminatory regimes. The central government would use its newfound wealth both as a carrot to entice states into accepting federal funds and as a stick to beat recalcitrant states and their officials into submission on matters of racial equality.

This carrot-and-stick strategy first became apparent in the interplay between the Civil Rights Act of 1964 and the Elementary and Secondary Education Act of 1965. Title VI of the Civil Rights Act gave the federal government the power to deny its funds to states and municipalities engaged in discriminatory practices— the first time in the twentieth century that the flow of federal resources was tied to the advance of civil rights. Interestingly, Title VI drew little attention and controversy in the congressional debates of 1964.[49]

Its significance came into focus in 1965, however, when Congress, through the Elementary and Secondary Education Act, committed $1.2 billion to public schools from kindergarten through the twelfth grade. A disproportionate amount of that billion-plus appropriation was to be made available to counties with high concentrations of poor schoolchildren. This meant that innumerable southern school districts qualified for substantial aid, with many standing to gain as much as 20 to 30 percent of their budgets from these federal dollars. But soon enough these school districts learned that the federal money would flow only if they complied with the nondiscrimination clauses of the Civil Rights Act of 1964. Suddenly, Title VI of the act became immensely important. Southern counties, to be eligible for these benefits, would have to eliminate racial discrimination from their schools, and this meant dismantling the dual school system—one set of schools for whites, and one for blacks—that despite *Brown*, still dominated the region.[50]

Outraged by this linkage of school aid to racial equality, white southerners beseeched Congress to loosen Title VI's compliance requirements, which were being enforced by Johnson's Department of Health, Education, and Welfare. The Johnson administration backed off for a time, though not for long, because of the countervailing support for dismantling Jim Crow within northern districts of the Democratic Party. These conflicts between northern and southern Democrats, and between the central government and the states, naturally ended up in federal courts, with predictable results given the Warren Court's commitment to ending Jim Crow. In *United States v. Jefferson County Board of Education* (1966 and 1967), *Green v. County School Board of New Kent County* (1968), and *Alexander v. Holmes* (1968), the Supreme Court ordered the dismantling of dual school systems in the South, and commanded southern school districts to adopt desegregation plans that not only displayed good intentions but also achieved quick and demonstrable results.[51]

The South's last best hope for escaping this imposition of federal power lay with the election of the Republican Richard Nixon in 1968, and his appointment of a new chief justice, Warren Burger, to succeed Warren in 1969.[52] Nixon played to the fears of southern whites in the 1968 election, allowing them to believe that putting him in the White House would stall the civil rights juggernaut. The optimism generated by Burger's appointment was quickly staunched as it became apparent that both the Nixon White House and Burger Court were determined, at least in the short term, to

finish the work of school desegregation in the South. White southerners contemplated but desisted from engaging in massive resistance as they had in the 1950s. Between 1969 and 1970, the de jure
system of separate schooling in the South collapsed. In the space
of one year, the percentage of African Americans in the South at-
tending integrated schools soared from less than a third to almost
90 percent.[53] The federal government had taken the authority given
it by Title VI of the Civil Rights Act, applied it to the Elementary
and Secondary Education Act, and in the words of education
scholar Gary Orfield, effected "a major social revolution" in southern schools.[54]

In other areas, too, the federal government began to encroach
on the states in ways it had shied from in previous eras of liberal
reform. Such was the case, as we have seen, with the 1965 Voting
Rights Act, which gave the federal government authority to reform
electoral rules that like public schools, had long been regarded as
the exclusive domain of state and local governments.[55] Likewise,
the Employment Equal Opportunity Act of 1972 extended the prohibition on employment discrimination from the private sector to
state and local governments themselves. The federal government
had never before sought to structure relations between individuals
and their local and state governments. Further, the impulse to compel states' submission to policies originating in Washington, DC,
spread far beyond racial matters. In 1965, for example, Congress
passed the Water Quality Act, which ordered individual states to
develop plans for maintaining adequate quality standards for interstate waters coursing through their states. If the states failed to develop appropriate plans, the central government would simply impose its own.[56]

Federal efforts to coerce the states in these ways ran into considerable resistance. Rearguard actions in Congress to roll back compliance requirements or deny new laws effective funding and enforcement machinery all played a part in delaying or frustrating
implementation. Legal challenges to the expansion of federal authority sometimes had similar results, as was the case in *Milliken v.
Bradley*, in which the Burger Court declared in 1974 that it would
not compel scores of white suburbs ringing Detroit to join the city

in a metropolitan-wide desegregation plan.[57] Nevertheless, states in the South and beyond were under siege. The assault even penetrated programs of public assistance, long a bastion of states' rights.

During the New Deal, southern states had insisted that new programs of federal public assistance, most notably Aid to Dependent Children, be left under state control, with each state free to determine its level of commitment. This allowed states to contribute almost nothing and sacrifice federal support in the process. Southern states generally opted for low-level contributions, which allowed them to divert state and federal welfare dollars away from the African American indigent in their midst. The "undeserving poor" were thereby denied assistance and kept at the bottom of the South's social hierarchy.[58]

A similar deference to the states seemed to inform the design of Medicaid. The federal government employed a uniform standard of matching funds for every state, but it left the level of appropriations to the discretion of individual states.[59] The amplitude of benefits quickly showed wide variations, with states in the South and increasingly the Southwest as well ranking among the stingiest. For example, by 1974 Missouri was spending only $274 per Medicaid recipient, less than a third of the sum, $911, paid out by Minnesota. States also had the opportunity to opt out of Medicaid altogether, which Arizona did until 1982.[60]

But even in the Medicaid program, the federal government encroached on the states in new ways. It determined whom among the poor would be eligible for Medicaid assistance, and it mandated that in return for accepting funds states were to commit to offering a basic slate of medical benefits.[61] At first, this included few services. But the principle that the federal government could make any of them obligatory on states was significant nonetheless. By the 1980s, the services required of states that accepted Medicaid funds had grown substantially, and the program became known as an exemplary instance of the federal government successfully imposing its "mandates" on the states.[62] In this way, the Great Society represented a departure from practices prevailing in the New Deal, which had allowed individual states far more control over the structure and delivery of welfare programs for the poor.

Attaching strings to the monies it dispensed was a second strategy used by Congress and presidents to subdue the states. Directly challenging the political elites that controlled state and local politics was a third. The actions of the executive branch and Congress along these lines can best be grasped by looking at the Community Action Program (CAP) authorized in 1964 by the Economic Opportunity Act.

CAP was the centerpiece of the War on Poverty. Envisioned as a small experimental program, Johnson made it the centerpiece of his War on Poverty and the recipient of nearly 40 percent of the Economic Opportunity Act's $800 million appropriation. Groups from across the country were invited to submit proposals to the federal government for funds to establish their own Community Action Agencies (CAA). By June 1965, 415 such agencies had been founded; a year later there were more than a thousand.[63] These agencies varied widely in their activities and organizational structures. They were all meant, however, to adhere to CAP's guiding principle that the poor had to be involved in designing and administering programs intended to alleviate their poverty and powerlessness. The slogan of community action was "maximum feasible participation" by the poor. Such participation, the thinking went, would counter their passivity and show them that they could change their life circumstances for the better. "Maximum feasible participation" would spark, in other words, self-improvement and economic gain. Poverty and its associated ills would fall away, and the poor would ascend, both economically and culturally, into the middle class.[64]

Most of those in the Johnson administration who embraced community action did so because it appeared to make poverty into a cultural problem that could be solved once the poor acquired the requisite cultural traits.[65] But some in the administration saw the intent of "maximum feasible participation" differently. The latter's ideological orientation was informed by the radical Columbia University–based sociologists Richard Cloward and Lloyd Ohlin, who argued that the poor's passivity arose not from deeply internalized cultural traits but rather from their lack of access to political power in their neighborhoods and communities. Give them power, these sociologists asserted, and the poor would transform their lives.[66]

Power was finite, however. Giving it to one group entailed taking it away from another, which engendered conflict. Cloward and Ohlin did not advocate class struggle in the traditional Marxist sense of workers confronting capitalists. The poor whom they studied had only intermittent involvement with employers and labor markets. Their strategy instead called for the poor to take control of local instruments of governance, and then use that control to funnel public and private resources into their own communities. This struggle would pit the poor against local and state sources of political power: mayors, governors, political machines, school boards, welfare agencies, and the police.[67]

These ideas, which had percolated during the Kennedy administration, held a strong appeal for Robert Kennedy's men in the Department of Justice who believed that government at all levels had become overly bureaucratized and too beholden to special interests.[68] In their eyes, the real impediments to meaningful change were state and municipal structures of government power that too often had fallen into the hands of inefficient and petty oligarchs. The idea of mobilizing the poor against these oligarchs was to them an especially alluring strategy. By 1961 and 1962, this mobilization was already happening in the South. Civil rights activists were marching on local courthouses, challenging local sheriffs, desegregating Greyhound Bus stations, and confronting southern governors. The resistance activists encountered fueled the Kennedy men's antipathy to local institutions of governance, especially in the South. What if the central government took on these institutions as well? CAP was a way to do just that.

Johnson knew little of this constellation of Department of Justice officials aligned with radical New York sociologists. In normal times, his lack of knowledge of minor administration figures would not have mattered. But in the tense and fluid political environment of 1963 and 1964, ideas and individuals on the margins could find their way to the center. Johnson was looking for new techniques and policies to undermine southern resistance to civil rights and antipoverty work. In CAP he saw a useful tool.

Not surprisingly, CAP immediately generated a level of conflict that Johnson and his aides had not anticipated. In summer 1965, the Child Development Group of Mississippi (CDGM) received CAP monies to launch Head Start, a new program to give disadvantaged preschoolers access to learning to prepare them for kindergarten and first grade. Hardened civil rights veterans fresh from fierce struggles with segregationist forces in Mississippi constituted the CDGM's leadership. They were determined to staff their program with the black poor, drawn from the ranks of Mississippi sharecroppers and domestic workers, and they did not shy from confronting the state's white educational establishment. In less than a year, these experienced organizers had opened eighty-three Head Start centers for nearly six thousand children across the state.

John Stennis, Mississippi's powerful senator and an archsegregationist, objected to the civil rights activists' foray into education and their use of federal funds to circumvent local school boards dominated by whites. Charging the CDGM with politicizing the educational process and misusing federal funds, Stennis campaigned to shut it down. Sargent Shriver, the head of the War on Poverty's administrative arm, bowed to Stennis's pressure and, in fall 1966, cut off CDGM's federal support. This action angered Head Start's northern supporters, and Shriver was forced to restore funds to the Mississippi activists in return for CDGM agreeing to include whites on its governing board and rework its accounting procedures and administrative practices.[69]

Established politicians in the North received Community Action Agencies almost as coolly as did their southern counterparts. In Syracuse, CAP funded a Saul Alinsky–style organization to mobilize welfare mothers and tenants of public housing against municipal authorities whom they accused of failing to serve the needs of the city's poor. The organization also conducted a voter registration drive among the city's minority poor for the purpose of defeating the Republican mayor, William Walsh, in the next municipal election. "We are experiencing a class struggle in the traditional

Karl Marx style," noted the incredulous director of the Syracuse Housing Authority, "and I do not like it."[70]

Mayor Richard Daley was determined to quash this kind of class struggle before it took root in Chicago, which he ruled with an iron fist. He skillfully turned local Community Action Agencies into extensions of his political machine, subjecting him to censure. Daley's refusal to put resources and power directly in the hands of the poor prompted a civil rights activist testifying before Congress to denounce him for turning a war on poverty into "more of the ancient galling war on the poor." Alinsky himself told a *Harper's* journalist that Daley's CAA was "a prize piece of political pornography."[71]

The way in which Great Society officials sought to ally themselves with local groups of activists in 1965 and 1966 was similar to what another group of federal government officials had attempted to do thirty years earlier during the New Deal. Then, Jerome Frank and his band of radical lawyers in the US Department of Agriculture's Legal Division sided with black sharecroppers in the South in their struggle against white landowners. That struggle had ended badly for both the sharecroppers and Frank's men. The white planters had mobilized their powerful network of supporters in southern statehouses, the agricultural extension schools of southern state universities, the farm bureaus, and Congress itself, and within days, had reversed prosharecropper policies and purged Frank's group from the USDA. It was an impressive display of white southern power, and Roosevelt dared not tangle with it again.[72]

The parallel countermobilization against CAP initiatives was not nearly so solid or effective, at least in the short term. Stennis had to settle for a compromise with Head Start in Mississippi. He and other critics did not succeed in eliminating the Office of Economic Opportunity altogether until 1974. During its decade of existence, the office supported hundreds of CAAs. Some CAAs became conventional social or educational service providers, more allies than antagonists of local government. But the spirit of maximum feasible participation survived in many places, and in some where it did not, a parallel spirit that we might call "maximum feasible service to the poor" emerged. Such was the case with Legal Services, a

CAA set up to provide legal assistance to the poor. The lawyers and staffs of Legal Services worked as advocates of the poor in scores of offices across the country into the 1980s and 1990s. That this policy insurgency lasted as long as it did is another sign of the central government's success in shaking up power structures in states and municipalities.

The reworking of the federal system emerging from Congress during the Great Society years was not as clear and decisive as that emerging from the Supreme Court. It could not be, for Congress, especially in the Senate, gave states a powerful role in making national policy. Invariably some states would use that power to protect both their own particular interests and uphold the interests of states in general. Thus Congress's efforts to take on the states was less one of steady advance, as it was in the federal courts, than one of advance, contestation, and sometimes retreat. The cumulative effect of Congress's assault on the states was impressive nonetheless. In the 1960s, Congress controlled the bulk of the revenue on which states had come to depend. It attached strings to most of this, meaning that state and local governments that used federal funds had to do so in a manner determined by Congress. Similar policies during the New Deal era left the states with much more discretion. That discretion had often been used to undercut the federal government's commitment to racial equality.

The story of CAP might appear to challenge this narrative of Washington's ever-increasing control. Yet if we keep in mind that among the federal government's intentions in launching the War on Poverty was the undermining of the independent power of states and municipalities as well as the oligarchs who allegedly ran many of them, then CAP perfectly fits this narrative. Considering Congress's assault on the states in combination with that of the Supreme Court, we can appreciate the magnitude of the federal government's campaign to contain and erode the power of the states.

The Cold War and the civil rights movement were the two biggest drivers of this campaign. The first provided the federal government with a level of resources, fiscal clout, and confidence that it had never possessed before. The second made the assault on the states a political and moral imperative. Racial equality could not triumph as long as states maintained their traditional control over matters of criminal justice, voting, marriage, education, and the disbursement of federal grant monies. In this struggle, the Supreme Court took the lead, supplying the critical constitutional legitimation for stripping the states of the powers they had long held. The Court became more conservative in the 1970s once its leadership passed from the liberal Warren to the conservative Burger, and once Nixon's other appointees began to influence rulings. This conservative tendency was especially apparent in the Court's refusal, in *Milliken v. Bradley*, to make the multiple municipalities that constituted the Detroit metropolitan area into a single school district for the purposes of implementing desegregation plans. In this decision, the Court respected rather than overturned the principles of local control that underlay federalism. The decision was a harbinger of rising conservative clout on the Court. Still, the Burger Court's moves against the Warren Court were initially limited, nothing like the Thermidor that the late nineteenth-century Supreme Court had executed against the Reconstruction-era centralizing state. The Burger Court allowed much of the work of the Warren Court to stand. The states were dealt a severe blow, while the power of the federal government was vastly augmented.[73]

States began to resist the federal government once they began to grasp the magnitude of its campaign against them. Some began mobilizing to roll back the expansion of federal power and restore states' rights, drawing on a large reservoir of anger toward the federal government among substantial portions of America's white population. Other states started maneuvering to enlarge their powers within the new system of Washington-based governance that suddenly engulfed them on all sides. They positioned themselves to receive more rather than less in the way of federal government grants and to find ways to circumvent Washington control in the process. They sought, too, to redress the imbalance of revenue between the central government and states by increasing their own revenue-raising capacity. The federalist system had always been a dynamic one, and the tussles between the states and central government did not cease. But the historic influence of the states, and the principle of police power on which it had rested, had been broken. Meanwhile, the Bill of Rights was finally enthroned, 180 years after it had formally become the law of the land.

10

CONSERVATIVE REVOLT

In the 1980s, as the New Right began its assault on "big government," Senator Fritz Hollings, a Democrat from South Carolina, delighted in telling the following story:

A veteran returning from Korea went to college on the GI Bill; bought his house with an FHA loan; saw his kids born in a VA hospital; started a business with an SBA loan; got electricity from the TVA and, later, water from an EPA project. His parents, on Social Security, retired to a farm, got electricity from the REA and had their soil tested by the USDA. When his father became ill, the family was saved from financial ruin by Medicare and a life was saved with a drug developed through the NIH. His kids participated in the school lunch program, learned physics from teachers trained in a NSF program and went to college with guaranteed student loans. He drove to work on the Interstate and moored his boat in a channel dredged by the Army engineers. When floods hit, he took Amtrak to Washington to apply for disaster relief, and spent some time in the Smithsonian museums. Then one day he got mad; he wrote his congressman an angry letter. "Get the government off my back," he wrote. "I'm tired of paying for all those programs created for ungrateful people."[1]

Hollings's words captured two key developments in the late twentieth-century United States: first, the expansion of the central state and the increasing range of services it provided, to the point where it was now woven into the life of nearly every citizen; and second, the widespread anger that this generated, which coalesced into a conservative political movement. The conviction that government had grown too large, expensive, and threatening to American liberties animated this new movement, the most significant development of the century's final decades. Conservatives held that government growth had to be staunched and then reversed, with the small central state of the nation's early years, its powers fragmented, the aspirational ideal. Many late twentieth-century conservatives in fact were eighteenth-century liberals, convinced that government posed the greatest threat to US liberty and the republic. Some opposed the exercise of government authority only at the federal level and were comfortable with the traditional notion that states themselves could exercise broad powers. Others, adopting a libertarian stance, opposed the exercise of government power at every level, championing the supremacy of individualism and free markets.

Conservatives were correct about the growth of federal government power and influence. Between 1970 and 1990, federal expenditures, adjusted for inflation, nearly doubled; unadjusted, the increase was from $334 million to in excess of an eye-popping $2 trillion.[2] The federal government's expanded reach and influence were equally impressive. Hollings's war veteran benefited from, among other programs, Social Security, Medicare, a federally assisted mortgage, loans for small businesses and for university students, environmental protection, and the National Institutes of Health. Not mentioned by Hollings were governmental regulation of workplaces in the interest of occupational safety and health, supervision of the safety of the country's food and drug supplies, care of national parks and monuments, and of course, maintenance of a vast national security state.

A full catalog of federal government capabilities would also include the powers that the government assumed in addressing racism—these, not surprisingly, also missing from the senator's story.

Apart from managing the capitalist economy to serve the public interest, the effort to achieve racial equality was the greatest social engineering project undertaken by the central state in the second half of the twentieth century. We have already seen the level of governmental activity this required: schools and public accommodations had to be integrated, states had to be stripped of long-held powers, and poverty, which disproportionately affected minorities, had to be remedied. To this already-formidable list, we must add the effort to eliminate discrimination from the workplace—a campaign that saw the federal government reordering employment practices across the entire economy in the 1970s and 1980s.

The crucial initiative in this regard was President Lyndon Baines Johnson's executive order 11246, little noticed when it was issued in 1965, which barred employers from "discriminating in employment decisions . . . on the basis of race, color, religion, sex, or national origins." The executive order required contractors with fifty-one or more employees and doing more than $50,000 per year worth of business with the federal government to develop affirmative action plans, based on whether analysis of their hiring practices showed disparities between the percentages of qualified minority and female applicants and the percentages actually hired.[3] These new rules applied to thousands of employers who together, controlled twenty-three million employees spread out among seventy-three thousand work sites. Johnson's executive order put pressure on the nation's large employers to alter not only their behavior during the hiring process but also the racial and gender composition of their workforces. The federal government had never before subjected so many employers to such intense scrutiny on matters involving discrimination. A number of subsequent laws, including the Equal Opportunity Employment Act of 1972 and the Age Discrimination in Employment Act of 1974, significantly widened the range of discriminatory behavior subject to federal government oversight.[4]

Altering hiring patterns necessitated counting and categorizing individuals by their race, gender, and other ascriptive characteristics. Not surprisingly, counting schemes proliferated, prompting the Office of Management and Budget in 1977 to issue statistical directive 15, which instructed all federal agencies to employ five racial categories to classify employees: white, black, American Indian, Asian and Pacific Islander, and Hispanic, the so-called ethnoracial pentagon. Penalties for noncompliance were substantial enough to persuade private institutions receiving federal funds to overhaul their hiring practices to ensure, at the least, apparent compliance.[5] The ethnoracial pentagon of racial classification powerfully influenced the terms in which antidiscrimination initiatives would be framed and pursued—and the way in which American society would be represented.[6] Sociologist Michael Mann has written about the ability of governments in the nineteenth and twentieth centuries to "cage" ever-expanding domains of social life.[7] The ways in which the American central state went about measuring and remedying racial injustice is exemplary of this caging power.

A broad overhaul of ancillary personnel practices also resulted from the central government's effort to extirpate racism from the workplace. Formal descriptions for jobs and regular performance reviews proliferated, as did complex salary classification systems designed to meet new demands for fairness and transparency. Increasingly intricate systems sent corporations seeking the services of human relations experts who, grouped into discrete human relations departments, intensified the drive to standardize racial classification and antidiscrimination practices in industry and government. The roots of human relations antedated the 1970s and 1980s, and were as much private as public. Still, the federal government's commitment to eliminating employment discrimination gave the field a big boost.[8]

The campaign against workplace discrimination was less successful than the bureaucratic transformation it had triggered. On the positive side, the federal contract compliance program that began with executive order 11246 is estimated to have opened new occupational opportunities to more than five million people of color and more than six million women between 1965 and 1995. On the negative side, patterns of employment and pay stratified by race and gender were too deeply entrenched to be readily remedied. The Civil Rights Act of 1964 authorized the establishment of the Equal Employment Opportunity Commission, an agency to which individual workers could address complaints about discrimination that employers failed to resolve. Yet the volume of cases overwhelmed the commission as soon as it became fully operational in the 1970s. As a result, many grievances either took too long to address or were never satisfactorily addressed at all. The commission's mixed record notwithstanding, central government efforts to eliminate discrimination had reorganized the terrain of employment, with significant consequences for the working lives of tens of millions of Americans.[9]

LEVIATHAN BESIEGED

Considering the reach of the post-1960s' central state into multiple spheres of life, including that of employment, allows us to account for the depth of the resistance it encountered. Resisters fall into three broadly construed categories: pragmatic, racial, and libertarian. The pragmatic opposition took shape around the belief that postwar liberalism, which had staked its reputation on the ability of the federal government to both manage the economy and achieve social harmony, no longer seemed to be working. The recession that struck in 1973 generated new problems—such as rising unemployment *and* rising interest rates—that the government's economic managers could not solve. Multiple factors converged to trigger this downturn, including the costs of the war in Vietnam, successful efforts of oil-producing countries to change the terms of trade with the industrialized world, and the emergence of Germany and Japan as serious economic rivals to the United States. Precisely because these factors were international in nature, they proved a difficult test for policies, Keynesian and otherwise, developed to manage the national economy in the 1950s and 1960s. Blame fell on the Democrats, because their philosophy of an activist government able to manage the business cycle as well as engineer economic and social well-being had driven American politics since the days of the Great Depression and World War II. Many who had long voted Democrat switched their vote to the Republicans in the

1980s, not necessarily because they subscribed to the GOP's new antigovernment ideology, but rather because they simply wanted a change.[10]

A second ground for opposing the power of the central government was racial. White southerners abandoned the Democratic Party en masse as they grasped the scale of the federal government's campaign to end regimes of white supremacy that had long defined their region. By the 1990s, the South had become as solidly red as it had once been firmly blue, with these new Republicans certain that the growth of central government power was an illegitimate interference into their way of life. White northerners were less inclined than southerners to speak the language of white supremacy or states' rights. They saw themselves as committed to America's belief in equality—for whites and blacks. Their quarrel with the federal government was that it had given blacks too much, in the process making working- and middle-class whites shoulder too much of the redistributive burden.

These racial grievances intensified in the 1970s and 1980s as the economic prospects for many white Americans dimmed, and as conservative ideologues elaborated a new populism that depicted working- and middle-class whites as the victims of an unholy Great Society alliance of federal government elites and the black poor. In this view, liberal elites designed racial remedies with little consideration for the havoc that they would unleash on long-established white neighborhoods and communities. White Americans flashed their populist anger first over busing plans to achieve school integration in America's cities. They then targeted welfare expenditures, which soared in the 1970s and 1980s as the economy weakened and many slipped into poverty. Reagan rode this wave of populist anger into the White House in 1981. He disparaged black female recipients of Aid to Dependent Children as "welfare queens," portraying them as hucksters who successfully played on liberal guilt to pry money from the federal government and then flaunted their takings. They were "ungrateful," in the words of Hollings's fictional constituent, and "undeserving" in the words of ever more white Americans. Populist anger also targeted affirmative action plans, seen as unfairly advancing under- or unqualified minorities.

Most northern whites now believed that racial discrimination in any form should be eliminated. But in the minds of some, eliminating prejudice was evolving to mean protecting whites against "reverse discrimination," the flip side of granting blacks affirmative action "privileges" on account of race. America, they insisted, should be truly "color blind." Let people rise and fall on their own merits, these critics declared, free of the central government's allegedly ham-fisted and discriminatory interventions.[11]

A fierce commitment to individual freedom and the free enterprise system generated a third ground for opposing big government. Although many gathered under this libertarian banner loathed the rules that the federal government was imposing on employment and other areas of American life in the name of racial remediation, they were not primarily motivated by a desire to secure white privilege. Rather, it was opposition to the central state's comprehensive regulatory apparatus governing capital, labor, finance, retirement, and health care that motivated them. This apparatus, in the eyes of these libertarian critics, was the work of a misguided (and liberal) government elite. It would never succeed in managing the economy in the interests of either efficiency or freedom. All such regulatory efforts would inevitably lead to some form of socialism, and hence to economic ruin and political tyranny. "We in America already have moved very far indeed toward some aspects of state socialism," lamented corporate lawyer Lewis Powell in a memo that he sent to the head of the US Chamber of Commerce in 1971. "The experience of the socialist and totalitarian states demonstrates," Powell continued, that "the contraction and denial of economic freedom is followed inevitably by governmental restrictions on other cherished rights." Powell argued that it was imperative to contest such overweening government power, and to find the will, ideology, and political muscle to roll it back.[12]

The vanguard of this emerging libertarian phalanx included University of Chicago economist Milton Friedman, Republican politicians Barry Goldwater and Reagan, and Republican insiders Powell and Nixon treasury secretary William Simon. They were no more favorably disposed to the power of the states than to that of the central government, and as such, had no desire to use their antigovernment rhetoric to restore regimes of Jim Crow in the South or pass laws regulating individuals' private lives. They viewed freedom, a product of the revolution of 1776, as America's great gift to the world. They believed that liberal and radical reformers from the 1930s through the 1960s had imperiled this gift, and opened the door to Soviet-style collectivism. Their task, as they saw it, was to halt the slide to collectivism and reinvigorate freedom, in both the short and long term. "Either we believe in our capacity for self-government," Reagan declared at the 1964 Republican National Convention, "or we abandon the American revolution and confess that an intellectual elite in a far-distant capitol [Washington, DC] can plan our lives for us better than we can plan them ourselves." America represented "the last best hope of man" in a world threatened everywhere by Communist tyranny. If Americans failed to preserve this hope, Reagan averred, they would be sentencing future generations to "a thousand years of darkness."[13]

These three distinct grounds of opposition to a large, centralized state—pragmatic, racial, and libertarian—coalesced in the late 1970s and early 1980s into a conservative movement that roared through American political life. Reagan was its tribune. His leadership would make him the most important Republican since Theodore Roosevelt. Even before Reagan was elected president in 1980, conservatives had launched antitax campaigns in multiple states to deny government the revenues on which its growth depended.[14] Influenced by the conservative-leaning Democratic president Jimmy Carter, Congress took the first steps in the 1970s toward deregulating the airlines, trucking, and telecommunications industries. On assuming office in 1981, Reagan immediately targeted two pillars of the New Deal: federal government support for collective bargaining and the progressive income tax. In 1981, he fired thousands of federally employed air traffic controllers who had gone on strike for better pay and improved working conditions. Reagan's bold move stunned the union, Professional Air Traffic Controllers Organization, and its members, and signaled to all public and private employers that Reagan would support a tougher stance toward unions than any administration since the 1920s.[15] Again in 1981, under Reagan's prodding, Congress passed the Economic

Recovery Tax Act, which reduced federal income taxes by an average of 23 percent and cut the highest marginal rate from 70 to 50 percent. A second tax bill, passed during Reagan's second term, further reduced the rate to 28 percent. In five years, then, Reagan and his congressional allies slashed the tax burden on America's highest-income earners by a remarkable 60 percent. These were the opening acts of a GOP initiative to both dramatically reduce the progressivity of the taxation system and deny the federal government the revenue on which its size and future growth depended.[16]

To further constrain the federal government, Reagan, on entering office, froze hiring at all civilian federal agencies and ordered them to refrain from issuing new regulatory rules. He appointed individuals known for their antigovernment zeal to one federal department after another. Reagan authorized these administrators to both curb the federal government's regulatory reach and assist private industry in expanding its economic operations without the "undue" influence of those who wished to protect the health of workers, quality of the environment, or even integrity of the financial system. The most headline-grabbing appointee was James Watt, secretary of the interior, who claimed that the biblical injunction "to occupy the land until He [Jesus] returns" meant that until the end of time, Americans should maximize the yield of oil, minerals, and timber from federal lands, even at the cost of damaging the environment.[17]

Watts was too outrageous a figure to last long, and he was gone from Interior by 1983. Not so Donald Regan, Reagan's secretary of the treasury from 1981 to 1985. Regan persuaded the Federal Home Loan Bank Board to advance the deregulation of savings and loan "thrift" associations (traditionally the most regulated sector of the financial industry) by allowing speculators to gain control of them and redirect capital resources to the highest-yielding investments, regardless of risk. With regulation removed, and the federal government still obligated by New Deal laws to bail out bank depositors in failed savings and loans, the stage was set for financial scandal and crisis. It came in 1987, with the crash of the savings and loan sector—a collapse that required a $370 billion bailout from the federal government.[18]

BATTLE FOR HEARTS AND MINDS

The animus against government had become so strong during the Reagan years that even the savings and loan fiasco could not temper it. It drew on a broad range of pragmatic, racial, and libertarian sources and advanced on multiple fronts. Powell, in his 1971 memo, had called on conservatives to undertake an ideological struggle to win the hearts and minds of Americans, especially the young ones on college campuses who would someday assume positions of leadership in society. Businesspeople and their allies, Powell insisted, had failed to challenge the liberal-leftist zeitgeist that had taken root on campuses and in the media in the 1960s. Conservatives had to become more outspoken, build organizations and campaigns to promote their values, and then vie for political power. "Such power," Powell declared, "must be assiduously cultivated; and . . . when necessary . . . used aggressively and with determination—without embarrassment."[19]

By the 1980s, a Powell-style conservative mobilization was emerging. A number of think tanks, such as the Heritage Foundation, American Enterprise Institute, Cato Institute, and Manhattan Institute, had been established or recast to serve as incubators of conservative ideas and policies. The hope was that they would become numerous and influential enough to constitute, in the words of journalist Sidney Blumenthal, a "counter-establishment" to challenge the hegemony of the liberal-dominated universities, liberal policymaking institutions such as the Brookings Institution, and liberal foundations such as Ford, Carnegie, and Russell Sage. Millionaires, corporations, and foundations, such as Pew, Olin, and Bradley, underwrote the costs of sustaining this counterestablishment. Convinced that liberals controlled the mainstream media, conservatives developed new ways to communicate their views to the American people and took advantage of novel technologies. Richard Viguerie pioneered direct mail techniques in the 1970s while Rush Limbaugh set radio airwaves ablaze with pugnacious conservative talk in the 1980s. Falwell, Pat Robertson, and other evangelical preachers were among the first to grasp the partisan potential of cable television, with their programs paving the way for the launch of Rupert Murdoch and Roger Ailes's fiercely conservative cable television network, Fox News, in the 1990s.[20]

Within this broader ideological and political offensive lay a quiet but crucial legal initiative advanced by conservative law professors and judges to overturn the jurisprudence that legitimated the radical work of the Warren Court. This campaign drew on widespread, popular sentiment that the Warren Court had moved too far and too fast in upending traditional practices of American government. Many white southerners were embittered by the Warren Court's destruction of states' rights. Others were less troubled by the diminution of the powers of the states per se than by the way the Court had wielded substantive due process, uncertainly in *Griswold v. Connecticut* and more confidently in *Roe v. Wade*, to argue that the Constitution guaranteed every American a right to privacy. As we have seen, the Warren Court used substantive due process to render an eighteenth-century Constitution "living" and relevant to the problems of modern life unanticipated by the founding fathers.

As early as 1971, Robert Bork, a Yale law professor, began attacking the principles on which "living constitution" jurisprudence rested. He denounced the doctrine of substantive due process from *Lochner v. New York* through *Griswold* as an illegitimate strategy of constitutional interpretation that allowed justices to make law based on their personal moral and policy preferences. He held that the nation could not long tolerate this kind of judicial activism, for it transferred the authority to make laws from the hands of legislatures elected by the people to a few unelected judges with lifetime tenure. In order for the judicial branch in the American system to maintain its "legitimate authority," it had to act within clear limits, which Bork defined as keeping constitutional interpretation closely aligned with what the founders had actually said and prescribed. It was a jurisprudential philosophy meant to strike at the heart of the Warren Court's achievements.[21]

The law students who gathered around Bork at Yale in the 1970s and 1980s began to use the term "originalism" to describe his jurisprudence. Their leader was Steven Calabresi, who founded the Federalist Society for Law and Public Policy Studies in 1982, and asked Bork to serve as faculty adviser. Two of Calabresi's Yale friends who had matriculated at the University of Chicago Law School started their own chapter of the society and chose Chicago law professor Antonin Scalia as their faculty sponsor.[22] They developed close connections to Edwin Meese, himself a former Yale man, and one of Reagan's longest-serving and most trusted advisers. Soon after becoming Reagan's attorney general in 1985, Meese assailed the Warren and Burger Courts, and called for a "jurisprudence of original intention." This jurisprudence, in Meese's view, would rest on three succinct principles. First, "where the language of the Constitution is specific, it must be obeyed." Second, "where there is a demonstrable consensus among the Framers and ratifiers as to a principle stated or implied by the Constitution, it should be followed." And third, "where there is ambiguity as to the precise meaning or reach of a constitutional provision, it should be interpreted and applied in a manner so as to at least not contradict the text of the Constitution itself."[23]

Meese secured appointments for members of the Federalist Society to numerous federal and judicial posts, and scored a big victory with Scalia's appointment to the Supreme Court in 1986 to take the place of William Rehnquist on the latter's elevation to chief justice. Republicans suffered a setback the following year when Bork's nomination to the Court was defeated in Congress, but achieved another significant victory in 1991 with the appointment of Clarence Thomas, who would prove to be even more an originalist than Scalia. The originalists targeted substantive due process and thereby threatened a major expansion of individual rights overseen by the Warren Court. They also took aim at liberal jurists' broad use of the commerce clause to justify the expansion of the government's regulatory power. The influence of Bork, Scalia, and others at America's top law schools, the success of Meese in seeding originalists throughout the federal government, and Scalia's boldness and analytic brilliance on the bench made originalism a major jurisprudential and policy force by the late 1980s. It provided a powerful set of justifications for rolling back the power of the federal government.[24]

Liberals were publicly contemptuous of the conservatives' jurisprudential challenge. Their defeat of Bork in his confirmation battle in the Senate and near defeat of Thomas gave them confidence that this challenge could be contained. But they knew they were vulnerable. Liberal lawyers and judges had themselves opposed the use of substantive due process for half a century, from the 1900s through the 1950s. Though a majority of liberal justices on the Warren Court appeared to abandon this opposition by invoking substantive due process as a justification for their decision in *Roe v. Wade* in 1973, several of them never entirely shed their discomfort with basing important decisions on what they had once regarded as a shaky foundation. In private, many liberal jurists were critical of the Warren Court's use of substantive due process in *Roe*, even as they believed America was a better place for having guaranteed women a right to an abortion. Few of the liberal jurists who accommodated themselves to substantive due process ever embraced it.[25]

The deeper problem facing liberals was that the Constitution offered them no tools adequate to the task of building a large regulatory state or expanding the rights of Americans beyond those enumerated in it. The best way for liberals to have expanded their tool kit was through constitutional amendment. An amendment guaranteeing privacy would have proven useful, as would one granting the federal government a power to act for the good and welfare of the commonwealth. However, amending the Constitution was such an arduous process—even a popular Equal Rights Amendment initiative in the 1970s failed to get the requisite 75 percent approval from state legislatures—that most liberals gave up on it, choosing instead to make creative use of tools already available. Liberal jurists were clever and sometimes ingenious in putting old clauses to new uses. But their discomfort in doing so spoke to a recognition that their jurisprudence and hence the Warren Court's achievements rested on an insecure foundation. By the late 1980s, conservatives had found several fissures in this foundation, and equipped with their jurisprudence of originalism, were chiseling to crack them wide open.

Substantive due process constituted one of those fissures. Another arose from the commerce clause, which liberal jurists had long before turned into a surrogate national police power endowing the federal government with comprehensive regulatory authority. The big liberal breakthrough had come in the 1930s and 1940s when the Supreme Court expanded the clause's regulatory sway to include not just commerce but also manufacturing, mining, agriculture, and labor relations. In the landmark *Wickard v. Filburn* decision (1942), the Court further increased the clause's power by ruling that all economic activities, even those that appeared to be local and uninvolved with commercial exchange, fell under its jurisdiction. In the 1960s, the Warren Court widened the authority of the commerce clause yet again by using it to affirm the constitutionality of the Civil Rights Act of 1964.[26]

That the Court felt compelled to justify its protection of civil (and human) rights on the basis of the federal government's authority to regulate commerce left several liberal justices uneasy—an unease discernible in the opinions they wrote for the cases deciding the constitutionality of the 1964 Civil Rights Act.[27] On the one hand, protecting civil rights was a project too far reaching to be framed by considerations of commerce; on the other hand, resorting to commerce to uphold civil rights made clear how far the Constitution was being stretched beyond its "original intent." This stretch was ripe for an attack. None came in the 1960s, when the authority of liberal jurisprudence seemed impregnable. But in the 1980s and 1990s, attacks did come, most powerfully from Richard Epstein, a University of Chicago law professor and rising star within the conservative legal firmament. The original regulatory import of the commerce clause, in Epstein's telling, was far narrower than twentieth-century liberal jurists had made it out to be. Properly construed, this clause limited the central government's regulatory authority to the realms of "interstate transportation, navigation, and sales." Epstein did not mince words: the uses that liberal justices had made of the commerce clause beginning in the New Deal were "extravagant" and constitutionally indefensible.[28]

Epstein's assault on liberal jurisprudence had more radical implications than did the attack on substantive due process, for it was meant to undercut the legitimacy of most regulatory activities undertaken by the central state since the 1930s. The logic of this position dictated that many of the regulatory institutions installed under the aegis of the commerce clause, including the National Labor Relations Act and the Civil Rights Act, might need to be dismantled. Epstein himself shrank from this conclusion not because he thought it was wrong but because he thought it would unleash too much chaos.[29] Other Republicans, however, did not shy from the consequences of Epstein's radicalism. By the 1980s, Grover Norquist was emerging as one of these radical Republicans' most forceful leaders.

Born in 1956, Norquist had been a conservative activist since 1968 when, at the age of twelve, he had volunteered to get out the vote for Nixon. He got his big break about twenty years later when Reagan appointed him to head Americans for Tax Reform, an organization set up to build grassroots support for Reagan's 1986 tax cut initiative. Norquist turned Americans for Tax Reform into a permanent organization dedicated to maintaining pressure on Congress to continue cutting federal taxes until the central state, starved for revenue, would perforce wither away. By the mid-1990s he was a major player on the Republican Right, an architect of Newt Gingrich's Contract for America in 1994, and the convener of a weekly breakfast, the Wednesday Morning series, that was rapidly becoming a leading site of GOP networking. Participation in these breakfasts was by invitation only. Participants had to sign a pledge permanently forswearing support for federal government tax hikes. As Republicans lined up to sign, Norquist spoke confidently about reducing the American Leviathan to its late-nineteenth century Lilliputian dimensions. He yearned for the time when William McKinley was still president and before Theodore Roosevelt had allegedly betrayed the Republican cause by committing the GOP to the idea of a powerful central state. Norquist was a provocateur, and he delighted in telling fellow Republicans and the press that his goal was to shrink the federal government to the point "where we can drown it in the bathtub."[30] The work of Epstein and like-minded originalist jurists provided Norquist and other radical Republican ideologues with the constitutional ammunition they needed to delegitimate America's federal state.

CONSERVATIVE CONTRADICTIONS

Even as conservatives exposed the vulnerability of liberal jurisprudence, they were unable to evade the contradictions of their own case for taking down big government. Most important, they were unwilling to contemplate placing limits on a major driver of the central state—the supersize military and military-industrial complex. Reagan entered office in 1981 determined to build up the military to overwhelm the Soviet enemy. He was prepared to spare no expense in doing so, increasing the Pentagon's budget as he cut federal taxes, in the process saddling the federal government with deficits that would triple over the course of his presidency. In his first year in office, Reagan persuaded Congress to increase the military's budget by 20 percent, arguably the largest such increase in US history excepting those moments when the nation was engaged in all-out war. By the end of his first term, defense appropriations had risen 34 percent, from $171 to $229 billion. Reagan matched this increased defense spending with an escalating rhetoric of confrontation with the Soviet Union. The era of détente and accommodation was over. Sensing the enemy's weakness, Reagan declared that the United States would undertake an arms race and military buildup that the Soviet Union could not possibly match, anticipating a "great revolutionary crisis" in the Communist homeland that would "leave Marxism-Leninism on the ash-heap of history." The United States would throw all its resources into this last, climactic battle with what Reagan liked to call the "evil empire."[31]

Reagan-era defense expenditures went toward expanding the ranks of military personnel as well as underwriting expensive new weapons programs—including the B-1 bomber, B-2 stealth bomber, cruise missiles, MX missile, and Strategic Defense Initiative—that involved lucrative contracts with defense manufacturers, augmenting further the country's military-industrial complex. As had been the case since the early years of the Cold War, defense work saw the government directing major sectors of the economy—a form of public influence on "private industry" as profound as that effected by the federal government's efforts to remedy workplace racial discrimination.[32] Spending for defense often became a form of surrogacy, since so many different kinds of expenditures could be justified by invoking the need to shield America from its enemies. National security was, in short, an enormous engine of government growth.

Small government ideologues in the GOP developed a handy rationale for justifying this sort of big central government, arguing that Communism had to be not only contained but also defeated. This goal achieved, America's big military would be shrunk and the military-industrial complex dismantled. By the 1980s, however, the militarized component of central state power had been integral to American government for more than forty years, and the Soviet Union's collapse—between 1989 and 1991—prompted few Republicans to contemplate a major reorientation. To the contrary, during the 1990s, against the backdrop of instability and war in the Balkans and the Middle East, William Kristol, Robert Kagan, Elliott Abrams, and other innovative Republican thinkers developed the doctrine of "preventive war." With this doctrine, they sought to justify maintaining a large defense sector during the post–Cold War era and a military capable, with a few months notice, of waging war anywhere in the world against states and groups threatening to the United States. Several of this group, including Donald Rumsfeld and Paul Wolfowitz, became principals in the George W. Bush administration and shaped the response to 9/11, which entailed keeping the nation on a war footing indefinitely. From the 1980s through the 2000s, the contradiction between their small government orientation and their commitment to a maintaining a large military was one that most Republicans preferred not to confront.[33]

Conservatives were also reluctant to face a similar contradiction in their preference for militarizing and federalizing the nation's police forces. "Law and order" had become a rallying cry for the conservative movement as far back as the late 1960s in response, first, to the urban insurrections of that decade, and then to the rising crime rates in America's cities. In the 1970s, this campaign focused on rapidly proliferating drug use among Americans and the crime associated with it. The resulting War on Drugs, launched by Nixon in 1971 and continued by every president since, had a foreign policy component, manifest in US efforts to destroy drugs grown overseas and the cartels that imported them. The War on Drugs also had a domestic state-building dimension in the form of the central government's conscription of state and local police into its work.[34] Initially, many states and municipalities were reluctant to join the federal War on Drugs, not because they were soft on crime, but instead because they wanted to keep control of crime fighting where they believed it belonged, with their own police forces. To overcome this resistance, the central government began supplying local law enforcement with money and equipment. Large grants were made available to municipal police departments to form narcotics task forces. The US Drug Enforcement Administration provided state highway patrols with free training and support for stopping motorists to inspect their cars for drugs. By the 1990s, the Pentagon was transferring surplus military hardware—helmets, night-vision goggles, grenade launchers, rifles, and helicopters—to these state and local police forces. In the space of ten years, for instance, the Pentagon gave Wisconsin police departments alone more than a hundred thousand pieces of military equipment. The availability of this firepower and technology accelerated the formation of units that could actually use both, and led to the proliferation of special weapons and tactics (SWAT) teams not only in large urban areas but also in small towns. SWAT deployments skyrocketed from three thousand per year in the early 1980s to thirty thousand by 1996.[35]

Civil rights and liberal groups were troubled by this militarization and federalization of local police forces, but most conservatives—and most white Americans—were not. By the 1980s, the War on Drugs was thoroughly racialized: black users of drugs and black (and minority) dealers were seen as the biggest threat to the welfare and safety of cities. Because "crack" cocaine was viewed as a "black" drug that rendered its users savage, Congress passed laws in the 1980s punishing the possession of crack with sentences one hundred times greater than that which the possession of powdered cocaine incurred.[36] Few white Americans paused to think what such intensification of the government's coercive powers might mean for them. They did not worry that SWAT teams might invade *their* neighborhoods and bang down *their* doors, and they did not fear long imprisonment for possessing small amounts of powdered cocaine. Thus few white Americans, even politically conservative ones, called for a federal government rollback in this area, or for reconsidering a social policy that by the 1990s had given the United States one of the largest incarcerated populations and prison complexes in the world. The "carceral state" was the kind of big government that many conservatives liked.[37]

White attitudes toward the federalization of crime fighting and mass incarceration exposed the complexity of popular thinking about government in America. Many Americans had become attached to various federal government programs and initiatives, especially those perceived as bringing them benefits. Social Security, Medicare, and support for basic research in science and medicine in addition to safe cities and harsh sentences for lawbreakers were among those that drew the most support. Conservative insistence on making the size and reach of government the central issue in American political life obscured rather than illuminated this variety and complexity.[38]

Many corporations and businessmen likewise drew close to federal government programs, though their eyes were drawn to a different kind of public benefit—lucrative contracts. From the 1940s to the 1990s, the federally fueled military-industrial complex sustained scores of corporations dependent on military contracts while raising up new men of power, especially in the South, Southwest, and West, who were devoted to the Republican Party.[39]

From the 1960s forward, federal funds also created numerous lucrative opportunities in the civilian economy, with the government hiring contractors to handle aspects of its work. New public programs, such as Medicare and Medicaid, responsible for enrolling millions of eligible beneficiaries, generated demands for data processing that the federal government was unprepared to meet. Clever entrepreneurs who grasped the potential of the emerging computer technology persuaded the government to turn such data processing over to them. Prominent in their ranks was a young Texan, H. Ross Perot, whose information processing on behalf of Medicare in the late 1960s laid the foundation for a business empire whose value had reached $2.5 billion by the 1980s. When Perot became active in politics in the late 1960s and early 1970s, he drew close not to the party that had passed Medicare and Medicaid—thereby making him rich—but instead to the one that cast itself in opposition to the Great Society and big government.[40]

As the central government became an operation that year in and year out generated billions of dollars for the private sector, ever-increasing numbers of lobbyists sought to influence political deliberations in Washington, both to shape the writing of legislation and win favor with Washington senators and congressmen who could throw contracts their clients' way. Washington's K Street, where lobbyists had long maintained offices, exploded in size in the 1980s and 1990s. "Antigovernment" Republicans turned out to be as effective as the Democrats, and often more so, in cutting new channels to direct the flow of federal money from the public to the private sector. Norquist joined forces with Texas Republican congressman (and majority whip) Tom DeLay in 1995 to launch the K Street Project, the ostensible purpose of which was to force lobbying firms to hire Republicans and in that way become more conservative in their dealings with Congress. But as a series of investigations in the early years of the twenty-first century revealed, the K Street Project was also deeply involved in directing government funds and favors to corporate and individual supporters of the GOP agenda.[41]

Awash in federal cash, metropolitan Washington grew steadily in wealth. By the first decade of the twenty-first century, it was home to six of the ten richest counties in the country.[42] It mattered little whether the national economy was booming or going bust, or whether Republicans or Democrats controlled Congress or the presidency. The business of government never seemed to dry up, which is why it attracted into its ranks not only those committed to public service but also those seeking to accumulate private fortunes. Throughout the 1990s and 2000s, the sums spent to finance political campaigns increased at an astronomical rate—a sure sign of the sizable economic dividends that big contributors expected in return from government policymakers.[43]

The national security state, militarization and federalization of crime fighting, and building of businesses and personal fortunes via central state contracts were forms of big government endorsed by conservative, antigovernment leaders and their followers. By the 1980s and 1990s, some conservatives, especially within the ranks of corporate America, had also come to see affirmative action as yet another good facilitated by an activist central government. Many political observers in the early 1980s believed at the time that the Supreme Court's 1978 decision to strike down quotas in university admissions (*Regents of the University of California v. Bakke*) marked the beginning of the end for affirmative action programs and the kind of racial engineering that these programs required at both universities and workplaces. But their forecast turned out to be wrong. Powell, the corporate lawyer who in 1971 had called on conservatives to mount an ideological offensive to delegitimate big government, now sat on the Supreme Court and delivered a surprisingly measured, even Solomonic decision in *Bakke*. Quotas were unconstitutional, he argued on behalf of the Court, but affirmative action in pursuit of "diversity" was a principle that employers and university admissions officers could legitimately deploy.[44] As a consequence of *Bakke*, quotas disappeared after 1978 while affirmative action programs as a whole strengthened their hold on employment and higher education. This strengthening occurred quietly, which is why William Bradford Reynolds, head of the Civil Rights Division in Reagan's Department of Justice, was stunned when he encountered it in 1985, as he and his boss, Attorney General Meese, were setting out to terminate the 1965 fiat (executive order 11246) that had launched affirmative action's career.

Grassroots conservative groups lined up to support Reynolds and Meese, while liberal organizations such as the National Association for the Advancement of Colored People and National Organization for Women ginned up the opposition. None of this surprised Reagan's top men. What did shock them was corporate America's reaction. The Business Roundtable declared that executive order 11246 had "served American society, workers, and government contractors well," and should be preserved. The historically archconservative National Association of Manufacturers agreed, calling this executive order "sound policy" and noting that it had drawn "enthusiastic support" from its members. These strong corporate endorsements were as much pragmatic as ideological. Having poured a great deal of energy and resources into creating employment and personnel management systems that featured diversity, manufacturers and other employers were not ready to see these systems torn apart by yet another political turn. The more internationally oriented executives in corporate ranks had also begun to glimpse the ways in which a diverse workforce could enhance a company's global appeal. For a variety of reasons, then, big business by the 1980s had accepted the reengineering of the American workplace that the federal government had undertaken in the 1960s and 1970s. With more than half of the Cabinet siding with corporate America on this issue, Reagan's Department of Justice backed down and executive order 11246—and the government-designed systems of hiring and promotion that it mandated—remained in force.[45]

DIVIDED GOVERNMENT, POLITICAL PARALYSIS

Surveying the full terrain across which the central state had become active in the last third of the twentieth century highlights the surprising diversity of attitudes toward government entertained by Americans. This diversity helps us to understand why for most of the 1980s and 1990s, voters repeatedly chose to divide control of the federal government between the Republicans and Democrats. Even during the height of Reagan's so-called revolution, the GOP never gained a majority in the House of Representatives and ceded its Senate majority to the Democrats in 1988. In the 1990s, a time of ostensible liberal resurgence centering on William J. Clinton's presidency, the Democrats failed from 1994 on to hold a majority in either house of Congress.

Divided government made politics challenging for both parties. They responded in intriguingly different ways: the Democrats with a politics of compromise, and the Republicans with a politics of principle and purity. President Clinton, who assumed office in 1993, led the Democrats' accommodationist campaign. After the spectacular failure of his national health care initiative that year and resulting repudiation of the Democratic Party by voters in the 1994 elections, Clinton embraced a role quite similar to the one that Eisenhower had assumed in the 1950s: restoring his party's political viability by persuading it to accept the core principles of the other party's ideology as its own. As president, Clinton lifted one idea after another from the GOP playbook. He declared that fiscal prudence had to take priority over social spending. He would end "welfare as we have come to know it" (and did just that by signing off on the Personal Responsibility and Work Opportunity Act of 1996). To promote law and order, he would put another hundred thousand policemen and women on America's streets. Most provocatively, Clinton declared that Democrats had to adjust to the reality that "the age of big government is over."[46]

In pursuit of this new Democratic goal of small government, Clinton signed legislation in 1998 repealing the Glass-Steagall Act of 1933, long regarded as one of the Democrats' signal achievements in using central state authority to impose much-needed discipline and stability on financial markets. A Democratic president therefore played a crucial role in "freeing" the financial sector from federal government control and unleashing the "animal spirits" that a mere decade later would trigger America's worst financial crash in eighty years. This kind of crash was precisely what the Glass-Steagall Act was meant to—and on several occasions did—forestall. Clinton's appropriation of conservative rhetoric and policy, a strategy he and his adviser Dick Morris labeled "triangulation," enraged Republicans, who saw it as a clever and opportunistic ruse to steal their policies, repackage them into Democratic proposals, and win presidential power. Republicans became obsessive in their determination to discredit Clinton, reveal to the public the questionable ethics that underlay his shape-shifting, and even, if possible, remove him from office. This last goal they almost accomplished in 1998 when the House of Representatives voted two articles of impeachment against Clinton for lying about a sexual encounter.[47]

Republicans also recognized, however, that Clinton's slipperiness alone could not explain why over a twenty-year period during which conservative ideology prevailed, progress toward their cherished goals of decreasing the size and influence of government had been slow and piecemeal. Increasingly they trained their ire on their own leaders, blaming them for not delivering on promises. Nixon, in this view, had betrayed the Republican cause by doing more to sustain than thwart the Great Society. Reagan now stood accused of overvaluing his friendship with Mr. Big Government himself, Tip O'Neill, the Democratic speaker of the House of Representatives for much of his presidency, compromising conservative principles when he should have stood firm. Conservatives were furious with George H. W. Bush for raising taxes after he had made a "read my lips" pledge not to do so under any circumstances.[48]

Well into the 1990s, conservatives believed that Gingrich, a brash, young congressman from Georgia, had the political backbone that his predecessors lacked. Gingrich's leadership of the 1994 electoral tsunami that gave the GOP control of both houses of Congress for the first time since 1954 augured well for the ascent of the Right.[49] Gingrich, though, was outfoxed by Clinton on several occasions, and then fell victim to his own bombastic tendencies and ethical lapses, forcing him to resign the house speakership in 1998 and his own congressional seat in 1999. GOP conservatives then embraced George W. Bush as their savior. The younger Bush's determination to enact a massive income tax cut and privatize Social Security as well as a broad array of social services appeared to reflect the depths of his conservative commitments. But he also disappointed purists, proving himself to be too much of a "compassionate conservative," and too willing to expand federal government power in the interest of improving education (with No Child Left Behind) and health care (via Medicare reform), implanting democracy in the Middle East (through nation building in Iraq), and once the 2008 financial crisis hit, restoring the economy to health. By the time Bush left office in 2009, conservatives despised him almost as much as did liberals.[50]

Conservatives also encountered disappointment with respect to the Supreme Court. Republican presidents appointed ten consecutive justices to the Court between 1969 and 1991 in a partisan run that exceeded that enjoyed by FDR, across four terms in office. Remarkably, that double-digit string of Republican appointments failed to produce the insurmountable Court majority for which they yearned. Powell of Virginia, selected by Nixon in 1971, became a defender, as we have seen, of nonquota forms of affirmative action. Sandra Day O'Connor of Arizona, appointed by Reagan in 1981, repeatedly antagonized conservatives by finding the middle ground between the Left and Right. Anthony Kennedy of California, chosen by Reagan in 1988 after the Senate refused to confirm Bork, gradually revealed such a strong commitment to individual rights that at times he seemed to be channeling the Warren Court. David Souter of New Hampshire, elevated to the Court by Bush in 1991, was an eclectic loner deeply at odds with all orthodoxies, including those that dominated the GOP. The Supreme Court of the 1990s did have redoubtable conservatives in Scalia, Thomas, and Chief Justice Rehnquist. But rarely could that conservative trio muster enough support from moderates O'Connor, Kennedy, and Souter to give conservatives what they wanted: ending affirmative action, overturning *Roe v. Wade*, and striking down *Miranda*, the 1960s' decision that conservatives charged granted criminal suspects outlandish rights and imperiled the safety of law-abiding citizens.[51]

Conservatives might have seen in their political and judicial defeats evidence that their beliefs were too extreme for the American people. They might have in effect agreed with the legal thinker Epstein, who held that actually imposing a full conservative agenda would upend too many institutions and generate too much upheaval. They might have admired O'Connor for insisting that a true conservative strategy for change ought to be gradual and respectful of how individuals, in any society, become embedded in institutions and accustomed to ways of living resistant to abrupt changes. An insistence on embeddedness had been a staple of conservative thought in Europe since Edmund Burke first articulated its principles in the eighteenth century, deploying them to argue that the radical tactics of the French revolutionaries would fail.[52] But American conservatives held Burke and his perspective in little regard; in temperament, they were closer to the French revolutionaries he despised. They blamed their only limited success not on the reluctance of "the people" to embrace radical change but rather on the failure of leaders to give "the people" what they wanted. And so in the 1990s and 2000s, American conservatives resolved to become more demanding of their leaders. They required all candidates for office to take irrevocable public oaths on major policy issues. They demanded that their legislators refuse the kinds of policy compromises that past Republican representatives had accepted, even if that meant risking electoral defeat. They expected their candidates to articulate core conservative principles and defend to them to the last.

This approach informed the Contract with America that Gingrich and his young insurgents offered to voters in the 1994 elections. It guided Norquist's determination to exact a pledge from every Republican legislator in Washington never under any circumstances to support an increase in the federal income tax. It justified DeLay's insistence that every lobbying organization on K Street put card-carrying conservative Republicans on its payrolls. And of course, it inspired Tea Party activists in 2010 and beyond to risk losing—which in fact happened—multiple elections by supporting candidates of conservative principles over Republicans whose ideological squishiness would have positioned them to prevail in general elections.[53]

In taking such stands on principle, organizations of the New Right actually began to resemble certain parties of the Old Left. Holding that a parliamentary politics of give-and-take had failed, old leftists, from the Jacobins of the eighteenth century to the anarchists and Communists of the twentieth, had turned instead to a purer and sterner politics of confrontation and conflict instead. They would do whatever they could to confront the old order at the price of considerable turmoil and chaos. They believed that struggle, ardently pursued, would yield a better world. With increasing fervor, they maintained that the world they wished to bring into being justified any political means. Conservative Republicans have not abandoned parliamentary politics as certain parties of the Old Left did, but they have shown a willingness to manipulate its procedures and obstruct its smooth functioning. Where they controlled statehouses, they gerrymandered to create multiple safe districts for their kind in the House of Representatives. They were equally determined to exclude, under the guise of state law, groups of Democratic-leaning voters from exercising their right to vote. In 2011, they brought the federal government to the edge of default by refusing to raise the debt ceiling on federal borrowing. If they had stayed true to this principle to the end, which they nearly did, they would have made it impossible for the federal government to pay bills it had already incurred, with possibly catastrophic results for its creditworthiness. Finally, in their efforts to enforce draconian budget cuts on government, Republican conservatives three times—in 1995, 1996, and 2013—refused to compromise with Democrats on appropriations bills that had to pass Congress in order for the federal government to continue its operations. Three times, as a consequence, the Republicans forced the federal government to shut its doors—for forty-three days all told. These shutdowns resulted in hundreds of thousands of federal employees going without pay and denied millions more regular government services. Popular anger at Republicans forced them to relent in order to allow the federal government to reopen its doors. Yet the defeats only temporarily stymied conservative militants, and did little to limit their ability to drive the GOP agenda.[54]

For the last two decades, the Republican conservatives' politics of principle and confrontation has been a more powerful force than the Democrats' politics of compromise and accommodation, with profound implications for public policy. Conservative Republicans have been so successful in demonizing income taxes that it is now impossible to imagine raising them to anywhere near the rates that prevailed from the 1940s through 1970s. By limiting the federal government's revenues in this way, the Republicans have undercut Congress's ability to launch major new domestic programs, even in cases such as infrastructural overhaul, immigration, and climate control where many argue they are necessary. As a result of pressures that Republicans have brought to bear on existing government programs, many public agencies have been hollowed out, and others meant to be regulators of industry have been turned into servants of the private sector. The ability of the central state to solve America's problems has declined, and public confidence in government has correspondingly eroded. That decline in confidence has, in turn, intensified pressure for privatizing many of the functions that government once regarded as its province, from military and intelligence work, on the one hand, to schooling and welfare, on the other. The central state, as we have seen, had since the nineteenth century been enlisting private groups and institutions to execute tasks that it was unable to accomplish on its own. But rarely was privatization as popular and celebrated as it became in the last decade of the twentieth century and the first decade of the twenty-first. All these developments reflect the success of the Republican Party in making its antigovernment ideology predominant.[55]

So too does the shape of President Barack Obama's most significant domestic achievement, the Affordable Care Act of 2010. Republicans loathed this bill and its commitment to making health insurance available to most Americans from the moment it took shape in Congress in 2009, and warned that its passage would herald the triumph of socialism in America. Their white-hot opposition has obscured one fact: that the 2010 act closely mirrors what the Republicans had proposed in 1993 as an alternative to the national health insurance bill that the Clinton White House was then drafting. The Affordable Care Act seeks to build on, not supplant, the private structure of insurance provision and to allow markets—called exchanges—to deliver insurance rather than enlisting the government to do this work itself. Obama conceived of his bill as offering an alternative to the single-payer system at work in Medicare in the United States, in which the government is the principal administrative player. In 2006, the then governor, Mitt Romney, supported the first rollout of this kind of plan in Massachusetts precisely because it was thought to embody Republican principles. That conservatives since then have felt emboldened to condemn this *Republican* plan as socialistic and have successfully persuaded many Americans of the same reveals how much further to the right they have moved political discourse since Clinton assumed office in 1993.[56]

Republicans' success in changing the zeitgeist has not spared them political defeat. They lost the presidency in 2008 and 2012 because of Bush's ill-advised and increasingly unpopular war in Iraq, and because the careless deregulation of the financial system that began under Clinton in 1998 metastasized under the younger Bush, precipitating the financial crash of 2008. Military and economic reversals created an opening for Democrats and a liberal surge led by Obama, remarkably only the fourth Democratic president in the last one hundred years to win reelection. Obama's success in passing a near trillion-dollar stimulus package in 2009, and the Affordable Care Act along with the Frank-Dodd Wall Street Reform and Consumer Protection Act in 2010, recalled some of the headiness of the Democratic Party's New Deal heyday. But no rout of conservatives, as occurred in Roosevelt's first midterm election in 1934, was in the offing. To the contrary, the Tea Party rebellion of 2010–12 killed Obama's momentum and has denied him the opportunity to pass meaningful domestic legislation during his second term in office. And though the GOP's chances of winning the presidency with a right-dominated Republican coalition are long, conservatives' strength in the House of Representatives will likely give them veto power over public policy for years to come. A veto is a limited yet nonetheless significant power, especially for a party committed first and foremost to preventing the growth of government.[57]

As successful as conservatives have been in promoting their antigovernment ideology, they have not come close to achieving their biggest goal of returning the central state to its pre–New Deal size and influence. It is one thing to stop the further expansion of government; it is quite another to dismantle what has been built, particularly when the federal government offers programs and benefits that many Americans on both sides of the Democratic-Republican divide want to preserve. Strong in the House of Representatives but stymied in their larger ambitions, Republicans have settled for a politics of paralysis in Washington, DC. Because Congress has done far too little to address the domestic challenges that the re-public of the twenty-first century confronts, many Americans have turned away from the central state in despair or disgust. This turn-ing away itself serves conservative purposes by underscoring the shortcomings of a large central state and reinforcing Republican claims that it serves no positive function.

REVIVAL OF THE STATES

America still has its Leviathan, but in domestic matters, it is an in-stitution besieged. Encircled and under fire, it has receded from the field of battle, allowing the incompletely vanquished states to reen-ter the fray.

Pundits have been predicting a resurgence in the states' power from the moment that the Warren Court and LBJ's Great Society broke it in the 1960s. Nixon proclaimed his commitment to a "new federalism" soon after assuming office in 1969.[58] Reagan did the same when he became president in 1981.[59] Rehnquist, elevated to the post of chief justice in 1986 by Reagan, intended to make the restoration of powers to the states his signature jurisprudential ac-complishment. But he effected nothing like the Thermidor of states' rights that the late nineteenth-century Supreme Court engineered, instead working around the edges of the Warren Court revolution and rarely challenging its core principles.[60] That Court had drasti-cally diminished the police power of the states, and no respectable politician, right or left, dared to challenge the incorporation doc-trine that it had used to enforce the Bill of Rights on the states. The 1960s' shift in power from the states to the federal government was far deeper and more enduring than the 1860s' shift had been.[61]

That situation may now be changing, for three reasons: first, paralysis in Congress; second, the realization by monied players in American politics that public policy advantage can be more easily secured in state capitals than in Washington; and third, a decision by the John Roberts's Supreme Court limiting the federal govern-ment's ability to conscript the states into its policy initiatives.

As congressional paralysis became the norm in the twenty-first century, state governments began to take urgent policy matters, ranging from immigration reform and climate control to raising the minimum wage and improving infrastructure, into their own hands. The Supreme Court beat back attempts in Arizona and Alabama to develop immigration regimes in their states at odds with federal policy, but thus far allowed legislative initiatives on other matters to go forward.[62]

The shift in the flow of campaign finance from the central government to the states is an unintended consequence of the Supreme Court's 2010 *Citizens United* decision, which removed restrictions on contributions from wealthy individuals to political candidates. In the decision's wake, the wealthy, as expected, dramatically increased the level of their contributions to presidential candidates and others seeking national office as well as the organizations supporting them. Once the 2012 Romney presidential campaign imploded and paralysis in Congress became manifest, however, the monied began to direct contributions to political contests in the states in the hopes of gaining some of the power and influence denied them at the federal level. The billionaire Koch brothers have pioneered this strategy, but Democratic donors are imitating them. The goal is to create "one-party states," where one party controls the governorship and both houses of the state legislature, enabling it to decisively influence policy on a wide range of matters: the legalization of same-sex marriage and marijuana; access to abortions and guns; the level of the minimum wage and rights of public sector employees; support for mass transit, climate control, and health care; the treatment of undocumented immigrants; and rules governing elections. The Republicans have had success turning Tennessee, Wisconsin, Alabama, and North Carolina into one-party states, while Democrats have built out from their California and Illinois strongholds to develop similar degrees of party control in Minnesota and Colorado. Both parties have been plotting takeovers of multiple other states.[63]

A key part of the Supreme Court's 2012 decision on the Affordable Care Act (ACA) has further stimulated the newly independent spirit of the states. While the decision upheld the act as a whole, it struck down a provision that penalizes states for refusing to play their assigned role in federal health insurance reform. The ACA required the states to provide their poorest citizens with insurance by expanding their Medicaid programs. The federal government agreed to fund the full cost of this expansion at the outset and, after three years, to continue paying 90 percent of states' costs. The Roberts Supreme Court ruled, however, that the federal government could not impose this Medicaid expansion on the states, even if it agreed to pick up almost the entire cost. "Congress may use its spending power," Roberts wrote in the majority opinion, "to create incentives for States to act in accordance with federal policies. But when 'pressure turns into compulsion,' . . . the legislation runs contrary to our system of federalism." The states, Roberts declared, are "independent sovereigns in our federal system," and their sovereignty must be protected. Failure to do so would turn "the two-government system established by the Framers" into "a system that vests power in one central government, and individual liberty would suffer."[64]

The immediate effect of this ruling was to permit states to opt out of the Medicaid-administered part of ACA, with the consequence that poor people living in those states would be denied access to health insurance that the legislation had authorized for them. One-party Republican states seized on this option, as did many states in which Republicans controlled two branches of state government. But the more significant effect was to give state legislators permission to once again imagine their polities as "independent sovereigns" over which the federal government had only limited control. In the years ahead, we can expect to see state legislatures testing in court the boundary between federal incentives (permitted) and federal coercion (prohibited), seeking to interpret as much as possible as coercive and thus to release themselves from the control that the federal government had achieved through the work of the Warren Court and Great Society.

How far will this incipient revival of the states go? It seems unlikely that the Roberts Court will allow it to unfold without limits, which would involve giving the states back the full extent of the police power that prevailed prior to the time, between the 1930s and 1960s, when the Court used the doctrine of incorporation to vitiate it. Chief Justice Roberts himself has shown a commitment to protecting the rights of corporations—a commitment that could be undermined if the revival of states' police power were to become too robust. Associate Justice Kennedy has an equally deep commitment to protecting the rights of individuals against encroachments by government—a principle that could also suffer if too much power were to be returned to the states. Should a Democratic candidate win the 2016 presidential election, and have a chance to make one or two Supreme Court appointments, the commitment to the regime of individual rights would likely only grow stronger.

A restoration of the states to the position of privilege they enjoyed in the nineteenth or early twentieth centuries seems improbable. States have positioned themselves, though, to serve as policy hothouses, with the capacity to trigger changes in national policy under the right circumstances. This process is already well advanced in connection to a variety of issues, including the legalization of gay marriage and marijuana, restrictions on the rights of public workers and availability of abortions, and raising the minimum wage. States have once again become "laboratories of democracy"—a phrase that Louis Brandeis once used to describe their work and importance during the Progressive era. Yet this revival of the states should not obscure the ad hoc nature of the project, nor the fact that it is a politics born as much out of desperation as by design. The recent turn toward the states, then, underscores the constraints imposed on the central state by an eighteenth-century Constitution and the near impossibility of altering the Constitution so as to give government in the United States new tools to address its twenty-first century problems. In this respect, America remains bound by its eighteenth-century origins.

CONCLUSION

America's system of governance has displayed both considerable strength and weakness across its 240-year history. Its strength is apparent first in its ability to embed its laws, institutions, and sovereignty across a vast continent. That no manifest destiny was involved in this process—to the contrary, multiple forces in the nineteenth century were pushing the new republic toward fragmentation and even failure—makes the force of its southern and western drive all the more impressive. Expansion involved war, violence, and conquest, as it has wherever governments have set it as a goal. The continent was not virgin land. The surprising part of the story is that the expansion was effected by a relatively small central state, and one with limited resources in both military and nonmilitary affairs. Military forces could be scaled up rapidly, but Congress showed an equal determination to scale those forces back after conflagrations ended. Congress did not support the formation of a large-scale, standing military until the nation committed itself to near-permanent war in the 1940s. How the United States managed expansion without a large centralized state is, I have suggested, among the most significant stories of American history.

The republic's embrace of a liberal Constitution meant to limit the size of government and orbit of its powers was the most formidable barrier to the formation of a large central state for most of its history. This liberal governing framework shaped not only processes of territorial expansion but also the manner in which the central state grew and the techniques it employed to address problems it faced. Between the 1880s and 1930s, countless state builders envisioned transforming the federal government into a colossus. At that time, every Western nation aspiring to greatness was thought to need such a state. Many in the United States turned toward Europe for instruction in constructing one; boatloads traveled across the Atlantic for inspiration and guidance. What they could accomplish in their native land, however, usually trailed far behind their European dreams. Liberal constitutional constraints enforced by vigilant Supreme Courts made thoroughgoing transformations in government difficult to achieve. These constraints did not halt efforts to increase the size and influence of the central state. But for a long time they prompted many supporters of expanded government power to abjure transformation in favor of improvisation. State builders developed a repertoire of techniques—those that I have labeled exemption, surrogacy, and privatization—to extend government power beyond the limits intended by the founders. These techniques, I have argued, empowered the federal government, enabling it to pursue a variety of aims: to build a transcontinental railroad, suppress cultural and political dissenters, campaign against social evils (such as drugs and prostitution), regulate manufacturing and industrial relations, administer colonies, and pursue racial equality. The turn toward improvisation gave the nation an effective central state while keeping it within the bounds permitted by a liberal and difficult-to-amend Constitution.

Improvisation was a source of weakness as well as strength. The government's heavy reliance on privatization made its agencies chronically susceptible to the influence of private and frequently monied interests. The foregoing chapters have shown the multiple realms through which this influence flowed—infrastructure and public works, political parties, and national security, to name only three—and the harm that it could do. Meanwhile, the excessive use of exemption eroded the liberal basis of the republic by sparing large swaths of government from constitutional scrutiny. And too great a use of surrogacy made the central government vulnerable to the charge of indirection—that it was doing one thing (such as regulating morals or promoting civil rights) while claiming to do another (delivering the mail or regulating commerce). Too large a gap between the federal government's stated and actual intentions put its legitimacy at risk. Indeed, in no other industrialized country has the central state been forced to fight for its legitimacy as doggedly as in the United States.

That the theory of power animating the states differed from that structuring the central government must be counted as a weakness as well. This contradiction has made it especially difficult for Americans to define the proper boundaries of government and grasp its purposes. One can find virtues in both theories of power: the first in its assertion that government (at the level of the states) has the responsibility to look after the good and welfare of the entire commonwealth; the second in its insistence on delineating a sphere for individual freedom on which no government, federal or state, could impinge. Yet the two theories, thrown together, have produced a great deal of incoherence in citizens' thinking about government. That incoherence is most apparent in the remarkably easy—and paradoxical—way in which Americans have proclaimed their determination to get the government off their backs while simultaneously seeking to wrap their fellow citizens' moral, cultural, and personal lives in thickets of government regulations. That such dissonant attitudes toward the use of public power have gotten so thoroughly entangled in the minds of countless Americans is rooted, I have suggested, in the nation's nearly two-hundred-year encounter (1789–1970) with profoundly different theories and practices of government at the federal and state levels.

The durability of both strengths and weaknesses in the US system has not prevented Americans from mounting campaigns to change their government. Improvisation made possible programs of piecemeal change that cumulatively enabled the central state to grow substantially in multiple directions, and to creatively solve a variety of economic and social problems. The broad charter of powers given to the individual states created opportunities for several of these miniature Leviathans to become at certain moments laboratories of democracy. Then in three intense decades bookended by the Great Depression and civil rights revolution, the American system of governance seemed on the verge of transformation. A central state that historically had been preoccupied with protecting negative liberty now cultivated positive liberty. As a result of this shift, the federal government gave farmers, workers, African Americans, and others unprecedented rights and opportunities. It gave most Americans access to an array of newly established social welfare benefits. It narrowed the gulf between rich and poor. And it broke the police power of the states, making the Bill of Rights the law of the entire polity for the first time in American history. These were momentous changes. In the process of making them, the federal government grew from a small institution with limited powers into a Leviathan with influence across numerous areas of American life.

Yet this transformation was incomplete, for important dimensions of the old nineteenth-century state survived into the new one. The ease with which wealthy groups of farmers reworked New Deal agricultural reform to their liking resembled the use nineteenth-century railroad magnates made of government to secure their privilege. The insurgent labor movement of the 1930s and 1940s regarded the old monied basis of American electoral politics to be so entrenched that not even during the zenith of its interwar power did it dare mount a challenge. At the same time, the dramatic growth in the orbit and powers of the federal government over these three decades occurred with few additions to the statecraft toolbox. To a large extent, those who built the state of positive liberty were still improvising with nineteenth-century strategies. Thus the Warren Court, for example, deployed surrogacy (in the form of the commerce clause) to uphold the Civil Rights Act of 1964 and substantive due process to establish a right to privacy. The use of these techniques not only allowed elements of the old regime to survive in the new political order but also exposed that order to attacks on its legitimacy. The federal government that emerged out of the convulsive midcentury decades had enormous capacity and influence but inadequate authority.

The way in which this new federal state departed most fully from the practices of the old one is to be found in its commitment to near-permanent war. The imperative of fighting Communism everywhere and forever impelled Republicans not only to acquiesce to the New Deal but to sign on to an open-ended program of federal government growth and resource enhancement. Liberals, in turn, fashioned calls for national security into a new form of surrogacy. Ambitious and costly plans for reform could now be justified as fortifying the nation in its struggle against Communism. These plans took legislative and jurisprudential shape during the years of the Great Society and Warren Court, resulting in major advances in civil rights and civil liberties, substantial expansion of social welfare, and creative efforts to empower the poor.

The yoking together of reform and war burdened Americans with having to grapple yet again with the old paradox of liberty amid coercion. The era of near-permanent war threw together in one government a judicial and executive apparatus devoted to expanding civil rights and civil liberties, and an equally vigorous national security apparatus driven by the imperatives of surveillance and secrecy. The Warren Court that did so much to secure the Bill of Rights did little to curb the growth of the imperial presidency and the ever-growing array of agencies tracking individuals and groups deemed insufficiently loyal in the struggle against Communism. Today, the Supreme Court's defense of gay rights and gay marriage defines one aspect of America's federal government while the National Security Agency's omniscient surveillance defines another. Once again a deep commitment to allowing individuals to live freely cohabits in one system of governance with a profound determination to police the population. The difference is that now the cohabitation of liberty and coercion involves not so much the federal government and the states but instead different sectors of the federal government itself.

The federal government that has grown into a Leviathan over the last fifty years is here to stay. It is intertwined with so many sectors of American life that to remove it would require a level of dislocation and hardship that a large majority of the nation's inhabitants are not willing to endure. This reluctance to dispense with big government rests on more than inertia. Many federal government programs, from Medicare to Social Security, national security to income tax deductions, and the Federal Reserve to disaster relief, are supported by large majorities of the population. A general suspicion of government is not a bad thing; when it leads to careful scrutiny of government programs—examining where the money is going, and how effectively and fairly it is being used—it becomes a positive good. But suspicion of government is one thing; unremitting hostility to the exercise of public power at the federal level is another. Such hostility has now all but paralyzed the federal government, curtailing its ability to address problems confronting the country in the twenty-first century.

Conservatives who have unleashed this hostility, and made it one of the most powerful forces in American politics these last forty years, have found a strong sanction in the Constitution, which was intended to limit and fragment federal power. They are the truest of eighteenth-century liberals. In light of the varieties of government tyranny that so disfigured the twentieth century, they are right to remind us of the concern for liberty that was so central to the thinking of the founding generation. The Bill of Rights was a prescient document. There are good reasons why it is so widely admired both in the United States and around the world today.

In sanctifying the founding moment, though, conservatives have endowed the Constitution with a species of perfection it never possessed. It sanctioned slavery. It established an array of measures, from the electoral college to the cloture rule in the Senate to the election of senators by state legislators, meant to limit democratic rule. While it sought to insulate the central government from popular passions, it indulged those same passions in the states, sanctioning in them the kind of majority rule that ran roughshod over individual liberties for three-quarters of the republic's history.

Given these flaws, why make originalism into a religious faith? Why not concede the limitations of the Constitution, and launch a discussion of how to improve it? For the last twenty years, liberal efforts along these lines have been notably weak. In the face of originalism's power, many liberals abandoned battles over ideology in hopes that clever tweaking of constitutional mechanisms would be sufficient to defend and even advance liberal causes. Gone is the confidence that informed Louis Brandeis's declaration that the Constitution must be treated as a living document in need of periodic reinterpretation to make its principles relevant to changing circumstances. The decline in Brandeisian confidence reflects a tacit acceptance that the tools fashioned over the last 150 years to render the Constitution living—surrogacy, privatization, and exemption—have been inadequate to the task at hand. The obvious alternative strategy is to reinvigorate the constitutional amendment process. There have been calls to do so the last few years.[1] But those initiatives are weighed down by knowledge of how tortuous and prone to failure the path toward amendment in the United States almost always has been.

It is nevertheless the path that liberals must pursue—not necessarily because it will yield a series of successful amendments. Instead, it will open up an ideological space that allows a belief in a living constitution to take root and grow. Americans will require such a belief in order to regain confidence that the problems of their governing system can be fixed.

Fixing the system does not mean that the paradoxes that have long shaped America's structure of public power will be resolved. The competing claims within the US state—indeed, within all liberal democratic states—to police populations, on the one hand, and create circumstances of liberty, on the other, run too deep. But fixing the system does mean giving Americans the tools and flexibility to fashion a government that works, and one that as members of a polity in which the people are meant to be sovereign, they deserve.

NOTES

INTRODUCTION

1. The Massachusetts blasphemy statute read in part: "Whoever wilfully blasphemes the holy name of God by denying, cursing or contumeliously reproaching God, His creation, government or final judging of the world, or by cursing or contumeliously reproaching Jesus Christ or the Holy Ghost . . . shall be punished." The target of the 1928 application of this law was Horace Kallen, a philosopher, cultural critic, and political activist who had uttered these words at a rally for Sacco and Vanzetti in Boston: "If Sacco and Vanzetti were anarchists, Jesus Christ was an anarchist." See Horace M. Kallen, "Fear and Freedom: With Special Reference to the Madness of Massachusetts," unpublished manuscript of a speech delivered by Kallen to the Open Forum in Baltimore, December 28, 1928, box 72, folder 2, Horace M. Kallen Papers, Manuscript Collection No. 1, American Jewish Archives, Cincinnati, OH.

2. A distinguished tradition of scholarship dating back to Edmund Morgan's seminal work *American Slavery, American Freedom* has been indispensable in capturing a portion of the paradoxical coexistence of liberty and coercion in the American experience. This book owes a large debt to the Morgan tradition even as it frames an analysis of liberty and coercion that diverges from it. Edmund S. Morgan, *American Slavery, American Freedom* (New York: W. W. Norton and Company, 1975).

3. For a monumental account of the centrality of transformation to the history of government in the United States, see Bruce Ackerman, *We the People, Volume I: Foundations* (Cambridge, MA: Harvard University Press, 1993);

Bruce Ackerman, *We the People, Volume II: Transformations* (Cambridge, MA: Harvard University Press, 1998); Bruce Ackerman, *We the People, Volume III: The Civil Rights Revolution* (Cambridge, MA: Harvard University Press, 2014).

4. Patrick Griffin, *American Leviathan: Empire, Nation, and Revolutionary Frontier* (New York: Hill and Wang, 2007).

CHAPTER 1. A LIBERAL CENTRAL STATE EMERGES

1. Ralph Waldo Emerson, "Concord Hymn: Sung at the Completion of the Battle Monument, April 19, 1836," in *Poems: Household Edition* (Boston: Houghton Mifflin Company, 1884), 139.

2. *Declaration of Independence*, http://www.archives.gov/exhibits/charters /declaration_transcript.html (accessed March 26, 2015); Thomas Bender, *A Nation among Nations: America's Place in World History* (New York: Hill and Wang, 2006), chap. 2; David Armitage, *The Declaration of Independence: A Global History* (Cambridge, MA: Harvard University Press, 2007); Laurent Dubois, *Avengers of the New World: The Story of the Haitian Revolution* (Cambridge, MA: Harvard University Press, 2004); Joanna Innes and Mark Philp, eds., *Re-Imagining Democracy in the Age of Revolutions: America, France, Britain, and Ireland* (New York: Oxford University Press, 2013); Eric Hobsbawm, *The Age of Revolution: Europe, 1789–1848* (New York: New American Library, 1962).

3. Seth Cotlar, "Languages of Democracy from the Revolution to the Election of 1800," in *Re-Imagining Democracy in the Age of Revolutions: America, France, Britain, and Ireland*, ed. Joanna Innes and Mark Philp (New York: Oxford University Press, 2013), 13–27; Mark Philp, "Talking about Democracy: Britain in the 1790s," in *Re-Imagining Democracy in the Age of Revolutions: America, France, Britain, and Ireland*, ed. Joanna Innes and Mark Philp (New York: Oxford University Press, 2013), 101–13; Jennifer Tolbert Roberts, *Athens on Trial: The Antidemocratic Tradition in Western Thought* (Princeton, NJ: Princeton University Press, 1994).

4. On the ideology of republicanism, see J.G.A. Pocock, *The Machiavellian Moment: Florentine Political Thought and the Atlantic Republican Tradition* (Princeton, NJ: Princeton University Press, 1975); Quentin Skinner, *The Foundations of Modern Political Thought*, 2 vols. (New York: Cambridge University Press, 1978); Gordon S. Wood, *The Creation of the American Republic, 1776–1787* (Chapel Hill: University of North Carolina Press, 1969); Maurizio Viroli, *Foundations of Modern Political Thought: Machiavelli* (New York: Oxford University Press, 1998); Bernard Bailyn, *The Ideological Origins of the American Revolution* (Cambridge, MA: Harvard University Press, 1967). On the democratic turn that republicanism took in America, see Eric Foner,

Tom Paine and Revolutionary America (New York: Oxford University Press, 1976); Sean Wilentz, *Chants Democratic: New York City and the Rise of the American Working Class* (New York: Oxford University Press, 1984).

5. On the liberalism of the American Revolution, see Gordon S. Wood, *The Radicalism of the American Revolution* (New York: Vintage Books, 1993); Joyce Appleby, *Liberalism and Republicanism in the Historical Imagination* (Cambridge, MA: Harvard University Press, 1992); Joyce Appleby, *Capitalism and a New Social Order* (New York: New York University Press, 1984); Andreas Kalyvas and Ira Katznelson, *Liberal Beginnings: Making a Republic for the Moderns* (New York: Cambridge University Press, 2008).

6. In addition to the principle of contractualism, Locke saw two others as essential to good government: first, that it contain mechanisms of representation, whereby those who had ceded rights to their state could ensure that their voices would be heard in the corridors of power; and second, that no state, not even one with robust representative institutions, could legitimately arrogate all power unto itself or spuriously invade private life. A government limited in this way and governed by the rule of law would protect individuals from state tyranny, and enhance the possibilities for free expression, movement, and exchange. John Locke, *Two Treatises of Government*, ed. Thomas I. Cook (New York: Macmillan Publishers, 1947).

7. A vigorous debate has played out these last fifty to sixty years regarding the influence of Lockean thought on the minds of American revolutionaries. Louis Hartz, writing in the 1950s, argued that Lockean thought was the only influence, becoming in post-revolutionary America the only political tradition that mattered. Bernard Bailyn, Gordon Wood, and Hannah Arendt challenged the Hartz "liberal hegemony" thesis in the 1960s, uncovering an alternative, republican tradition, and contending that it was more important than anyone thought. Their work ignited a thirty-year effort to reconstruct the republican tradition in America and demonstrate its influence in the eighteenth and nineteenth centuries. From the mid-1980s to the mid-1990s, the "republican hegemony" school was in ascendance. More recent scholarship has challenged it from a variety of positions. Some have reasserted the primacy of liberalism. A second group has asked whether republicanism in America was ever coherent enough as an ideology to constitute a political tradition. A third has asserted that both republican and liberal traditions were present in the late eighteenth century, and that they were deeply entangled with each other. I incline toward to this last view. To follow this debate, see Louis Hartz, *The Liberal Tradition in America: An Interpretation of American Political Thought since the Revolution* (New York: Harcourt, Brace and World, Inc., 1955); Bailyn, *Ideological Origins*; Wood, *Creation of the American Republic*; John Dunn, "The Politics of Locke in England and America in the Eighteenth Century," in *John Locke: Problems and Perspectives, A Collection of New Essays*, ed. John W. Yolton (Cambridge: Cambridge University Press, 1969), 45–80; Dorothy Ross, "The Liberal Tradition Revisited and the Republican Tradition Addressed," in *New Directions in American Intellectual History*, ed. John Higham and Paul K.

Conkin (Baltimore: Johns Hopkins University Press, 1979), 116–31; Yuhtaro Ohmori, "The Artillery of Mr. Locke: The Use of Locke's Second Treatise in Pre-Revolutionary America" (PhD diss., Johns Hopkins University, 1988); Quentin Skinner, *Liberty before Liberalism* (Cambridge: Cambridge University Press, 1998); Daniel T. Rodgers, "Republicanism: The Career of a Concept," *Journal of American History* 79 (1992): 11–38; James T. Kloppenberg, *The Virtues of Liberalism* (New York: Oxford University Press, 1998); Desmond King and Marc Stears, "Capitalism, Democracy, and the Missing State in Louis Hartz's America," in *The American Liberal Tradition Reconsidered: The Contested Legacy of Louis Hartz*, ed. Mark Hulluing (Lawrence: University Press of Kansas, 2010), 125–48; Kalyvas and Katznelson, *Liberal Beginnings*; Appleby, *Liberalism and Republicanism in the Historical Imagination*. See also Mark Goldie, introduction to *The Reception of Locke's Politics*, ed. Mark Goldie (London: Pickering and Chatto Ltd., 2000), 1:xlix–lix.

8. Adam Smith, *An Inquiry into the Nature and Causes of the Wealth of Nations*, ed. Edwin Cannan (1776; repr., New York: Modern Library, 1965), 13, 651.

9. The emancipatory character of liberal thought, in its eighteenth-century guise, is often underestimated. See Istvan Hont and Michael Ignatieff, "Needs and Justice in the Wealth of Nations: An Introductory Essay," in *Wealth and Virtue: The Shaping of Political Economy in the Scottish Enlightenment*, ed. Istvan Hont and Michael Ignatieff (New York: Cambridge University Press, 1983), 1–44; Gary Gerstle, "The Protean Character of American Liberalism," *American Historical Review* 99 (October 1994): 1043–73.

10. Kalyvas and Katznelson, *Liberal Beginnings*. The debate on the relative significance of liberalism and republicanism in eighteenth-century America has also surfaced in connection to Smith. Was he a progenitor of liberalism, or is he more properly seen as himself being immersed in a civic humanist, republican world? I find Kalyvas and Katznelson's answer to this question a compelling one: that Smith "found and deployed attractive elements from within the republican tradition," but deemed republicanism as a whole inadequate to the task of interpreting the political economy emerging around him. Ibid., 50, more generally 18–50. On Republican revisionism and Smith, see David Winch, *Adam Smith's Politics: An Essay in Historiographic Revision* (New York: Cambridge University Press, 1978); John Dwyer, "Virtue and Improvement: The Civic World of Adam Smith," in *Adam Smith Reviewed*, ed. Peter Jones and Andrew J. Skinner (Edinburgh: Edinburgh University Press, 1992), 190–216. For rebuttals, see John Robertson, "Scottish Political Economy beyond the Civic Tradition: Government and Economic Development in the Wealth of Nations," *History of Political Thought* 4 (Winter 1983): 451–82; Michael Ignatieff, "Smith, Rousseau, and the Republic of Needs," in *Scotland and Europe, 1200–1850*, ed. T. C. Smouth (Edinburgh: John Donald, 1986), 187–206. Evidence for the republican Smith is usually gleaned from his earlier work in the 1750s and 1760s, beginning with *The Theory of Moral Sentiments* (1759; repr., Indianapolis: Liberty Press, 1976). There Smith did write about how the noneconomic dimensions of human interaction—most notably a ca-

pacity for sympathy and desire to be loved—shaped morality and ethics in ways that drew on the civic humanist tradition.

11. On the Articles of Confederation, see Wood, *Creation of the American Republic*, 354–63; Jack N. Rakove, *Original Meanings: Politics and Ideas in the Making of the Constitution* (New York: Alfred A. Knopf, 1996), 23–34; Max Farrand, *The Framing of the Constitution of the United States* (1913; repr., New Haven, CT: Yale University Press, 1976), 1–12.

12. Rakove, *Original Meanings*; Wood, *Creation of the American Republic*, 469–564; Gordon S. Wood, *Empire of Liberty: A History of the Early Republic, 1789–1815* (New York: Oxford University Press, 2009), chaps. 1–2; Farrand, *Framing of the Constitution of the United States*; Max M. Edling, *A Revolution in Favor of Government: Origins of the U.S. Constitution and the Making of the American State* (New York: Oxford University Press, 2003); Woody Holton, *Unruly Americans and the Origins of the Constitution* (New York: Hill and Wang, 2007).

13. On the ratification process, see Pauline Maier, *Ratification: The People Debate the Constitution, 1787–88* (New York: Simon and Schuster, 2010); Holton, *Unruly Americans*, chap. 14.

14. Holton, *Unruly Americans*, 435–68; Michael Kent Curtis, *No State Shall Abridge: The Fourteenth Amendment and the Bill of Rights* (Durham, NC: Duke University Press, 1986); Wood, *Empire of Liberty*, 65–72; Akhil Reed Amar, *The Bill of Rights* (New Haven, CT: Yale University Press, 1998); Ralph Ketcham, *Framed for Posterity: The Enduring Philosophy of the Constitution* (Lawrence: University Press of Kansas, 1993), 87–108.

15. Several scholars have argued that Americans took little cognizance of the Bill of Rights as a distinct part of their Constitution, and as one empowering individuals vis-à-vis their government until the late nineteenth and early twentieth century. See, for example, Amar, *Bill of Rights*, 284–87. While this argument is true in terms of the usage of the phrase "Bill of Rights," it overlooks the degree to which the first ten amendments, from the early nineteenth century on, shaped a view of the central government as limited in its powers. See, for example, the Supreme Court's 1833 decision in *Barron v. the Mayor and City Council of Baltimore*, in which Chief Justice John Marshall, writing for the court, noted repeatedly that a key purpose of the Constitution and the first ten amendments had been the "limitation or restraining" [of] . . . the power of the general government." *Barron v. Baltimore*, 32 U.S. (7 Pet.) (1833). This decision will be discussed in chapter 2.

16. Maier, *Ratification*, 435–68; Wood, *Empire of Liberty*, 65–72; Amar, *Bill of Rights*, 44–45. On laws to curb religious liberty in the early republic, specifically in Massachusetts, see Johann N. Neem, *Creating a Nation of Joiners: Democracy and Civil Society in Early National Massachusetts* (Cambridge, MA: Harvard University Press, 2008), chaps. 1–2.

17. For Madison's views on the inevitability of dissent, disagreement, and factionalism in a republic, see Alexander Hamilton, James Madison, and John Jay, *The Federalist Papers* (1777–78; repr., New York: New American Library, 1961), 77–83.

18. Helen E. Veit, Kenneth R. Bowling, and Charlene Bangs Bickford, eds., *Creating the Bill of Rights: The Documentary Record from the First Federal Congress* (Baltimore: Johns Hopkins University Press, 1991), 188–89. See also Rakove, *Original Meanings*, 310–38.

19. For two recent and exhaustive accounts of the early republic that reconstruct the struggle between Hamilton and Jefferson along with the parties they represented (the Federalists and later the Whigs, on the one side, and the Democratic-Republicans, on the other), see Sean Wilentz, *The Rise of American Democracy: From Jefferson to Lincoln* (New York: W. W. Norton and Company, 2005); Daniel Walker Howe, *What Hath God Wrought: The Transformation of America, 1815–1848* (New York: Oxford University Press, 2007). Wilentz favors the Jeffersonians, and Howe leans toward the Hamiltonians. For an early twentieth-century rendering of this story, see Herbert Croly, *The Promise of American Life* (1909; repr., Boston: Northeastern University Press, 2009).

20. My framing of these questions has been influenced by three important works: John Brewer, *The Sinews of Power: War, Money, and the English States, 1688–1783* (Cambridge, MA: Harvard University Press, 1988); Ira Katznelson, "Flexible Capacity: The Military and Early American Statebuilding," in *Shaped by War and Trade: International Influences on American Political Development*, ed. Ira Katznelson and Martin Shefter (Princeton, NJ: Princeton University Press, 2002), 83–110; Brian Balogh, *A Government Out of Sight: The Mystery of National Authority in Nineteenth-Century America* (New York: Cambridge University Press, 2009).

21. See, for example, Tom Paine, *Common Sense* (1776; repr., Mineola, NY: Dover Publications, 1997), 24–39, passim.

22. Wood, *Empire of Liberty*, 44–46.

23. Nor should we disregard a baser motive for expansion: the opportunity it presented to individuals to accumulate land and become rich. The various founding fathers (George Washington) or fathers of the founding fathers (Peter Jefferson) who became surveyors were not doing this work simply because they loved the science of measurement. They were acquisitive men who saw in land speculation a pathway toward wealth. Woody Holton, *Forced Founders: Indians, Debtors, Slaves, and the Making of the American Revolution in Virginia* (Chapel Hill: University of North Carolina Press, 1999). On the geopolitical imperatives shaping politics in the new nation, see Edling, *Revolution in Favor of Government*; Alan Taylor, *The Civil War of 1812: American Citizens, British Subjects, and Indian Allies* (New York: Alfred A. Knopf, 2010); Richard White, *The Middle Ground: Indians, Empires, and Republics in the Great Lakes Regions, 1650–1815* (New York: Cambridge University Press, 1991); Jane G. Landers, *Atlantic Creoles in the Age of Revolutions* (Cambridge, MA: Harvard University Press, 2010).

24. Marion Clawson, *The Land System of the United States: An Introduction to the History and Practice of Land Use and Land Tenure* (Lincoln: University of Nebraska Press, 1968), 36; Aristide R. Zolberg, *A Nation by Design:*

Immigration Policy in the Fashioning of America (Cambridge, MA: Harvard University Press, 2006), 68–69.

25. Later laws would expand this one section per township to two and then to four. Clawson, *Land System of the United States*, 59. See also Harold M. Hyman, *American Singularity: The 1787 Northwest Ordinance, the 1862 Homestead and Morrill Acts, and the 1944 G.I. Bill* (Athens: University of Georgia Press, 1986), 18–34; Balogh, *Government Out of Sight*, 180–83.

26. On the variety of systems of surveying still extant in the new nation, see Andro Linklater, *Measuring America: How an Untamed Wilderness Shaped the United States and Fulfilled the Promise of Democracy* (New York: Walker and Co., 2002), 161–75, passim.

27. Ibid., 145–59.

28. Clawson, *Land System of the United States*, 54.

29. Jerry L. Mashaw, "Reluctant Nationalists: Federal Administration and Administrative Law in the Republican Era, 1801–1829," *Yale Law Journal* 116 (June 2007): 1700.

30. Balogh, *Government Out of Sight*, 178–83.

31. Linklater, *Measuring America*, 175; Stephen Aron, *How the West Was Lost: The Transformation of Kentucky from Daniel Boone to Henry Clay* (Baltimore: Johns Hopkins University Press, 1996); Malcolm J. Rohrbough, *The Land Office Business: The Settlement and Administration of American Public Lands, 1789–1837* (New York: Oxford University Press, 1968); Walter Johnson, *River of Dark Dreams: Slavery and Empire in the Cotton Kingdom* (Cambridge, MA: Harvard University Press, 2013), 34–40.

32. Balogh, *Government Out of Sight*, 178–83; Daniel Feller, *The Public Lands in Jacksonian Politics* (Madison: University of Wisconsin Press, 1984).

33. Hyman, *American Singularity*, 18–34.

34. Peter J. Kastor, *The Nation's Crucible: The Louisiana Purchase and the Creation of America* (New Haven, CT: Yale University Press, 2004); Adam Rothman, *Slave Country: American Expansion and the Origins of the Deep South* (Cambridge, MA: Harvard University Press, 2005).

35. Zolberg, *Nation by Design*, 24–57; Appleby, *Capitalism and a New Social Order*.

36. Zolberg, *Nation by Design*, 24–57.

37. Ibid., 58–98; James H. Kettner, *The Development of American Citizenship, 1608–1870* (Chapel Hill: University of North Carolina Press, 1978); US Cong., Sess. 2, Chap. 3, March 1, 1790, 103–4, http://memory.loc.gov/cgi-bin/ampage?collId=llsl&fileName=001/llsl001.db&recNum=226 (accessed February 4, 2015).

38. The good character clause became the basis for denying citizenship to paupers.

39. Zolberg, *Nation by Design*, 66–68.

40. Peter H. Schuck and Rogers M. Smith, *Citizenship without Consent: Illegal Aliens in the American Polity* (New Haven, CT: Yale University Press, 1985), chaps. 1–2.

41. US Cong., Sess. 2, Chap. 3, March 1, 1790, 103–4, http://memory.loc
.gov/cgi-bin/ampage?collId=llsl&fileName=001/llsl001.db&recNum=226 (accessed February 4, 2015).

42. Gary Gerstle, "America's Encounter with Immigrants," in *In Search of Progressive America*, ed. Michael Kazin (Philadelphia: University of Pennsylvania Press, 2008), 37–53.

43. Richard R. John, *Spreading the News: The American Postal System from Franklin to Morse* (Cambridge, MA: Harvard University Press, 1995), 3.

44. Ibid., 5.

45. Ibid., passim.

46. Benedict Anderson, *Imagined Communities: Reflections on the Origin and Spread of Nationalism* (London: Verso, 1991).

47. On slavery in North America in the eighteenth and early nineteenth centuries, see Ira Berlin, *Many Thousands Gone: The First Two Centuries of Slavery in North America* (Cambridge, MA: Harvard University Press, 1998); Johnson, *River of Dark Dreams*; Rothman, *Slave Country*; David Waldstreicher, *Slavery's Constitution: From Revolution to Ratification* (New York: Hill and Wang, 2009); Edward E. Baptist, *The Half Has Never Been Told: Slavery and the Making of American Capitalism* (New York: Basic Books, 2014). On the 1792 Fugitive Slave Law, see Don E. Fehrenbacher, *The Slaveholding Republic: An Account of the United States Government's Relations to Slavery*, completed and ed. Ward M. McAfee (New York: Oxford University Press, 2001), 209–13, passim.

48. Linda K. Kerber, *Women of the Republic: Ideology and Intellect in Revolutionary America* (Chapel Hill: University of North Carolina Press, 1980); Nancy F. Cott, *The Bonds of Womanhood: "Woman's Sphere" in New England, 1780–1835* (New Haven, CT: Yale University Press, 1977); Rosemary Zagarri: *Revolutionary Backlash: Women and Politics in the Early Republic* (Philadelphia: University of Pennsylvania Press, 2007); David R. Roediger, *The Wages of Whiteness: Race and the Making of the American Working Class* (London: Verso, 1991); Matthew Frye Jacobson, *Whiteness of a Different Color: European Immigrants and the Alchemy of Race* (Cambridge, MA: Harvard University Press, 1998).

49. Kerber, *Women of the Republic*; Berlin, *Many Thousands Gone*; Wood, *Radicalism of the American Revolution*; Armitage, *Declaration of Independence*; Wilentz, *Chants Democratic*; Foner, *Tom Paine and Revolutionary America*; Alfred F. Young, ed., *The Radicalism of the American Revolution* (DeKalb: Northern Illinois University Press, 1976); Gary Nash, *The Unknown American Revolution: The Unruly Birth of Democracy and the Struggle to Create America* (New York: Viking, 2005); Wood, *Creation of the American Republic*; Charles A. Beard, *An Economic Interpretation of the Constitution* (1913; repr., New York: Dover Publications, 2004), chap. 1; Stephen Kantrowitz, *More Than Freedom: Fighting for Black Citizenship in a White Republic, 1829–1889* (New York: Penquin Press, 2012).

50. Christopher Tomlins, *Freedom Bound: Law, Labor, and Civic Identity in English America, 1580–1865* (New York: Cambridge University Press, 2010);

Morton J. Horwitz, *The Transformation of American Law, 1780–1860* (Cambridge, MA: Harvard University Press, 1977); Amy Dru Stanley, *From Bondage to Contract: Wage Labor, Marriage, and the Market in the Age of Slave Emancipation* (New York: Cambridge University Press, 1998); C. B. Macpherson, *The Political Theory of Possessive Individualism: Hobbes to Locke* (1962; repr., New York: Oxford University Press, 2011); David Harvey, *A Brief History of Neoliberalism* (New York: Oxford University Press, 2005).

51. See chapters 6 and 7 of this book.

52. Brewer, *Sinews of Power*, 30–33; Katznelson, "Flexible Capacity."

53. After the Civil War, these militia units metamorphosed into the National Guard. John Whiteclay Chambers II, *To Raise an Army: The Draft Comes to Modern America* (New York: Free Press, 1987), chap. 1; Lawrence Cress, *Citizens in Arms: The Army and the Militia in American Society to the War of 1812* (Chapel Hill: University of North Carolina Press, 1982); John K. Mahon, *History of the Militia and National Guard* (New York: Free Press, 1983).

54. Katznelson, "Flexible Capacity," 91.

55. As historian John Chambers has written, these units would be "funded by the U.S. government and directed by federally appointed generals," but "locally raised and officered." Chambers, *To Raise an Army*, 29.

56. Ibid., 42. In the Civil War, more than 90 percent of the two million men serving in the Union Army were raised in this way. Only in 1898, in the midst of the Spanish-American War, did the federal government rethink this decentralized, private, and ad hoc way of raising an army.

57. Theodore J. Crackel, *Mr. Jefferson's Army: Political and Social Reform of the Military Establishment, 1801–1809* (New York: New York University Press, 1987); Robert M. S. McDonald, *Thomas Jefferson's Military Academy: The Founding of West Point* (Charlottesville: University of Virginia Press, 2004).

58. John Shy, *A People Numerous and Armed: Reflections on the Military Struggle for American Independence* (Ann Arbor: University of Michigan Press, 1990).

59. Ibid.

60. Taylor, *Civil War of 1812*; Kastor, *Nation's Crucible*; Landers, *Atlantic Creoles in the Age of Revolutions*. Moreover, it was apparent that the US government could not always count on the loyalty of its own citizens. The Whiskey rebels and New England secessionists of the Hartford Convention are examples of groups of citizens either disregarding their government or turning on it, each spurred by the conviction that it (the government) had failed to represent them and their interests. Many of the most serious challenges to the young republic arose in these moments. On the Whiskey Rebellion and other instances of settler rebellion, see Patrick Griffin, *American Leviathan: Empire, Nation, and the Revolutionary Frontier* (New York: Hill and Wang, 2007); Thomas P. Slaughter, *The Whiskey Rebellion: Frontier Epilogue to the American Revolution* (New York: Oxford University Press, 1986). On the Hartford Convention, see James M. Banner Jr., *To the Hartford Convention: The Federalists and the Origins of Party Politics in Massachusetts, 1789–1815* (New

York: Alfred A. Knopf, 1969); Richard Buel Jr., *America on the Brink: How the Political Struggle over the War of 1812 Almost Destroyed the Young Republic* (New York: Palgrave Macmillan, 2005); Sveinn Johannesson, "Securing the State: Coercion, Rebellion, and the Making of a Liberal Central State in Post-Revolutionary America" (graduate seminar paper, Vanderbilt University, 2014).

61. Rothman, *Slave Country*, 74; Daniel Rasmussen, *American Uprising: The Untold Story of America's Largest Slave Revolt* (New York: Harper Perennial, 2011); Johnson, *River of Dark Dreams*, chap. 1.

62. Kastor, *Nation's Crucible*, pt. I.

63. Burr failed in his effort, but Stephen F. Austin, Sam Houston, Sam Bowie, Davy Crockett, and their friends would later succeed, creating the Republic of Texas. After a decade of independence, Anglo-Texans would bring that republic into the United States. But had such a republic been established in 1805, when the United States was a weaker and less imposing entity than it subsequently became, it might well have remained independent, becoming a hemispheric rival to the United States and competitor for the sparsely settled lands of the trans-Mississippi West. Such a republic might have seized Mexico's northwest territory, including California, and incorporated it into a North-South Anglo empire in North America; alternatively, Anglo settlers of the trans-Mississippi West might have fought to establish a nation independent of the United States, Texas, and Mexico, choosing instead to fashion a third and perhaps fourth Anglo republic. Rothman, *Slave Country*; Nancy Isenberg, *Fallen Founder: The Life of Aaron Burr* (New York: Penguin Group, 2007); T. R. Fehrenbach, *Lone Star: A History of Texas and Texans* (1968; repr., New York: Collier, 1980); David J. Weber, *The Mexican Frontier, 1821–1846: The American Southwest under Mexico* (Albuquerque: University of New Mexico Press, 1982); Pekka Hämäläinen, *The Comanche Empire* (New Haven, CT: Yale University Press, 2008); Johnson, *River of Dark Dreams*, chap. 1.

64. Katznelson, "Flexible Capacity."

65. J.C.A. Stagg, *Mr. Madison's War: Politics, Diplomacy, and Warfare in the Early American Republic, 1783–1830* (Princeton, NJ: Princeton University Press, 1983); Robert V. Remini, *Andrew Jackson* (New York: Palgrave Macmillan, 2008), 34–36; H. W. Brands, *Andrew Jackson: His Life and Times* (New York: Anchor Books, 2006), 174–87.

66. Remini, *Andrew Jackson*, 60; Robert V. Remini, *Andrew Jackson and His Indian Wars* (New York: Viking, 2001); Fred Anderson and Drew Cayton, *The Dominion of War: Empire and Liberty in North America, 1500–2000* (New York: Viking Penguin), 207–46.

67. Remini, *Andrew Jackson*; Rothman, *Slave Country*; Johnson, *River of Dark Dreams*, 28–31.

68. Brands, *Andrew Jackson*, 238–39; Rothman, *Slave Country*, 143–46.

69. Rothman, *Slave Country*, 143–46.

70. Rothman, *Slave Country*, 161; Howe, *What Hath God Wrought*, 8; Remini, *Andrew Jackson*, 120.

71. And had the British won and taken New Orleans before news of the peace treaty arrived, these facts on the ground may have forced an alteration in the terms of the peace.

72. Quoted in Remini, *Andrew Jackson*, 124.

73. Rothman, *Slave Country*, 161; Howe, *What Hath God Wrought*, 8; Remini, *Andrew Jackson*, 120; Stephen Watts, *The Republic Reborn: War and the Making of Liberal America, 1790–1820* (Baltimore: Johns Hopkins University Press, 1987); Stagg, *Mr. Madison's War*.

74. Landers, *Atlantic Creoles in the Age of Revolutions*.

75. Remini, *Andrew Jackson*, 129–74; Landers, *Atlantic Creoles in the Age of Revolutions*, 95–137, 175–203; Francis Paul Prucha, *Sword of the Republic: The United States Army on the Frontier, 1783–1846* (New York: Macmillan, 1968), 132–36.

76. Prucha, *Sword of the Republic*, 151–53; John C. Calhoun, "Reduction of the Army," 16th Cong., 2nd Sess., December 12, 1820; Katznelson, "Flexible Capacity."

77. On preemptions, see Mashaw, "Reluctant Nationalists."

78. Quoted in Mashaw, "Reluctant Nationalists," 1714. This parsimonious attitude made it difficult to attract the best people to federal government service. Territorial government was full of second-raters. See Kastor, *Nation's Crucible*; Leonard D. White, *The Jeffersonians: A Study in Administrative History, 1801–1829* (New York: Macmillan, 1951).

79. Mashaw, "Reluctant Nationalists."

80. Ibid.

81. Pekka Hämäläinen, *The Comanche Empire* (New Haven, CT: Yale University Press, 2008).

82. Prucha, *Sword of the Republic*, passim; David Andrew Nichols, *Red Gentleman and White Savages: Indians, Federalists, and the Search for Order on the American Frontier* (Charlottesville: University of Virginia Press, 2008); Lynn Hudson Parsons, " 'A Perpetual Harrow upon My Feelings': John Quincy Adams and the American Indian," *New England Quarterly* 46 (September 1973): 339–79; Reginald Horseman, *Race and Manifest Destiny: The Origins of Racial Anglo-Saxonism* (Cambridge, MA: Harvard University Press, 1981); Francis Paul Prucha, *The Great Father: The United States Government and the American Indians*, vol. 1 (Lincoln: University of Nebraska Press, 1984); Robert F. Berkhofer Jr., *Salvation and the Savage: An Analysis of Protestant Missions and American Indian Response, 1787–1862* (Lexington, KY: Atheneum, 1965).

83. As Prucha has written, "The smallness of the military force . . . was no doubt the primary cause of the failure to enforce completely the prohibitions against settling in the Indian country." Prucha, *Sword of the Republic*, 199.

84. Philip St. George Cooke, *Scenes and Adventures in the Army; or, Romance of Military Life* (1857; repr., New York: Arno Press, 1973), 158.

85. On the power of the state governments in the nineteenth century, see chapter 2.

86. Prucha, *Sword of the Republic*, 222–23; John W. Hall, *Uncommon Defense: Indian Allies in the Black Hawk War* (Cambridge, MA: Harvard University Press, 2009); St. George Cooke, *Scenes and Adventures in the Army*, passim. One student of the Black Hawk War wrote in 1893 that it was "a bloody and costly contest, characterized on our part by heartlessness, bad faith, and gross mismanagement." Reuben Gold Thwaites, "The Story of the Black Hawk War," *Wisconsin Historical Collections* 12 (1892): 50.

87. Prucha, *Sword of the Republic*; Landers, *American Creoles in the Age of Revolutions*. On the volatility of the Canadian border, see Taylor, *Civil War of 1812*.

88. Quoted in Parsons, "Perpetual Harrow upon My Feelings," 374.

89. Brands, *Andrew Jackson*; Remini, *Andrew Jackson*.

90. On the savagery of warfare on the frontier, see Griffin, *American Leviathan*; Peter Silver, *Our Savage Neighbors: How Indian War Transformed Early America* (New York: W. W. Norton and Company, 2008); Ned Blackhawk, *Violence over the Land: Indians and Empires in the Early American West* (Cambridge, MA: Harvard University Press, 2006); Theodore Roosevelt, *The Winning of the West: An Account of the Exploration and Settlement of Our Country from the Alleghanies to the Pacific* (1890), in *Works of Theodore Roosevelt*, ed. Hermann Hagedorn, nat. ed. (New York: C. Scribner's Sons, 1926), vols. 8 and 9; Richard Slotkin, *Regeneration through Violence: The Mythology of the American Frontier, 1600–1860* (Norman: University of Oklahoma Press, 1973).

91. Howe, *What Hath God Wrought*, passim.

CHAPTER 2. THE STATES AND THEIR POLICE POWER

A small part of this chapter was previously published in Gary Gerstle, "The Resilient Power of the States across the Long Nineteenth Century: An Inquiry into a Pattern of American Governance," in *The Unsustainable American State*, ed. Lawrence Jacobs and Desmond King (New York: Oxford University Press, 2009), 61–87; reproduced by permission of Oxford University Press, http://global.oup.com/?cc=us (accessed February 5, 2015).

1. The marginalization of the states and federalism in the study of the American state now seems to be changing. See, for example, Kimberley S. Johnson, *Governing the American State: Congress and the New Federalism, 1877–1929* (Princeton, NJ: Princeton University Press, 2007); Amy Bridges, "Managing the Periphery in the Gilded Age: Writing Constitutions for the Western States," *Studies in American Political Development* 22 (Spring 2008): 32–58; Paul Emerson Herron, "Southern State Constitutions, Federalism, and American Political Development, 1860–1965" (PhD diss., Brandeis University, 2014); Noam Maggor, "To 'Coddle and Caress These Great Capitalists': Eastern Money and the Politics of Market Integration in the Great American West" (paper in au-

thor's possession). On the importance of reintegrating the states into the conversation, see Martha Derthick, *Keeping the Compound Republic: Essays on American Federalism* (Washington, DC: Brookings Institution Press, 2001).

2. This is, of course, a play on the famous phrase and book authored by Theda Skocpol and her colleagues. See Theda Skocpol, Dietrich Reuschemeyer, and Peter B. Evans, *Bringing the State Back In* (New York: Cambridge University Press, 1985).

3. See, for example, Daniel J. Elazar, *American Federalism: A View from the States*, 2nd ed. (New York: Crowell, 1972); Morton Grodzins, *The American System: A New View of Government in the United States*, ed. Daniel J. Elazar (Chicago: Rand McNally, 1966).

4. William J. Novak, *The People's Welfare: Law and Regulation in Nineteenth-Century America* (Chapel Hill: University of North Carolina Press, 1996), 46, 80.

5. J.G.A. Pocock, *The Machiavellian Moment: Florentine Political Thought and the Atlantic Republican Tradition* (Princeton, NJ: Princeton University Press, 1975); Quentin Skinner, *The Foundations of Modern Political Thought*, 2 vols. (New York: Cambridge University Press, 1978); Gordon S. Wood, *The Creation of the American Republic, 1776–1787* (Chapel Hill: University of North Carolina Press, 1969); Maurizio Viroli, *Foundations of Modern Political Thought: Machiavelli* (New York: Oxford University Press, 1998). The literature on republicanism in America is vast. For reviews and syntheses, see Robert Shalhope, "The Emergence of an Understanding of Republicanism in Early American Historiography," *William and Mary Quarterly* 29 (1972): 49–80; Daniel T. Rodgers, "Republicanism: The Career of a Concept," *Journal of American History* 79 (1992): 11–38. See also Andreas Kalyvas and Ira Katznelson, *Liberal Beginnings: Making a Republic for the Moderns* (New York: Cambridge University Press, 2008).

6. US Constitution, amendment 10; Jack N. Rakove, *Original Meanings: Politics and Ideas in the Making of the American Constitution* (New York: Alfred A. Knopf, 1996), 192.

7. Alexander Hamilton, James Madison, and John Jay, *The Federalist Papers* (New York: New American Library, 1961), 292–93.

8. Quoted in Jack N. Rakove, *Original Meanings*, 192.

9. On the experience of colonies as partially self-governing entities, see Jack Greene, *The Constitutional Origins of the American Revolution* (New York: Cambridge University Press, 2001); Craig Yirush, *Settlers, Liberty, and Empire: The Roots of Early American Political Theory* (New York: Cambridge University Press, 2011); Peter Onuf, *The Origins of the Federal Republic: Jurisdictional Controversies in the United States, 1775–1787* (Philadelphia: University of Pennsylvania Press, 1983). On the formidable powers accumulating to the states in the early republic, see Forrest McDonald, *States' Rights and the Union: Imperium in Imperio, 1776–1876* (Lawrence: Kansas University Press, 2000); Douglas Bradburn, *The Citizenship Revolution: Politics and the Creation of the American Union, 1774–1804* (Charlottesville: University of Virginia Press, 2009). For a set of reflections on Europe's longer and broader

experience with sovereign parts and wholes, see J. H. Elliott, "A Europe of Composite Monarchies," *Past and Present* 137 (November 1992): 48–71. On America's experience broadly construed, see John L. Brooke, "Cultures of Nationalism, Movements of Reform, and the Composite-Federal Polity: From Revolutionary Settlement to Antebellum Crisis," *Journal of the Early Republic* 29 (Spring 2009): 1–33.

10. Alexis de Tocqueville, *The Ancien Régime and the French Revolution*, trans. and ed. Gerald Bevan (London: Penguin Books, 2008).

11. William Blackstone, *Commentaries on the Laws of England* 162 (1769; repr., Oxford: Clarendon Press, 1770). More generally, see Markus Dirk Dubber, *The Police Power: Patriarchy and the Foundations of American Government* (New York: Columbia University Press, 2005). See also Gordon J. Schochet, *Patriarchalism in Political Thought: The Authoritarian Family and Political Speculation and Attitudes Especially in Seventeenth-Century England* (New York: Oxford University Press, 1975).

12. Commonwealth v. Alger, 7 Cush. 53 (Mass., 1851), 85.

13. "The people of this Commonwealth have the sole and exclusive right of governing themselves, as a free, sovereign, and independent state; and do, and forever hereafter shall, exercise and enjoy every power, jurisdiction, and right, which is not, or may not hereafter be, by them expressly delegated to the United States of America, in Congress assembled." "Constitution or Form of Government for the Commonwealth of Massachusetts," in *Federal and State Constitutions, Colonial Charters, Other Organic Laws of the States, Territories, and Now or Heretofore Forming the United States of America*, comp. and ed. Francis Newton Thorpe (Washington, DC: Government Printing Office, 1889–1909), 3:1890.

14. *Commonwealth v. Alger*, 93.

15. That royal doctrines partially underlay the powers possessed by the states helps us to understand what recent critics of the republican tradition have pointed out: stalwart nineteenth-century advocates of republicanism seemed to have had little trouble reinscribing hierarchy into their governing practices. Thus, in the early nineteenth century, many republicans had little difficulty justifying slavery or arguing for women's servile status. The "people" whom republicanism most clearly empowered were white men who either were or could look forward to becoming heads of household. With power went responsibility. And just as the king of England was obligated to look after his kingdom, so too were America's white men required to look after their small kingdoms. See Linda Kerber, *Women of the Republic: Intellect and Ideology in Revolutionary America* (Chapel Hill: University of North Carolina Press, 1980). On republicanism and slavery, see David R. Roediger, *Wages of Whiteness: Race and the Making of the American Working Class* (New York: Verso, 1991). See also Laura Edwards, *The People and Their Peace: Legal Culture and the Transformation of Inequality in the Post-Revolutionary South* (Chapel Hill: University of North Carolina Press, 2009). For a different though intriguingly parallel argument about the survival of eighteenth-century royalist conceptions of governance in the new nation, see Eric Nelson, *The Royalist Revolution:*

Monarchy and the American Founding (Cambridge, MA: Harvard University Press, 2014).

16. For a nineteenth-century survey of the many different ways in which a state could deploy its police power, see Thomas M. Cooley, *A Treatise on the Constitutional Limitations upon the Legislative Power of the States of the American Union*, 5th ed. (1883; repr., Union, NJ: Lawbook Exchange, 1998), 707–46.

17. *Commonwealth v. Alger*, 85.

18. Carter Goodrich, *Government Promotion of American Canals and Railroads, 1800–1890* (New York: Columbia University Press, 1960), 268. The $7 million figure somewhat underestimates federal contributions because it does not count federal land or federal budget surpluses distributed to the states. Even if these transfers are included, the total federal government contribution would still not approximate the cumulative expenditures of the states.

19. L. Ray Gunn, *The Decline of Authority: Public Economic Policy and Political Development in New York, 1800–1860* (Ithaca, NY: Cornell University Press), 37, 14.

20. Louis Hartz, *Economic Policy and Democratic Thought: Pennsylvania, 1776–1860* (Cambridge, MA: Harvard University Press, 1948), 149.

21. Ibid., 89, 290; John Wallis, "American Government Finance in the Long Run, 1790–1900," *Journal of Economic Perspectives* 14 (Winter 2000): 61–82; John Wallis, "Early American Federalism and Economic Development, 1790–1840," in *Environmental and Public Economics: Essays in Honor of Wallace E. Oates*, ed. Arvind Panagariya, Paul R. Portnoy, and Robert M. Schwab (Northampton, MA: Edward Elgar Press, 1999), 283–309.

22. Hartz, *Economic Policy and Democratic Thought*, 46–47, 291; Oscar Handlin and Mary Handlin, *Commonwealth: A Study of the Role of Government in the American Economy: Massachusetts, 1774–1861* (New York: New York University Press, 1947), 53–193. The process of petitioning state governments for charters could, of course, encourage corruption, with state officials directing corporate charters to those who paid a premium for them. This temptation may have influenced Massachusetts to move away (in the 1820s) from charters as privileges to charters as a basic right available to all. On corruption as a problem in government, see John Wallis, "The Concept of Systematic Corruption in American Economic and Political History," in *Corruption and Reform: Lessons from America's Economic History*, ed. Edward L. Glaeser and Claudia Goldin (Chicago: University of Chicago Press, 2006), 23–62.

23. Hartz, *Economic Policy and Democratic Thought*, 292, 289. In addition to the works already cited, see Harry N. Scheiber, "Government and Economy: Studies of the 'Commonwealth' Policy in Nineteenth-Century America," *Journal of Interdisciplinary History* 3 (Summer 1972): 135–51; Milton Heath, *Constructive Liberalism: The Role of the State in the Economic Development of Georgia to 1860* (Cambridge, MA: Harvard University Press, 1954); James Willard Hurst, *Law and the Conditions of Freedom in the Nineteenth-Century United States* (Madison: University of Wisconsin Press, 1956); Goodrich, *Government Promotion of American Canals and Railroads*; Harry N. Scheiber,

Ohio Canal Era: A Case Study of Government and Economy, 1820–1861 (Athens: Ohio University Press, 1969); Lee Benson, *Merchants, Farmers, and Railroads: Railroad Regulation and New York Politics, 1850–1887* (Cambridge, MA: Harvard University Press, 1955).

24. This list is drawn from Novak, *The People's Welfare*, 3–6.

25. In many instances it was municipal governments that passed these kinds of laws. But legally, municipalities (as the example of Chicago demonstrates) received their power to regulate the people's welfare from the state governments, which were authorized to charter and oversee them.

26. Robert C. Allen, *Horrible Prettiness: Burlesque and American Culture* (Chapel Hill: University of North Carolina Press, 1991); Paul Johnson, *A Shopkeeper's Millennium: Society and Revivals in Rochester, New York, 1815–1837* (New York: Hill and Wang, 1978).

27. The power of communities was felt not just in the regulation of these activities but also in the manner in which offenders were punished. In 1853, the overseers of the poor in Portland, Maine, placed two single women, a mother and daughter, in a workhouse because they were alleged paupers " 'living a dissolute, vagrant life' whose home was 'reputed to be a house of ill-fame.' " The accused women received no opportunity to defend themselves; they had no lawyer and were given no trial. They were simply arrested and committed indefinitely. Novak, *The People's Welfare*, 168. See also Kunal M. Parker, "Citizenship and Immigration Law, 1800–1924: Resolutions of Membership and Territory," in *The Cambridge History of Law in America*, ed. Michael Grossberg and Christopher Tomlins (New York: Cambridge University Press, 2008), 2:168–203.

28. Oscar Handlin and Mary Handlin introduced the phrase "humanitarian police state" to describe the moral surveillance undertaken by Massachusetts local and state authorities in the 1840s and 1850s. The Handlins did not explain why they chose this seemingly anachronistic phrase to capture the scope of state rule, but perhaps they were trying to grasp the modern character of governance in the Bay State. Handlin and Handlin, *Commonwealth*, 218.

29. US Constitution, article 1, section 9; Don E. Fehrenbacher, *The Slaveholding Republic: An Account of the United States Government's Relations to Slavery*, completed and ed. Ward M. McAfee (New York: Oxford University Press, 2001), 29.

30. US Constitution, article 1, section 2. Fehrenbacher, *Slaveholding Republic*, passim; David Waldstreicher, *Slavery's Constitution: From Revolution to Ratification* (New York: Hill and Wang, 2009).

31. Paul Finkelman, *An Imperfect Union: Slavery, Federalism, and Comity* (Chapel Hill: University of North Carolina Press, 1981).

32. US Constitution, amendments 1–10.

33. Ibid., amendment 1.

34. Barron v. Baltimore, 32 U.S. (7 Pet.) (1833), 249–50.

35. Cooley, *Constitutional Limitations*, 414–17n1, 467–69n1–2.

36. On the extension of rights to free blacks in Massachusetts, see Stephen Kantrowitz, *More Than Freedom: Fighting for Black Citizenship in a White*

Republic, 1829–1889 (New York: Penguin Press, 2012), chap. 1. See also Andrew W. Robertson, "Democracy: America's Other 'Peculiar Institution,'" in *Democracy, Participation, and Contestation: Civil Society, Governance, and the Future of Liberal Democracy*, ed. Emmanuelle Avril and Johann N. Neem (London: Routledge, 2014), 69–80.

37. *Barron v. Baltimore*, 243. See also William E. Leuchtenberg, "The Birth of America's Second Bill of Rights," in *The Supreme Court Reborn: The Constitutional Revolution in the Age of Roosevelt* (New York: Oxford University Press, 1995), 237–58. Douglas Bradburn has argued that even in situations in which the federal government believed it had the right to intervene in the affairs of particular states, it often did not, believing that its overstretched federal court system was not always capable of "enforc[ing] the federal government's will." Bradburn, *Citizenship Revolution*, 285.

38. In some places, marrying couples could escape the eye of the state or win a community's tacit approval of a marriage—say, across the color line—formally barred by law. See Daniel J. Sharfstein, *The Invisible Line: Three American Families and the Secret Journey from Black to White* (New York: Penguin Press, 2011); Edwards, *People and Their Peace*. For a comprehensive history of marriage law and practices along with how they were changing across the nineteenth century, see Michael Grossberg, *Governing the Hearth: Law and the Family in Nineteenth-Century America* (Chapel Hill: University of North Carolina Press, 1985).

39. Gunn, *Decline of Authority*, 169. On the scarcity of skills to manage large-scale enterprises in the early nineteenth century, see Sidney Pollard, *The Genesis of Modern Management: A Study of the Industrial Revolution in Great Britain* (Cambridge, MA: Harvard University Press, 1965).

40. Hendrik Hartog, *Man and Wife in America: A History* (Cambridge, MA: Harvard University Press, 2000).

41. Ibid., especially chap. 1.

42. Albert Hirschman, *Exit, Voice, Loyalty: Responses to Decline in Firms, Organizations, and States* (Cambridge, MA: Harvard University Press, 1970).

43. Adam Rothman, "The 'Slave Power' in the United States, 1783–1865," in *Ruling America: A History of Wealth and Power in a Democracy*, ed. Steve Fraser and Gary Gerstle (Cambridge, MA: Harvard University Press, 2005), 64–69. On the sway of southerners in Congress, see also Robin Einhorn, *American Taxation, American Slavery* (Chicago: University of Chicago Press, 2006).

44. Berlin, *The Long Emancipation: The Demise of Slavery in the United States* (Cambridge, MA: Harvard University Press, 2015).

45. Fehrenbacher, *Slaveholding Republic*, chaps. 2 and 7.

46. Kantrowitz, *More Than Freedom*, chap. 2.

47. Fehrenbacher, *Slaveholding Republic*, chaps. 7–8. See also Sally E. Hadden, *Law and Violence in Virginia and the Carolinas*, Harvard Historical Studies 138 (Cambridge, MA: Harvard University Press, 2001).

48. Fehrenbacher, *Slaveholding Republic*, chap. 9; Don E. Fehrenbacher, *The Dred Scott Case: Its Significance in American Law and Politics* (New York:

Oxford University Press, 1978); Paul Finkelman, *Dred Scott v. Sandford: A Brief History with Documents* (Boston: Bedford St. Martin's, 1997).

49. David Ericson, *Slavery in the American Republic: Developing the Federal Government, 1791–1861* (Lawrence: University of Kansas Press, 2011); Einhorn, *American Taxation, American Slavery.*

50. Fehrenbacher, *Slaveholding Republic*, chap. 10; Harold W. Thatcher, "Calhoun and Federal Reinforcement of State Laws," *American Political Science Review* 36 (October 1941): 873–80; Richard K. Cralle, ed., *Reports and Public Letters of John C. Calhoun* (New York: D. Appleton and Co., 1888), 5:200–202; Richard R. John, "Hiland Hall's 'Report on the Incendiary Publications': A Forgotten Nineteenth-Century Defense of the Constitutional Guarantee of the Freedom of the Press," *American Journal of Legal History* 41 (January 1997): 94–125. See also Lacy K. Ford, *Deliver Us from Evil: The Slavery Question in the Old South* (New York: Oxford University Press, 2009), 481–504; Michael Kent Curtis, *Free Speech, "The People's Darling Privilege": Struggles for Freedom of Expression in American History* (Durham, NC: Duke University Press, 2000), 155–81; Clement Eaton, *Freedom of Thought in the Old South* (Durham, NC: Duke University Press, 1940).

51. Fehrenbacher, *Slaveholding Republic*, 302.

52. Finkelman, *Dred Scott v. Sandford*; Thatcher, "Calhoun and Federal Reinforcement of State Laws."

53. Theda Skocpol, *Protecting Soldiers and Mothers: The Political Origins of Social Policy in the United States* (Cambridge, MA: Harvard University Press, 1992), 105–15.

54. On the change in federal governance stimulated by the Civil War, see Eric Foner, *Reconstruction: America's Unfinished Revolution, 1863–1877* (New York: Harper and Row, 1988); Richard Franklin Bensel, *Yankee Leviathan: The Origins of Central State Authority in America, 1859–1877* (New York: Cambridge University Press, 1990); Bruce Ackerman, *We the People: Transformations* (Cambridge, MA: Harvard University Press, 1998), 2:99–252.

55. US Constitution, amendment 14, section 1.

56. Substantive due process will be discussed at length in chapter 9. Cooley, *Constitutional Limitations*; Edward S. Corwin, *Liberty against Government* (Baton Rouge: Louisiana State University Press, 1948); Sidney Fine, *Laissez-Faire and the General Welfare State: A Study in Conflict in American Thought, 1865–1901* (Ann Arbor: University of Michigan Press, 1956); Benjamin R. Twiss, *Lawyers and the Constitution: How Laissez-Faire Came to the Supreme Court* (Princeton, NJ: Princeton University Press, 1942); Edward S. Corwin, "The Supreme Court and the Fourteenth Amendment," *Michigan Law Review* 7 (1908–9): 643–772; Charles W. McCurdy, "Justice Field and the Jurisprudence of Government-Business Relations: Some Parameters of Laissez-Faire Constitutionalism, 1863–1897," *Journal of American History* 61 (March 1975): 970–1005; Christopher Tomlins, "To Improve the State and Condition of Man: The Power to Police and the History of American Governance," *Buffalo Law Review* 53 (2005–6): 1215–71; Howard J. Graham, *Everyman's Constitution: Historical Essays on the Fourteenth Amendment, the 'Conspiracy*

Theory,' and American Constitutionalism (Madison: University of Wisconsin Press, 1968); Morton Keller, *Affairs of State: Public Life in Late Nineteenth-Century America* (Cambridge, MA: Harvard University Press, 1977); Richard Franklin Bensel, *The Political Economy of American Industrialization, 1877–1900* (New York: Cambridge University Press, 2000).

57. Santa Clara County v. Southern Pacific Railroad, 118 U.S. 356 (1886); Wabash, St. Louis, and Pacific Railway Company v. Illinois, 118 U.S. 557 (1886); Chicago Milwaukee and St. Paul Railway Co. v. Minnesota, 134 U.S. 418 (1890); Allgeyer v. Louisiana, 165 U.S. 578 (1897). See also Jack Beatty, *Age of Betrayal: The Triumph of Money in America, 1865–1900* (New York: Alfred A. Knopf, 2007), chap. 6.

58. For works that attempt to grasp the impressive scope of state activity during the postbellum years, see William R. Brock, *Investigation and Responsibility: Public Responsibility in the United States, 1865–1900* (New York: Cambridge University Press, 1984); Melvin I. Urosky, "Myth and Reality: The Supreme Court and the Protective Legislation in the Progressive Era," *Yearbook—Supreme Court Historical Society* (1983): 53–72; Melvyn I. Urosky, "State Courts and Protective Legislation during the Progressive Era: A Reevaluation," *Journal of American History* 72 (June 1985): 63–91; Johnson, *Governing the American State*.

59. Opinion written for Barbier v. Connolly, 113 U.S. 27 (1885). For contemporary opinions on the rising influence of the police power doctrine, see Ernst Freund, *The Police Power: Public Policy and Constitutional Rights* (Chicago: Callaghan and Company, 1904); A. H. Robbins, "Taking the Lid Off the Police Power," 75 *Central Law Journal* 314 (1912), 314–15; Charles Warren, "A Bulwark to the State Police Power—the United States Supreme Court," *Columbia Law Review* 13 (December 1913): 667–95; George W. Wickersham, "The Police Power, a Product of the Rule of Reason," *Harvard Law Review* 27 (February 1914): 297–316.

In stressing the importance of the police power in the postbellum era, I am contributing to a revisionist interpretation of the Gilded Age that questions how quickly and completely laissez-faire constitutionalism triumphed during those years. I also believe, however, that aspects of this revisionism have gone too far, most notably in treating what was once considered a landmark antilabor case, the 1905 *Lochner* decision, as an aberration or inconsequential. (The case declared unconstitutional a New York law limiting the numbers of hours that bakers could work.) The Court's antilabor bias is still apparent in its reluctance to regulate manufacturing (as opposed to commerce) and the alacrity with which it issued injunctions against unions engaged in strikes. For an indispensable work in this regard, see William E. Forbath, *Law and the Shaping of the American Labor Movement* (Cambridge, MA: Harvard University Press, 1991). For an unusually thoughtful piece on how postbellum courts dealt with the labor question, see Karen Orren, "The Laws of Industrial Organization," in *The Cambridge History of Law in America, Volume II: The Long Nineteenth Century (1789–1920)*, ed. Michael Grossberg and Christopher Tomlins (New York: Cambridge University Press, 2008), 568–603. My own investigation of the labor question will unfold in chapter 7. For a good introduction to *Lochner* revisionism, see Gary D. Rowe, "Lochner Revisionism Revisited," *Law and Social Inquiry* 24 (Winter 1999): 221–52.

60. Tomlins, "To Improve the State and Condition of Man," 1248–49.

61. These regulations were necessary, Field once conceded, to help the "under fellow" gain "a show in this life." McCurdy, "Justice Field," 979.

62. Nancy F. Cott, *Public Vows: A History of Marriage and the Nation* (Cambridge, MA: Harvard University Press, 2000); Grossberg, *Governing the Hearth*; Laura Edwards, "Status without Rights: African Americans and the Tangled History of Law and Governance in the Nineteenth-Century South," *American Historical Review* 112 (2007): 365–93; Rachel Moran, *Interracial Intimacy: The Regulation of Race and Romance* (Chicago: University of Chicago Press, 2001); Martha Hodes, *White Women, Black Men: Illicit Sex in the Nineteenth-Century South* (New Haven, CT: Yale University Press, 1997); Paul S. Boyer, *Urban Masses and Moral Order in America, 1820–1920* (Cambridge, MA: Harvard University Press, 1978).

63. Jill Elaine Hasday argues otherwise in "Federalism and the Family Reconstructed," *UCLA Law Review* 45 (1997–98): 1297–1400. But the evidence in her article can be read to mean that after a surge in federal control during Reconstruction, the states reasserted their predominant control in the late nineteenth century.

64. Plessy v. Ferguson, 163 U.S. 537 (1896). For a history of the case in the context of judicial interpretations, see Owen M. Fiss, *Troubled Beginnings of the Modern State, 1888–1910* (New York: Maxwell Macmillan International, 1993). See also Brook Thomas, "Introduction: The Legal Background," in *Plessy v. Ferguson: A Brief History with Documents* (Boston: Bedford Books, 1997), 1–38.

65. Lochner v. New York, 198 U.S. 45 (1905).

66. For a trenchant analysis of the contradictoriness of liberal thought in America, and resulting entanglement of liberal and illiberal principles (and policies), see Desmond King, *In the Name of Liberalism: Illiberal Social Policy in the United States and Britain* (New York: Oxford University Press, 1999).

67. Barbara Young Welke, *Recasting American Liberty: Gender, Race, Law, and the Railroad Revolution, 1865–1920* (New York: Cambridge University Press, 2001), 351.

Another solution to the puzzle of how the same Supreme Court could have issued both the *Plessy* and *Lochner* rulings has come from the libertarian "law and economics" group led by Richard Epstein at the University of Chicago. Convinced that the true jurisprudence of the Supreme Court since the days of Marshall has been a laissez-faire one, the law and economics scholars have viewed *Plessy* as a "tragic misstep" that *Lochner* and other subsequent rulings began to remedy. They blame this misstep on the Court's infatuation with "sociological jurisprudence," a new approach to legal interpretation associated with Progressivism's rise that relied not on felicity to constitutional principles but instead on the need to adapt law to public opinion and desires, or what the 1896 Supreme Court *Plessy* majority called the "established usages, customs, and traditions of the people." Because, as David E. Bernstein has argued, the court had "assimilated the contemporary social science notion that blacks and whites, as members of distinct races, were instinctively hostile to one another," it ruled that a state government endeavoring to keep the two races apart was acting well within the boundaries of its police power.

Many who read Bernstein along with Epstein and other members of the law and economics group will be rightfully skeptical of their claim that Progressivism is to blame for *Plessy*, and that the problems of racial inequality would have been substantially solved had the Court only adhered to the superior constitutional regime of property, contracts, and personal liberty. Moreover, a careful reading of their writings on the place of *Plessy* in the history of constitutional law reveals that Bernstein and Epstein themselves understand how much *Plessy* rested not on a new doctrine of sociological jurisprudence but rather on the Court's respect for the old doctrine of police power that inhered in state governments. Indeed, their writings, unwittingly perhaps, draw our attention to the vitality of the police power doctrine in the late nineteenth century, and how decisions such as *Plessy* ensured its centrality to conceptions of American governance for much of the twentieth century as well. See David E. Bernstein, "Philip Sober Controlling Philip Drunk: *Buchanan v. Warley* in Historical Perspective," *Vanderbilt Law Review* 51 (1997–98): 797–879; quote from 824. See also Richard J. Epstein, "Lest We Forget: *Buchanan v. Warley* and the Constitutional Jurisprudence of the 'Progressive Era,'" *Vanderbilt Law Review* 51 (1997–98): 787–96.

68. Grossberg, *Governing the Hearth*, 75–182; Cott, *Public Vows*; Edwards, "Status without Rights"; Barbara Young Welke, *Law and the Borders of Belonging in the Long Nineteenth-Century United States* (New York: Cambridge University Press, 2010).

69. Quoted in Moran, *Interracial Intimacy*, 79.

70. Peggy Pascoe, "Miscegenation Law, Court Cases, and Ideologies of 'Race' in Twentieth-Century America," *Journal of American History* 83 (June 1996): 49, 59; Peggy Pascoe, *What Comes Naturally: Miscegenation Law and the Making of Race in America* (New York: Oxford University Press, 2009).

71. Pascoe, *What Comes Naturally*.

72. Leuchtenberg, "America's Second Bill of Rights," 243.

73. Brandeis's role in developing a right to privacy that no government could touch will be discussed in chapter 9.

74. See Jason L. Bates, "Reconfiguring Citizenship and Growing the State: Anti-Narcotics Law and Race in the United States, 1870–1930" (PhD diss., Vanderbilt University, 2016).

75. Meyer v. Nebraska, 262 U.S., 390 (1923), 399. See also Pierce v. Society of Sisters, 268 U.S. 510 (1925); Farrington v. Tokushige, 273 U.S. 284 (1927).

76. Gitlow v. New York, 268 U.S. 652 (1925), 666. On *Gitlow*, see also Marc Lendler, *Gitlow v. New York: Every Idea an Incitement* (Lawrence: University of Kansas Press, 2012).

77. Near v. Minnesota, 283 U.S. 697 (1931), 707.

78. The decision overturning bans on miscegenation was *Loving v. Virginia*, 388 U.S. 1 (1967); the one overturning bans on contraception was *Griswold v. Connecticut*, 381 U.S. 479 (1965).

79. George Chauncey, *Gay New York: Gender, Urban Culture, and the Making of the Gay Male World, 1890–1940* (New York: Basic Books, 1994); George Chauncey, *Why Marriage? The History Shaping Today's Debate over Gay Equality* (New York: Basic Books, 2004); Canaday, *The Straight State: Sexuality and Citizenship in Twentieth-Century America* (Princeton, NJ: Princeton University Press, 2011).

80. Martha Derthick, "Crossing the Thresholds: Federalism in the 1960s," in *Keeping the Compound Republic: Essays on American Federalism* (Washington, DC: Brookings Institution Press, 2001), 138–52; Edward S. Corwin, "The Passing of Dual Federalism," *Virginia Law Review* 36 (1950): 1–24.

81. Leuchtenburg, "America's Second Bill of Rights."

CHAPTER 3. STRATEGIES OF LIBERAL RULE

1. Quoted in Robert Eugene Cushman, "The National Police Power under the Commerce Clause of the Constitution," *Minnesota Law Review* 3 (1919): 292.

2. For a new work on one dimension of this antistatist ideology, framed in terms of opposition to federal taxation, see Romain Huret, *American Tax Resisters* (Cambridge, MA: Harvard University Press, 2014).

3. Richard Bensel, *Yankee Leviathan: The Origins of Central State Authority in America* (New York: Cambridge University Press, 1995).

4. For an important exception to this trend, see Kimberley S. Johnson, *Governing the American State: Congress and the New Federalism, 1877–1929* (Princeton, NJ: Princeton University Press, 2007).

5. Geoffrey Stone, *Perilous Times: Free Speech in Wartime from the Sedition Act of 1798 to the War on Terrorism* (New York: W. W. Norton and Company, 2005); John Fabian Witt, *Lincoln's Code: The Laws of War in American History* (New York: Free Press, 2013); Mary L. Dudziak, *War-Time: An Idea, Its History, Its Consequences* (New York: Oxford University Press, 2012); Rachel Maddow, *Drift: The Unmooring of American Military Power* (New York: Crown Publishers, 2012); Andrew J. Bacevich, *Washington Rules: America's Path to Permanent War* (New York: Metropolitan Books, 2010); Francis Paul Prucha, *Sword of the Republic: The United States Army on the Frontier, 1783–1846* (New York: Macmillan, 1968). For efforts to theorize exemption, or "state of exception," see Carl Schmitt, *Political Theology: Four Chapters on the Concept of Sovereignty* (Chicago: University of Chicago Press, 2005), and Giorgio Agamben, *State of Exception* (Chicago: University of Chicago Press, 2005).

6. See, for example, Pekka Hämäläinen, *The Comanche Empire* (New Haven, CT: Yale University Press, 2008); Brian Delay, *War of a Thousand Deserts:*

Indian Raids and the U.S.-Mexican War (New Haven, CT: Yale University Press, 2008); Richard Slotkin, *Regeneration through Violence: The Mythology of the American Frontier, 1600–1860* (Norman: University of Oklahoma Press, 1973).

7. For the territorial policies inaugurated by the Northwest Ordinances, see chapter 1.

8. As US Army general Barr McCaffrey noted in 2006, "The great value of the platform of Guantanamo was that it was a military space in which no Federal District Court had primary jurisdiction." Quoted in Jonathan M. Hansen, *Guantanamo: An American History* (New York: Hill and Wang, 2011), 352–53. See also Michael J. Strauss, *The Leasing of Guantanamo Bay* (Westport, CT: Praeger Security International, 2009); Paul Kramer, *The Blood of Government: Race, Empire, the United States, and the Philippines* (Chapel Hill: University of North Carolina, 2006); Alexander Aleinikoff, *Semblances of Sovereignty: The Constitution, the State, and American Citizenship* (Cambridge, MA: Harvard University Press, 2002); Christina Duffy Burnett and Burke Marshall, eds., *Foreign in a Domestic Sense: Puerto Rico, American Expansion, and the Constitution* (Durham, NC: Duke University Press, 2000); Gary Lawson and Guy Seidman, *The Constitution of Empire: Territorial Expansion and American Legal History* (New Haven, CT: Yale University Press, 2004); Linda C. Noel, *Debating American Identity: Southwestern Statehood and Mexican Immigration* (Tucson: University of Arizona Press, 2014); Robert W. Larson, *New Mexico's Quest for Statehood, 1846–1912* (Albuquerque: University of New Mexico Press, 1968); Howard R. Lamar, *The Far Southwest: A Territorial History, 1846–1912* (Albuquerque: University of New Mexico Press, 2000); George H. Alden, "The Evolution of the American System of Forming and Admitting New States into the Union," *Annals of the American Academy of Political and Social Science* 18 (November 1901), 79–89; Sarah Barringer Gordon, *The Mormon Question: Polygamy and Constitutional Conflict in Nineteenth-Century America* (Chapel Hill: University of North Carolina Press, 2002); Nancy F. Cott, *Public Vows: A History of Marriage and the Nation* (Cambridge, MA: Harvard University Press, 2000); Christopher Tomlins, "The Supreme Sovereignty of the State: A Genealogy of Police in American Constitutional Law, from the Founding Era to *Lochner*," in *Police and the Liberal State*, ed. Markus D. Dubber and Mariana Valverde (Stanford, CA: Stanford Law Books, 2008), 43–46.

9. Aristide Zolberg, *A Nation by Design: Immigration Policy and the Fashioning of a Nation* (New York: Russell Sage Foundation, 2006); Aleinikoff, *Semblances of Sovereignty*, chaps. 2 and 7; Kunal Parker, "Citizenship and Immigration Law, 1800–1924: Resolutions of Membership and Territory," in *The Cambridge History of Law in America, Volume II: The Long Nineteenth Century (1789–1920)*, ed. Michael Grossberg and Christopher Tomlins (New York: Cambridge University Press, 2008), 168–203; Hidetaka Hirota, " 'The Great Entrepot of Mendicants': Foreign Poverty and Immigration Control in New York State to 1882," *Journal of American Ethnic History* 33 (Winter 2014): 5–32.

10. Gary Gerstle, *American Crucible: Race and Nation in the Twentieth Century* (Princeton, NJ: Princeton University Press, 2001), chap. 3.

11. Gary Gerstle, "Inclusion, Exclusion, and American Nationality" in *Handbook on American Immigration and Ethnicity*, ed. Ronald Bayor (New York: Oxford University Press, forthcoming); Lucy E. Salyer, *Laws Harsh as Tigers: Chinese Immigrants and the Shaping of Modern Immigration Law* (Chapel Hill: University of North Carolina Press, 1995); Rogers M. Smith, *Civic Ideals: Conflicting Visions of Citizenship in U.S. History* (New Haven, CT: Yale University Press, 1997); Desmond King, *Making Americans: Immigration, Race, and the Origins of the Diverse Democracy* (Cambridge, MA: Harvard University Press, 2000).

12. Quoted in *Congressional Record*, March 17, 1924, 4389.

13. Aleinikoff, *Semblances of Sovereignty*, chap. 7.

14. The few who did usually had to find a judge willing to certify that they possessed certain key attributes, cultural or physical, of whiteness. The Supreme Court closed that loophole with its *Ozawa* and *Thind* decisions of 1922 and 1923, respectively. See Ian F. Haney Lopez, *White by Law: The Legal Construction of Race* (New York: New York University Press, 1991); Ozawa v. United States, 260 U.S. 178 (1922); United States v. Thind, 261 U.S. 204 (1923). See also James H. Kettner, *The Development of American Citizenship, 1608–1870* (Chapel Hill: University of North Carolina Press, 1978); Matthew Jacobson, *Whiteness of a Different Color: European Immigrants and the Alchemy of Race* (Cambridge, MA: Harvard University Press, 1998); Mae Ngai, *Impossible Subjects: Illegal Aliens and the Making of Modern America* (Princeton, NJ: Princeton University Press, 2004); Erika Lee, *At America's Gates: Chinese Immigration during the Exclusion Era, 1882–1943* (Chapel Hill: University of North Carolina Press, 2003).

15. US Constitution, amendment 14, section 1; Eric Foner, *Reconstruction: America's Unfinished Revolution, 1863–1877* (New York: Harper and Row, 1988); Eric Foner, *The Story of American Freedom* (New York: W. W. Norton and Company, 1988); Garrett Epps, "The Citizenship Clause: A 'Legislative History,'" *American University Law Review* 60 (December 2010): 331–91; Gerald L. Neuman, *Strangers to the Constitution: Immigrants, Borders, and Fundamental Law* (Princeton, NJ: Princeton University Press, 1996). See also United States v. Wong Kim Ark, 169 U.S. 649 (1898).

16. Quoted in *Congressional Globe*, 39th Cong., 1st Sess., 498 (1866).

17. Ibid. Only some groups of Indians were to be excluded from birthright citizenship, and for reasons of jurisdiction rather than race or culture: through treaties, the US government had granted these groups rights of self-government, which meant that they were not fully subject to the jurisdiction of American laws.

18. *United States v. Wong Kim Ark.*

19. On the complexities of the situation confronting Chinese and Japanese communities from the 1870s to 1950s, see Andrew Gyory, *Closing the Gate: Race, Politics, and the Chinese Exclusion Act* (Chapel Hill: University of North Carolina Press, 1998); Salyer, *Laws Harsh as Tigers*; Lee, *At America's*

Gates; Yuji Ichioka, *The Issei: The World of the First-Generation Japanese Immigrants, 1880–1924* (London: Collier Macmillan Publishers, 1988); Yuji Ichioka, *Before Internment: Essays in Prewar Japanese American History*, ed. Gordon H. Chang and Eiichiro Azuma (Palo Alto, CA: Stanford University Press, 2006); Ngai, *Impossible Subjects*; Scott Kurashige, *The Shifting Grounds of Race: Black and Japanese Americans in the Making of Multiethnic Los Angeles* (Princeton, NJ: Princeton University Press, 2010); Ellen D. Wu, *The Color of Success: Asian Americans and the Origins of the Model Minority* (Princeton, NJ: Princeton University Press, 2013).

20. Christopher Tomlins uses the term "proxy" to describe the process that I am here calling surrogacy. See Tomlins, "Supreme Sovereignty of the State," 39, 46.

21. Jason L. Bates, "Reconfiguring Citizenship and Growing the State: Anti-Narcotics Law and Race in the United States, 1870–1930" (PhD diss., Vanderbilt University, 2016).

22. The phrase "definite constitutional peg" appears in Cushman, "National Police Power under the Commerce Clause of the Constitution," 296. See also David J. Langum, *Crossing over the Line: Legislating Morality and the Mann Act* (Chicago: University of Chicago Press, 1994); Bates, "Reconfiguring Citizenship and Growing the State"; Kathleen J. Frydl, *The Drug Wars in America, 1940–1973* (New York: Cambridge University Press, 2013), 19.

23. Richard R. John, *Network Nation: Inventing American Telecommunications* (Cambridge, MA: Harvard University Press, 2010).

24. On Comstock, obscenity, and morals regulation, see Nicola Beisel, *Imperiled Innocents: Anthony Comstock and Family Reproduction in Victorian America* (Princeton, NJ: Princeton University Press, 1997); Timothy J. Gilfoyle, *City of Eros: New York City, Prostitution, and the Commercialization of Sex, 1790–1920* (New York: W. W. Norton and Company, 1992); Helen Lefkowitz Horowitz, *Rereading Sex: Battles of Sexual Knowledge and Suppression in Nineteenth-Century America* (New York: Alfred A. Knopf, 2002); George Chauncey, *Gay New York: Gender, Urban Culture, and the Making of the Gay Male World, 1890–1940* (New York: Basic Books, 1994), 146; Paul Boyer, *Urban Masses and Moral Order in America, 1820–1920* (Cambridge, MA: Harvard University Press, 1978), 120; Leslie J. Reagan, *When Abortion Was a Crime: Women, Medicine, and Law in the United States, 1867–1973* (Berkeley: University of California Press, 1997); Linda Gordon, *Woman's Body, Woman's Right* (New York: Penguin Books, 1977), 24, 64–65, 167, 214; Janet Farrell Brodie, *Contraception and Abortion in Nineteenth-Century America* (Ithaca, NY: Cornell University Press, 1994), 255–66; 281–88; James A. Morone, *Hellfire Nation: The Politics of Sin in American History* (New Haven, CT: Yale University Press, 2003); Paul Starr, *The Creation of the Media; Political Origins of Modern Communication* (New York: Basic Books, 2004), 240–50.

25. The complete elimination of "obscenity" was, of course, impossible. On the limits of the campaign, see Andrea Tone, *Devices and Desires: A History of Contraception in America* (New York: Hill and Wang, 2001).

26. Daniel Carpenter, *The Forging of Bureaucratic Autonomy: Reputations, Networks, and Policy Innovation in Executive Agencies, 1862–1928* (Princeton, NJ: Princeton University Press, 2001), 94–162.

27. United States v. E. C. Knight Co., 156 U.S. 1 (1895); Karen Orren, "The Laws of Industrial Organization, 1870–1920," in *The Cambridge History of Law in America*, ed. Michael Grossberg and Christopher Tomlins (New York: Cambridge University Press, 2008), 2:531–67.

28. Lochner v. New York, 198 U.S. 45 (1905).

29. On the need to protect miners, see Holden v. Hardy, 169 U.S. 366 (1898). On women, see Muller v. Oregon, 208 U.S. 412 (1908). On the context in which these rulings emerged, see Melvin I. Urosky, "Myth and Reality: The Supreme Court and Protective Legislation in the Progressive Era," *Yearbook 1983* (Washington, DC: Supreme Court Historical Society, 1983), 53–72.

30. Robert Eugene Cushman, "The National Police Power under the Commerce Clause of the Constitution, Part IV: Regulations Denying the Privileges of Interstate Commerce to Harmless Goods Produced under Objectionable Conditions—The Federal Child Labor Law," *Minnesota Law Review* 4 (1920): 452–83.

31. Ernst Freund, *The Police Power: Public Policy and Constitutional Rights* (Chicago: University of Chicago Press, 1904).

32. Cushman, "The National Police Power under the Commerce Clause of the Constitution," *Minnesota Law Review* 3, 291; Cushman, "National Police Power under the Commerce Clause of the Constitution," *Minnesota Law Review* 4, 452, 483.

33. Cushman, "National Police Power under the Commerce Clause of the Constitution," *Minnesota Law Review* 3, 294–95.

34. I read Cushman somewhat differently than does William Novak, who emphasizes the success rather than the limitation of the surrogacy strategy for achieving a full-fledged national police power. See William J. Novak, "Police Power and the Hidden Transformation of the American State," in *Police and the Liberal State*, ed. Markus D. Dubber and Mariana Valverde (Stanford, CA: Stanford University Press, 2008), 54–73.

Michelle Landis Dauber's recent work on disaster relief can be interpreted as uncovering an intriguing form of federal action that drew on both exemption and surrogacy. When confronted with the destruction caused by a natural disaster (such as a drought, flood, fire, earthquake, or epidemic), the federal courts were inclined to interpret the federal government's constitutional authority to act for the "general welfare" (and thus to offer relief to disaster victims) more expansively than they did in normal circumstances. Progressives sought to enlarge this exemption from limited government by arguing that the central state possessed equally expansive authority when responding to man-made disasters such as economic depressions. They "hung" this authority on the constitutional peg of taxation, long associated by jurists with the general welfare. This yoking together of exemption and surrogacy would prove a potent tool, especially in the 1930s, for forging the nation's welfare state. Michelle Landis

Dauber, *The Sympathetic State: Disaster Relief and the Origins of the American Welfare State* (Chicago: University of Chicago Press, 2013).

35. My work on privatization draws on the thought of others who have explored the intersection of public and private power in nineteenth-century and early twentieth-century America. See, for example, Brian Balogh, *A Government Out of Sight: The Mystery of National Authority in Nineteenth-Century America* (New York: Cambridge University Press, 2009); William J. Novak, "Public-Private Governance: A Historical Introduction," in *Government by Contract: Outsourcing and American Democracy*, ed. Judy Freeman and Martha Minow (Cambridge, MA: Harvard University Press 2009), 23–40; William J. Novak, "The Pluralist State: The Convergence of Public and Private Power in America," in *American Public Life and the Historical Imagination*, ed. Wendy Gamber, Michael Grossberg, and Hendrik Hartog (South Bend, IN: University of Notre Dame Press, 2003), 27–48; Morton Horwitz, "The History of the Public/Private Distinction," *University of Pennsylvania Law Review* 130 (June 1982): 1423–28; Theda Skocpol, Marshall Ganz, and Ziad Munson, "A Nation of Organizers: The Institutional Origins of Civic Voluntarism in the United States," *American Political Science Review* 94 (September 2000): 527–46.

36. *Congressional Globe*, 35th Cong., 2nd Sess., 55 (1858); Lewis H. Haney, *A Congressional History of Railways in the United States* (1908; repr., New York: Augustus M. Kelley Publishers, 1968), 2:153; Maury Klein, *Union Pacific: Birth of a Railroad, 1862–1893* (Garden City, NY: Doubleday, 1987), 16; Robert William Fogel, *The Union Pacific Railroad: A Case in Premature Enterprise* (Baltimore: Johns Hopkins University Press, 1960), 58.

37. Fogel, *Union Pacific Railroad*, 18. These numbers expand greatly if we include all the transcontinental routes that the US government subsidized in the second half of the nineteenth century.

38. Klein, *Union Pacific*, 14–15.

39. Ibid.

40. The publicly appointed commissioners did scrape together enough investors to take the Union Pacific private within a year, but general interest in Union Pacific stock remained so low that the company could not raise enough additional money to build the road.

41. Klein, *Union Pacific*, 31; Fogel, *Union Pacific Railroad*, 50.

42. Steve Fraser, *Every Man a Speculator: A History of Wall Street in American Life* (New York: HarperCollins, 2005), 118.

43. Klein, *Union Pacific*, 108–28; Nelson Trottman, *History of the Union Pacific: A Financial and Economic Survey* (1923; repr., New York: Augustus M. Kelly, 1966), 32–35; Noam Maggor, "Politics of Property: Urban Democracy in the Age of Capital, 1865–1900" (PhD diss., Harvard University, 2010); Richard White, *Railroaded: The Transcontinentals and the Making of Modern America* (New York: W. W. Norton and Company, 2011), 93–133; Fraser, *Every Man a Speculator*, 117–19.

44. During the same period (1866–69) the Central Pacific had covered "only" 881 miles from Sacramento to Utah, but it had had to contend with nightmarish construction conditions in the Sierra Nevada. White, *Railroaded*, 37.

45. Ibid., passim.

46. Ibid., 458–59. See also Robert S. Henry, "The Railroad Land Grant Legend in American History Texts," *Mississippi Historical Review* 32 (September 1945): 191.

47. On the impact of the telegraph, see John, *Network Nation*.

48. White, *Railroaded*, 455–56; Hämäläinen, *The Comanche Empire*; Katherine Benton Cohen, *Borderline Americans: Racial Division and Labor War in the Arizona Borderlands* (Cambridge, MA: Harvard University Press, 2009).

49. White, *Railroaded*; Noam Maggor, "Politics of Property."

50. Kevin Starr, *California: A History* (New York: Modern Library, 2005), 78–83; Kevin Starr, *Americans and the California Dream, 1850–1915* (New York: Oxford University Press, 1973), 49.

51. Some historians, such as Robert Howard and Nelson Trottman, give the Pacific Railway too much credit for western economic growth, and others, like Robert Fogel, counter the notion that railroads were specifically responsible for the United States' western expansion. But most agree that railroads enabled economic, technological, and population growth in the American West. Klein, *Union Pacific*, xi; Alfred D. Chandler Jr., *The Railroads: The Nation's First Big Business* (New York: Harcourt, Brace and World, Inc., 1965), 22–23, 43–44; William Cronon, *Nature's Metropolis: Chicago and the Great West* (New York: W. W. Norton and Company, 1991), 80–81, 325, passim; Robert West Howard, *The Great Iron Trail: The Story of the First Transcontinental Railroad* (New York: G. P. Putnam's Sons, 1962), 344, 349; Trottman, *History of the Union Pacific*, 101–2, 203; Robert William Fogel, *Railroads and American Economic Growth: Essays in Econometric History* (Baltimore: Johns Hopkins University Press, 1964); John F. Stover, *American Railroads*, 2nd ed. (1961; repr., Chicago: University of Chicago Press, 1997), 94–95, 164–65; John Debo Galloway, *The First Transcontinental Railroad* (New York: Simmons-Boardman, 1950), 13; Henry, "Railroad Land Grant Legend," 191; Stewart H. Holbrook, *The Story of American Railroads* (New York: Crown Publishers, 1947), 3–5, 8, 10, 13–14, 16–18.

52. White, *Railroaded*, 455–93.

53. Fogel estimates that between 1870 and 1879, the Union Pacific was a "highly profitable venture": the average private rate of return—the rate of return to the company on the construction expenditure—was a healthy 11.6 percent. As to the promoters, Fogel calculates the range of their profits at $13 to $16.5 million. He argues that this range was close to justified based on the amount of risk they took on. According to Fogel, a "reasonable" profit based on the risk and capital invested would have been around $11.1 million. Fogel, *Union Pacific Railroad*, 97, 70–71, 85.

54. White, *Railroaded*, 415–52.

55. Jack Beatty, *Age of Betrayal: The Triumph of Money in America, 1865–1900* (New York: Alfred A. Knopf, 2007), 148–91; Paul Kens, *Justice Stephen Field: Shaping Liberty from the Gold Rush to the Gilded Age* (Lawrence: University of Kansas Press, 1997); Carl Brent Swisher, *Stephen J. Field: Craftsman of the Law* (Washington, DC: Brookings Institution Press, 1930); William E.

Forbath, *Law and the Shaping of the American Labor Movement* (Cambridge, MA: Harvard University Press, 1991).

56. Fogel, *Union Pacific Railroad*, 107–10. Carter Goodrich agrees, suggesting that had public opinion accepted a government road, it would have been a better option than the public-private solution. For support he calls on Charles Francis Adams, who said, as quoted by Goodrich, " 'In any other country' . . . an undertaking like the Union Pacific 'would have been built by the Government as a military road.' " Carter Goodrich, *Government Promotion of American Canals and Railroads, 1800-1890* (New York: Columbia University Press, 1960), 201.

57. Letter from C. P. Huntington to Senator George F. Edmunds, April 3, 1876, quoted in *House Report No. 440*, 44th Cong., 1st Sess., 103 (1876).

58. Alexis de Tocqueville, *Democracy in America*, ed. J. P. Mayer (Garden City, NY: Anchor Books, Doubleday, 1969), 2:513.

59. Ibid., 513–17. See also Johann N. Neem, *Creating a Nation of Joiners: Democracy and Civil Society in Early Massachusetts* (Cambridge, MA: Harvard University Press, 2008).

60. David B. Truman, *The Governmental Process: Political Interests and Public Opinion* (New York: Alfred A. Knopf, 1971); Arthur M. Schlesinger Jr., *The Vital Center: The Politics of Freedom* (Boston: Houghton Mifflin Company, 1949).

61. James M. Banner, "The Problem of South Carolina," in *The Hofstadter Aegis: A Memorial*, ed. Stanley Elkins and Eric McKitrick (New York: Alfred A. Knopf, 1974), 75.

62. Jürgen Habermas, *The Structural Transformation of the Public Sphere: An Inquiry into a Category of Bourgeois Society* (Cambridge, MA: MIT Press, 1989); Jason L. Bates, "Public Spheres, Subaltern Counterpublics, and Voluntary Associations: Locating Civil Society in the United States" (graduate seminar paper, Vanderbilt University, 2011).

63. Arthur M. Schlesinger, "Biography of a Nation of Joiners," *American Historical Review* 50 (October 1944): 21.

64. Theda Skocpol, *Protecting Soldiers and Mothers: The Political Origins of Social Policy in the United States* (Cambridge, MA: Belknap Press of Harvard University Press, 1992); Theda Skocpol, Marshall Ganz, and Ziad Munson, "A Nation of Organizers: The Institutional Origins of Civic Voluntarism in the United States," *American Political Science Review* 94 (September 2000): 527–46.

65. Linda K. Kerber, *Women of the Republic: Intellect and Ideology in Revolutionary America* (Chapel Hill: University of North Carolina Press, 1980); Mary P. Ryan, *Women in Public: Between Banners and Ballots, 1825–1880* (Baltimore: Johns Hopkins University Press, 1990); Mary P. Ryan, *Civic Wars: Democracy and Public Life in the American City during the Nineteenth Century* (Berkeley: University of California Press, 1997); Elisabeth S. Clemens, *The People's Lobby: Organizational Innovation and the Rise of Interest Group Politics in the United States, 1890–1925* (Chicago: University of Chicago Press, 1997); Nancy F. Cott, *The Bonds of Womanhood: "Woman's Sphere" in New England, 1780–1835* (New Haven, CT: Yale University Press, 1977); Paula

Baker, "The Domestication of Politics: Women and American Political Society, 1780–1920," *American Historical Review* 89 (June 1984): 620–47; Paula Baker, *The Moral Frameworks of Public Life: Gender, Politics, and the State in Rural New York, 1870–1930* (New York: Oxford University Press, 1991); Robyn Muncy, *Creating a Female Dominion in American Reform, 1890–1935* (New York: Oxford University Press, 1991).

66. William E. Channing, "Remarks on Associations," in *Works* (Boston: American Unitarian Association, 1875), 149. This Channing article appeared first, unsigned, in *Christian Examiner and General Review* 7 (September 1829): 105–40.

67. John Whiteclay Chambers II, *To Raise an Army: The Draft Comes to Modern America* (New York: Free Press, 1987).

68. William Quentin Maxwell, *Lincoln's Fifth Wheel: The Political History of the United States Sanitary Commission* (New York: Longmans, Green, and Company, 1956), 310, passim; George M. Fredrickson, *The Inner Civil War: Northern Intellectuals and the Crisis of the Union* (New York: Harper Torchbooks, 1965), 98–112; Lori D. Ginzberg, *Women and the Work of Benevolence: Morality, Politics, and Class in the Nineteenth-Century United States* (New Haven, CT: Yale University Press, 1990), chap. 5.

69. Foster Rhea Dulles, *The American Red Cross: A History* (New York: Harper and Brothers, 1950), 2.

70. On the Committee of Fourteen, see George Chauncey, *Gay New York: Gender, Urban Culture, and the Making of the Gay Male World, 1890–1940* (New York: Basic Books, 1994), 131–77.

71. Linda Gordon, *The Great Arizona Orphan Abduction* (Cambridge, MA: Harvard University Press, 1999); Anthony Lukas, *Big Trouble: A Murder in a Small Western Town Sets Off a Struggle for the Soul of America* (New York: Simon and Schuster, 1997).

72. Gerstle, *American Crucible*, 61; Theodore Roosevelt to Philander Chase Knox, February 8, 1909, in Elting E. Morison, ed., *The Letters of Theodore Roosevelt* (Cambridge, MA: Harvard University Press, 1951–54), 6:1511–12; Theodore Roosevelt to Henry Cabot Lodge, July 10, 1907, in Elting E. Morison, ed., *The Letters of Theodore Roosevelt* (Cambridge, MA: Harvard University Press, 1951–54), 5:710.

CHAPTER 4. LESSONS OF TOTAL WAR

1. David Kennedy, *Over Here! The First World War and American Society* (New York: Oxford University Press, 1982); James T. Kloppenberg, *Uncertain Victory: Social Democracy and Progressivism in European and American Democracies* (New York: Oxford University Press, 1986); Robert H. Wiebe, *The Search for Order, 1877–1920* (New York: Hill and Wang, 1967); James Weinstein, *The Corporate Ideal in the Liberal State, 1900–1918* (Boston: Beacon Press, 1968); Alan Dawley, *Struggles for Justice: Social Responsibility and*

the Liberal State (Cambridge, MA: Harvard University Press, 1991); Ronald Schaffer, *America in the Great War: The Rise of the War Welfare State* (New York: Oxford University Press, 1991); Charles Forcey, *The Crossroads of Liberalism: Croly, Weyl, Lippmann, and the Progressive Era, 1900–1925* (New York: Oxford University Press, 1961); David W. Levy, *Herbert Croly of the New Republic: The Life and Thought of an American Progressive* (Princeton, NJ: Princeton University Press, 1985).

2. Kennedy, *Over Here!*

3. Ibid.

4. Ibid.; Horace C. Peterson and Gilbert C. Fite, *Opponents of War, 1917–1918* (Madison: University of Wisconsin Press, 1957); Nick Salvatore, *Eugene V. Debs: Citizen and Socialist* (Champaign: University of Illinois Press, 1984); William Preston Jr., *Aliens and Dissenters: Federal Suppression of Radicals, 1903–1933* (Cambridge, MA: Harvard University Press, 1963); John Milton Cooper Jr., *The Warrior and the Priest: Woodrow Wilson and Theodore Roosevelt* (Cambridge, MA: Harvard University Press, 1983).

5. Irving Howe, *Socialism and America* (San Diego, CA: Harcourt Brace, 1985); David Montgomery, *The Fall of the House of Labor: The Workplace, the State, and American Labor Activism, 1865–1925* (New York: Cambridge University Press, 1987); Steve Fraser, *Labor Will Rule: Sidney Hillman and the Rise of American Labor* (New York: Free Press, 1993); Joseph A. McCartin, *Labor's Great War: The Struggle for Industrial Democracy and the Origins of Modern American Labor Relations, 1912–1921* (Chapel Hill: University of North Carolina Press, 1997); John Higham, *Strangers in the Land: Patterns of American Nativism, 1865–1925* (New Brunswick, NJ: Rutgers University Press, 1984); Frederick C. Luebke, *Bonds of Loyalty: German-Americans and World War I* (DeKalb: Northern Illinois University Press, 1974), 194–263; Gary Gerstle, *American Crucible: Race and Nation in the Twentieth Century* (Princeton, NJ: Princeton University Press, 2001), chap. 3.

6. Geoffrey R. Stone, *Perilous Times: Free Speech in Wartime, from the Sedition Act of 1798 to the War on Terrorism* (New York: W. W. Norton and Company, 2004), chap. 3.

7. John Whiteclay Chambers II, *To Raise an Army: The Draft Comes to Modern America* (New York: Free Press, 1987), chaps. 5–8.

8. Kimberley Johnson, *Governing the American State: Congress and the New Federalism, 1877–1929* (Princeton, NJ: Princeton University Press, 2007), 125–32.

9. Ellis W. Hawley, *The Great War and the Search for Modern Order: A History of the American People and Their Institutions* (1992; repr., Prospect Heights, IL: Waveland Press, Inc., 1997), chap. 2; Robert D. Cuff, *The War Industries Board: Business-Government Relations during World War I* (Baltimore: Johns Hopkins University Press, 1973); Jordan A. Schwarz, *The Speculator, Bernard M. Baruch in Washington, 1917–1965* (Chapel Hill: University of North Carolina Press, 1981), chap. 2; Barry D. Karl, *The Uneasy State: The United States from 1915 to 1945* (Chicago: University of Chicago Press, 1983), chap. 3; Dawley, *Struggles for Justice*; Kennedy, *Over Here!* chap. 2.

10. Olivier Zunz, *Philanthropy in America: A History* (Princeton, NJ: Princeton University Press, 2012), 58. Red Cross volunteer collectors numbered more than eight million.

11. Ibid.

12. Foster Rhea Dulles, *The American Red Cross: A History* (New York: Harper and Brothers, 1950), 157–71, 173–88.

13. C. Howard Hopkins, *History of the Y.M.C.A. in North America* (New York: Association Press, 1951), 487–92, passim; William H. Taft and Frederick Morgan Harris, *Service with Fighting Men: An Account of the Work of the American Young Men's Christian Associations in the World War* (New York: Association Press, 1922), 1:204–5, plate V, passim; Nina Mjagkij, *Light in the Darkness: African Americans and the YMCA, 1852–1946* (Lexington: University Press of Kentucky, 1994), chap. 6; Owen E. Pence, *The Y.M.C.A. and Social Need* (New York: Association Press, 1939); Mayer N. Zald, *Organizational Change: The Political Economy of the YMCA* (Chicago: University of Chicago Press, 1970).

14. Christopher Capozzola, *Uncle Sam Wants You: World War I and the Making of the Modern American Citizen* (New York: Oxford University Press, 2010), chap. 3.

15. Gerstle, *American Crucible*, chap. 3; Gary Gerstle, "The Immigrant as Threat to American Security: A Historical Perspective," in *From Arrival to Incorporation: Migrants to the U.S. in a Global Era*, ed. Elliott R. Barkan, Hasia Diner, and Alan M. Kraut (New York: New York University Press, 2008), 217–45.

16. Emerson Hough, *The Web: The Authorized History of the American Protective League* (Chicago: Reilly and Lee, 1919), 28.

17. Capozzola, *Uncle Sam Wants You*, passim; Stephen Meyer III, *The Five-Dollar Day: Labor Management and Social Control of the Ford Motor Company, 1908–1921* (Albany: State University of New York Press, 198), 169–94.

18. Stone, *Perilous Times*, 590n85; Paul L. Murphy, *World War I and the Origin of Civil Liberties in the United States* (New York: W. W. Norton and Company, 1979), 89–90; Hough, *Web*, 28. Gregory wrote that enlisting voluntary groups "enables us . . . to investigate hundreds of thousands of complaints and to keep scores of thousands of persons under observation. We have representatives at all meetings of any importance." Thomas Gregory, "Suggestions of Attorney-General Gregory to Executive Committee in Relation to the Department of Justice," *American Bar Association Journal* 4 (1918): 309.

19. Preston, *Aliens and Dissenters*; James Weinstein, *The Decline of Socialism in America, 1912–1925*, 2nd ed. (New Brunswick, NJ: Rutgers University Press, 1986); Melvyn Dubofsky, *We Shall Be All: A History of the IWW* (New York: Quadrangle Press, 1969); Michael Kazin, *American Dreamers: How the Left Changed a Nation* (New York: Alfred A. Knopf, 2011), chap. 4; Curt Gentry, *J. Edgar Hoover: The Man and the Secrets* (New York: W. W. Norton and Company, 1991), 71–73; Kenneth Ackerman, *The Young J. Edgar: Hoover, the Red Scare, and the Assault on Civil Liberties* (New York: Carroll and Graf Publishers, 2007), 20.

20. Trenton and Atlantic City (New Jersey), Galveston (Texas), and San Francisco and Sacramento (California) were among the cities targeted. Capozzola, *Uncle Sam Wants You*, chap. 1; Hough, *Web*, 143.

21. Gentry, *J. Edgar Hoover*, 72; Ackerman, *Young J. Edgar*, 19.

22. Quoted in "Draft Raids Here Anger Senators," *New York Times*, September 6, 1918, http://query.nytimes.com/gst/abstract.html?res=F4081FFA3F5D1 47A93C4A91782D85F4C8185F9 (accessed June 16, 2011).

23. Capozzola, *Uncle Sam Wants You*, 52–53; Meyer, *Five-Dollar Day*, 169–94.

24. William Pencak, *For God and Country: The American Legion, 1919– 1941* (Boston: Northeastern University Press, 1989); Lisa McGirr, *The War on Alcohol: Prohibition and the Rise of the American State* (New York: W. W. Norton and Company, 2015); Michael A. Lerner, *Dry Manhattan: Prohibition in New York City* (Cambridge, MA: Harvard University Press, 2007), 61–95.

25. Murphy, *World War I and the Origins of Civil Liberties in the United States*; Gary Gerstle, "The Protean Character of American Liberalism," *American Historical Review* 99 (October 1994): 1043–73.

26. Herbert Croly, *The Promise of American Life* (1909; repr., Boston: Northeastern University Press, 2009); Theodore Roosevelt, "The New Nationalism," in *The New Nationalism* (New York: Outlook Company, 1910), 3–33; Kathryn Kish Sklar, *Florence Kelley and the Nation's Work: The Rise of Woman's Political Culture, 1830–1900* (New Haven, CT: Yale University Press, 1997); Steve Fraser, "The 'Labor Question,' " in *The Rise and Fall of the New Deal Order, 1930–1980*, ed. Steve Fraser and Gary Gerstle (Princeton, NJ: Princeton University Press, 1989), 55–84; Christopher Lasch, *The American Liberals and the Russian Revolution* (New York: McGraw-Hill, 1962); Stanley Shapiro, "The Great War and Reform: Liberals and Labor, 1917–1919," *Labor History* 12 (Summer 1971): 114–45; John Dewey, *Liberalism and Social Action* (1935; repr., Amherst, NY: Prometheus Books, 1999); Gerstle, "Protean Character of American Liberalism."

27. Gentry, *J. Edgar Hoover*, 63, 67, 127; Ackerman, *Young J. Edgar*, 3–4, 41–43, 45, 367–68; William B. Breuer, *J. Edgar Hoover and His G-Men* (Westport, CT: Praeger, 1995), 12; Diarmuid Jeffreys, *The Bureau: Inside the Modern FBI* (Boston: Houghton Mifflin Company, 1995), 56.

28. Claire Bond Potter, *War on Crime: Gangsters, G-Men, and the Politics of Mass Culture* (New Brunswick, NJ: Rutgers University Press, 1998), 2–3, 35–39; Breuer, *J. Edgar Hoover and His G-Men*, 13, 98–99, 232; Gentry, *J. Edgar Hoover*, 129–30.

29. Robert K. Murray, *Red Scare: A Study in National Hysteria, 1919–1920* (Minneapolis: University of Minnesota Press, 1955); Preston, *Aliens and Dissenters*; Stone, *Perilous Times*, chap. 3.

30. Murray, *Red Scare*, 239–62; Stanley Coben, *A. Mitchell Palmer: Politician* (New York: Columbia University Press, 1963); Stone, *Perilous Times*, chap. 3. Hoover was even forced to dismantle the General Intelligence Division in 1924. And the funds for the army's Military Intelligence Unit dried up after

the war, too. Richard D. Challener, *United States Military Intelligence, 1917–1927* (New York: Garland, 1979), 1:v–xii; Kenneth Reilly, *Hoover and the Un-Americans: The FBI, HUAC, and the Red Menace* (Philadelphia: Temple University Press, 1983), 18.

31. David Burner, *Herbert Hoover: A Public Life* (New York: Alfred A. Knopf, 1979); Joan Hoff Wilson, *Herbert Hoover: Forgotten Progressive* (Boston: Little, Brown and Company, 1975).

32. Zunz, *Philanthropy in America*, chap. 2.

33. Ibid., 104–5.

34. Herbert Hoover, *American Individualism* (Garden City, NY: Doubleday, Page and Company, 1923), 43.

35. Ellis W. Hawley, "Herbert Hoover, the Commerce Secretariat, and the Vision of an 'Associative State,' 1921–1928," *Journal of American History* 61 (June 1974): 116–40; Ellis W. Hawley, "Herbert Hoover and American Corporatism, 1929–1933," in *The Hoover Presidency: A Reappraisal*, ed. Martin L. Fausold and George T. Mazuzan (Albany: State University of New York Press, 1974), 101–19; Dawley, *Struggles for Justice*.

36. Zunz, *Philanthropy in America*, chap. 4.

37. John M. Barry, *Rising Tide: The Great Mississippi Flood of 1927 and How it Changed America* (New York: Simon and Schuster, 1997), 382.

38. Eric Foner, *Reconstruction: America's Unfinished Revolution, 1863–1877* (New York: Harper and Row, 1988), 228–411.

39. M. R. Werner, *Julius Rosenwald: The Life of a Practical Humanitarian* (New York: Harper and Brothers, 1939), 353.

40. Ibid., 293.

41. Zunz, *Philanthropy in America*, chap. 4.

CHAPTER 5. PARTIES, MONEY, CORRUPTION

1. US Constitution, article 1, section 4.

2. Gordon S. Wood, *The Creation of the American Republic, 1776–1787* (Chapel Hill: University of North Carolina Press, 1969); J.G.A. Pocock, *The Machiavellian Moment: Florentine Political Thought and the Atlantic Republican Tradition* (Princeton, NJ: Princeton University Press, 1975); Quentin Skinner, *The Foundations of Modern Political Thought*, 2 vols. (New York: Cambridge University Press, 1978); Maurizio Viroli, *Foundations of Modern Political Thought: Machiavelli* (New York: Oxford University Press, 1998); Andreas Kalyvas and Ira Katznelson, *Liberal Beginnings: Making a Republic for the Moderns* (New York: Cambridge University Press, 2008).

3. Stephen Skowronek, *Building a New American State: The Expansion of National Administrative Capacities, 1877–1920* (New York: Cambridge University Press, 1982), 26.

4. On the development of parties, and their role in nineteenth-century governance, see Jean H. Baker, *Affairs of Party: The Political Culture of Northern Democrats in Mid-Nineteenth-Century America* (Ithaca, NY: Cornell University Press, 1983).

5. Alexander Keyssar, *The Right to Vote: The Contested History of Democracy in the United States* (New York: Basic Books, 2000): Linda K. Kerber, *Women of the Republic: Intellect and Ideology in Revolutionary America* (Chapel Hill: University of North Carolina Press, 1980); Nancy F. Cott, *The Bonds of Womanhood: 'Woman's Sphere' in New England, 1780–1835* (New Haven, CT: Yale University Press, 1977); Rosemarie Zagarri, *Revolutionary Backlash: Women and Politics in the Early American Republic* (Philadelphia: University of Pennsylvania Press, 2007); Stephen Kantrowitz, *More Than Freedom: Fighting for Black Citizenship in a White Republic, 1829–1889* (New York: Penquin Books, 2012); Reeve Huston, "Rethinking 1828: The Emergence of Competing Democracies in the United States," in *Democracy, Participation, and Contestation: Civil Society, Governance, and the Future of Liberal Democracy*, ed. Emmanuel Avril and Johann N. Neem (New York: Routledge, 2015), 13–24; Andrew W. Robertson, "Democracy: America's Other 'Peculiar Institution,'" in *Democracy, Participation, and Contestation: Civil Society, Governance, and the Future of Liberal Democracy*, ed. Emmanuel Avril and Johann N. Neem (New York: Routledge, 2015), 69–80.

6. Rhode Island and South Carolina were partial holdouts, with the former requiring a property qualification for immigrants to gain the right to vote and South Carolina requiring, for those without property, a minimum period of residence in the state. Keyssar, *Right to Vote*, 348–49.

7. Gary J. Kornblith and John M. Murrin, "The Dilemmas of Ruling Elites in Revolutionary America," in *Ruling America: A History of Wealth and Power in a Democracy*, ed. Steve Fraser and Gary Gerstle (Cambridge, MA: Harvard University Press, 2005), 27–63; Matthew Josephson, *The Politicos, 1865–1896* (New York: Harcourt, 1938), 64–68; Leonard D. White, *The Jeffersonians: A Study in Administrative History, 1801–1829* (New York: Macmillan, 1951); Leonard D. White, *The Jacksonians: A Study in Administrative History, 1829–1861* (New York: Macmillan, 1954).

8. Kornblith and Murrin, "Dilemmas of Ruling Elites in Revolutionary America."

9. Sean Wilentz, *The Rise of American Democracy: Jefferson to Lincoln* (New York: W. W. Norton and Company, 2005), 307–15, passim. The number of eligible voters who cast ballots rose from 27 percent in 1824 to 58 percent in 1832, and then to 80 percent in 1840—a level it maintained for most of the nineteenth century.

10. Gordon S. Wood, *The Radicalism of the American Revolution* (New York: Alfred A. Knopf, 1992), 232, passim.

11. Daniel Walker Howe, *What Hath God Wrought: The Transformation of America, 1815–1848* (New York: Oxford University Press, 2007); Richard Bensel, *The American Ballot Box in the Mid-Nineteenth Century* (New York: Cambridge University Press, 2004).

12. M. Ostrogorski, *Democracy and the Organization of Political Parties*, trans. (from French) Frederick Clarke (New York: Macmillan Company, 1902), 2:47.

13. Ibid., 2:612–14.

14. Wilentz, *Rise of American Democracy*, 514–18.

15. Joel H. Silbey, *Martin Van Buren and the Emergence of American Popular Politics* (Lanham, MD: Rowman and Littlefield, 2002), 82; Wilentz, *Rise of American Democracy*, 516; Richard McCormick, "Political Development and the Second Party System," in *The American Party Systems*, ed. William Nisbet Chambers and Walter Dean Burnham, 2nd ed. (New York: Oxford University Press, 1975), 90–116; Arthur M. Schlesinger Jr., "The Short Happy Life of American Political Parties," in *The Cycles of American History* (Boston: Houghton Mifflin Company, 1986), 256–76; E. E. Schattschneider, *Party Government* (New York: Holt, Rinehart and Winston, 1942).

16. James Bryce, preface to *Democracy and the Organization of Political Parties*, by M. Ostrogorski, trans. (from French) Frederick Clarke (New York: Macmillan Company, 1902), 1:xlii.

17. Josephson, *Politicos*, 69.

18. *Nation* 1204, July 26, 1888, 66; Richard L. McCormick, *The Party Period and Public Policy: American Politics from the Age of Jackson to the Progressive Era* (New York: Oxford University Press, 1986); McCormick, "Political Development and the Second Party System"; Michael McGerr, *The Decline of Popular Politics: The American North, 1865–1928* (New York: Oxford University Press, 1986); Joel H. Silbey, *The American Political Nation, 1838–1893* (Stanford, CA: Stanford University Press, 1991); Silbey, *Martin Van Buren and the Emergence of American Popular Politics*; Ronald P. Formisano, *The Birth of Mass Political Parties: Michigan, 1827–1861* (Princeton, NJ: Princeton University Press, 1971); Robert Vincent Remini, *Martin Van Buren and the Making of the Democratic Party* (New York: Columbia University Press, 1959); Josephson, *Politicos*; Bensel, *American Ballot Box*.

19. These values are nineteenth-century dollars. The equivalent costs today, in current dollars, would be far higher. Thomas E. Will, "Political Corruption: How Best to Oppose," *Arena* 10 (November 1894): 846; Jesse Macy, *Party Organization and Machinery* (New York: Century Company, 1904), 220–22; Louise Overacker, *Money in Elections* (1932; repr., New York: Arno Press, 1974), 31.

20. Silbey, *Martin Van Buren and the Emergence of American Popular Politics*; Remini, *Martin Van Buren and the Making of the Democratic Party*; John Niven, *Martin Van Buren: The Romantic Age of American Politics* (New York: Oxford University Press, 1983); Donald B. Cole, *Martin Van Buren and the American Political System* (Princeton, NJ: Princeton University Press, 1983); Ted Widmer, *Martin Van Buren* (New York: Times Books, 2005); Edward Morse Shepard, *Martin Van Buren* (1899; repr., New York: AMS, 1972).

21. US Congress, House, Select Committee of Investigation, Defalcations of Samuel Swartout and Others, Collectors and Receivers of Public Money, *Report No. 313*, 25th Cong., 3rd Sess., February 27, 1839, 249–50, http://congressional

.proquest.com.ezp-prod1.hul.harvard.edu/congressional/docview/t47.d48.352_h .rp.313?accountid=11311 (accessed March 28, 2015); Robert E. Mutch, *Campaigns, Congress, and Courts: The Making of Federal Campaign Finance Law* (New York: Praeger, 1988), xvi.

22. Ostrogorski, *Democracy and the Organization of Political Parties*, 2:143–47.

23. Albert Bigelow Paine, *Thomas Nast: His Period and His Pictures* (Princeton, NJ: Pyne Press, 1904), 459.

24. M. L. Cooke, *The Political Assessment of Officeholders: A Report on the System as Practised by the Republican Organization in the City of Philadelphia, 1883–1913* (Philadelphia: Department of Public Works, 1913).

25. William Mills Ivins, *Machine Politics and Money in Elections in New York City* (1887; repr., New York: Arno Press, 1970), 54–57.

26. Josephson, *Politicos*, 133; John McDonald, *Secrets of the Great Whiskey Ring* (Chicago: Belford Clarke and Co., 1880).

27. G. F. Howe, *Chester A. Arthur: A Quarter-Century of Machine Politics* (New York: Dodd, Mead, and Company, 1934), 49; William Hartman, "Politics and Patronage: The New York Customs' House, 1852–1901" (PhD diss., Columbia University, 1952), 352.

28. Josephson, *Politicos*, 94–95.

29. Ibid., 136.

30. McDonald, *Secrets of the Great Whiskey Ring*, 51. Morton didn't personally ask for the funds; a Republican operative, Henry T. Blow, made the actual request a few days after Morton's visit. But McDonald understood that the purpose of Morton's visit was to prepare the ground for Blow's arrival.

31. Ostrogorski, *Democracy and the Organization of Political Parties*, 2: 285–86, 292.

32. C. K. Yearley, *The Money Machines: The Breakdown and Reform of Governmental and Party Finance in the North, 1860–1920* (Albany: State University of New York Press, 1970), 104.

33. Ibid., 104–5; Jack Beatty, *Age of Betrayal: The Triumph of Money in America, 1865–1900* (New York: Alfred A. Knopf, 2007), passim.

34. Yearley, *Money Machines*, 104; James A. Kehl, *Boss Rule in the Gilded Age: Matt Quay of Pennsylvania* (Pittsburgh: University of Pittsburgh Press, 1981), 98, passim; Macy, *Party Organization and Machinery*, 124.

35. Ivins, *Machine Politics*, 58, passim. See also Bensel, *American Ballot Box*, 11–13.

36. Alfred Connable and Edward Silberfarb offer the county courthouse figures in *Tigers of Tammany: Nine Men Who Ran New York* (New York: Holt, Rinehart and Winston, 1967), 158–59. For more on the courthouse, including varying estimates on total costs from $12 to $13 million, see Gustavus Myers, *The History of Tammany Hall*, 2nd ed. (New York: Boni and Liveright, 1917), 238–41; Alexander B. Callow, *The Tweed Ring* (New York: Oxford University Press, 1966), 200; M. R. Werner, *Tammany Hall* (New York: Doubleday, Doran and Co., 1928), 371.

Regarding Tweed's total plunder, Callow and Seymour J. Mandelbaum acknowledged the impossibility—due to dubious accounting, stealthy wealth management, and missing records—of determining the exact amount the Tweed ring stole. An early investigation into the ring frauds by Judge James Emott yielded an estimate of $15 million, while John Townsend, one of Tweed's lawyers, claimed the haul was $30 million. At the other end of the spectrum, Myers, a comprehensive Tammany historian, contended that "those who have had the best opportunity for knowing" estimated the ring's plunder at over $100 million, and Matthew O'Rourke, an anti-Tammany employee of the comptroller's office who leaked evidence against the ring, proposed a total of $200 million. The most reasonable guess as to how much the Tweed ring stole is between $45 and $60 million—a range suggested by Henry F. Taintor, who was hired by a special aldermanic committee to examine the ring frauds and spent six years studying financial records. Callow, *Tweed Ring*, 164–65; Denis Tilden Lynch, *"Boss" Tweed: The Story of a Grim Generation* (New York: Boni and Liveright, 1927), 370–71, 406; Seymour J. Mandelbaum, *Boss Tweed's New York* (New York: Wiley, 1965), 86; Myers, *History of Tammany Hall*, 248–49; John D. Townsend, *New York in Bondage* (New York, 1901), 102.

37. Yearley, *Money Machines*, 112–16.

38. For the $7 million figure, see Werner, *Tammany Hall*, 371. For the $25 million figure, see Yearley, *Money Machines*, 266. Yearley also estimates that Tammany made $2.5 to $10 million per year from liquor establishments. Yearley, *Money Machines*, 116.

39. Werner, *Tammany Hall*, 417.

40. Ivins, *Machine Politics*, 30–38.

41. Yearley, *Money Machines*, 113–16; Steven P. Erie, *Rainbow's End: Irish-Americans and the Dilemmas of Urban Machine Politics, 1840–1985* (Berkeley: University of California Press, 1988), 28, 68–69, 71, 87–91. On the Tammany way of doing business, in the words of one of its lieutenants, see *Plunkitt of Tammany Hall: A Series of Very Plain Talks on Very Practical Politics, Delivered by Ex-Senator George Washington Plunkitt, the Tammany Philosopher, from his Rostrum—the New York County Court House Bootblack Stand—and Recorded by William L. Riordon*, intro. Roy V. Peel (New York: Alfred A. Knopf, 1948).

42. On the work of party bosses in other locations, see G. Wayne Dowdy, *Mayor Crump Don't Like It: Machine Politics in Memphis* (Jackson: University Press of Mississippi, 2006); Walton Bean, *Boss Ruef's San Francisco: The Story of the Union Labor Party, Big Business, and the Graft Prosecution* (Berkeley: University of California Press, 1968); Tom M. Reddig, *Tom's Town: Kansas City and the Pendergast Legend* (Philadelphia: J. B. Lippincott, 1948); Jack Beatty, *The Rascal King: The Life and Times of James Michael Curley (1874–1958)* (1992; repr., New York: Da Capo Press, 2000); Robert Penn Warren, *All the King's Men* (New York: Harcourt, 1946).

43. Kehl, *Boss Rule in the Gilded Age*, 62–64. The Quay machine in Pennsylvania was also supposed to have developed a list of all eight hundred thousand Republican voters in the state, organized into three groups: reliable, unreli-

able, and "those accustomed to 'fumble in the booth.'" Decisions about how to deploy party resources during elections were made accordingly. Macy, the author of these words, also wrote that scrutinizing this many voters was an undertaking involving "minute and careful subdivision of labor among trained and skilled agents." This work was constant, but would reach "its highest level efficiency" during a "heated campaign, every tenth or every fifth man in the party is given an official position . . . to learn the exact political opinions and intentions of the few voters assigned to his observation." Electioneering, in the hands of bosses like Quay, had become something akin to a political science. Macy, *Party Organization and Machinery*, 120–22.

44. Herbert Croly, *Marcus Alonzo Hanna: His Life and Work* (New York: Macmillan Company, 1912); James Moore and Wayne Slater, *Bush's Brain: How Karl Rove Made George W. Bush Presidential* (Hoboken, NJ: John Wiley and Sons, 2003); Lou Dubose and Jan Reid, *The Hammer Comes Down: The Nasty, Brutish, and Shortened Life of Tom DeLay* (New York: Public Affairs, 2009); David Plouffe, *The Audacity to Win: The Inside Story and Lessons of Obama's Historic Victory* (New York: Viking Penquin, 2009).

45. Kehl, *Boss Rule in the Gilded Age*, 98–112.

46. The switch in unit of machine representation from ward to district assembly seems to have occurred in 1871. A resolution passed at the 1871 Democratic State Convention required all delegates from New York County, in order to be recognized by the convention, to be elected by an assembly district committee. "Following this resolution, the Democratic General Committee of the County of New York was reorganized and the basis of representation in the Committee was changed from the Ward to the Assembly District." Edwin P. Kilroe, Abraham Kaplan, and Joseph Johnson, *The Story of Tammany* (New York: New York County Democratic Organization, 1928), 50.

47. This group of about 840 individuals would grow considerably after the incorporation of Brooklyn, Queens, and Staten Island into New York City in 1897 and 1901.

48. Ivins, *Machine Politics*, 11–12; Roy V. Peel, *The Political Clubs of New York City* (New York: G. P. Putnam's Sons, 1935), 67–68; Roy V. Peel, "The Political Machine of New York City," *American Political Science Review* 27 (August 1933): 611–18.

49. In addition to providing a range of social services to needy constituents and organizing community social events, Tammany cadre would sponsor mass political meetings, canvass for votes, and both get out and monitor the vote on Election Day. Ivins, *Machine Politics*, 12–15.

50. P. Tecumseh Sherman, *Inside the Machine: Two Years in the Board of Alderman, 1898–1899: A Study of the Legislative Features of the City Government of New York City under the Greater New York Charter* (New York: Cooke and Fry, 1901), 77–78.

51. Joseph B. Bishop, "The Price of Peace," *Century Illustrated Magazine* 48 (September 1894): 667–72.

52. David M. Scobey, *Empire City: The Making and Meaning of the New York City Landscape* (Philadelphia: Temple University Press, 2002), 204–9.

53. Sven Beckert, *The Monied Metropolis: New York City and the Consolidation of the American Bourgeoisie, 1850–1896* (New York: Cambridge University Press, 2001).

54. Schattschneider, *Party Government*, 134–42.

55. Daniel T. Rodgers, *Atlantic Crossings: Social Politics in a Progressive Age* (Cambridge, MA: Harvard University Press, 1998), 152–59.

56. On civil service reform, see Carl Russell Fish, *The Civil Service and the Patronage* (1904; repr., New York: Russell and Russell, Inc., 1963); Ari Hoogenboom, *Outlawing the Spoils: A History of the Civil Service Reform Movement, 1865–1883* (Champaign: University of Illinois Press, 1961); Margaret Susan Thompson, *The "Spider Web": Congress and Lobbying in the Age of Grant* (Ithaca, NY: Cornell University Press, 1985). On other efforts to reform the political system, see John W. Cell, *The Highest Stage of White Supremacy: The Origins of Segregation in South Africa and the American South* (New York: Cambridge University Press, 1982); Keyssar, *Right to Vote*, 87–221; Yearley, *Money Machines*, chaps. 6–10; Robert H. Wiebe, *The Search for Order, 1877–1920* (New York: Hill and Wang, 1967); Arthur Stanley Link and Richard L. McCormick, *Progressivism* (Arlington Heights, IL: Harlan Davidson, Inc., 1983). On the maternalist politics of suffrage, see Robyn Muncy, *Creating a Female Dominion in American Reform, 1890–1935* (New York: Oxford University Press, 1991); Linda Gordon, *Pitied But Not Entitled: Single Mothers and the History of Welfare, 1890–1935* (New York: Free Press, 1994); Sonya Michel and Seth Koven, eds., *Mothers of a New World: Maternalist Politics and the Origins of Welfare States* (New York: Routledge, 1993).

57. George also received more votes than the Republican candidate, Theodore Roosevelt. Kenneth Finegold, *Experts and Politicians: Reform Challenges to Machine Politics in New York, Cleveland, and Chicago* (Princeton, NJ: Princeton University Press, 1995), 38.

58. On the Progressive campaign against Tammany, see ibid., 35–54; Augustus Cerillo Jr., "The Impact of Reform Ideology: Early Twentieth-Century Municipal Government in New York City," in *The Age of Urban Reform: New Perspectives on the Progressive Era*, ed. Michael H. Ebner and Eugene M. Tobin (Port Washington, NY: Kennikat Press, 1977), 68–85; Erie, *Rainbow's End*, 85–91, 216–17. See also John F. McClymer, "Of Mornin' Glories and 'Fine Old Oaks': John Purroy Mitchel, Al Smith, and Irish-American Political Aspiration," in *The New York Irish*, ed. Timothy Meagher and Ronald Bayor (Baltimore: Johns Hopkins University Press, 1996), 374–94.

59. Martin Shefter, "The Electoral Foundations of the Political Machine: New York City, 1884–1897," in *The History of American Electoral Behavior*, ed. Joel H. Silbey, Allen G. Bogue, and William H. Flanigan (Princeton, NJ: Princeton University Press, 1978), 290–91.

60. On the way in which elite-populist divisions shaped urban politics in late nineteenth- and early twentieth-century Boston, see Noam Maggor, *Brahmin Capitalism: Bankers, Populists, and the Making of the Modern American Economy* (Cambridge, MA: Harvard University Press, forthcoming).

61. Erie, *Rainbow's End*, 85; Yearley, *Money Machines*, chaps. 6–10.

62. James C. Scott, "Corruption, Machine Politics, and Political Change," *American Political Science Review* 63 (December 1969): 1144.

63. Erie, *Rainbow's End*, 97–99.

64. Another unintended result of state-produced ballots was the strengthening of party bosses. The new ballots weakened district leaders' ability to "bolt"; they could no longer change ballots in their districts to go against the party line. State-produced ballots, then, increased the bosses' control over party candidates for city offices. David C. Hammack, *Greater New York at the Turn of the Century* (New York: Russell Sage Foundation, 1982), 128–29.

65. Ostrogorski, *Democracy and the Organization of Political Parties*, 2:502–4.

66. McGerr, *Decline of Popular Politics*; Overacker, *Money in Elections*; George Thayer, *Who Shakes the Money Tree? American Campaign Financing Practices from 1789 to the Present* (New York: Simon and Schuster, 1973), 56–57.

67. The Pendleton Act of 1883 created a class of federal employees who could only be placed in office by virtue of their having passed an objective and competitive examination. This was the origin of the US Civil Service. Paul P. Van Riper, *History of the United States Civil Service* (Evanston, IL: Row, Peterson and Company, 1958), 96–112.

68. Josephson, *Politicos*, 350.

69. In 1896, Hanna attempted to regularize and standardize corporate contributions by assessing banks at one-quarter of 1 percent of their capital. Croly, *Marcus Alonzo Hanna*, 218–20.

70. Thayer, *Who Shakes the Money Tree?* 53–55; Overacker, *Money in Elections*, 240.

71. Chester Lloyd Jones, "Spoils and the Party," *Annals of the American Academy of Political and Social Science* 64 (March 1916): 66–76.

72. Henry George, "Money and Elections," *North American Review* 136 (February 1883): 201, 206.

73. Henry George, *Progress and Poverty* (San Francisco: W. M. Hinton and Co., 1879).

74. George, "Money and Elections."

75. Mutch, *Campaigns, Congress, and Courts*, 35.

76. Theodore Roosevelt, "Seventh Annual Message," December 3, 1907, http://millercenter.org/scripps/archive/speeches/detail/3779 (accessed August 6, 2009).

77. Mutch, *Campaigns, Congress, and Courts*, 12. See also US Congress, Senate, "Campaign Contributions: Testimony before a Subcommittee of the Committee on Privileges and Elections, June 14, 1912, to February 25, 1913, Pursuant to S. Res. 79," 62nd Cong., 2nd Sess. (Washington, DC: Government Printing Office, 1913), passim; Henry F. Pringle, *Theodore Roosevelt: A Biography* (New York: Harcourt, Brace and Company, 1931), 357–58.

78. Jones, "Spoils and the Party," 74; Colorado State Legislature, "An Act concerning Campaign Expenses of Political Parties and Contributing Thereto," in *Session Laws of Colorado*, chap. 141 (1909), 303–5.

79. Overacker, *Money in Elections*, 202.

80. Ivins, *Machine Politics*, 53.

81. Walter E. Weyl, "The Democratization of Party Finance," *American Political Science Review* 7 (February 1913): 178–82.

82. He may have been transfixed by the example of the German Social Democratic Party, which used this system to raise millions of deutsche marks from its multimillion-person membership. See Overacker, *Money in Elections*, 145, 201.

83. Thayer, *Who Shakes the Money Tree?* 54; Overacker, *Money in Elections*, 238.

84. Overacker, *Money in Elections*, 249–88; Thayer, *Who Shakes the Money Tree?* 62–63.

85. Frank R. Kent, *The Great Game of Politics: An Effort to Present the Elementary Human Facts about Politics, Politicians, and Political Machines, Candidates and Their Way, for the Benefit of the Average Citizen* (1923; repr., New York: Doubleday, Doran, and Company, 1940), 114.

86. Overacker, *Money in Elections*, 372.

CHAPTER 6. AGRARIAN PROTEST AND THE NEW LIBERAL STATE

1. Franklin D. Roosevelt, "Annual Message to Congress," January 4, 1935, http://www.presidency.ucsb.edu/ws/index.php?pid=14890 (accessed June 19, 2014).

2. Ibid.

3. See Steve Fraser, "The 'Labor Question,'" in *The Rise and Fall of the New Deal Order, 1930–1980*, ed. Steve Fraser and Gary Gerstle (Princeton, NJ: Princeton University Press, 1989), 55–84.

4. On the outsize influence of the South in Congress, see Ira Katznelson, *Fear Itself: The New Deal and the Origins of Our Time* (New York: Liveright Publishing Corporation, 2013); Anthony J. Badger, *The New Deal: The Depression Years, 1933–1940* (New York: Hill and Wang, 1989); James Patterson, *Congressional Conservatism and the New Deal: The Growth of the Conservative Coalition in Congress, 1933–1939* (Lexington: University of Kentucky Press, 1967).

5. The literature on agrarian protest of the late nineteenth century is vast and varied. See John Donald Hicks, *The Populist Revolt: A History of the Farmers' Alliance and the People's Party* (Lincoln: University of Nebraska Press, 1961); Lawrence Goodwyn, *The Populist Moment: A Short History of the Agrarian Revolt in America* (New York: Oxford University Press, 1978); Charles Postel, *The Populist Vision* (New York: Oxford University Press, 2007); Michael Kazin, *The Populist Persuasion: An American History* (Ithaca, NY: Cornell University Press, 1998); Michael Kazin, *A Godly Hero: The Life of William Jennings Bryan* (New York: Alfred A. Knopf, 2006); Donna A. Barnes, *Farmers in Rebellion: The Rise and Fall of the Southwest Farmers' Alliance and*

the People's Party in Texas (Austin: University of Texas Press, 1984); Richard White, *Railroaded: The Transcontinentals and the Making of Modern America* (New York: W. W. Norton and Company, 2010); Elizabeth Sanders, *Roots of Reform: Farmers, Workers, and the American State, 1877–1917* (Chicago: University of Chicago Press, 1999); Elisabeth S. Clemens, *The People's Lobby: Organizational Innovation and the Rise of Interest Group Politics* (Chicago: University of Chicago Press, 1997); Robert H. Wiebe, *The Search for Order, 1877–1920* (New York: Hill and Wang, 1967); Richard Hofstadter, *The Age of Reform from Bryan to FDR* (New York: Vintage Books, 1960).

6. It was a reasonable move for a plebeian group in a democracy to make. The Kansan Populist William Peffer declared in 1891 that "the Government of the United States" really was "the agent of the people," and that through it, the people could and should exercise "intense political power" and "make common cause until we have restored the Government to its rightful place." William A. Peffer, *The Farmer's Side: His Troubles and Their Remedy* (1891; repr., Westport, CT: Hyperion, 1976), 132, 170–71.

7. Omaha Platform, July 1892, in Hicks, *Populist Revolt*, appendix F, 441.

8. The Populists also set the agenda on other issues. They called for currency reform and better management of financial markets; a progressive income tax to redistribute some wealth to those who needed it; the elimination of the tariff on imported goods, which both hurt agricultural exports and was a source of government corruption; and the direct election of senators. The Populists, finally, brought back into American politics the proposition that the Civil War had interred: that the railroads were simply too important to national well-being to be left to private enterprise. Instead, they ought to be nationalized, regulated, and operated by the federal government. All this is evident in the Omaha Platform.

9. John D. Hicks, "The Sub-Treasury Plan: A Forgotten Plan for the Relief of Agriculture," *Mississippi Valley Historical Review* 15 (December 1928): 355–73; Charles Postel, *Populist Vision*, 153–55; Omaha Platform.

10. Sanders, *Roots of Reform*, 158.

11. On La Follette, see David Thelen, *Robert M. La Follette and the Insurgent Spirit* (Boston: Little, Brown and Company, 1976).

12. Daniel P. Carpenter, *The Forging of Bureaucratic Autonomy: Reputations, Networks, and Policy Innovation in Executive Agencies, 1862–1928* (Princeton, NJ: Princeton University Press, 2001); Edward Danforth Eddy Jr., *Colleges for Our Land and Time: The Land-Grant Idea in American Education* (New York: Harper and Brothers, 1956); Allan Nevins, *The Origins of the Land-Grant Colleges and State Universities: A Brief Account of the Morrill Act of 1862 and Its Results* (Washington, DC: Civil War Centennial Commission, 1962). On the early history of the agricultural experiment stations, and on the scientists who worked in them, see Charles E. Rosenberg, *No Other Gods: On Science and American Social Thought*, rev. ed. (Baltimore: Johns Hopkins University Press, 1997), 135–99.

13. Kimberley S. Johnson, *Governing the American State: Congress and the New Federalism, 1877–1929* (Princeton, NJ: Princeton University Press, 2007).

14. Jordan Schwarz, *The New Dealers: Power Politics in the Age of Roosevelt* (New York: Alfred A. Knopf, 1993); Harold Pinkett, *Gifford Pinchot, Private and Public Forester* (Urbana: University of Illinois Press, 1970); Char Miller, *Gifford Pinchot and the Making of Modern Environmentalism* (Washington, DC: Island Press, 2001); Brian Balogh, "Scientific Forestry and the Roots of the Modern American State: Gifford Pinchot's Path to Progressive Reform," *Environmental History* 7 (2002): 198–225; Bernard Sternsher, *Rexford Tugwell and the New* Deal (New Brunswick, NJ: Rutgers University Press, 1964); Michael Namorato, *Rexford G. Tugwell: A Biography* (New York: Praeger, 1988); Edward Scapsmeier, *Henry A. Wallace of Iowa: The Agrarian Years, 1910–1940*, 1st ed. (Ames: Iowa State University Press, 1968); Norman Markowitz, *The Rise and Fall of the People's Century: Henry A. Wallace and American Liberalism, 1941–1948* (New York: Free Press, 1973); John Culver and John Hyde, *American Dream: The Life and Times of Henry A. Wallace* (New York: W. W. Norton and Company, 2000). See also Christopher Loss, *Between Citizens and the States: The Politics of American Higher Education in the Twentieth Century* (Princeton, NJ: Princeton University Press, 2011), chap. 3.

15. Carpenter, *Forging of Bureaucratic Autonomy*, passim; Loss, *Between Citizens and the State*, chap. 3.

16. Carpenter, *Forging of Bureaucratic Autonomy*, 288–91, passim.

17. Sanders, *Roots of Reform*, 391.

18. Grant McConnell, *The Decline of Agrarian Democracy* (Berkeley: University of California Press, 1953), 32.

19. Carpenter, *Forging of Bureaucratic Autonomy*, 256–302; Loss, *Between Citizens and the State*, chap. 3; Gilbert C. Fite, *American Agriculture and Farm Policy since 1900* (Washington, DC: Service Center for Teachers of History, 1967); Murray R. Benedict, *Farm Policies of the United States, 1790–1950: A Study of Their Origin and Development* (New York: Twentieth Century Fund, 1953), chap. 7.

20. Joseph Cannon Bailey, *Seaman A. Knapp: Schoolmaster of American Agriculture* (New York: Columbia University Press, 1945).

21. McConnell, *Decline of Agrarian Democracy*, 44–45. See also Kenneth Finegold and Theda Skocpol, *State and Party in America's New Deal* (Madison: University of Wisconsin Press, 1995), 56–59; Carpenter, *Forging of Bureaucratic Autonomy*, 291–301.

22. Finegold and Skocpol, *State and Party in America's New Deal*, 58–59.

23. Grant McConnell, *Private Power and American Democracy* (New York: Alfred A. Knopf, 1966), 78–79.

24. Quoted in Bailey, *Seaman A. Knapp*, 202.

25. McConnell, *Private Power and American Democracy*, 44–45.

26. On the rise of the AFBF, see Orville Kile, *The Farm Bureau through Three Decades* (Baltimore: Waverly Press, 1948); Christina McFayden, *The Farm Bureau and the New Deal: A Study of the Making of National Farm Policy* (Champaign: University of Illinois Press, 1962); Samuel Berger, *Dollar Harvest: The Story of the Farm Bureau* (Lexington, MA: Heath Lexington Books, 1971).

27. McConnell, *Decline of Agrarian Democracy*, 52–53. See also US Congress, House, Committee on Banking and Currency, "Statement of Mr. Gray Silver, Washington Representative of the American Farm Bureau Federation and Member of the Executive Committee," Hearings on Farm Organizations, 66th Cong., 3rd Sess., January 21, 1921 (Washington, DC: Government Printing Office, 1922), 25–42.

28. On the AFBF as the model pressure group, see John Mark Hansen, *Gaining Access: Congress and the Farm Lobby, 1919–1981* (Chicago: University of Chicago Press, 1991).

29. Theodore Saloutos and John D. Hicks, *Agricultural Discontent in the Middle West, 1900–1939* (Madison: University of Wisconsin Press, 1951), 87–110.

30. Ibid., 100.

31. Ibid., 254–58; McConnell, *Decline of Agrarian Democracy*, 51.

32. Saloutos and Hicks, *Agricultural Discontent*, 149–254; Herbert Earle Gaston, *The Nonpartisan League* (New York: Harcourt, Brace, and Howe, 1920); Charles Edward Russell, *The Story of the Nonpartisan League: A Chapter in American Evolution* (New York: Harper and Brothers, 1920); Andrew A. Bruce, *Non-Partisan League* (New York: Macmillan Company, 1921); Robert L. Morlan, *Political Prairie Fire: The Nonpartisan League, 1915–1922* (Minneapolis: University of Minnesota Press, 1955); Carol E. Jenson, *Agrarian Pioneer in Civil Liberties: The Nonpartisan League in Minnesota during World War I* (New York: Garland, 1986).

33. Saloutos and Hicks, *Agricultural Discontent*, 335–66.

34. American Presidency Project, "Election of 1924," http://www.presidency .ucsb.edu/showelection.php?year=1924 (accessed June 19, 2014). On La Follette's Farmer Labor Party and its subsequent history, see Thelen, *Robert M. La Follette*; Stuart Arthur Rice, *Farmers and Workers in American Politics* (New York: Columbia University Press, 1924); Millard L. Gieske, *Minnesota Farmer-Laborism: The Third Party Alternative* (Minneapolis: University of Minnesota Press, 1979); John Earl Haynes, *Dubious Alliance: The Making of Minnesota's DFL Party* (Minneapolis: University of Minnesota Press, 1984); Richard M. Valelly, *Radicalism in the States: The Minnesota Farmer-Labor Party and the American Political Economy* (Chicago: University of Chicago Press, 1989).

35. US Congress, House, Committee on Banking and Currency, "Statement of Mr. J. R. Howard, President, American Farm Bureau Federation, Chicago, Illinois," Hearings on Farm Organizations, 66th Cong., 3rd Sess., July 20, 1921 (Washington, DC: Government Printing Office, 1922), 227.

36. James C. Scott, *Seeing Like a State: How Certain Schemes to Improve the Human Condition Have Failed* (New Haven, CT: Yale University Press, 1998), 196–201.

37. Gilbert C. Fite, *George N. Peek and the Fight for Farm Parity* (Norman: University of Oklahoma Press, 1954).

38. Ibid.

39. Ibid.

40. One such leftist figure was Lewis Cecil Gray, who had studied agricultural economics under socialist Richard Ely at the University of Wisconsin and

was, in 1919, appointed to head the Land Economics Division of the Bureau of Agricultural Economics—a post he held until 1935. A pioneering figure in land use planning, Gray wanted to extend the regulatory reach of the central state to take unsuitable lands out of cultivation, restrain the urge in America to turn every piece of land into an extensively exploited commodity, and achieve a better ecology—a better balance between people and their natural surroundings. Donald Worster, *Dust Bowl: The Southern Plains in the 1930s* (New York: Oxford University Press, 1979), 189–92.

41. Fite, *George N. Peek*, 185–242.

42. Arthur M. Schlesinger Jr., *The Coming of the New Deal, 1933–1935*, vol. 2 (Boston: Houghton Mifflin Company, 1959), pt. I; Badger, *New Deal*, chap. 4; Finegold and Skocpol, *State and Party in America's New Deal*, 104–14; Benedict, *Farm Policies of the United States*, 277–315.

43. Saloutos and Hicks, *Agricultural Discontent*, 469.

44. Theodore Saloutos, *The American Farmer and the New Deal* (Ames: Iowa State University Press, 1982), 103; Henry I. Richards, *Cotton and the AAA* (Washington, DC: Brookings Institution Press, 1936), 43–66.

45. Christiana McFayden Campbell, *The Farm Bureau and the New Deal: A Study in the Making of National Farm Policy, 1933–1940* (Urbana: University of Illinois Press, 1962); Saloutos, *American Farmer and the New Deal*, 48; Saloutos and Hicks, *Agricultural Discontent*, 470–72.

46. Worster, *Dust Bowl*, 161.

47. Saloutos and Hicks, *Agricultural Discontent*, 472; Finegold and Skocpol, *State and Party in America's New Deal*, 17.

48. McConnell, *Decline of Agrarian Democracy*, 74.

49. Paul H. Landis, "Agents on the Air," *Extension Services Review* 7 (February 1936): 18; Wayne D. Rasmussen, *Taking the University to the People: Seventy-Five Years of Cooperative Education* (Ames: Iowa State University Press, 1989), 100; Loss, *Between Citizens and the State*, chap. 3.

50. Worster, *Dust Bowl*, 157.

51. Ibid., 159.

52. Saloutos and Hicks, *Agricultural Discontent*, 497–523.

53. Susan Levine, *School Lunch Politics: The Surprising History of America's Favorite Welfare Program* (Princeton, NJ: Princeton University Press, 2008).

54. http://www.gsa.gov/portal/ext/html/site/hb/method/post/category/25431 (accessed February 15, 2015).

55. Lester Thurow, *The Zero-Sum Solution: Building a World-Class American Economy* (New York: Simon and Schuster, 1985), 270–72.

56. Franklin D. Roosevelt, "Address at Omaha, Nebraska," October 10, 1936, http://www.presidency.ucsb.edu/ws/index.php?pid=15163&st=agricultural+adjustment+act&st1=#ixzz1TKu4h9aq (accessed June 19, 2014).

57. Worster, *Dust Bowl*, 154.

58. Isaiah Berlin, "Two Concepts of Liberty," in *Liberty*, ed. Henry Hardy (New York: Oxford University Press, 2002), 166–217. Berlin was skeptical about regimes of positive liberty, believing that most would produce some sort of tyranny. It is possible, however, to adopt Berlin's conception of the two liberties

without attaching to positive liberty the negative connotation that he assigned it. See, for example, Charles Taylor, "What's Wrong with Negative Liberty," in *Law and Morality: Readings in Legal Philosophy*, ed. David Dyzenhaus, Sophia Reibetanz Moreau, and Arthur Ripstein, 2nd ed. (Toronto: University of Toronto Press, 2001), 359–68.

59. Carey McWilliams, *Factories in the Field: The Story of Migratory Farm Labor in California* (Boston: Little, Brown and Company, 1939); Deborah Fitzgerald, *Every Farm a Factory: The Industrial Ideal in American Agriculture* (New Haven, CT: Yale University Press, 2003).

60. Worster, *Dust Bowl*, 158.

61. This is a conservative estimate: *Historical Statistics* lists 3.6 million farm owners in 1930, plus 2.7 million farm tenants and 0.8 million sharecroppers in the South. That leaves 9.1 million who were either unpaid family members or hired agricultural laborers from outside the family. *Historical Statistics* does not break down this 9.1 million total into family and hired labor. I am estimating the agricultural labor portion to be a conservative 1 million, giving us a total population of farm tenants, sharecroppers, and laborers of approximately 4.4 million. US Department of Commerce Bureau of the Census, "Farms, by Race and Tenure of Operator, and Acreage and Value, by Tenure of Operator: 1880–1969," in *Historical Statistics of the United States, Colonial Times to 1970* (White Plains, NY: Kraus International Publications, 1989), series K 109–53, 465. Another set of statistics from *Historical Statistics* puts the total number of hired workers on farms at 3.2 million in 1930. This figure includes sharecroppers and migrant workers, but not tenant farmers. If we add tenant farmers to the mix, the number of agriculturalists who did not own land rises to 5.9 million, or 47 percent of the 1930 total. US Department of Commerce Bureau of the Census, "Farm Employment: 1910–1999," in *Historical Statistics of the United States, Millennial Edition Online*, table Da612–14, https://hsus.cambridge.org/HSUSWeb/toc/showTablePdf.do?id=Da612-614 (accessed February 15, 2015). See also David Eugene Conrad: *The Forgotten Farmers: The Story of the Sharecroppers in the New Deal* (Urbana: University of Illinois Press, 1965).

62. Quoted in Richards, *Cotton and the AAA*, 140–41.

63. Saloutos, *American Farmer and the New Deal*, 99–100.

64. Ibid., 52, 92; Finegold and Skocpol, *State and Party in America's New Deal*, 144–45. Risa Lauren Goluboff, *The Lost Promise of Civil Rights* (Cambridge, MA: Harvard University Press, 2007).

65. Saloutos, *American Farmer and the New Deal*, passim; Donald H. Grubbs, *Cry from Cotton: The Southern Tenants Farmers' Union and the New Deal* (Fayetteville: University of Arkansas Press, 2000). On the Southern Tenant Farmers' Union, see Ted Rosengarten, *All God's Dangers: The Life of Nate Shaw* (New York: Alfred A. Knopf, 1974); Howard Kester, *Revolt among the Sharecroppers* (Knoxville: University of Tennessee Press, 1997); Robin D. G. Kelley, *Hammer and Hoe: Alabama Communists during the Great Depression* (Chapel Hill: University of North Carolina Press, 1990).

66. Saloutos, *American Farmer and the New Deal*, 66–67. See also Patterson, *Congressional Conservatism and the New Deal*; Julian E. Zelizer, *On Capitol Hill: The Struggle to Reform Congress and Its Consequences, 1948–2000* (New York: Cambridge University Press, 2004); Katznelson, *Fear Itself*; McConnell, *Private Power and American Democracy*, 232–43.

67. Rexford G. Tugwell, *The Stricken Land: The Story of Puerto Rico* (New York: Doubleday, 1947), 24; Sternsher, *Rexford Tugwell and the New Deal*, 205.

68. US Department of Commerce Bureau of the Census, "Farms, by Race and Tenure of Operator, and Acreage and Value, by Tenure of Operator: 1880–1969," 465.

69. Bruce J. Schulman, *From Cotton Belt to Sunbelt: Federal Policy, Economic Development, and the Transformation of the South, 1938–1980* (New York: Oxford University Press, 1991).

70. James N. Gregory, *American Exodus: The Dust Bowl Migration and the Okie Culture in California* (New York: Oxford University Press, 1989), xvii.

71. US Department of Commerce Bureau of the Census, "Farm Population, Farms, Land in Farms, and Value of Farm Property and Real Estate: 1850 to 1970," in *Historical Statistics of the United States, Colonial Times to 1970* (White Plains, NY: Kraus International Publications, 1989), series K 1–16, 457.

72. Nicholas Lemann, *The Promised Land: The Great Black Migration and How It Changed America* (New York: Alfred A. Knopf, 1991); Miriam Pawel, *The Crusades of Cesar Chavez* (New York: Bloomsbury Press, 2014).

73. On the transmutation of farmers from agrarian democrats at the edge of dispossession to a privileged interest group, see McConnell, *American Democracy and Private Power*; V. O. Key Jr., *Politics, Parties, and Pressure Groups* (New York: Crowell, 1952); Hansen, *Gaining Access*. For more benign and positive views on the emergence of interest group politics in the United States in this period, see David B. Truman, *The Governmental Process: Political Interests and Public Opinion* (New York: Alfred A. Knopf, 1951); Earl Latham, "The Group Basis of Politics: Notes for a Theory," *American Political Science Review* 46 (June 1952): 376–97; William P. Browne, *Private Interests, Public Policy, and American Agriculture* (Lawrence: University Press of Kansas, 1988). For a work that attempts to encompass both sides of this debate, see Robert A. Dahl, *Who Governs? Power and Democracy in an American City* (New Haven, CT: Yale University Press, 1961).

74. John Lauck, *American Agriculture and the Problem of Monopoly: The Political Economy of Grain Belt Farming, 1953–1980* (Lincoln: University of Nebraska Press, 1991); E. Welsey G. Peterson, *A Billion Dollars a Day: The Economics and Politics of Agricultural Subsidies* (Malden, MA: Wiley-Blackwell, 2009); A. Gordon Ball and Earl O. Heady, eds., *Size, Structure, and Future of Farms* (Ames: Iowa State University Press, 1971); Michael Pollan, *The Omnivore's Dilemma: A Natural History of Four Meals* (New York: Penguin Press, 2006).

75. Robert Michels, *Political Parties: A Sociological Study of the Oligarchical Tendencies of Modern Democracy* (Glencoe, IL: Free Press, 1949).

NOTES TO CHAPTER 7   401

CHAPTER 7. RECONFIGURING
LABOR-CAPITAL RELATIONS

1. Alexander Keyssar, *Out of Work: The First Century of Unemployment in Massachusetts* (New York: Cambridge University Press, 1986); David Montgomery, *The Fall of the House of Labor: The Workplace, the State, and American Labor Activism, 1865–1925* (New York: Cambridge University Press, 1987); Herbert Gutman, *Work, Culture, and Society in Industrializing America: Essays in American Working-Class and Social History* (New York: Alfred A. Knopf, 1976); Bruce Laurie, *Artisans into Workers: Labor in Nineteenth-Century America* (New York: Noonday Press, 1989); Leon Fink, *Workingman's Democracy: The Knights of Labor and American Politics* (Champaign: University of Illinois Press, 1983); Robert H. Wiebe, *The Search of Order, 1877–1920* (New York: Hill and Wang, 1967); Francis Couvares, *The Remaking of Pittsburgh: Class and Culture in an Industrializing City, 1877–1919* (Albany: State University Press of New York, 1984); Richard White, *Railroaded: The Transcontinentals and the Making of Modern America* (New York: W. W. Norton and Company, 2011); Herbert Gutman, *Power and Culture: Essays on the American Working Class* (New York: New Press, 1987).

2. White, *Railroaded*; Robert Bruce, *1877: Year of Violence* (Indianapolis: Bobbs-Merrill, 1959); Philip Foner, *The Great Labor Uprising of 1877* (New York: Monad Press, 1977); David O. Stowell, *Streets, Railroads, and the Great Strike of 1877* (Chicago: University of Chicago Press, 1999); Michael Bellesiles, *1877: America's Year of Living Violently* (New York: New Press, 2010); Couvares, *Remaking of Pittsburgh*; Walter Licht, *Working for the Railroad: The Organization of Work in the Nineteenth Century* (Princeton, NJ: Princeton University Press, 1983); Jeremy Brecher, *Strike!* rev. ed. (Boston: South End Press, 1997). On the building of armories, see Robert Fogelson, *America's Armories: Architecture, Society, and Public Order* (Cambridge, MA: Harvard University Press, 1989).

3. Almont Lindsey, *The Pullman Strike: The Story of a Unique Experiment and of a Great Labor Upheaval* (Chicago: University of Chicago Press, 1942); Nick Salvatore, *Eugene V. Debs: Citizen and Socialist* (Champaign: University of Illinois Press, 1982); Richard Schneirov, Shelton Stromquist, and Nicholas Salvatore, eds., *The Pullman Strike and the Crisis of the 1890s: Essays on Labor and Politics* (Champaign: University of Illinois Press, 1999); Cheryl Hudson, "Making Modern Citizens: Political Culture in Chicago, 1890–1930" (PhD diss., Vanderbilt University, 2011); Ray Ginger, *The Bending Cross: A Biography of Eugene Victor Debs* (New Brunswick, NJ: Rutgers University Press, 1949); Ray Ginger, *Altgeld's America: The Lincoln Ideal versus Changing Realities* (New York: Funk and Wagnalls Co., 1958); Donald L. McMurry, *Coxey's Army: A Study in the Industrial Army Movement of 1894* (Boston: Little, Brown and Company, 1929).

4. Fink, *Workingmen's Democracy*; Matthew Hild, *Greenbackers, Knights of Labor, and Populists: Farmer-Labor Insurgency in the Late Nineteenth-*

Century South (Athens: University of Georgia Press, 2007); Craig Phelan, *Grand Master Workman: Terence Powderly and the Knights of Labor* (Westport, CT: Greenwood Press, 2000); Robert Weir, *Knights Unhorsed: Internal Conflict in a Gilded Age Social Movement* (Detroit: Wayne State University Press, 2000); Robert Weir, *Beyond Labor's Veil: The Culture of the Knights of Labor* (University Park: Pennsylvania State University Press, 1996); Kim Voss, *The Making of American Exceptionalism: The Knights of Labor and Class Formation in the Nineteenth Century* (Ithaca, NY: Cornell University Press, 1993); Richard Schneirov, *Labor and Urban Politics: Class Conflict and the Origins of Modern Liberalism in Chicago, 1864–97* (Champaign: University of Illinois Press, 1998); Richard Oestreicher, *Solidarity and Fragmentation: Working People and Class Consciousness in Detroit, 1875–1900* (Champaign: University of Illinois Press, 1986); Robin Archer, *Why Is There No Labor Party in America?* (Princeton, NJ: Princeton University Press, 2007); James Green, *Death in the Haymarket: A Story of Chicago, the First Labor Movement, and the Bombing That Divided Gilded Age America* (New York: Random House, 2006).

5. For more on liberty of contract discourse, see chapters 2 and 3 of this book.

6. William E. Forbath, *Law and the Shaping of the American Labor Movement* (Cambridge, MA: Harvard University Press, 1991), 54, passim; Stuart Kaufmann, *Gompers and the American Federation of Labor, 1848–1896* (Westport, CT: Greenwood Press, 1973); Montgomery, *Fall of the House of Labor*; Julie Greene, *Pure and Simple Politics: The American Federation of Labor and Political Activism, 1881 to 1917* (New York: Cambridge University Press, 1998); Samuel Gompers, *Seventy Years of Life and Labor: An Autobiography*, 2 vols. (New York: E. P. Dutton and Company, 1925); Samuel Gompers, "Judicial Vindication of Labor's Claims," *American Federationist* 7 (1901): 283, 284.

7. Forbath, *Law and the American Labor Movement*, chap. 3.

8. Salvatore, *Debs*; Forbath, *Law and the American Labor Movement*, 73–79.

9. In re Debs, 158 U.S. 564 (1895).

10. Forbath, *Law and the American Labor Movement*, chap. 3; David Bensman, *The Practice of Solidarity: American Hat Finishers in the Nineteenth Century* (Champaign: University of Illinois Press, 1985).

11. Forbath, *Law and the American Labor Movement*, 96; Montgomery, *Fall of the House of Labor*; David Montgomery, "The 'New Unionism' and the Transformation of Workers' Consciousness in America, 1909–22," *Journal of Social History* 7 (Summer 1974): 509–29; Anthony Lukas, *Big Trouble: A Murder in a Small Western Town Sets Off a Struggle for the Soul of America* (New York: Simon and Schuster, 1997); Melvyn Dubofsky, *We Shall Be All: A History of the Industrial Workers of the World*, abr. ed. (Champaign: University of Illinois Press, 2000); David Brody, *Workers in Industrial America: Essays on the Twentieth-Century Struggle* (New York: Oxford University Press, 1980); David Brody, *Steelworkers in America: The Nonunion Era* (Cambridge, MA: Harvard University Press, 1960); James Green, *The World of the Worker: Labor*

in Twentieth-Century America (New York: Hill and Wang, 1980); Selig Perlman, *A History of Trade Unionism in the United States* (New York: Macmillan Company, 1929); Selig Perlman, *A Theory of the Labor Movement* (New York: Macmillan Company, 1928), chap. 10; Aristide R. Zolberg, "How Many Exceptionalisms?" in *Working-Class Formation: Nineteenth-Century Patterns in Western Europe and the United States*, ed. Ira Katznelson and Aristide R. Zolberg (Princeton, NJ: Princeton University Press, 1986), 397–456; David Corbin, *Life, Work, and Rebellion in the Coal Fields: The Southern West Virginia Miners, 1880–1922* (Champaign: University of Illinois Press, 1981); Thomas G. Andrews, *Killing for Coal: America's Deadliest Labor War* (Cambridge, MA: Harvard University Press, 2008).

12. My comparative frame for thinking about workers and farmers is indebted to the scholarship of Theda Skocpol and Kenneth Finegold. See Theda Skocpol, *Protecting Mothers and Children: The Political Origins of Social Policy in the United States* (Cambridge, MA: Belknap Press of Harvard University Press, 1992); Theda Skocpol and Kenneth Finegold, *State and Party in America's New Deal* (Madison: University of Wisconsin Press, 1995).

13. Joseph McCartin, *Labor's Great War: The Struggle for Industrial Democracy and the Origins of Modern American Labor Relations, 1912–1921* (Chapel Hill: University of North Carolina Press, 1997); Steve Fraser, *Labor Will Rule: Sidney Hillman and the Rise of American Labor* (New York: Free Press, 1991); David Brody, *Labor in Crisis: The Steel Strike of 1919*, 1st ed. (Philadelphia: Lippincott, 1965); Montgomery, *Fall of the House of Labor*; Lizabeth Cohen, *Making a New Deal: Industrial Workers in Chicago, 1919–1939* (New York: Cambridge University Press, 1990).

14. Ellis W. Hawley, *The New Deal and the Problem of Monopoly: A Study in Economic Ambivalence* (Princeton, NJ: Princeton University Press, 1966); Anthony Badger, *The New Deal: The Depression Years, 1933–1940* (New York: Hill and Wang, 1989), chap. 2.

15. Ellis W. Hawley, *The Great War and the Search for a Modern Order: A History of the American People and Their Institutions, 1917–1933* (1992; repr., Prospect Heights, IL: Waveland Press, 1997), chaps. 11–13.

16. Arthur M. Schlesinger Jr., *The Coming of the New Deal, 1933–1935*, vol. 2 (Boston: Houghton Mifflin Company, 1959), chap. 2; William E. Leuchtenberg, *Franklin D. Roosevelt and the New Deal, 1932–1940*, 1st ed. (New York: Harper and Row, 1963); David M. Kennedy, *Freedom from Fear: The American People in Depression and War* (New York: Oxford University Press 1999), chaps. 5–7; Robert McElvaine, *The Great Depression: America, 1929–1941* (New York: Times Books, 1984).

17. National Industrial Recovery Act, Chap. 90, 48 Stat. 195, Title I, Sec. 7(a).

18. James A. Gross, *The Making of the National Labor Relations Board: A Study in Economics, Politics, and the Law* (Albany: State University of New York Press, 1974); Gary Gerstle, *Working-Class Americanism: The Politics of Labor in a Textile City, 1914–1960* (New York: Cambridge University Press, 1989), 95–150; Nelson Lichtenstein, *State of the Union: A Century of American Labor* (Princeton, NJ: Princeton University Press, 2002), chap. 1; Irving

Bernstein, *The Turbulent Years: A History of the American Worker, 1933–1941* (Boston: Houghton Mifflin Company, 1970).

19. Bernstein, *Turbulent Years*; Robert H. Zieger, *The CIO, 1935–1955* (Chapel Hill: University of North Carolina Press, 1997); Melvyn Dubofsky and Warren van Tine, *John L. Lewis: A Biography* (New York: Quadrangle, 1977); Gerstle, *Working-Class Americanism*, 127–50; Elizabeth Faue, *A Community of Suffering and Struggle: Women, Men, and the Labor Movement in Minneapolis, 1915–1945* (Chapel Hill: University of North Carolina Press, 1991); Bruce Nelson, *Workers on the Waterfront: Seamen, Longshoremen, and Unionism in the 1930s* (Champaign: University of Illinois Press, 1988); Joshua B. Freeman, *In Transit: The Transport Workers Union in New York City, 1933–1966* (New York: Oxford University Press, 1989); Fraser, *Labor Will Rule*, chaps. 11–12; Steve Fraser, "The 'Labor Question,'" in *The Rise and Fall of the New Deal Order, 1930–1980*, ed. Steve Fraser and Gary Gerstle (Princeton, NJ: Princeton University Press, 1989), 55–84.

20. Quoted in Irving Bernstein, *The New Deal Collective Bargaining Policy* (Berkeley: University of California Press, 1950), 88. See also Schlesinger, *Coming of the New Deal*, 489–507.

21. In 1937 the CIO was renamed the Congress of Industrial Organizations. Harvey Klehr, *The Heyday of American Communism: The Depression Decade* (New York: Basic Books, 1984); Maurice Isserman and Dorothy Ray Healey, *California Red: A Life in the American Communist Party* (Champaign: University of Illinois Press, 1993); Zieger, *CIO*, chaps. 1–3; Fraser, *Labor Will Rule*, chaps. 11–12; Dubofsky and van Tine, *John L. Lewis*.

22. Gross, *Making of the National Labor Relations Board*; Dubofsky and van Tine, *John L. Lewis*, chaps. 11–12; Christopher L. Tomlins, *The State and the Unions: Labor Relations, Law, and the Organized Labor Movement in America, 1880–1960* (New York: Cambridge University Press, 1985), chap. 4.

23. Gross, *Making of the National Labor Relations Board*.

24. Milton Derber, *The American Idea of Industrial Democracy, 1865–1965* (Champaign: University of Illinois Press, 1970); Nelson Lichtenstein and Howell Harris, eds., *Industrial Democracy in America: The Ambiguous Promise* (Washington, DC: Woodrow Wilson Center Press, 1993); Lichtenstein, *State of the Union*, chap. 1; Gerstle, *Working-Class Americanism*, 196–229.

25. Gross, *Making of the National Labor Relations Board*, 132–39; Bernstein, *New Deal Collective Bargaining Policy*.

26. Karl E. Klare, "Judicial Deradicalization of the Wagner Act and the Origins of Modern Legal Consciousness, 1937–1941," *Minnesota Law Review* 62 (March 1978): 265–340; Tomlins, *State and the Unions*, 103–47.

27. On Witt and his influence in the NLRB, see Gross, *Making of the National Labor Relations Board*, passim; James A. Gross, *The Reshaping of the National Labor Relations Board: National Labor Policy in Transition, 1937–1947* (Albany: State University of New York Press, 1981), passim.

28. Sidney Fine, *Sit-down: The General Motors Strike of 1936–1937* (Ann Arbor: University of Michigan Press, 1969); Nelson Lichtenstein, *The Most Dangerous Man in Detroit: Walter Reuther and the Fate of American Labor* (New York: Basic Books, 1995), chap. 5.

29. Legal and political historians have engaged in spirited debate about whether the Supreme Court's 1937 ruling was more the product of long-developing jurisprudential thinking or a response to the political pressures of the moment. It seems clear to me that it was both. For an introduction to this debate, see "AHR Forum: The Debate over the Constitutional Revolution of 1937," *American Historical Review* 110 (November 2005): 1046–115. See also Barry Cushman, *Rethinking the New Deal Court: The Structure of a Constitutional Revolution* (New York: Oxford University Press, 1998); William G. Ross, "The Hughes Court (1930–1941): Evolution and Revolution," in *The United States Supreme Court: The Pursuit of Justice*, ed. Christopher Tomlins (New York: Houghton Mifflin Company, 2005), 223–48; Burt Solomon, *FDR v. the Constitution: The Court-Packing Fight and the Triumph of Democracy* (New York: Walker and Co., 2009); Jeff Shesol, *Supreme Power: Franklin Roosevelt vs. the Supreme Court* (New York: W. W. Norton and Company, 2010).

30. Gross, *Making of the National Labor Relations Board*, 237–40.

31. Ibid., 243.

32. Ibid., 108; Gerstle, *Working-Class Americanism*, 196–229.

33. Two new members of the NLRB, William Lieserson and Harry Millis, were themselves liberals, but saw their role on the NLRB less in terms of the promotion of labor's rights than as umpires whose job it was to resolve disputes between capital and labor in neutral ways. The third new board member, Gerard D. Reilly, was the first real conservative to sit on the board and to inject his politics into board decisions. Tomlins, *State and the Unions*, chap. 6. On the presence of Communists in the labor movement, see Bert Cochran, *Labor and Communism: The Conflict That Shaped American Unions* (Princeton, NJ: Princeton University Press, 1977); Gerstle, *Working-Class Americanism*, 153–95.

34. Gross, *Reshaping of the National Labor Relations Board*, 65; Tomlins, *State and the Unions*, chap. 5.

35. Lichtenstein, *State of the Union*, 102.

36. Ibid., 54–56.

37. Ibid., 57.

38. Paul Krugman, *The Conscience of a Liberal* (New York: W. W. Norton and Company, 2007), 46–47. On declines in wealth inequality, see also Thomas Piketty, *Capital in the Twenty-First Century* (Cambridge, MA: Harvard University Press, 2014).

39. Lichtenstein, *State of the Union*, 59.

40. Gary Gerstle, "Inclusion, Exclusion, and the Making of American Nationality," in *The Oxford Handbook on American Immigration and Ethnicity*, ed. Ronald Bayor (New York: Oxford University Press, forthcoming).

41. Gerstle, *Working-Class Americanism*, 311–18; Katherine van Wezel Stone, "The Post-War Paradigm in American Labor Law," *Yale Law Journal* 90 (1981): 1509–80; Christopher Tomlins, *State and the Unions*, chaps. 7–9; Howell Harris, *The Right to Manage: Industrial Relations Policies of American Business in the 1940s* (Madison: University of Wisconsin Press, 1982).

42. In Wickard v. Filburn, 317 U.S. 111 (1942), the Supreme Court ruled that the commerce clause endowed the central government with virtually unlimited authority to regulate the economy.

43. Alice Kessler-Harris, *In Pursuit of Equity: Women, Men, and the Quest for Citizenship in 20th-Century America* (New York: Oxford University Press, 2001), chaps. 1–2; Dorothy Sue Cobble, *The Other Women's Movement: Workplace Justice and Social Rights in Modern America* (Princeton, NJ: Princeton University Press, 2004); Dorothy Sue Cobble, *The Sex of Class: Women Transforming American Labor* (Ithaca, NY: ILR Press, 2007); Mae Ngai, *Impossible Subjects, Illegal Aliens and the Making of Modern America* (Princeton, NJ: Princeton University Press, 2004).

44. Social Security, in its earliest form, did exclude 55 percent of African American workers and 80 percent of women workers; these exclusions dropped significantly as a result of subsequent amendments to the act. Lichtenstein, *State of the Union*, 96; Edward D. Berkowitz, *America's Welfare State: From Roosevelt to Reagan* (Baltimore: Johns Hopkins University Press, 1991), chaps. 1–2; Edward D. Berkowitz, *Mr. Social Security: The Life of Wilbur J. Cohen* (Lawrence: University of Kansas Press, 1995), chaps. 1–4. The social assistance provisions of Social Security also varied widely by state, as states were given a major role in deciding the benefit levels. See Suzanne Mettler, *Dividing Citizens: Gender and Federalism in New Deal Public Policy* (Ithaca, NY: Cornell University Press, 1998).

45. Nelson Lichtenstein, "From Corporatism to Collective Bargaining: Organized Labor and the Eclipse of Social Democracy in the Postwar Era," in *The Rise and Fall of the New Deal Order, 1930–1980*, ed. Steve Fraser and Gary Gerstle, 122–52. On failed efforts at health care reform, see Colin Gordon, *Dead on Arrival: The Politics of Health Care in Twentieth-Century America* (Princeton, NJ: Princeton University Press, 2003); Paul Starr, *Remedy and Reaction: The Peculiar American Struggle over Health Care Reform* (2011; repr., New Haven, CT: Yale University Press, 2013), chap. 1.

46. Lichtenstein, *State of the Union*, chap. 3.

47. Lichtenstein, *Most Dangerous Man in Detroit*, chap. 13.

48. Jacob S. Hacker, *The Divided Welfare State: The Battle over Public and Private Social Benefits in the United States* (New York: Cambridge University Press, 2002), 85–173; Jennifer Klein, *For All These Rights: Business, Labor, and the Shaping of America's Public-Private Welfare State* (Princeton, NJ: Princeton University Press, 2003).

49. Fraser, "'Labor Question'"; Lichtenstein, *State of the Union*, chap. 3; Zieger, *CIO*, chaps. 8–9; Tomlins, *State and the Unions*, chaps. 7–8; Jean-Christian Vinel, *The Employee: A Political History* (Philadelphia: University of Pennsylvania Press, 2013).

50. Fraser, *Labor Will Rule*, 370; Dubofsky and van Tine, *John L. Lewis*, 252; Louise Overacker, "Campaign Funds in the Presidential Election of 1936," *American Political Science Review* 31 (June 1937): 490.

51. Louise Overacker, "American Government and Politics: Presidential Campaign Funds, 1944," *American Political Science Review* 39 (October 1945): 899–925, 919–92.

52. Overacker, "Campaign Funds in the Presidential Campaign of 1936," 485.

53. Ibid., 492.

54. Ibid., 487.

55. Fraser, "'Labor Question.'"

56. Overacker, "Campaign Funds in the Presidential Election of 1936," 487–90; Thomas Ferguson, "Industrial Conflict and the Coming of the New Deal: The Triumph of Multinational Liberalism in America," in *The Rise and Fall of the New Deal Order, 1930–1980*, ed. Steve Fraser and Gary Gerstle (Princeton, NJ: Princeton University Press, 1989), 3–31; Fraser, "'Labor Question'"; Steve Fraser and Gary Gerstle, introduction to *Ruling America: A History of Wealth and Power in a Democracy* (Cambridge, MA: Harvard University Press, 2005), 22–24; Steve Fraser, *Every Man a Speculator: A History of Wall Street in American Life* (New York: HarperCollins, 2005), 468; Jordan Schwarz, *The New Dealers: Power Politics in the Age of Roosevelt* (New York: Alfred A. Knopf, 1993), 264–84; Robert A. Caro, *The Years of Lyndon Johnson: The Path to Power* (New York: Alfred A. Knopf, 1982), 531–671.

57. Franklin D. Roosevelt, "Inaugural Address, March 4, 1933," in *The Public Papers and Addresses of Franklin D. Roosevelt*, comp. Samuel I. Rosenman (New York: Random House, 1938), 2:12.

CHAPTER 8. AN ERA OF NEAR-PERMANENT WAR

1. Susan B. Carter, Scott Sigmund Gartner, Michael R. Haines, Alan L. Olmstead, Richard Sutch, and Gavin Wright, eds., *Historical Statistics of the United States, Millennial Edition Online* (New York: Cambridge University Press, 2008), Appendix A: Military Personnel on Active Duty, by Branch of Service and Sex, 1789–1995, table Ed26–47.

2. The chapter subhead, "Warfare State," is drawn from James T. Sparrow, *Warfare State: World War II Americans and the Age of Big Government* (New York: Oxford University Press, 2011). The United States did not embrace universal military training, which would have required every American male to be trained for military service and be placed in a reserve unit liable to be called up. But it did maintain the World War II system of Selective Service from 1946 to 1973 (except for a one-year hiatus in 1947)—a draft scheme that required every American male to register with the military at age eighteen, and allowed the US Armed Forces to "select" those it needed to staff its ranks. Ibid.; Carter et al., *Historical Statistics of the United States*, Military Personnel and Casualties, by War and Branch of Service, 1775–1991, table Ed1–5. On universal military training and conscription, see Michael J. Hogan, *A Cross of Iron: Harry S. Truman and the Origins of the National Security State, 1945–1954* (New York: Cambridge University Press, 1998); Arthur Ekirch Jr., *The Civilian and the Military* (New York: Oxford University Press, 1956).

3. It also created the lesser-known National Resources Board along with the Research and Development Board. Hogan, *Cross of Iron*, 65–66. See also Ira

Katznelson, *Fear Itself: The New Deal and the Origins of Our Time* (New York: Liveright Publishing Corporation, 2013); Michael Sherry, *In the Shadow of War: The United States since the 1930s* (New Haven, CT: Yale University Press, 1995). On military unification, see Demetrios Caraley, *The Politics of Military Unification: A Study of Conflict and the Policy Process* (New York: Columbia University Press, 1966); Laurence J. Legere, *Unification of the Armed Forces* (New York: Garland, 1988).

4. Athan G. Theoharis, Tony Poveda, Susan Rosenfeld, and Richard Gid Powers, *The FBI: A Comprehensive Reference Guide* (Phoenix: Oryx Press, 1999), 4–5.

5. Katznelson, *Fear Itself*, 431.

6. Hogan, *Cross of Iron*; Jonathan Bell, *The Liberal State on Trial: The Cold War and American Politics in the Truman Years* (New York: Columbia University Press, 2004); Julian E. Zelizer, *Arsenal of Democracy: The Politics of National Security: From World War II to the War on Terrorism* (New York: Basic Books, 2010), 60–120.

7. Harold Lasswell, "The Garrison State," *American Journal of Sociology* 46 (1941): 455–68. See also Aaron L. Friedberg, *In the Shadow of the Garrison State: American Anti-Statism and Its Cold War Grand Strategy* (Princeton, NJ: Princeton University Press, 2000); Zelizer, *Arsenal of Democracy*; Hogan, *Cross of Iron*; Gary Gerstle, "A State Both Strong and Weak," *American Historical Review* 115 (2010): 779–85; Arthur M. Schlesinger Jr., *The Imperial Presidency* (Boston: Houghton Mifflin Company, 1989); John Yoo, *Crisis and Command: The History of Executive Power from George Washington to George W. Bush* (New York: Kaplan Publishers, 2009); Dana D. Nelson, *Bad for Democracy: How the Presidency Undermines the Power of the People* (Minneapolis: University of Minnesota Press, 2008).

8. Carter et al., *Historical Statistics of the United States*, Federal Government Employees, by Government Branch and Location to the Capital: 1816–1992, table Ea894–903; Carter et al., *Historical Statistics of the United States*, National Defense Outlays and Veterans' Benefits: 1915–1995, table Ed146–54.

9. Melvyn P. Leffler, *A Preponderance of Power: National Security, the Truman Administration, and the Cold War* (Stanford, CA: Stanford University Press, 1992); John Lewis Gaddis, *The United States and the Origins of the Cold War, 1941–1947* (New York: Columbia University Press, 1972); John Lewis Gaddis, *Strategies of Containment: A Critical Appraisal of Postwar American National Security Policy*, rev. ed. (New York: Oxford University Press, 2005); John Lewis Gaddis, *George F. Kennan: An American Life* (New York: Penguin, 2011); John Lewis Gaddis, *We Now Know: Rethinking Cold War History* (New York: Oxford University Press, 1997); Gar Alperovitz, *Atomic Diplomacy: Hiroshima and Potsdam: The Use of the Atomic Bomb and the American Confrontation with Soviet Power* (New York: Penguin, 1985); Vladislav Zubok and Constantine Pleshekov, *Inside the Kremlin's Cold War: From Stalin to Khrushchev* (Cambridge, MA: Harvard University Press, 1996); Vladislav Zubok, *A Failed Empire: The Soviet Union in the Cold War from Stalin to Gorbachev* (Chapel Hill: University of North Carolina Press,

2007); Bruce Cumings, *The Origins of the Korean War*, 2 vols. (Princeton, NJ: Princeton University Press, 1981–90); William Stueck, *The Road to Confrontation: American Policy toward China and Korea, 1947–1950* (Chapel Hill: University of North Carolina Press, 1981); William Stueck, *The Korean War: An International History* (Princeton, NJ: Princeton University Press, 1995).

10. National Security Council, "NSC 68: United States Objectives and Programs for National Security," April 14, 1950, https://www.mtholyoke.edu /acad/intrel/nsc-68/nsc68-1.htm (accessed July 2, 2014); Hogan, *Cross of Iron*, 291–314; Gaddis, *Strategies of Containment*, 87–124.

11. Compiled from Carter et al., *Historical Statistics of the United States*, Military Personnel on Active Duty, by Branch of Service and Sex, 1789–1995, table Ed26-47; Carter et al., *Historical Statistics of the United States*, Table 1: Civilian Defense Employees as Percentage of Federal Civilian Employees, 1909–1992, in Federal Government Employees by Government Branch and Location Relative to the Capital, 1816–1992, table Ea894–903; Carter et al., *Historical Statistics of the United States*, National Defense Outlays and Veterans Benefits: 1915–1995, table Ed146–54. Twenty years earlier, 70 percent of a far-smaller federal state had worked either for the post office or Department of Agriculture.

12. Richard Immerman, *The Hidden Hand: A Brief History of the CIA* (Malden, MA: Wiley-Blackwell, 2014); John Prados, *The Family Jewels: The CIA, Secrecy, and Presidential Power* (Austin: University of Texas Press, 2013); Tim Weiner, *Legacy of Ashes: The History of the CIA* (New York: Doubleday, 2007); David M. Barrett, *The CIA and Congress: The Untold Story from Truman to Kennedy* (Lawrence: University of Kansas Press, 2005); David F. Rudgers, *Creating the Secret State: The Origins of the Central Intelligence Agency* (Lawrence: University of Kansas Press, 2000); Rhodri Jeffrey-Jones, *The CIA and American Democracy* (New Haven, CT: Yale University Press, 1989); John Ranelagh, *The Agency: The Rise and Decline of the CIA* (New York: Simon and Schuster, 1986); Britt L. Snider, *The Agency and the Hill: CIA's Relationship with Congress, 1946–2004* (Washington, DC: Center for the Study of Intelligence, Central Intelligence Agency, 2008).

13. Alien Registration Act of 1940, 18 USC § 2385, 76 Cong., 3rd Sess. (1940).

14. Michael Belknap, *Cold War Political Justice: The Smith Act, the Communist Party, and American Civil Liberties* (Westport, CT: Greenwood Press, 1977). More generally on the anti-Communist crusade, see Ellen Schrecker, *Many Are the Crimes: McCarthyism in America* (Boston: Little, Brown and Company, 1998); David Caute, *The Great Fear: The Anti-Communist Purge under Truman and Eisenhower* (New York: Simon and Schuster, 1978); David Oshinsky, *A Conspiracy So Immense: The World of Joe McCarthy* (New York: Free Press, 1983); Richard Rovere, *Senator Joe McCarthy* (New York: Harcourt, Brace and World, Inc., 1959); Stanley I. Kutler, *The American Inquisition: Justice and Injustice in the Cold War* (New York: Hill and Wang, 1982); Dennis v. United States, 341 U.S. 494 (1951); Geoffrey R. Stone, *Perilous Times: Free Speech in Wartime: From the Sedition Act of 1798 to the War on Terrorism* (New York: W. W. Norton and Company, 2004), 395–415; Arthur Sabin, *In Calmer Times: The Supreme Court and Red Monday* (Philadelphia:

University of Pennsylvania Press, 1999); Richard H. Pells, *The Liberal Mind in a Conservative Age: American Intellectuals in the 1940s and 1950s* (New York: Harper and Row, 1985), 262–345.

15. On the FBI, see Athan Theoharis, *Spying on Americans: Political Surveillance from Hoover to the Huston Plan* (Philadelphia: Temple University Press, 1978); Athan Theoharis and John Stuart Cox, *The Boss: J. Edgar Hoover and the Great American Inquisition* (Philadelphia: Temple University Press, 1988); Rhodri Jeffreys-Jones, *The FBI: A History* (New Haven, CT: Yale University Press, 2007); Curt Gentry, *J. Edgar Hoover: The Man and the Secrets* (New York: W. W. Norton and Company, 1991); Schrecker, *Many Are the Crimes*, 203–39; Katznelson, *Fear Itself*, 403–66.

16. Stone, *Perilous Times*, 184–234, 248–58.

17. Ibid., 311–426; Schlesinger, *Imperial Presidency*, 127–76; Clinton Rossiter, *Constitutional Dictatorship: Crisis Government in the Modern Democracies* (Princeton, NJ: Princeton University Press, 1948).

18. Theoharis et al., *FBI*, 4–5; Shrecker, *Many Are the Crimes*, 106, 206–11; Kutler, *American Inquisition*, passim.

19. Hogan, *Cross of Iron*; Landon R. Y. Storrs, *The Second Red Scare and the Unmaking of the New Deal Left* (Princeton, NJ: Princeton University Press, 2013); Schrecker, *Many Are the Crimes*, 106, 206–11; Leffler, *Preponderance of Power*; Kutler, *American Inquisition*; Theoharis and Cox, *Boss*, 157–300; Ellen Schrecker, *No Ivory Tower: McCarthyism and the Universities* (New York: Oxford University Press, 1986); Caute, *Great Fear*; Neal Gabler, *An Empire of Their Own: How the Jews Invented Hollywood* (New York: Crown Publishers, 1988), 351–86; Bert Cochran, *Between Labor and Communism: The Conflict That Shaped American Unions* (Princeton, NJ: Princeton University Press, 1977); Harvey A. Levenstein, *Communism, Anticommunism, and the CIO* (Westport, CT: Greenwood Press, 1981); Stephen J. Whitfield, *The Culture of the Cold War*, 2nd ed. (Baltimore: Johns Hopkins University Press, 1996); Oshinsky, *Conspiracy So Immense*; Stone, *Perilous Times*, 411–26.

20. Stephen E. Ambrose, *Eisenhower: The President* (New York: Simon and Schuster, 1984), 2:91–107, 186–89; Fred I. Greenstein, *The Hidden-Hand Presidency: Eisenhower as Leader* (Baltimore: Johns Hopkins University Press, 1982), 155–227; Oshinsky, *Conspiracy So Immense*; Stone, *Perilous Times*, 411–26; Sabin, *Calmer Times*; Belknap, *Cold War Political Justice*. The four cases in which the Supreme Court overturned convictions of Communists under the Smith Act were: Service v. Dulles, 354 U.S. 363 (1957); Watkins v. United States, 354 U.S. 178 (1957); Sweezy v. New Hampshire, 354 U.S. 354 (1957); Yates v. United States, 354 U.S. 298 (1957). The Supreme Court handed down all these rulings on one day, June 17, 1957, dubbed "Red Monday" by anti-Communists who thought that the Court's decisions would boost the spirits and fortunes of the American Communist Party.

21. Katznelson, *Fear Itself*, 451, 470.

22. Joshua B. Freeman, *American Empire: The Rise of a Global Power, the Democratic Revolution at Home, 1945–2000* (New York: Viking, 2012), 87.

23. Gaddis, *Strategies of Containment*, 125–61; Walter A. McDougall, *The Heavens and the Earth: A Political History of the Space Age* (New York: Basic Books, 1985), 137–230; Friedberg, *Shadow of the Garrison State*; Sherry, *In the Shadow of War*, 188–236.

24. Dwight D. Eisenhower, "Farewell Radio and Television Address to the American People," January 17, 1961, *Public Papers of the Presidents of the United States: Dwight D. Eisenhower, 1960–61* (Washington, DC: Government Printing Office, 1961), 1035–40. More generally, see James Ledbetter, *Unwarranted Influence: Dwight D. Eisenhower and the Military-Industrial Complex* (New Haven, CT: Yale University Press, 2011).

25. Eisenhower, "Farewell Radio and Television Address."

26. Katznelson, *Fear Itself*, 427.

27. Bruce J. Schulman, *From Cotton Belt to Sunbelt: Federal Policy, Economic Development, and the Transformation of the South, 1938–1980* (New York: Oxford University Press, 1991), 147.

28. Matthew Owen, " 'For the Progress of Man': The TVA, Electric Power, and the Environment" (PhD diss., Vanderbilt University, 2014); Leland Johnson and Daniel Schaffer, *Oak Ridge National Laboratory: The First Fifty Years* (Knoxville: University of Tennessee Press, 1994); Russell Olwell, *At Work in the Atomic City: A Labor and Social History of Oak Ridge, Tennessee* (Knoxville: University of Tennessee Press, 2004).

29. Friedberg, *Shadow of the Garrison State*; Schulman, *From Cotton Belt to Sunbelt*, 147–49; Elizabeth Tandy Shermer, *Sunbelt Capitalism: Phoenix and the Transformation of American Politics* (Philadelphia: University of Pennsylvania Press, 2013); T. Andrew Needham, *Power Lines: Phoenix and the Making of the Modern Southwest* (Princeton, NJ: Princeton University Press, 2014); Robert A. Caro, *The Years of Lyndon Johnson: Master of the Senate* (New York: Alfred A. Knopf, 2002); Anthony Champagne, *Congressman Sam Rayburn* (New Brunswick, NJ: Rutgers University Press, 1984); McDougall, *Heavens and the Earth*, 157–76.

30. Roger Lotchin, *Fortress California, 1910–1961: From Warfare to Welfare* (New York: Oxford University Press, 1992); Ann Markusen, Peter Hall, Scott Campbell, and Sabina Deitrick, *The Rise of the Gunbelt: The Military Remapping of Industrial America* (New York: Oxford University Press, 1991); Schulman, *From Cotton Belt to Sunbelt*; Paul Koistinen, *The Military-Industrial Complex: A Historical Perspective* (New York: Praeger, 1980); Gregory Hooks, "The Rise of the Pentagon and the US State Building: The Defense Programs as Industrial Policy," *American Journal of Sociology* 96 (September 1990): 358–404; John Clayton, "The Impact of the Cold War on the Economies of California and Utah," *Pacific Historical Journal* 36 (November 1967): 449–73; William Hartung, *Prophets of War: Lockheed Martin and the Making of the Military-Industrial Complex* (New York: Nation Books, 2011); Jacob Vander Meulen, *The Politics of Aircraft: Building an American Military Industry* (Lawrence: University Press of Kansas, 1991); Needham, *Power Lines*; Shermer, *Sunbelt Capitalism*.

31. Richard White, *"It's Your Misfortune and None of My Own": A History of the American West* (Norman: University of Oklahoma Press, 1991); Needham, *Power Lines*; Owen, "'Progress of Man'"; Johnson and Schaffer, *Oak Ridge National Laboratory*.

32. Federal-Aid Highway Act of 1956, Public Law 627, June 29, 1956; Tom Lewis, *Divided Highways: Building the Interstate Highways, Transforming American Life* (Ithaca, NY: Cornell University Press, 2013); Earl Swift, *The Big Roads: The Untold Story of the Engineers, Visionaries, and Trailblazers Who Created the American Superhighways* (Boston: Houghton Mifflin Company, 2011); Owen D. Gutfreund, *Twentieth-Century Sprawl: Highways and the Reshaping of the American Landscape* (New York: Oxford University Press, 2004); David James St. Clair, *The Motorization of American Cities* (New York: Praeger, 1986); Dianne Perrier, *Onramps and Overpasses: A Cultural History of Interstate Travel* (Gainesville: University of Florida Press, 2009). On the growth of suburbs, see Kenneth T. Jackson, *The Crabgrass Frontier: The Suburbanization of the United States* (New York: Oxford University Press, 1985); Lizabeth Cohen, *A Consumers' Republic: The Politics of Mass Consumption in Postwar America* (New York: Alfred A. Knopf, 2003).

33. Katznelson, *Fear Itself*, 456; Schulman, *From Cotton Belt to Sunbelt*, 148–73; Jessica Wang, *American Science in an Age of Anxiety: Scientists, Anticommunism, and the Cold War* (Chapel Hill: University of North Carolina Press, 1999); Margaret Pugh O'Mara, *Cities of Knowledge: Cold War Science and the Search for the Next Silicon Valley* (Princeton, NJ: Princeton University Press, 2004); McDougall, *Heavens and the Earth*, 97–176.

34. Kathleen J. Frydl, *The GI Bill* (New York: Cambridge University Press, 2009), 3; Keith Olson, "The G. I. Bill and Higher Education: Success and Surprise," *American Quarterly* 25 (December 1973): 596–610; Keith Olson, *The G.I. Bill, the Veterans, and the Colleges* (Lexington: University Press of Kentucky, 1974); Ira Katznelson, *When Affirmative Action Was White: An Untold Story of Racial Inequality in Twentieth-Century America* (New York: W. W. Norton and Company, 2005); Suzanne Mettler, *Soldiers to Citizens: The G.I. Bill and the Making of the Greatest Generation* (New York: Oxford University Press, 2005); US Department of Education, *120 Years of American Education: A Statistical Portrait* (Washington, DC: Office of Educational Research and Improvement, National Center for Education Statistics, January 1993), 75.

35. Wang, *American Science in an Age of Anxiety*, 44–182; Martin Sherwin and Kai Bird, *American Prometheus: The Triumph and Tragedy of J. Robert Oppenheimer* (New York: Alfred A. Knopf, 2005), 323–565; Ray Monk, *Inside the Centre: The Life of J. Robert Oppenheimer* (London: Jonathan Cape, 2012), 531–624; Abraham Pais, *J. Robert Oppenheimer: A Life* (New York: Oxford University Press, 2006), 144–271; Katznelson, *Fear Itself*, 482–84.

36. Quoted in Katznelson, *Fear Itself*, 455.

37. Toby A. Appel, *Shaping Biology: The National Science Foundation and American Biological Research, 1945–1975* (Baltimore: Johns Hopkins University Press, 2000); Dian Olson Belanger, *Enabling American Innovation: Engineering and the National Science Foundation* (West Lafayette, IN: Purdue

University Press, 1998); J. Merton England, *A Patron for Pure Science: The National Science Foundation's Formative Years, 1945–57* (Washington, DC: National Science Foundation, 1982).

38. David C. Engerman, *Know Your Enemy: The Rise and Fall of America's Soviet Experts* (New York: Oxford University Press, 2009); Howard Brick: *Age of Contradiction: American Thought and Culture in the 1960s* (New York: Twayne Publishers, 1998); Joy Rohde, *Armed with Expertise: The Militarization of American Society Research during the Cold War* (Ithaca, NY: Cornell University Press, 2013); Mark Solovey and Hamilton Cravens, eds., *Cold War Social Science: Knowledge Production, Liberal Democracy, and Human Nature* (New York: Palgrave Macmillan, 2012); Joel Isaac, "Tangled Loops: Theory, History, and the Human Sciences in Modern America," *Modern Intellectual History* 6 (2009): 397–424; Joel Isaac, "The Human Sciences in Cold War America," *Historical Journal* 50 (2007): 725–46; Christopher P. Loss, *Between Citizens and the State: The Politics of American Higher Education in the Twentieth Century* (Princeton, NJ: Princeton University Press, 2012), 121–64.

39. Carter et al., *Historical Statistics of the United States*, Federal Income Tax Returns—Individual: 1940–1992, table Ea740–47; Carter et al., *Historical Statistics of the United States*, Federal Income Tax Returns—Individual: 1913–1943, table Ea748–57; Carter et al., *Historical Statistics of the United States*, Population: 1790–2000 [annual estimates], table Aa6–8; Carter et al., *Historical Statistics of the United States*, Labor Force, Employment, and Unemployment: 1890–1990, table Ba470–77; Military Personnel on Active Duty, by Branch of Service and Sex: 1789-1995, table Ed26-47.

40. For taxation in America, see Sheldon Pollack, *War, Revenue, and State Building: Financing the Development of the American State* (Ithaca, NY: Cornell University Press, 2009); W. Elliot Brownlee, *Federal Taxation in America: A Short History*, 2nd ed. (Washington, DC: Woodrow Wilson Center Press, 2004); W. Elliot Brownlee, ed., *Funding the Modern American State, 1941–1995: The Rise and Fall of the Era of Easy Finance* (Washington, DC: Woodrow Wilson Center Press, 1996); Sidney Ratner, *American Taxation: Its History as a Social Force in Democracy* (New York: W. W. Norton and Company, 1942); Sidney Ratner, *Taxation and Democracy in America* (New York: Wiley, 1967); Carolyn Jones, "Class Tax to Mass Tax: The Role of Propaganda in the Expansion of the Income Tax during World War II," *Buffalo Law Review* 37 (1988–89): 685–738; Mark Leff, *The Limits of Symbolic Reform: The New Deal and Taxation, 1933–1939* (New York: Cambridge University Press, 1984); John Witte, *The Politics and Development of the Federal Income Tax* (Madison: University of Wisconsin Press, 1985); Julian E. Zelizer, *Taxing America: Wilbur D. Mills, Congress, and the State, 1945–1975* (New York: Cambridge University Press, 1998). See also Sven Steinmo, *Taxation and Democracy: Swedish, British, and American Approaches to Financing the Modern Welfare State* (New Haven, CT: Yale University Press, 1993); Ajay K. Mehrotra, *Making the Modern American Fiscal State: Law, Politics, and the Rise of Progressive Taxation, 1877–1929* (New York: Cambridge University Press, 2013).

41. These totals reflect revenues received exclusively from personal income tax paid. Corporate taxes brought in another $16 billion, up from $1.2 billion in 1940. Carter et al., *Historical Statistics of the United States*, Federal Government Revenue, by Source: 1934–1999 [Office of Management and Budget], table Ea683–97; Pollack, *War, Revenue, and State Building*, 261–62.

42. Pollack, *War, Revenue, and State Building*, 262–63; Lawrence Zelenak, "The Federal Retail Sales Tax That Wasn't: An Actual History and an Alternate History," *Law and Contemporary Problems* 73 (2010): 164; Ratner, *Taxation and Democracy in America*, 517.

43. Carter et al., *Historical Statistics of the United States*, Federal Income Tax Returns—Individual: 1940–1992, table Ea 740–47; Carter et al., *Historical Statistics of the United States*, Federal Income Tax Returns—Individual: 1913–1943, table Ea 748–57; Carter et al., *Historical Statistics of the United States*, Population: 1790–2000 [annual estimates], table Aa6–8; Carter et al., *Historical Statistics of the United States*, Labor Force, Employment, and Unemployment: 1890–1990, table Ba470–77; Carter et al., *Historical Statistics of the United States*, Military Personnel on Active Duty, by Branch of Service and Sex: 1789–1995, table Ed26–47.

44. Wilbur D. Mills, "Are You a Pet or a Patsy?" *Life*, November 23, 1959, 62.

45. Romain Huret, *American Tax Resisters* (Cambridge, MA: Harvard University Press, 2014).

46. This new exemption strategy would, in fact, become an ever more prominent feature of America's tax code between the 1950s and 1980s.

47. Dwight D. Eisenhower, "Radio and Television Address to the American People on the Tax Program," March 15, 1954, *Public Papers of the Presidents of the United States: Dwight D. Eisenhower, 1954* (Washington, DC: Government Printing Office, 1960), 313–18. See also Witte, *The Politics and Development of the Federal Income Tax*, 146–50; Iwan W. Morgan, *Eisenhower versus "the Spenders": The Eisenhower Administration, the Democrats, and the Budget, 1953–60* (New York: St. Martin's Press, 1990).

48. Eisenhower, "Radio and Television Address to the American People on the Tax Program."

49. Ibid.

50. Godfrey Hodgson, *America in Our Time: From World War II to Nixon—What Happened and Why* (New York: Vintage Books, 1978), 67–98.

CHAPTER 9. BREAKING THE
POWER OF THE STATES

1. The literature on the civil rights movement is vast. For a sampling, see Richard Kluger, *Simple Justice: The History of Brown v. Board of Education and Black America's Struggle for Equality* (New York: Random House, 1975); Richard Klarman, *From Jim Crow to Civil Rights: The Supreme Court and the*

Struggle for Racial Equality (New York: Oxford University Press, 2004); James T. Patterson, *Brown v. Board of Education: A Civil Rights Milestone and Its Troubled Legacy* (New York: Oxford University Press, 2002); Robert Weisbrot, *Freedom Bound: A History of America's Civil Rights Movement,* (New York: W. W. Norton and Company, 1989); David J. Garrow, *Bearing the Cross: Martin Luther King, Jr., and the Southern Christian Leadership Conference* (New York: William Morrow and Company, 1986); Howell Raines, *My Soul Is Rested: Movement Days in the Deep South Remembered* (New York: Penguin Books, 1983); Raymond Arsenault, *Freedom Riders: 1961 and the Struggle for Racial Justice* (New York: Oxford University Press, 2006); Clayborne Carson, *In Struggle: SNCC and the Black Awakening of the 1960s* (Cambridge, MA: Harvard University Press, 1995); Wesley Hogan, *Many Minds, One Heart: SNCC's Dream for a New America* (Chapel Hill: University of North Carolina Press, 2009); George Lewis, *Massive Resistance: The White Response to the Civil Rights Movement* (New York: Oxford University Press, 2006); Numan V. Bartley, *Massive Resistance: Race and Politics in the South during the 1950s* (Baton Rouge: Louisiana State University Press, 1999); Thomas J. Sugrue, *Sweet Land of Liberty: The Forgotten Struggle for Civil Rights in the North* (New York: Random House, 2008); Dan Carter, *The Politics of Rage: George Wallace, the Origins of the New Conservatism, and the Transformation of American Politics* (Baton Rouge: Louisiana State University Press, 2000); Carl Brauer, *John F. Kennedy and the Second Reconstruction* (New York: Columbia University Press, 1977); Jonathan Rieder, *Gospel of Freedom: Martin Luther King Jr.'s Letter from Birmingham Jail and the Struggle That Changed a Nation* (New York: Bloomsbury Press, 2013); Nicholas Lemann, *The Promised Land: The Great Black Migration and How It Changed America* (New York: Alfred A. Knopf, 1991); Philip A. Klinker and Rogers M. Smith, *The Unsteady March: The Rise and Decline of Racial Equality in America* (Chicago: University of Chicago Press, 1999), chaps. 7–8; Robert A. Caro, *The Years of Lyndon Johnson: The Passage of Power* (New York: Alfred A. Knopf, 2012), pt. V; Clay Risen, *The Bill of the Century: The Epic Battle for the Civil Rights Act* (New York: Bloombury, 2014).

2. Susan B. Carter, Scott Sigmund Gartner, Michael R. Haines, Alan L. Olmstead, Richard Sutch, and Gavin Wright, eds., *Historical Statistics of the United States, Millennial Edition Online* (New York: Cambridge University Press, 2013), Total Government Revenue and Expenditure, by Level: 1902–1995, table Ea10–23, http://hsus.cambridge.org/HSUSWeb/toc/showTable.do?id=Ea1-583 (accessed February 18, 2015).

3. US Constitution, amendment 14, section 1.

4. This had been the intent of two architects of the Fourteenth Amendment, Congressman John A. Bingham and Senator Jacob M. Howard. See Alexander M. Bickel, "The Original Understanding and the Segregation Decision," *Harvard Law Review* 69 (1955): 1–65; Raoul Berger, *Government by Judiciary: The Transformation of the Fourteenth Amendment* (Cambridge, MA: Harvard University Press, 1977). Twentieth-century conservatives have construed Congress's intent in ratifying the Fourteenth Amendment differently. According to

Charles Fairman, it is uncertain whether the rest of the Congress agreed with Bingham and Howard's expansive view of the Fourteenth Amendment. See, for instance, Charles Fairman, "Does the Fourteenth Amendment Incorporate the Bill of Rights? The Original Understanding," *Stanford Law Review* 2 (December 1949): 5–139; Earl M. Maltz, "The Fourteenth Amendment as Political Compromise: Section One in the Joint Committee on Reconstruction," *Ohio State Law Journal* 45 (Fall 1984): 933–80.

5. Slaughterhouse Cases, 83 U.S. 36 (1873); United States v. Cruikshank, 92 U.S. 542 (1876); Civil Rights Cases, 109 U.S. 3 (1883); Hurtado v. California, 110 U.S. 516 (1884).

6. Gitlow v. New York, 268 U.S. 652 (1925); Near v. Minnesota, 283 U.S. 697 (1931).

7. Associate Justice Benjamin Cardozo was among those justices who supported the doctrine of "selective incorporation," which held that only the "fundamental rights" that were essential to "a scheme of ordered liberty" needed to be incorporated. Palko v. Connecticut, 302 U.S. 319 (1937), 320–27.

8. Richard Cortner, *The Supreme Court and the Second Bill of Rights: The Fourteenth Amendment and the Nationalization of Civil Liberties* (Madison: University of Wisconsin Press, 1981); Michael Kent Curtis, *No State Shall Abridge: The Fourteenth Amendment and the Bill of Rights* (Durham, NC: Duke University Press, 1986); Chester J. Antieau, *The Original Understanding of the Fourteenth Amendment* (Tucson, AZ: Mid-America Press, 1981); Judith A. Baer, *Equality under the Constitution: Reclaiming the Fourteenth Amendment* (Ithaca, NY: Cornell University Press, 1983); Berger, *Government by Judiciary*; Bryan Wildenthal, "The Lost Compromise: Reassessing the Early Understanding in Court and Congress on Incorporation of the Bill of Rights in the Fourteenth Amendment," *Ohio State Law Journal* 61 (2000): 1051–174; Bryan Wildenthal, "Nationalizing the Bill of Rights: Revisiting the Original Understanding of the Fourteenth Amendment in 1866–67," *Ohio State Law Journal* 68 (2007): 1509–626; George C. Thomas III, "The Riddle of the Fourteenth Amendment: A Reply to Professor Wildenthal," *Ohio State Law Journal* 68 (2007): 1626–58.

9. Lochner v. New York, 198 U.S. 45 (1905). Field himself did not live long enough to savor this triumph (he died in 1899), but he had been instrumental in laying the groundwork for the 1905 decision. In the 1880s, laissez-faire constitutionalists had already turned corporations into persons who could avail themselves of Fourteenth Amendment protections. It also should be noted that the laissez-faire group was not hostile to all protective labor laws, as long as those laws were limited to two groups of workers: first, women and child laborers who for reasons of gender or age were thought to be incapable of defending their liberty; and second, male workers who labored at exceptionally dangerous work sites such as mines. In both cases, public health was thought to trump the freedom of individual employers and employees to negotiate the terms of employment. A notable example of this kind of protective legislation was *Muller v. Oregon*, 208 U.S. 412 (1908), in which the Court upheld an Oregon state law that restricted the number of hours women could work.

10. Erwin Chemerinsky, "Substantive Due Process," *Touro Law Review* 15 (1999): 1501–34; James Ely Jr., "The Oxymoron Reconsidered: Myth and Reality in the Origins of Substantive Due Process," *Constitutional Commentary* 16 (1999): 315–46; Herbert Hovenkamp, "The Political Economy of Substantive Due Process," *Stanford Law Review* 40 (1988): 379–447; Benjamin Wright, *The Growth of American Constitutional Law* (Boston: Houghton Mifflin Company, 1942); Monrad Paulsen, "The Persistence of Due Process in the States," *Minnesota Law Review* 34 (1950): 91–118; Daniel Conkle, "The Second Death of Substantive Due Process," *Indiana Law Journal* 62 (1986–87): 215–42; Edward S. Corwin, *Court over Constitution: A Study of Judicial Review as an Instrument of Popular Government* (Princeton, NJ: Princeton University Press, 1938); Robert Cushman, *The Supreme Court and the Constitution* (Washington, DC: Public Affairs Committee, 1936); Laurence Tribe, "Pursuing the Pursuit of Happiness," *New York Review of Books*, September 24, 1998, http://www.nybooks.com.ezp-prod1.hul.harvard.edu/articles/archives/1998/sep/24/pursuing-the-pursuit-of-happiness/ (accessed March 26, 2015); John Hart Ely, *Democracy and Distrust: A Theory of Judicial Review* (Cambridge, MA: Harvard University Press, 1980); Robert G. Dixon Jr., "The 'New' Substantive Due Process and the Democratic Ethic: A Prolegomenon," *BYU Law Review* 43 (1976): 43–88; Richard A. Epstein, "The Mistakes of 1937," *George Mason University Law Review* 11 (1988): 5–20; Wayne McCormack, "Economic Substantive Due Process and the Right to Livelihood," *Kentucky Law Journal* 82 (1993–94), 397–463; Ryan C. Williams, "The One and Only Substantive Due Process Clause," *Yale Law Journal* 120 (December 2010): 408–689; G. Edward White, *The Constitution and the New Deal* (Cambridge, MA: Harvard University Press, 2000); Howard Gillman, *The Constitution Besieged: The Rise and Demise of Lochner Era Police Powers Jurisprudence* (Durham, NC: Duke University Press, 1993); Victoria Nourse, "A Tale of Two Lochners: The Untold History of Substantive Due Process and the Idea of Fundamental Rights," *California Law Review* 97 (2009), 751–99.

11. Samuel Warren and Louis Brandeis, "The Right to Privacy," *Harvard Law Review* 4 (December 1890): 220.

12. Olmstead v. United States, 277 U.S. 438, 472 (1928) (Brandeis, J., dissenting), 473.

13. On Brandeis and privacy, see Neal M. Richards, "The Puzzle of Brandeis, Privacy, and Speech," *Vanderbilt Law Review* 63 (2010): 1295–352.

14. Meyer v. Nebraska, 232 U.S. 390 (1923), 399; Pierce v. Society of Sisters, 268 U.S. 510 (1924). Lawrence Tribe has called Meyer and Pierce "the two sturdiest pillars of the substantive due process temple." Lawrence Tribe, "Lawrence v. Texas: The 'Fundamental Right' That Dare Not Speak Its Name," *Harvard Law Review* 117 (April 2004): 1934. See also Chemerinsky, "Substantive Due Process," 1501–8.

15. The critical cases overturning *Lochner* and the substantive due process doctrine in the economic realm were *National Labor Relations Board v. Jones and Laughlin Steel Corporation*, 301 U.S. 1 (1937); *West Coast Hotel Co. v.*

Parrish, 300 U.S. 379 (1937); *United States v. Carolene Products Company*, 304 U.S. 144 (1938).

16. Eisenhower's second Supreme Court appointment, sandwiched between Warren and Brennan, was John Marshall Harlan II, appointed in 1955.

17. On Black, see Tony Allan Freyer, *Hugo L. Black and the Dilemma of American Liberalism*, 2nd ed. (New York: Pearson Longman, 2008); Steve Suitts, *Hugo Black of Alabama: How His Roots and Early Career Shaped the Great Champion of the Constitution* (Montgomery, AL: New South Books, 2005); Howard Ball, *Hugo L. Black: Cold Steel Warrior* (New York: Oxford University Press, 1996); Howard Ball, *The Vision and the Dream of Justice Hugo L. Black: An Examination of a Judicial Philosophy* (Tuscaloosa: University of Alabama Press, 1975); Roger K. Newman, *Hugo Black: A Biography* (New York: Pantheon Books, 1994); Tinsley E. Yarbrough, *Mr. Justice Black and His Critics* (Durham, NC: Duke University Press, 1988); James F. Simon, *The Antagonists: Hugo Black, Felix Frankfurter, and Civil Liberties in Modern America* (New York: Simon and Schuster, 1989); James J. Magee, *Mr. Justice Black: Absolutist on the Court* (Charlottesville: University Press of Virginia, 1980); Gerald T. Dunne, *Hugo Black and the Judicial Revolution* (New York: Simon and Schuster, 1977). On the way in which the Roosevelt appointees began to reshape the Court, and on the activist wing of that Court led by Black and opposed by Frankfurter, see Arthur M. Schlesinger Jr., "The Supreme Court: 1947," *Fortune*, January 1947, 73–79, 201–11; Noah Feldman, *Scorpions: The Battles and Triumphs of FDR's Greatest Supreme Court Justices* (New York: Twelve, 2010); Jeffrey D. Hockett, *New Deal Justice: The Constitutional Jurisprudence of Hugo L. Black, Felix Frankfurter, and Robert H. Jackson* (Lanham, MD: Rowman and Littlefield, 1996); Howard Ball, *Of Power and Right: Hugo Black, William O. Douglas, and America's Constitutional Revolution* (New York: Oxford University Press, 1992).

18. In his first reelection bid in 1946, Warren was so popular that he secured the nominations of both the Republican and Democratic parties.

19. James C. Derieux, "Will Warren Pivot to the Presidency?" *Colliers*, January 19, 1952, 48; G. Edward White, *Earl Warren: A Public Life* (New York: Oxford University Press, 1982), 327–36; Ed Cray, *Chief Justice: A Biography of Earl Warren* (New York: Simon and Schuster, 1997), 19, 27–31; Bernard Schwartz, *Super Chief, Earl Warren, and His Supreme Court—A Judicial Biography* (New York: New York University Press, 1983), 8; John Weaver, *Warren: The Man, the Court, the Era* (Boston: Little, Brown and Company, 1967), 344. On Warren and the Warren Court, see also Jim Newton, *Justice for All: Earl Warren and the Nation He Made* (New York: Riverhead Books, 2006); Michael Belknap, *The Supreme Court under Earl Warren, 1953–1969* (Columbia: University of South Carolina Press, 2005); Melvin Urofsky, *The Warren Court: Justices, Rulings, and Legacy* (Santa Barbara, CA: ABC-CLIO, 2001); Lucas A. Powe Jr., *The Warren Court and American Politics* (Cambridge, MA: Belknap Press of Harvard University Press, 2000); Bernard Schwartz, *The Warren Court: A Retrospective* (New York: Oxford University Press, 1996); Mark Tushnet, ed., *The Warren Court in Historical and Political Perspective*

(Charlottesville: University Press of Virginia, 1993); Bruce Ackerman, *We the People, Volume 3: The Civil Rights Revolution* (Cambridge, MA: Harvard University Press, 2014).

20. Letter from Earl Warren to Robert Kenny, July 20, 1938, reproduced in *National Lawyers' Guild Review* 14 (1954–55), quoted in White, *Earl Warren*, 223.

21. Derieux, "Will Warren Pivot to the Presidency?" 18, 48, 51; Earl Warren, "The Law and the Future," *Fortune*, November 1955, 226, 229.

22. Stephen Wermiel and Seth Stern, *Justice Brennan: Liberal Champion* (Boston: Houghton Mifflin Harcourt, 2010).

23. Mapp v. Ohio, 367 U.S. 643 (1961); Gideon v. Wainwright, 372 U.S. 335 (1963); Malloy v. Hogan, 378 U.S. 1 (1964); Miranda v. Arizona, 384 U.S. 436 (1966); Parker v. Gladden, 385 U.S. 363 (1966); Duncan v. Louisiana, 391 U.S. 145 (1968).

24. Baker v. Carr, 369 U.S. 186 (1962). Brennan was a key player in this decision as well. See Alexander Keyssar, *The Right to Vote: The Contested History of Democracy in the United States* (New York: Basic Books, 2000), chap. 8; Schwartz, *Super Chief*, 336–72.

25. Loving v. Virginia, 388 U.S. 1 (1967).

26. Peggy Pascoe, *What Comes Naturally: Miscegenation Law and the Making of Race in America* (New York: Oxford University Press, 2009), chap. 8.

27. *Loving v. Virginia*, 12.

28. Griswold v. Connecticut, 381 U.S. 479 (1965).

29. Poe v. Ullman, 367 U.S. 497, 543 (1961) (Harlan, J., dissenting).

30. David J. Garrow, *Liberty and Sexuality: The Right to Privacy and the Making of Roe v. Wade* (Berkeley: University of California Press, 1998), 241–54.

31. Griswold v. Connecticut, 507–27; Garrow, *Liberty and Sexuality*, 196–269.

32. Eisenstadt v. Baird, 405 U.S. 438 (1972); Roe v. Wade, 410 U.S. 113 (1973); Garrow, *Liberty and Sexuality*, 473–599. "The basic thing is that the government has no business making that choice for a woman," Supreme Court justice Ruth Bader Ginsberg stated in a 2009 interview. Quoted in Emily Bazelon, "The Place of Women on the Court," *New York Times*, July 7, 2009, http://www.nytimes.com/2009/07/12/magazine/12ginsburg-t.html?_r=0 (accessed March 25, 2015).

33. Arthur Goldberg took Frankfurter's place. Goldberg served until 1965, when he left to become the US ambassador to the United Nations. Abe Fortas replaced Goldberg. Both men became major players in the Warren Court. On Goldberg, see David Stebenne, *Arthur J. Goldberg: New Deal Liberal* (New York: Oxford University Press, 1996). On Fortas, see Laura Kalman, *Abe Fortas: A Biography* (New Haven, CT: Yale University Press, 1990).

34. Engel v. Vitale, 370 U.S. 421 (1962). On the precedent for *Engel*, see Everson v. Board of Education, 330 U.S. 1 (1947).

35. "The Inaugural Address of Governor George C. Wallace," January 14, 1963, Montgomery, Alabama, typescript, 6–7, Alabama Department of Archives

and History, http://digital.archives.alabama.gov/cdm/singleitem/collection/voices/id/2952/rec/5 (accessed June 30, 2014).

36. Quoted in Darren Dochuk, *From Bible Belt to Sun Belt: Plain-Folk Religion, Grassroots Politics, and the Rise of Evangelical Conservatism* (New York: W. W. Norton and Company, 2011), 240; William Martin, *With God on Our Side: The Rise of the Religious Right in America* (New York: Broadway Books, 1996), 77–78.

37. Kevin Schultz, *Tri-Faith America: How Catholics and Jews Held Postwar America to Its Protestant Promise* (New York: Oxford University Press, 2011); Joseph Crespino, *In Search of Another Country: Mississippi and the Conservative Counterrevolution* (Princeton, NJ: Princeton University Press, 2007); David Sehat, *The Myth of American Religious Freedom* (New York: Oxford University Press, 2011), 235–54; Jerry Falwell, *Strength for the Journey: An Autobiography* (New York: Simon and Schuster, 1987), 356–81.

38. Quoted in Schwartz, *Super Chief*, 438–43.

39. Ansley Lillian Quiros, "'God's on Our Side, Today': Lived Theology in the Civil Rights Movement in Americus, Georgia, 1942–1976" (PhD diss., Vanderbilt University, 2014).

40. "News Conference with Chief Justice—Earl Warren Talks about the 'Warren Court,'" *U.S. News and World Report*, July 15, 1968, 64.

41. William Nelson Cromwell Foundation, *Mr. Justice Jackson: Four Lectures in His Honor* (New York: Columbia University Press, 1969), 60.

42. Laura Kalman has written insightfully about the legacy of this anxiety and concern within legal liberal circles from the 1970s to 1990s. See Laura Kalman, *The Strange Career of Legal Liberalism* (New Haven, CT: Yale University Press, 1999).

43. On its passage, see Caro, *Years of Lyndon Johnson*, 558–605; Risen, *Bill of the Century*.

44. The Great Society has generated a huge literature. For a sampling, see Allen J. Matusow, *The Unraveling of America: A History of Liberalism in the 1960s*, 1st ed. (New York: Harper and Row, 1984); Steve Fraser and Gary Gerstle, eds., *The Rise and Fall of the New Deal Order, 1930–1980* (Princeton, NJ: Princeton University Press, 1989); Sar A. Levitan, William B. Johnston, and Robert Taggart, *Still a Dream: The Changing Status of Blacks since 1960* (Cambridge, MA: Harvard University Press, 1975); Frances Fox Piven and Richard A. Cloward, *Regulating the Poor: The Functions of Public Welfare*, 1st ed. (New York: Pantheon Books, 1971); Frances Fox Piven and Richard A. Cloward, *Poor People's Movements: Why They Succeed, How They Fail*, 1st ed. (New York: Pantheon Books, 1977); Thomas J. Sugrue, *The Origins of the Urban Crisis: Race and Inequality in Postwar Detroit* (Princeton, NJ: Princeton University Press, 1996); Desmond S. King, *In the Name of Liberalism: Illiberal Social Policy in the USA and Britain* (New York: Oxford University Press, 1999); Caro, *Years of Lyndon Johnson*; Doris Kearns Goodwin, *Lyndon Johnson and the American Dream* (New York: St. Martin's Press, 1991); Robert Dallek, *Lyndon B. Johnson: Portrait of a President* (New York: Oxford University Press, 2005); Lemann, *Promised Land*; Julian E. Zelizer,

Taxing America: Wilbur D. Mills, Congress, and the State, 1945–1975 (New York: Cambridge University Press, 1998); Godfrey Hodgson, *America in Our Time: From World War II to Nixon—What Happened and Why*, 1st pbk. ed. (Princeton NJ: Princeton University Press, 2005); Michael B. Katz, *The Price of Citizenship: Redefining the American Welfare State* (New York: Metropolitan Books, 2001); Michael B. Katz, *The Undeserving Poor: America's Enduring Confrontation with Poverty*, 2nd ed. (New York: Oxford University Press, 2013); Charles Noble, *Welfare as We Knew It: A Political History of the American Welfare State* (New York: Oxford University Press, 1997); Jacob S. Hacker, *The Divided Welfare State: The Battle over Public and Private Social Benefits in the United States* (New York: Cambridge University Press, 2002); Edward D. Berkowitz, *America's Welfare State from Roosevelt to Reagan* (Baltimore: Johns Hopkins University Press, 1991); Julian E. Zelizer, *The Fierce Urgency of Now: Lyndon Johnson, Congress, and the Battle for the Great Society* (New York: Penquin Press, 2015); Brian Balogh, "Making Pluralism 'Great': Beyond a Recycled History of the Great Society," in *The Great Society and the High Tide of Liberalism*, ed. Sidney Milkis and Jerome M. Miller (Amherst: University of Massachusetts Press, 2005), 145–82.

45. Ira Katznelson, "Was the Great Society a Lost Opportunity?" in *The Rise and Fall of the New Deal Order, 1930–1980*, ed. Steve Fraser and Gary Gerstle (Princeton, NJ: Princeton University Press, 1989), 185–211. A stream of works has argued that this was not the case: that New Deal possibilities were still very much alive in the 1960s and were only extinguished in the 1970s. I would grant that the afterglow of the New Deal burned longer and brighter than previously thought, but still, that efforts to curb corporate power in the 1960s fell short of New Deal attempts. See Kevin Boyle, *The UAW and the Heyday of American Liberalism, 1945–1968* (Ithaca, NY: Cornell University Press, 1995); Jefferson Cowie, *Stayin' Alive: The 1970s and the Last Days of the Working Class* (New York: New Press, 2010); Judith Stein, *Pivotal Decade: How the United States Traded Factories for Finance in the Seventies* (New Haven, CT: Yale University Press, 2010); Stebenne, *Arthur J. Goldberg*.

46. Susan B. Carter, Scott Sigmund Gartner, Michael R. Haines, Alan L. Olmstead, Richard Sutch, and Gavin Wright, eds., *Historical Statistics of the United States, Millennial Edition Online* (New York: Cambridge University Press, 2013), State Government Revenue by Source: 1902–1996, table Ea348–84, http://hsus.cambridge.org/HSUSWeb/toc/showTablePdf.do?id=Ea348-384 (accessed February 19, 2015). Taking inflation into account, the twenty-seven-fold increase still represented a 700 percent increase in federal contributions to state and local governments. Ibid.; US Inflation Calculator, http://www.us inflationcalculator.com/ (accessed February 19, 2015); David Nice, *Federalism: The Politics of Intergovernmental Relations* (New York: St. Martin's Press, 1987), 55.

47. Matusow, *Unraveling of America*, 189; Martha Derthick, "Crossing Thresholds: Federalism in the 1960s," in *Keeping the Compound Republic: Essays on American Federalism* (Washington, DC: Brookings Institution Press, 2001), 146.

48. Kimberley S. Johnson, *Governing the American State: Congress and the New Federalism, 1877–1929* (Princeton, NJ: Princeton University Press, 2007); Paul Dommel, *The Politics of Revenue Sharing* (Bloomington: Indiana University Press, 1974), 12–13; Martha Derthick, *The Influence of Federal Grants* (Cambridge, MA: Harvard University Press, 1970); Daniel J. Elazar, *American Federalism: A View from the States* (New York: Harper and Row, 1984); Philip Moneypenny, "Federal Grants-in-Aid to State Governments: A Political Analysis," *National Tax Journal* 13 (March 1960): 1–16; Richard Nathan and Fred Doolittle, *Reagan and the States* (Princeton, NJ: Princeton University Press, 1987); Alice Rivlin, *Reviving the American Dream: The Economy, the States, and the Federal Government* (Washington, DC: Brookings Institution Press, 1992); Edwin Corbin, "The Passing of Dual Federalism," *Virginia Law Review* 36 (February 1950): 1–24; Kimberly Morgan and Andrea Louise Campbell, *The Delegated Welfare State: Medicare, Markets, and the Governance of Social Policy* (New York: Oxford University Press, 2011); Nice, *Federalism*; Lawrence J. O'Toole Jr., ed., *American Intergovernmental Relations: Foundations, Perspectives, and Issues*, 2nd ed. (Washington, DC: CQ Press, 1993); Michael Danielson, Alan Hershey, and John Boyne, *One Nation, So Many Governments* (Lexington, MA: Lexington Books, 1977).

49. Hugh Davis Graham, *The Civil Rights Era: Origins and Development of National Policy* (New York: Oxford University Press, 1990), 82–83, 125–53.

50. Gareth Davies, *See Government Grow: Education Politics from Johnson to Reagan* (Lawrence: University Press of Kansas, 2007), chaps. 2 and 5.

51. United States v. Jefferson County Board of Education, 372 F. 2d. 836 (1966); United States v. Jefferson County Board of Education, 380 F. 2d. 385 (1967); Green v. County School Board of New Kent County, 391 U.S. 430 (1968); Alexander v. Holmes, 396 U.S. 20 (1968).

52. Nixon's opportunity to appoint his own chief justice came about because Congress had refused to confirm Fortas, selected by LBJ to continue the Warren tradition. Kalman, *Abe Fortas*.

53. The actual figures were 32 and 86 percent. Davies, *See Government Grow*, 120.

54. Gary Orfield, *The Reconstruction of Southern Education: The Schools and the 1964 Civil Rights Act* (New York: Wiley-Interscience, 1969), 46; Davies, *See Government Grow*, 109–40; Patterson, *Brown v. Board of Education*, 155. Of course, indirect resistance to integration in the South (and North) continued through white flight to private schools and suburbs, which in the early 1970s, the Supreme Court ruled were independent of the heavily minority cities that they frequently abutted. See Matthew Lassiter, *The Silent Majority: Suburban Politics in the Sunbelt South* (Princeton, NJ: Princeton University Press, 2006); Kevin Michael Kruse, *White Flight: Atlanta and the Making of Modern Conservatism* (Princeton, NJ: Princeton University Press, 2005).

55. Derthick, "Crossing the Thresholds," 138–52.

56. Ibid., 144–45.

57. Milliken v. Bradley, 418 U.S. 717 (1974).

58. Anthony Badger, *The New Deal: The Depression Years* (New York: Hill and Wang, 1989), 190–244; Ira Katznelson, *Fear Itself: The New Deal and the Origins of Our Time* (New York: W. W. Norton and Company, 2013), 260; Suzanne Mettler, *Dividing Citizens: Gender and Federalism in New Deal Public Policy* (Ithaca, NY: Cornell University Press, 1998); Katz, *Undeserving Poor.*

59. The federal government would pay $1 to $1.50 for every $2 that a state spent. But states had control over how much they chose to spend and discretion over which medical services they wished to cover. Paul Starr, *Remedy and Reaction: The Peculiar American Struggle over Health Care Reform* (New Haven, CT: Yale University Press, 2013), 47.

60. Matusow, *Unraveling of America*, 231; Starr, *Remedy and Reaction*, 47.

61. By the late 1960s, too, the federal government was determining eligibility requirements for Aid to Families with Dependent Children, one of the original Social Security programs, to an unprecedented degree. Derthick, "Crossing the Thresholds," 146.

62. Ibid., 144, 146.

63. Matusow, *Unraveling of America*, 245.

64. On the War on Poverty more generally, see Matusow, *Unraveling of America*; Gareth Davies, *From Opportunity to Entitlement: The Transformation and Decline of Great Society Liberalism* (Lawrence: University Press of Kansas, 1996); Katz, *Undeserving Poor*, chap. 3; Lemann, *Promised Land*, 109–222; Annelise Orleck and Lisa Gayle Hazirjian, eds., *The War on Poverty: A New Grassroots History, 1964–1980* (Athens: University of Georgia Press, 2011); Susan Youngblood Ashmore, *Carry It On: The War on Poverty and the Civil Rights Movement in Alabama* (Athens: University of Georgia Press, 2008).

65. Anthropologist Oscar Lewis was influential here. His work on Mexican peasants had allegedly revealed an all-encompassing "culture of poverty" among the poor. The key to solving poverty, according to Lewis, was to dissolve this culture and replace it with one that would position the poor to seize opportunities made available to them. Lewis's theory drew support from across the political spectrum, from liberals and conservatives alike, and thus promised to give Johnson's program a strong and bipartisan base of support. Oscar Lewis, *Five Families: Mexican Case Studies in the Culture of Poverty* (1959; repr., New York: Basic Books, 1975).

66. Richard A. Cloward and Lloyd E. Ohlin, *Delinquency and Opportunity: A Theory of Delinquent Gangs* (New York: Free Press, 1960).

67. Ibid.

68. Kennedy's men included David Hackett, Robert's school chum; assistant attorney generals Nicholas Katzenbach and John Doar, and Doar's assistant, John Siegenthaler; and Richard Boone, a sociologist trained at the University of Chicago who turned political operative. Matusow, *Unraveling of America*, 244–45; Lemann, *Promised Land*, 152–53.

69. Matusow, *Unraveling of America*, 253–54.

70. Ibid., 248. Quote from *New York Times*, June 24, 1965, 13.

71. Daley words quoted in Matusow, *Unraveling of America*, 249; Marion K. Sanders, "Conversations with Saul Alinksy, part II: A Professional Radical Moves in on Rochester," *Harper's* 231 (July 1965), 54.

72. Katznelson, *Fear Itself*, chap. 5.

73. Gary Gerstle, "The Resilient Power of the States across the Long Nineteenth Century: An Inquiry into a Pattern of American Governance," in *The Unsustainable American State*, ed. Lawrence Jacobs and Desmond King (New York: Oxford University Press, 2009), 78–80.

CHAPTER 10. CONSERVATIVE REVOLT

1. Quoted in James T. Sparrow, *Warfare State: World War II Americans and the Age of Big Government* (New York: Oxford University Press, 2011), 259.

2. Susan B. Carter, Scott Sigmund Gartner, Michael R. Haines, Alan L. Olmstead, Richard Sutch, and Gavin Wright, eds., *Historical Statistics of the United States, Millennial Edition Online* (New York: Cambridge University Press, 2013), Federal Government Expenditure, by Major Function: 1934–1999 [Office of Management and Budget], table Ea704–25, http://hsus.cambridge.org /HSUSWeb/toc/tableToc.do?id=Ea748-757 (accessed February 20, 2015). Real costs calculated using Consumer Price Index information provided by the Federal Reserve Bank of Minneapolis, https://www.minneapolisfed.org/community _education/teacher/calc/hist1913.cfm (accessed February 20, 2015).

3. The federal courts affirmed the constitutionality of executive order 11246 in 1970 and 1971. See David Golland, *Constructing Affirmative Action: The Struggle for Equal Employment Opportunity* (Lexington: University Press of Kentucky, 2011), 143–70.

4. Nancy MacLean, *Freedom Is Not Enough: The Opening of the American Workplace* (New York: Russell Sage Foundation, 2006), pt. I.

5. Frank Dobbin, John R. Sutton, John W. Meyer, and W. Richard Scott, "Equal Opportunity and the Construction of Internal Labor Markets," *American Journal of Sociology* 99 (September 1993): 396–427.

6. David A. Hollinger, *Postethnic America: Beyond Multiculturalism* (New York: Basic Books, 1995), 19–50.

7. Michael Mann, *The Sources of Social Power, Volume II: The Rise of Classes and Nation-States* (New York: Cambridge University Press, 1993), 58–61. For an important work on the role of science, expertise, and federal power in facilitating this caging process, see Daniel Carpenter, *Reputation and Power: Organizational Image and Pharmaceutical Regulation at the FDA* (Princeton, NJ: Princeton University Press, 2010).

8. On the history of human relations, see Frank Dobbin and Frank R. Sutton, "The Strength of a Weak State: The Rights Revolution and the Rise of Human Resources Management Divisions," *American Journal of Sociology* 104 (1998): 441–76.

9. MacLean, *Freedom Is Not Enough*, 111–13, 317; Jonathan D. Skrentny, *The Minority Rights Revolution* (Cambridge, MA: Harvard University Press, 2002); Jonathan D. Skrentny, *After Civil Rights: Racial Realism in the Workplace* (Princeton, NJ: Princeton University Press, 2014). The slowness of the Equal Employment Opportunity Commission's process raised questions about the government's reliance on the individual employee's appeal as a mechanism of redress. In many respects, the collective bargaining model that unions had pioneered over the first half of the twentieth century was a superior tool for remedying problems at the workplace. But many unions remained burdened by a long history of racial and gender discriminatory behavior in which they themselves had engaged, and even those unions that had escaped this burden found themselves fighting for their lives in a politically conservative environment that had become deeply hostile to their mission. Thus the commission remained an important mechanism for redress into the 1980s and 1990s, its limitations consequential for the struggle against discrimination. See Nelson Lichtenstein, *The State of the Union: A Century of American Labor* (Princeton, NJ: Princeton University Press, 2013), chap. 5; Judith Stein, *Running Steel, Running America: Race, Economic Policy, and the Decline of Liberalism* (Chapel Hill: University of North Carolina Press, 1998). For a provocative, contrary view of the commission's work, see Robert C. Lieberman, "Private Power and American Bureaucracy: The State, the EEOC, and Civil Rights Enforcement," in *Boundaries of the State in U.S. History*, ed. James T. Sparrow, Stephen W. Sawyer, and William J. Novak (Chicago: University of Chicago Press, 2015), 259–94.

10. Samuel Freedman, *The Inheritance: How Three Families and the American Political Majority Moved from Left to Right* (New York: Simon and Schuster, 1996); Jefferson Cowie, *Stayin' Alive: The 1970s and the Last Days of the Working Class* (New York: New Press, 2010); Stanley B. Greenberg, *Middle-Class Dreams: The Politics and Power of the New American Majority* (New York: Random House, 1995).

11. Ronald P. Formisano, *Boston against Busing: Race, Class, and Ethnicity in the 1960s and 1970s* (Chapel Hill: University of North Carolina Press, 1991); J. Anthony Lukas, *Common Ground: A Turbulent Decade in the Lives of Three American Families* (New York: Random House, 1986); Matthew D. Lassiter, *The Silent Majority: Suburban Politics in the Sunbelt South* (Princeton, NJ: Princeton University Press, 2006); Jonathan Rieder, *Canarsie: The Jews and Italians of Brooklyn against Liberalism* (Cambridge, MA: Harvard University Press, 1985). On right-wing populism, see Michael Kazin, *The Populist Persuasion: An American History* (Ithaca, NY: Cornell University Press, 1995), chaps. 9–10; Dan T. Carter, *The Politics of Rage: George Wallace, the Origins of the New Conservatism, and the Transformation of American Politics* (New York: Simon and Schuster, 1995). On the rise of colorblindness, see MacLean, *Freedom Is Not Enough*, 225–61; Michelle Alexander, *The New Jim Crow: Mass Incarceration in the Age of Colorblindness* (New York: New Press, 2010); Desmond King and Rogers Smith, *Still a House Divided: Race and Politics in Obama's America* (Princeton, NJ: Princeton University Press,

2011). See also Ken Auletta, *The Underclass*, rev. ed. (Woodstock, NY: Overlook Press, 1999); Michael Katz, *The Undeserving Poor: From the War on Poverty to the War on Welfare* (New York: Pantheon Books, 1989).

12. Lewis F. Powell Jr., "Confidential Memo [to Eugene B. Sydnor Jr., US Chamber of Commerce]: Attack on American Free Enterprise System," August 23, 1971, http://law.wlu.edu/deptimages/Powell%20Archives/Powell MemorandumTypescript.pdf (accessed February 20, 2015); Kim Phillips-Fein, *Invisible Hands: The Making of the Conservative Movement from the New Deal to Reagan* (New York: W. W. Norton and Company, 2009); Daniel Stedman Jones, *Masters of the Universe: Hayek, Friedman, and the Birth of Neoliberal Politics* (Princeton, NJ: Princeton University Press, 2012); Angus Burgin, *The Great Persuasion: Reinventing Free Markets since the Depression* (Cambridge, MA: Harvard University Press, 2012).

13. Ronald Reagan, "A Time for Choosing" (speech at 1964 Republican Convention, October 27, 1964), in Ronald Reagan, *A Time for Choosing: The Speeches of Ronald Reagan, 1961–1982* (Chicago: Regnery Gateway, 1983), 43, 57; Barry M. Goldwater, *Conscience of a Conservative* (Princeton, NJ: Princeton University Press, 2007); Milton Friedman, *Capitalism and Freedom* (Chicago: University of Chicago Press, 1962); Powell, "Confidential Memo"; William Simon, *A Time for Truth* (New York: Berkeley Books, 1978); William Simon, *A Time for Action* (New York: McGraw-Hill Book Company, 1980); Rick Perlstein, *The Invisible Bridge: The Fall of Nixon and the Rise of Reagan* (New York: Simon and Schuster, 2014); Gil Troy, *Morning in America: How Ronald Reagan Invented the 1980s* (Princeton, NJ: Princeton University Press, 2005); Lou Cannon, *Governor Reagan: His Rise to Power* (New York: Public Affairs, 2003); Lou Cannon, *President Reagan: The Role of a Lifetime* (New York: Simon and Schuster, 1991); Alice O'Connor, "Financing the Counterrevolution," in *Rightward Bound: Making America Conservative in the 1970s*, ed. Bruce Schulman and Julian E. Zelizer (Cambridge, MA: Harvard University Press, 2008), 148–68; Bethany Moreton, "Make Payroll, Not War: Business Culture as Youth Culture," in *Rightward Bound: Making America Conservative in the 1970s*, ed. Bruce Schulman and Julian E. Zelizer (Cambridge, MA: Harvard University Press, 2008), 52–70; Phillips-Fein, *Invisible Hands*; Stedman Jones, *Masters of the Universe*.

14. Romain D. Huret, *American Tax Resisters* (Cambridge, MA: Harvard University Press, 2014), 208–40; Howard Jarvis and Robert Pack, *I'm Mad as Hell: The Exclusive Story of the Tax Revolt and Its Leader* (New York: Times Books, 1979); Daniel Smith, "Howard Jarvis: Populist Entrepreneur: Reevaluating the Causes of Proposition 13," *Social Science History* 23 (1999): 173–210.

15. Joseph A. McCartin, *Collision Course: Ronald Reagan, the Air Traffic Controllers, and the Strike That Changed America* (New York: Oxford University Press, 2011).

16. W. Elliot Brownlee, *Federal Taxation in America: A Short History*, 2nd ed. (Washington, DC: Woodrow Wilson International Center for Scholars, 2004), 147–77; Cathie Jo Martin, "American Business and the Taxing

State: Alliances for Growth in the Postwar Period," in *Funding the Modern American State, 1941–1995: The Rise and Fall of the Era of Easy Finance*, ed. W. Elliott Brownlee (Washington, DC: Woodrow Wilson Center Press, 1996), 379–406; Herbert Stein, *Presidential Economics: The Making of Economic Policy from Roosevelt to Clinton*, 3rd rev. ed. (Washington, DC: American Enterprise Institute for Public Policy Research, 1994), 235–411; John F. Witte, *The Politics and Development of the Federal Income Tax* (Madison: University of Wisconsin Press, 1985), 220–43; Sheldon D. Pollack, *The Failure of U.S. Tax Policy: Revenue and Politics* (University Park: Pennsylvania State University Press, 1996), 87–115.

17. Sean Wilentz, *The Age of Reagan: A History, 1974–2008* (New York: HarperCollins, 2008), 140.

18. Ibid., 196–200.

19. Powell, "Confidential Memo," 26.

20. Phillips-Fein, *Invisible Hands*; O'Connor, "Financing the Counterrevolution"; Sidney Blumenthal, *The Rise of the Counter-Establishment: From Conservative Ideology to Political Power* (New York: Harper and Row, 1986); Gabriel Sherman, *The Loudest Voice in the Room: How the Brilliant, Bombastic Roger Ailes Built Fox News—and Divided a Country* (New York: Random House, 2014); Jerry Falwell, *Strength for the Journey: An Autobiography* (New York: Simon and Schuster, 1987).

21. Robert J. Bork, "Neutral Principles and Some First Amendment Problems," *Indiana Law Journal* 47 (1971): 1–34; Robert J. Bork, "We Suddenly Feel That the Law Is Vulnerable," *Fortune*, December 1971, 115–17, 136–38, 143; Robert J. Bork, *The Tempting of America: The Political Seduction of the Law* (New York: Free Press, 1990). See also Keith Whittington, "The New Originalism," *Georgetown Journal of Law and Public Policy* 2 (2004): 599–614; Jonathan O'Neill, "Shaping Modern Constitutional Theory: Bickel and Bork Confront the Warren Court," *Review of Politics* 65 (2003): 325–54; Daniel T. Rodgers, *Age of Fracture* (Cambridge, MA: Harvard University Press, 2011), 232–42.

22. Steven M. Teles, *The Rise of the Conservative Legal Movement: The Battle for Control of the Law* (Princeton, NJ: Princeton University Press, 2008), chap. 5; Jeffrey Toobin, *The Nine: Inside the Secret World of the Supreme Court* (New York: Doubleday, 2007), 12–13.

23. Quoted in Laura Kalman, *The Strange Career of Legal Liberalism* (New Haven, CT: Yale University Press, 1996), 132.

24. Teles, *Rise of the Conservative Legal Movement*, chaps. 5–6.

25. Kalman, *Strange Career of Legal Liberalism*, 7.

26. Wickard v. Filburn, 317 U.S. 111 (1942); Heart Motel of Atlanta Inc. v. United States, 379 U.S. 241 (1964); Katzenbach v. McClung, 379 U.S. 294 (1964).

27. On liberal discomfort, see Heart Motel of Atlanta Inc. v. United States, 379 U.S. 279 (1964) (Douglas, J, concurring); Heart Motel of Atlanta Inc. v. United States, 379 U.S. 291 (1964) (Goldberg, J, concurring). More generally, see Bernard Schwartz, *Super Chief: Earl Warren and His Supreme Court—A*

Judicial Biography (New York: New York University Press, 1983), 508–25, 552–55. Bruce Ackerman has argued that Brennan engineered the Court's turn to the commerce clause as part of his and Warren's efforts to secure a unanimous decision on the Civil Rights Act. Had the Court looked to the Fourteenth Amendment (and its equal protections clause) instead, the Civil Rights Act would still have passed muster but possibly with the narrowest (five to four) of margins. Ackerman admires Brennan's handiwork, for it put the full weight of the Court behind the legislation and made additional acts of massive resistance by white southerners harder to justify. There is, in fact, much to admire here, although Brennan's tactical success cannot obscure the long-term strategic weakness of relying so heavily on the commerce clause. Progressive era reformers such as Robert Cushman had been aware of this weakness in the 1910s; by the 1950s and 1960s, expansive use of the commerce clause had become so routine that many regarded it as an unassailable judicial practice. They would soon learn that it was not. Bruce Ackerman, *We the People, Volume III: The Civil Rights Revolution* (Cambridge, MA: Harvard University Press, 2014), 141–53.

28. Richard A. Epstein, "The Proper Scope of the Commerce Power," *Virginia Law Review* 73 (November 1987): 1454, 1451. Others who share this restrictive view of the powers granted to Congress by the commerce clause include Albert Abel, "The Commerce Clause in the Constitutional Convention and in Contemporary Comment," *Minnesota Law Review* 25 (1941): 432–94; Raoul Berger, "Judicial Manipulation of the Commerce Clause," *Texas Law Review* 74 (1995–96): 695–717; Grant Nelson and Robert Pushaw, "Rethinking the Commerce Clause: Applying First Principles to Uphold Federal Commercial Regulations but Preserve State Control over Social Issues," *Iowa Law Review* 85 (1999–2000): 1–173; Randy Barnett, "The Original Meaning of the Commerce Clause," *University of Chicago Law Review* 68 (2001): 101–47; Randy Barnett, "New Evidence on the Original Meaning of the Commerce Clause," *Arkansas Law Review* 55 (2003): 847–900.

29. Epstein, "Proper Scope of the Commerce Clause," 1455.

30. William Grieder, "The Right's Grand Ambition: Rolling Back the Twentieth Century," *Nation*, May 12, 2003, 2, quote from 16. See also Grover Norquist, *Leave Us Alone: Getting the Government's Hands Off Our Money, Our Guns, Our Lives* (New York: William Morrow, 2008).

31. Ronald Reagan, "Address to the Members of the British Parliament," June 8, 1982, http://www.reagan.utexas.edu/search/speeches/speech_srch.html (accessed March 26, 2015); Wilentz, *Age of Reagan*, 154, 206; Rachel Maddow, *Drift: The Unmooring of American Military Power* (New York: Crown Books, 2012), 64; Julian E. Zelizer, *Arsenal of Democracy: The Politics of National Security—from World War II to the War on Terrorism* (New York: Basic Books, 2010), 300–354; Michael Sherry, *In the Shadow of War: The United States since the 1930s* (New Haven, CT: Yale University Press, 1995), chap. 8; John Lewis Gaddis, *Strategies of Containment: A Critical Appraisal of American National Security Policy during the Cold War*, rev. ed. (New York: Oxford University Press, 2005), 342–79.

32. Ira Katznelson, *Fear Itself: The New Deal and the Origins of Our Time* (New York: W. W. Norton and Company, 2013), 367–402.

33. On preventive war and the Bush doctrine, see James Mann, *The Rise of the Vulcans: The History of Bush's War Cabinet* (New York: Viking, 2004); Zelizer, *Arsenal of Democracy*, 411–14; George Packer, *The Assassin's Gate: America in Iraq* (New York: Farrar, Straus and Giroux, 2006). Ron Paul and Rand Paul represent exceptions, but lonely ones, to this dominant Republican position. On the drift toward permanent war, and acceptance of an expanded role for presidential and executive power, see Mary L. Dudziak, *War Time: An Idea, Its History, Its Consequences* (New York: Oxford University Press, 2012). See also Julian E. Zelizer, "How Conservatives Learned to Stop Worrying and Love Presidential Power," in *The Presidency of George W. Bush: A First Historical Assessment*, ed. Julian E. Zelizer (Princeton, NJ: Princeton University Press, 2010), 15–38.

34. Kathleen Frydl, *The Drug Wars in America, 1940–1973* (New York: Cambridge University Press, 2013), 418–39.

35. Alexander, *New Jim Crow*, 71–83.

36. Ibid., 109–10.

37. On the rise of the carceral state, see ibid.; Ruth Wilson Gilmore, *Golden Gulag: Prisons, Surplus, Crisis, and Opposition in Globalizing California* (Berkeley: University of California Press, 2007); Robert T. Chase, "Rioting Peacefully in Carceral States: Rethinking Prison Uprisings in the Sunbelt after Attica, 1970–1985" (paper presented at William P. Clements Center for Southwest Studies annual symposium, Southern Methodist University, Dallas, TX, March 24, 2012); Heather Thompson, "Why Mass Incarceration Matters: Rethinking Crisis, Decline, and Transformation in Postwar American History," *Journal of American History* 97 (December 2010): 703–34; Robert Perkinson, *Texas Tough: The Rise of America's Prison Empire* (New York: Metropolitan Books, 2010); Marie Gottschalk, *The Prison and the Gallows: The Rise of Mass Incarceration in America* (New York: Cambridge University Press, 2006); Marie Gottschalk, *Caught: The Prison State and the Lockdown of American Politics* (Princeton, NJ: Princeton University Press, 2015). On white Americans' support for law and order politics, see Michael W. Flamm, *Law and Order: Street Crime, Civil Unrest, and the Crisis of Liberalism in the 1960s* (New York: Columbia University Press, 2005).

38. For an interesting argument for why many Americans have had so much difficulty expressing support for aspects of government they like, see Suzanne Mettler, *The Submerged State: How Invisible Government Policies Undermine American Democracy* (Chicago: University of Chicago Press, 2011). See also Christopher Howard, *The Hidden Welfare State: Tax Expenditures and Social Policy in the United States* (Princeton, NJ: Princeton University Press, 1997).

39. Michael Lind, "Conservative Elites and the Counterrevolution against the New Deal," in *Ruling America: A History of Wealth and Power in a Democracy*, ed. Steve Fraser and Gary Gerstle (Cambridge, MA: Harvard University Press, 2005), 250–85; Kirkpatrick Sale, *Power Shift: The Rise of the Southern*

Rim and Its Challenge to the Eastern Establishment (New York: Random House, 1975); Sherry, *Shadow of War*, 391–497, passim; Elizabeth Tandy Shermer, *Sunbelt Capitalism: Phoenix and the Transformation of American Politics* (Philadelphia: University of Pennsylvania Press, 2013); Andrew Needham, *Power Lines: Phoenix and the Making of the Modern Southwest* (Princeton, NJ: Princeton University Press, 2014); Bruce Schulman, *From Cotton Belt to Sunbelt: Federal Policy, Economic Development, and the Transformation of the South, 1938–1980* (New York: Oxford University Press, 1991); Aaron Friedberg, *In the Shadow of the Garrison State: America's Anti-Statism and Its Cold War Grand Strategy* (Princeton, NJ: Princeton University Press, 2000).

40. Gerald Posner, *Citizen Perot: His Life and Times* (New York: Random House, 1966), 38–39, passim.

41. On DeLay and the K Street Project, see Nicholas Confessore, "Welcome to the Machine: How the GOP Disciplined K Street and Made Bush Supreme," *Washington Monthly*, July–August 2003, http://www.washingtonmonthly.com /features/2003/0307.confessore.html (accessed February 20, 2015); Jeremy Scahill, "Exile on K-Street: Scandals Abound in the Smoking Remains of the Alexander Strategy Group," *Nation*, February 20, 2006, http://www.thenation .com/article/exile-k-street (accessed February 20, 2015).

42. Maddow, *Drift*, 6; Andrew Friedman, *Covert Capital: Landscapes of Denial and the Making of U.S. Empire in the Suburbs of Northern Virginia* (Berkeley: University of California Press, 2013).

43. On the funds coursing through lobbying and campaign finance in the 1990s and 2000s, see Benjamin C. Waterhouse, *Lobbying America: The Politics of Business from Nixon to NAFTA* (Princeton, NJ: Princeton University Press, 2014); Lawrence Lessig, *Republic Lost: How Money Corrupts Congress—and a Plan to Stop It* (New York: Twelve, 2011); Robert G. Kaiser, *So Damn Much Money: The Triumph of Lobbying and the Corrosion of American Government* (New York: Alfred A. Knopf, 2009); John Nichols and Robert W. McChesney, *Dollarocracy: How the Money and Media Election Complex Is Destroying America* (New York: Nation Books, 2013); Jay Cost, *Spoiled Rotten: How the Politics of Patronage Corrupted the Once Noble Democratic Party and Now Threatens the American Republic* (New York: Broadside Books, 2012).

44. Regents of the University of California v. Bakke, 438 U.S. 265 (1978).

45. MacLean, *Freedom Is Not Enough*, 302–14; Anne B. Fisher, "Businessmen Like to Hire by the Numbers," *Fortune*, September 16, 1985, 26.

46. Wilentz, *Age of Reagan*, 323–407. On Clinton, see William Chafe, *Bill and Hillary: The Politics of the Personal* (New York: Farrar, Straus and Giroux, 2012); David Maraniss, *First in His Class: A Biography of Bill Clinton* (New York: Touchstone, 1995); William C. Berman, *From the Center to the Edge: The Politics and Policies of the Clinton Presidency* (Lanham, MD: Rowman and Littlefield, 2001); Haynes Johnson, *The Best of Times: America in the Clinton Years* (New York: Harcourt, 2001); Joe Klein, *The Natural: The Misunderstood Presidency of Bill Clinton* (New York: Doubleday, 2002); Alex

Waddan, *Clinton's Legacy? A New Democrat in Governance* (New York: Palgrave, 2002); Nigel Hamilton, *Bill Clinton: An American Journey—Great Expectations* (New York: Random House, 2003); John F. Harris, *The Survivor: Bill Clinton in the White House* (New York: Random House, 2005); Nigel Hamilton, *Bill Clinton: Mastering the Presidency* (New York: Public Affairs, 2007); Jack Godwin, *Clintonomics: How Bill Clinton Reengineered the Reagan Revolution* (New York: American Management Associations, 2009).

47. This, of course, was the Monica Lewinsky affair. See Wilentz, *Age of Reagan*, 381–94, 399–400; Michael Isikoff, *Uncovering Clinton: A Reporter's Story* (New York: Crown Publishers, 1999).

48. Donald T. Critchlow, *The Conservative Ascendancy: How the GOP Right Made Political History* (Cambridge, MA: Harvard University Press, 2007); Theda Skocpol and Vanessa Williamson, *The Tea Party and the Remaking of Republican Conservatism* (New York: Oxford University Press, 2012); Sam Tanenhaus, *The Death of Conservatism* (New York: Random House, 2009); Michael Kazin, "From Hubris to Despair: George W. Bush and the Conservative Movement," in *The Presidency of George W. Bush: A First Historical Assessment*, ed. Julian E. Zelizer (Princeton, NJ: Princeton University Press, 2010), 282–302.

49. Newt Gingrich, *To Renew America* (New York: HarperCollins, 1995).

50. Gary Gerstle, "Minorities, Multiculturalism, and the Presidency of George W. Bush," in *The Presidency of George W. Bush: A First Historical Assessment*, ed. Julian E. Zelizer (Princeton, NJ: Princeton University Press, 2010), 252–81; see also Gary Gerstle, "The GOP in the Age of Obama: Will the Tea Party and Republican Establishment Unite or Fight?" *New Labor Forum* 19 (Fall 2010): 23–31; Robert Dreyfuss, "Grover Norquist: 'Field Marshall' of the Bush Tax Plan," *Nation*, May 14, 2001, 11–16.

51. Jeffrey Toobin, *Nine*; Bob Woodward and Scott Armstrong, *The Brethren: Inside the Supreme Court* (New York: Simon and Schuster, 1979).

52. David Bromwich, *The Intellectual Life of Edmund Burke: From the Sublime and Beautiful to American Independence* (Cambridge, MA: Harvard University Press, 2014); Conor Cruise O'Brien, *The Great Melody: A Thematic Biography of Edmund Burke* (Chicago: University of Chicago Press, 1992); Gertrude Himmelfarb, *The De-Moralization of Society: From Victorian Virtues to Modern Values* (New York: Alfred A. Knopf, 1995); Gertrude Himmelfarb, *One Nation, Two Cultures* (New York: Alfred A. Knopf, 1999); Tanenhaus, *Death of Conservatism*, 18–20.

53. On the radicalization of Republicans, see Wilentz, *Age of Reagan*, chaps. 13–14; Skocpol and Williamson, *Tea Party*; Corey Robin, *The Reactionary Mind: Conservatism from Edmund Burke to Sarah Palin* (New York: Oxford University Press, 2011).

54. On 1990s' government shutdowns, see Wilentz, *Age of Reagan*, 355–73. On the 2011 debt default crisis and 2013 shutdown, see Jackie Calmes, "Behind Battle over Debt, a War over Government," *New York Times*, July 14, 2011, http://www.nytimes.com/2011/07/15/us/politics/15deficit.html (accessed

June 11, 2014); Timothy Egan, "Anarchists and Tasseled Loafers," *New York Times*, July 14, 2011, http://opinionator.blogs.nytimes.com/2011/07/14/anarchists-and-tasseled-loafers/ (accessed June 11, 2014); Zeke Miller, "Hidden Hand: How Heritage Action Drove DC to Shut Down," *Time*, September 30, 2013, http://swampland.time.com/2013/09/30/hidden-hand-how-heritage-action-drove-dc-to-shut-down/ (accessed June 11, 2014); Zachary Goldfarb, "Tea Party Lawmakers See the Culmination of Years of Effort in Shutdown," *Washington Post*, October 2, 2013, http://www.washingtonpost.com/politics/with-shutdown-tea-party-lawmakers-see-the-culmination-of-years-of-effort-to-downsize-government/2013/10/02/3207126a-2ab3-11e3-8ade-a1f23cda135e_story.html (accessed June 11, 2014); Sheryl Gay Stolberg and Mike McIntire, "A Federal Budget Crisis Months in the Planning," *New York Times*, October 5, 2013, http://www.nytimes.com/2013/10/06/us/a-federal-budget-crisis-months-in-the-planning.html/?pagewanted=all&_r=0 (accessed June 11, 2014).

55. On the resurgence of interest in privatization, see Maddow, *Drift*; P. W. Singer, *Corporate Warriors: The Rise of the Privatized Military Industry* (Ithaca, NY: Cornell University Press, 2003); Kimberly J. Morgan and Andrea Louise Campbell, *The Delegated Welfare State: Medicare, Markets, and the Governance of Social Policy* (New York: Oxford University Press, 2011); Jacob Hacker, *The Divided Welfare State: The Battle over Public and Private Benefits in the United States* (New York: Cambridge University Press, 2002); Jody Freeman and Martha Minow, eds., *Government by Contract: Outsourcing and American Democracy* (Cambridge, MA: Harvard University Press, 2009); Martha Minow, "Outsourcing Power: How Privatizing Military Efforts Challenges Accountability, Professionalism, and Democracy," *Boston College Law Review* 46 (2004–5): 989–1026; Clifford Winston, *Last Exit: Privatization and Deregulation of the US Transportation System* (Washington, DC: Brookings Institution Press, 2010).

56. Paul Starr, *Remedy and Reaction: The Peculiar American Struggle over Health Care Reform* (New Haven, CT: Yale University Press, 2013); Lawrence R. Jacobs and Theda Skocpol, *Health Care Reform and American Politics: What Everyone Needs to Know* (New York: Oxford University Press, 2010); Steven Brill, *America's Bitter Pill: Money, Politics, Backroom Deals, and the Fight to Fix Our Broken Healthcare System* (New York: Random House, 2015); Mitch McConnell, "Congressional Republicans Resolved to Repeal Obamacare," *Washington Times*, June 6, 2012, B1; John Boehner, "Congressional Republicans Resolved to Repeal Obamacare," *Washington Times*, June 6, 2012, B1; Jonah Goldberg, "Live Free and Uninsured," *National Review*, July 4, 2012; James Delingpole, "Socialized Medicine, from a Survivor: What to Expect from America's Version of Britain's NHS," *Washington Times*, June 3, 2012, B1; William McGurn, "Chief Justice Roberts Taxes Credibility," *Wall Street Journal*, July 2, 2012, http://search.proquest.com.ezp-prod1.hul.harvard.edu/docview/1022993104?accountid=11311 (accessed March 26, 2015); Rich Lowry, "Obamacare: It's Not Over," *National Review*, July 3, 2012,

http://www.nationalreview.com/article/304649/obamacare-its-not-over-rich
-lowry (accessed March 26, 2015); Thomas Sowell, "Judicial Betrayal," *National
Review*, July 3, 2012, http://www.nationalreview.com/article/304619/judicial
-betrayal-thomas-sowell (accessed March 26, 2015); John Yoo, "Chief Justice
Roberts and His Apologists," *Wall Street Journal*, June 29, 2012, http://search
.proquest.com.ezp-prod1.hul.harvard.edu/docview/1022643662/abstract
/503D52B74BE84502PQ/1?accountid=11311 (accessed March 26, 2015).

57. Skocpol and Williamson, *Tea Party*. On the Obama administration, see
Thomas J. Sugrue, *Not Even Past: Barack Obama and the Burden of Race* (Prince-
ton, NJ: Princeton University Press, 2010); James T. Kloppenberg, *Reading
Obama: Dreams, Hope, and the American Political Tradition* (Princeton, NJ:
Princeton University Press, 2011); David Remnick, *The Bridge: The Life and
Rise of Barack Obama* (New York: Alfred A. Knopf, 2010); William Bunch,
*The Backlash: Right-wing Radicals, Hi-Def Hucksters, and Paranoid Politics
in the Age of Obama* (New York: Harper, 2010); Iwan Morgan, *Broken Gov-
ernment? American Politics in the Obama Era* (London: Institute for the Study
of the Americas, 2012); John Wright, *The Obama Haters: Behind the Right-
wing Campaign of Lies, Innuendo, and Racism* (Washington, DC: Potomac
Books, 2011); James Thurber, *Obama in Office* (Boulder, CO: Paradigm Pub-
lishers, 2011); Gary Dorrien, *The Obama Question: A Progressive Perspective*
(Lanham, MD: Rowman and Littlefield, 2012); Bob Woodward, *The Price of
Politics* (New York: Simon and Schuster, 2012); Terry Smith: *Barack Obama,
Post-Racialism, and the New Politics of Triangulation* (New York: Palgrave
Macmillan, 2012); David Corn, *Showdown: The Inside Story of How Obama
Battled the GOP to Set Up the 2012 Election* (New York: William Morrow,
2012); Michael Grunwald, *The New New Deal: The Hidden Story of Change
in the Obama Era* (New York: Simon and Schuster, 2012); Richard Minter,
*Leading from Behind: The Reluctant President and the Advisors Who Decide
for Him* (New York: St. Martin's Press, 2012); Jonathan Alter, *The Center
Holds: Obama and His Enemies* (New York: Simon and Schuster, 2013).

58. James M. Naughton, "Urges US Aid States and Cities," *New York Times*,
August 9, 1969, http://search.proquest.com.proxy.library.vanderbilt.edu/doc
view/118498684?accountid=1481 (accessed February 22, 2015); "Nixon Pro-
poses Revenue Sharing without Strings," *New York Times*, August 14, 1969,
http://search.proquest.com.proxy.library.vanderbilt.edu/docview/118618941
?accountid=14816 (accessed February 22, 2015); Richard R. Dommel, *The
Politics of Revenue Sharing* (Bloomington: Indiana University Press, 1974);
Richard Nixon, "Text of Nixon Message on Fund-Sharing," *New York Times*,
August 14, 1969, A24.

59. B. Drummond Ayres Jr., "Reagan's Acts Renew, with Vigor, Nation's Debate about Federalism, *New York Times*, June 1, 1981, A1, A13; Richard P.
Nathan and Fred C. Doolittle, *Reagan and the States* (Princeton, NJ: Princeton
University Press, 1987). See also Timothy Conlan, *New Federalism: Intergovernmental Reform from Nixon to Reagan* (Washington, DC: Brookings Institution Press, 1988); Timothy Conlan, *From New Federalism to Devolution:*

Twenty-Five Years of Intergovernmental Reform (Washington, DC: Brookings Institution Press, 1998); Richard S. Williamson, *Reagan's Federalism: His Efforts to Decentralize Government* (New York: University Press of America 1990); David Nice, *Federalism: The Politics of Intergovernmental Relations* (New York: St. Martin's Press, 1987).

60. Rehnquist achieved a few successes in restoring rights to the states, especially during cases decided in the late 1990s. But his larger goal remained out of reach. For his successes, see *United States v. Lopez*, 514 U.S. 549 (1995); *United States v. Morrison*, 529 U.S. 598 (2000). For his limitations, see Bernard Schwartz, "Chief Justice Rehnquist, Justice Jackson, and the 'Brown' Case," *Supreme Court Review* 1988 (1988): 245–67. See also Jeffrey Rosen, "Rehnquist the Great?" *Atlantic Monthly*, April 2005, http://www.theatlantic.com/magazine/archive/2005/04/rehnquist-the-great/303820/ (accessed February 22, 2015).

61. Gary Gerstle, "The Resilient Power of the States across the Long Nineteenth Century: An Inquiry into a Pattern of American Government," in *The Unsustainable American State*, ed. Lawrence Jacobs and Desmond King (New York: Oxford University Press, 2009), 61–87; Larry Gerston, *American Federalism: A Concise Introduction* (New York: M. E. Sharpe, Inc., 2006), 107, 70.

62. Bruce Katz and Jennifer Bradley, *The Metropolitan Revolution: How Cities and Metros Are Fixing Our Broken Politics and Fragile Economy* (Washington, DC: Brookings Institution Press, 2013). On the immigration laws and fight against them, see Alabama HB 65 and Arizona SB 1070; American Civil Liberties Union, "ACLU and Civil Rights Coalition File Lawsuit Charging Alabama's Racial Profiling Law Is Unconstitutional," July 8, 2011, http://www.aclu.org/immigrants-rights/aclu-and-civil-rights-coalition-file-lawsuit-charging-alabamas-racial-profiling (accessed June 11, 2014); Center for American Progress, "100 Reasons Why Alabama's Immigration Law Is a Disaster," November 21, 2011, http://americanprogress.org/issues/immigration/news/2011/11/21/10674/100-reasons-why-alabamas-immigration-law-is-a-disaster/ (accessed June 11, 2014); editorial, "Nation's Cruelest Immigration Law," *New York Times*, August 28, 2011, http://www.nytimes.com/2011/08/29opinion/the-nations-cruelest-immigration-law.html?_r=4&ref=opinion& (accessed June 11, 2014); Pamela Constable, "A Tough New Alabama Law Targets Illegal Immigrants and Sends Families Fleeing," *New York Times*, October 8, 2011, http://www.washingtonpost.com/local/a-tough-new-alabama-law-targets-illegal-immigrants-and-sends-families-fleeing/2011/10/07/gIQAtZuPWL_story_1.html (accessed June 11, 2014).

63. Citizens United v. Federal Election Commission, 558 U.S. 310 (2010); Mark Tushnet, *In the Balance: Law and Politics on the Roberts Court* (New York: W. W. Norton and Company, 2013), chap. 7; Nick Confessore, "A National Strategy Funds State Political Monopolies, *New York Times*, January 12, 2014, 1, 20–21.

64. National Federation of Independent Business v. Sebelius, 567 U.S. ___ (2012).

CONCLUSION

1. See, for example, Sanford Levinson, *Our Undemocratic Constitution: Where the Constitution Goes Wrong (and How We the People Can Correct It)* (New York: Oxford University Press, 2006); John Paul Stevens, *Six Amendments: How and Why We Should Change the Constitution* (Boston: Little, Brown and Company, 2014); Lawrence Lessig, "A Real Step to Fix Democracy," *Atlantic*, May 30, 2014, http://www.theatlantic.com/politics/archive/2014/05/a-real-step -to-fix-democracy/371898/ (accessed February 22, 2015).

INDEX